AF607890

CROSSING CENTRAL EUROPE

Continuities and Transformations, 1900 and 2000

Crossing Central Europe

Continuities and Transformations, 1900 and 2000

Edited by HELGA MITTERBAUER
and CARRIE SMITH-PREI

UNIVERSITY OF TORONTO PRESS
Toronto Buffalo London

Toronto Buffalo London
www.utorontopress.com

ISBN 978-1-4426-4914-9

Library and Archives Canada Cataloguing in Publication

Crossing Central Europe : continuities and transformations, 1900 and 2000 / edited by Helga Mitterbauer and Carrie Smith-Prei.
Includes bibliographical references and index.
ISBN 978-1-4426-4914-9 (hardcover)

1. Europe, Central – Civilization – 20th century. I. Mitterbauer, Helga, editor II. Smith-Prei, Carrie, 1975–, editor

DAW1024.C76 2017 943.0009'049 C2017-902387-X

The editors acknowledge the financial assistance of the Faculty of Arts, University of Alberta; the Wirth Institute for Austrian and Central European Studies, University of Alberta; and Philixte, Centre de recherche de la Faculté de Lettres, Traduction et Communication, Université Libre de Bruxelles.

University of Toronto Press acknowledges the financial assistance to its publishing program of the Canada Council for the Arts and the Ontario Arts Council, an agency of the Government of Ontario.

Canada Council for the Arts
Conseil des Arts du Canada

Funded by the Government of Canada
Financé par le gouvernement du Canada

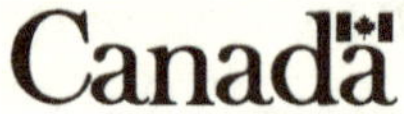

Contents

Part Two: 2000

Introduction: Crossings and Encounters

HELGA MITTERBAUER AND CARRIE SMITH-PREI

Central Europe has experienced strong vicissitudes in politics, geographical borders, and ethnic diversity. Around 1900, large parts of it belonged to the Austro-Hungarian Monarchy or the German Empire; some parts formed the borderlands of the Russian Empire and were territories of transition between the West and the East. In general, the nineteenth century was the time when nation-states evolved – a process that led to radical transformations. After the First World War, instead of a few large empires, the map of Europe showed a great number of smaller states, most of which had been transformed from monarchies into republics with thoroughly changed social structures. The middle class – which had gained economic power over the course of the Industrial Revolution – increased its political power and become a strong patron of the arts. As a result of the collapse of established structures, Central Europe found itself locked in a long-term battle among different ideologies – capitalist, fascist, communist, nationalist, and other movements – all of which led to the Second World War. That war, in turn, led to mass genocides and to the region's sharp division by the "Iron Curtain." Only the revolutions of 1989 and the collapse of the Soviet Union reopened this territory to the West. New nation-states appeared on the European map, although the transition did not happen peacefully in all of these countries, as the Yugoslav wars and the conflicts in Ukraine demonstrate.

One could read these changes as a unidimensional development towards nationalism. However, this trend is offset by a strong transnational tendency, particularly in literature, art, and music. In the late nineteenth century, Central Europe was on the periphery of a broad network of relations in European arts, with Paris as an important centre. Scholars such as French sociologist Pascale Casanova view that metropolis as having been the world capital of literature – a perspective that ignores the fact that London, Scandinavian cities, Vienna, and Berlin also played pivotal roles in this "république mondiale de lettres" (Casanova). This perspective also overlooks the importance of Russian literature, art, and music (St. Petersburg) and of Central European cities (Prague, Budapest, Zagreb, Warsow, Lviv, Chernivtsi, and so on), whose artists, writers, and musicians formed regional networks and also engaged in transnational encounters. Some of these people were highly successful in Western Europe. At the same time, the audiences in Central European cities showed great interest in new trends from the region as well as from other parts of Europe.

Crossing Central Europe focuses on these transcultural connections. It concentrates first on transnational and transcultural relations around 1900 and then on how these relations were re-created and new ones formed after 1989. It is based on the thesis that the Central European networks of artists, writers, and musicians were shaken by the world wars and then wracked by the Cold War, but that after the fall of the Iron Curtain, memories of the nineteenth century formed a solid base for re-establishing transnational relations. This volume does not claim to be exhaustive; it approaches its goal through case studies from the mid-nineteenth to the early twenty-first century.

In this volume, we accept that many different notions of Central Europe have developed historically and that different disciplines and scholars in various countries continue to hold divergent notions of this place (Feichtinger and Cohen). As it is not our goal to add a new definition to the already existing ones, but rather to emphasize the transnational and transcultural encounters, we engage with Central Europe as an imaginary landscape rather than a geographic territory. However, the articles place a strong emphasis on the former Austro-Hungarian Monarchy and the mythologized memory of it. Focusing on transnational relations requires us to take into account the relations reaching beyond the Habsburg Empire when analysing the network of Central European arts, literature, and music. This fluid notion of the space allows us to accommodate the diverse ideas about Central Europe found in the chapters of this volume.

The multi-ethnic condition of Central Europe has persisted since the nineteenth century despite all the historical upheavals.[1] After the First World War, Viennese writer Alfred Polgar emphasized that just as the Danube River has never conformed to the blue colour evoked in the famous waltz by Johann Strauss, Austria has never been an exclusively German-speaking country (209).[2] This statement can also be applied to Austria in the twenty-first century – as of 2014, 12 per cent of the people living in Austria held foreign citizenship.[3]

In the 1900s the Austro-Hungarian Monarchy did not find enthusiasm for the idea of a modern nation-state based on linguistic and ethnic unity. From the present perspective, we understand empire as a laboratory for a proto-globalized human condition, with all its conflicts and contradictions (Czaky). Such continuities and transformations are found at the heart of this volume, which sets out to uncover the political, historical, and social developments in transcultural relations among writers, artists, and musicians, and their works. The chapters identify motifs, topics, and modes of artistic creation characteristic of the region, such as the instability of national borders and the permeability of transcultural identity. They locate such developments in the late nineteenth century and then explore the resonance of that transcultural legacy today, since the fall of the Iron Curtain, thereby engaging the notion of a "longue durée" (Braudel) in these interrelations.

In the nineteenth century, industrialization, migration, and advances in health care led to the accelerating growth of cities like Vienna, Prague, and Budapest.[4] Increasing wealth and rising education among the middle class fostered a cosmopolitan stratum of intellectuals, writers, artists, and musicians, who generated modernist movements in the Central European cities that would gain international recognition – movements in areas such as psychoanalysis (Sigmund Freud, Alfred Adler), medicine (Theodor Billroth), political philosophy (Hans Kelsen), philosophy (Ernst Mach, Fritz Mauthner, Ludwig Wittgenstein), music as in the Second Viennese School of Music (Arnold Schönberg, and others), Symbolist and Expressionist art (Alfons Mucha, Gustav Klimt, Egon Schiele, Oskar Kokoschka), and writing (Arthur Schnitzler, Rainer Maria Rilke, and Franz Kafka). Many of them spent most of their life in Vienna, although born in different parts of Central Europe or descended from families who had earlier migrated to Vienna. Stefan Zweig described this pervasive habitus of the educated and transnationally active members of the intellectual bourgeoisie (*Bildungsbürger*) in his autobiography *The World of Yesterday*: in his family – as in many others of those times – the parents came from different parts of Europe and spoke several languages (6–10). The subtitle of Zweig's original German version reads "Memoirs of a European," further illuminating the transborder identity to which he ascribed in his book. Especially in art, music, and literature, the ethnic and cultural plurality supported by travels to the centres of modernist movements (to Paris, but also to London, and occasionally even to the United States) led to creative innovation. By exchanging journals, reading newly released books, attending performances of travelling theatre companies, and building international relations based on personal encounters and correspondence, an educated middle class established a worldwide network of cultural transfers and exchanges. Central Europe played a pivotal role in this process.

So it is unsatisfactory to study Austrian literature only in the context of Western literature, as Ernst Grabovszki and James Hardin do when they emphasize the "massive import of German, French, Italian, Scandinavian, and American influences" as well as the importance of Nietzsche and Wagner to Austrian music and literature at the turn of the century (4). In basing their study exclusively on texts in the German language, Grabovszki and Hardin follow Claudio Magris's influential study *Il mito absburgico nella letteratura austriaca moderna* (The Habsburg Myth in Modern Austrian Literature, 1963).

Vienna was not influenced solely by the West; it was also closely linked to the Central, Eastern, and Southeastern European modernist movements. It is striking, for instance, that nearly 40 per cent of the articles in the literary section of the Vienna-based weekly *Die Zeit* (The Times, 1894–1904) covered non-German literatures, with a strong emphasis on writers and books in Slavic languages (Moser and Zand). In 1902 the writer and journalist Jakob Julius David wrote that not only Western literature but also, indeed primarily, "Slavic literature" (Fyodor Dostoevsky, Leo Tolstoy) had affected the Viennese *fin de siècle* (121). Modernist writers such as Tadeusz/Thaddaeus Rittner (Polish-Galician), Ivan Franko (Ukrainian-Galician), and Ivan Cankar (Slovenian) had studied at the University of Vienna, got in touch with the local circles, and become part of these by publishing in Vienna's most important journals. Sometimes political conflicts instigated a cultural transfer; this was the case with the Croatian modernist movement around the journal *Mladost* (Youth), edited by Vladimir Vidrić and Milivoj Dežman, who protested against the opening ceremony of the Croatian National Theatre in Zagreb (1895). The Hungarian *ban* (governor) to Croatia ordered that a mound of Hungarian soil be built up for Emperor Francis Josef I to stand on as he performed the ceremony. The members of the *Mladost* group who protested this insult to their national feelings were dismissed from Zagreb University and continued their education in Vienna, where they published *Mladost* following modernist Viennese models. Journals such as *Die Zeit* and *Österreichische Rundschau* (Austrian Review, 1904–24) served as hot spots documenting Czech decadence as well as Polish, Ukrainian, and Bosnian modernist movements. They transmitted these developments not only to their readers across the Austro-Hungarian Monarchy but also to the rest of Europe and beyond.

Thus, before the First World War, Central Europe was a space of communication where cultural features were interwoven beyond nationalities and ethnicities. The railway stations, school buildings, and theatres designed by the famous Viennese architects Hermann Helmer and Ferdinand Fellner are among the many examples of overlapping aesthetic manifestations specific to Central Europe. For this reason, the region must be thought of more in terms of changes and transformations, or as a fluid structure with blurred edges, rather than as a territory with clear borders. There are few places in the world where national borders have changed so frequently over the past century as Central Europe: borders drawn within the Austro-Hungarian Monarchy were redrawn as countries reflecting the Paris treaties after the First World War, only to be redrawn again repeatedly during occupation by Nazi Germany, the division of the territory during the Cold War, and the revolutions and wars attending the painful processes of creating new states after the fall of the Iron Curtain. After 1989, a kind of Austrian nostalgia – one could call this process "austrostalgia" in the style of "ostalgia," the nostalgia for the former East Germany – appeared on both sides of the former borders (Bucur and Wingfield; Schwartz; Schlipphacke). Indeed, the Austrian government established an array of scholarship programs and Austrian libraries to improve academic cooperation with Central European partner institutions.[5] Meanwhile, some people in the countries of the former Austro-Hungarian Monarchy have expressed the sentiment that the shared past before the First World War was preferable to the political systems that followed. Although the monarchy treated its peripheries less well than the centres, in the 1990s one could hear many voices emphasizing those infrastructural and cultural connections established in the late nineteenth century. In keeping with this historical longing, Eastern Central European cities such as Chernivtsi have restored monuments to Emperor Francis Josef I and use the architecture and the memory of the monarchy as a means to attract tourists from around the world. In contrast, writers like Martin Pollack see a new wall replacing the Iron Curtain in the form of the borders of the European Union, which block access to the cultural richness of the regions in the East, including those diverse literatures less well-known to Western Europe.[6]

Scholarly analysis of the region, therefore, must consider these historical and contemporary transnational relations as well as their integral relationship to the processes of nation building; even if categories such as the nation-state remain in the foreground of discursive thought, an territory and structure of the respective countries of Central Europe have changed many times over the past century.

The chapters that follow examine these processes by engaging in an imbrication of historical and transnational perspectives on arts. This volume includes contributions from a variety of disciplinary perspectives – literature, film, music, architecture, media studies – and has two sections. The first focuses on the historical framework and investigates transcultural relations in the nineteenth and early twentieth centuries. The studies point to a complex trans-ethnic network of ideas and motifs spreading throughout the region, thus demonstrating the inadequacy of nationally bound perspectives in cultural studies. Following from this foundation, the authors in the second section examine interrelations in the late twentieth and early twenty-first centuries. They discuss both transnational and regional connections and correlations in context of globalization with its electronic mass media and its intensified migration, as well as the ruptures in aesthetic expression that have followed the end of the Cold War. The time periods comprising the two sections may appear static; better, though, to view them not as fixed but as resonating to each other. Furthermore, the chapters in each section are neither chronologically organized nor grouped around national identities; instead, they are built around theoretical and aesthetic affinities. Thus the imbrications occur within and across chapters so as to highlight historical returns and cultural ruptures.

Chapter 1 provides an overview of recent theories of transcultural studies, emphasizing the concept of cultural transfer. It describes the widespread network of intercultural and intertextual references in Central European arts, music, and literature around 1900. Viewing cultural transfers as a network unveils contradictions, phenomena of non-simultaneity, and power constellations resulting from the ethnic, medial, technical, economic, and ideological contexts of these processes. Helga Mitterbauer highlights the fact that literature, arts, and music were already strongly transculturally interconnected at the turn of the century. Many journals spread each new idea to a proto-globalized world that was concentrated on Europe but also reached far beyond; theatre and the new medium of film inspired writers and artists to constantly develop new artistic movements, which were later summarized under the umbrella term "modernism." A case study about the *fin de siècle* play *King Harlequin* (1900) by Austro-Hungarian journalist and playwright Rudolph Lothar shows the transfer of the symbolist character Pierrot and its pivotal role in literature and art.

In chapter 2, Agatha Schwarz and Helga Thorson emphasize how mobility and interculturality impacted the dramatic shifts in aesthetics around 1900. They investigate modernism as a transcultural phenomenon; their focus is on women writers representing different languages and parts of the Austro-Hungarian Monarchy (Grete Meisel-Hess, Terka Lux, Olha Kobylianska, Nafija Sarajlić, Zofka Kveder). Their analysis is based on the concept of "geomodernism" and thus emphasizes the importance of location and interconnections, showing the complexity of voices as well as the shifting boundaries of the Danube Monarchy. Among the results of this study is the observation that movements within the Monarchy – in this case, feminist organizations – tended to migrate out towards peripheries rather than in towards Vienna and Budapest. Analysis of the voices of female writers – a group largely neglected in the research on the *fin de siècle* – has far-reaching repercussions for the theory of modernism, for it shifts the focus beyond the dominant narratives describing formal characteristics towards a more differentiated cultural history.

Chapter 3 illuminates how music contributes to the social construction of space. According to Gregor Kokorz, because of its fluidity, semantic openness, and power to appeal to collectives, music played a pivotal role in the process of nationalism in the mid-nineteenth century. Starting with Felix Mendelssohn-Bartholdy's experience of the Italian border in 1830, Kokorz emphasizes the simultaneity of various ethnicities and cultures within the Austro-Hungarian Monarchy. The 1839–40 concert tour to Buda and Pest by Franz/Ferenc Liszt serves as a second example with regard to the construction of national identity. The Hungarian-born composer and conductor was of German ethnicity and spoke mostly French, yet on the eve of 1848 Revolution, Hungarians celebrated him as a national hero. Liszt became a figure of national identification because he represented the modern European world. The 1848 Revolution confronted the multi-ethnic condition in the port city of Trieste. In this situation, music played a part in the nationalistic competition for the urban space as it was transferred from the opera houses and concert halls to the streets.

In chapter 4, Imre Szeman analyses the reading play *The Tragedy of Man* (1862) by Hungarian writer Imre Madách as "a document of an interregnum" of blocked nationalist and socialist desires between the 1848 Revolution and the First World War (96). That revolution's failure sharply undermined intellectuals' and writers' faith in their role in political transformation. The reading play, as a literary form, responded to this social and political disappointment by questioning the relationship between politics and literature – in particular, the political ambitions of literature. A comparison with similar texts by Goethe, Flaubert, Karl Kraus, and James Joyce reveals that the double-crisis – the political one and the one resulting from the realization that politics cannot be adequately represented in literature – was a constitutive moment for the paradoxical literary form – that is, for plays could not be brought to the stage because they exceeded the limits of performance. Viewed as an intellectual thought experiment whose results could not be reapplied to the world, the reading play reflected dissociation from actual politics and a turn to a humanism detached from history.

Sarah McGaughey in chapter 5 turns to the development of architectural space and design in Central Europe, focusing on the representation of the modern kitchen in literature during the interwar period. She analyses texts by Franz Kafka, Ernst Weiß, Joseph Roth, Kurt Tucholsky, and Jakob Wassermann alongside international developments in the home, in particular Margarete (Grete) Schütte-Lihotzky's Frankfurt kitchen, and suggests a challenge to the national, aesthetic, and theoretical boundaries that determine how the modern kitchen is usually understood. She shows how a look at literary descriptions of the kitchen uncovers the development and circulation of the "modern aesthetic imagination" and how the kitchen becomes a creative space for authors as well as readers (102). Her chapter illustrates how, in the Central European kitchen, old meets new to offer alternative approaches and responses resonating in architecture, literature, and everyday practice.

The second section of this volume focuses on the period following the end of the Cold War and the fall of the Iron Curtain. Identity politics and identity formation in the post-totalitarian societies of East Central Europe are situated in a broader context of shifting political, cultural, and geophysical spaces. In chapter 6, Irene Sywenky examines the peripheral space of Lemberg/Lwów/Lvov/Lviv as a city shaped by the movement of languages and cultures across a variety of historical moments, including transfer from the Kingdom of Poland to the Austro-Hungarian Empire, to the Second Polish Republic, to the Soviet Union. Her analysis accents literary examples by Józef Wittlin, Stanisław Lem, Zbigniew Herbert, Adam Zagajewski, and Iurii Andrukhovych to show how Lviv remains a space marked by the desire for – and impossibility of – notions of belonging and home, and how it offers a potentially phantasmic location for the search for a bounded cultural identity.

Chapter 7 also examines the literary expressions of fluid identity as destabilizing geophysical space, but this time moving from the periphery to the centre. Sandra Vlasta analyses texts by Doron Rabinovici, Julya Rabinowich, and Vladimir Vertlib, all of which are set partly in Vienna. The city, however, through cultural transfer and travel, becomes linked to a broader range of Central European cities and is thus opened up to reflect not only local but also global concerns. Vlasta reads these texts in particular for their descriptions of transcultural collective memory, identities, and experiences, of which Jewishness is a shared part. Due to the ambiguities around both historical time and national space, she argues for their consideration not as works of Austrian literature but as Central European literature, and even world literature.

Chapter 8 picks up on and deepens these themes of movement, identity, and cultural transfer. Michael Boehringer's analysis of the novel *Engelszungen* (Tongues of Angels) by Dimitré Dinev places that novel within Austrian discussions around intercultural literature. His analysis revolves around the depiction of masculine norms and behaviours, especially their failures and ruptures, as representative of the destabilization of patriarchal structures of Central Europe, including the dominant narratives of communism and nationhood. This failure is rooted in imaginary notions of home, in terms of both origins (for Dinev, Bulgaria) and conflict with migration (here in Austria). Boehringer demonstrates how transcultural processes impact culturally based identity formations and negations of subjectivity. Gender becomes a means to display the coming together of historical and transnational approaches to self, national identity, and difference.

If the previous chapters of the second section show how transcultural processes resonate in literary depictions of identity struggles determined by movement across and within geophysical and national-imaginary spaces, chapter 9 shows how these processes also find their way into popular media, such as music, and take an intertextual form. Stefan Simonek examines the music of the Slovene band Laibach for their use of a broad range of national and transnational references, including their aesthetic appropriation of international avant-garde art movements from the early twentieth century: Russian opera, Nazi art, rock music, and disco. Using the notion of remixing, Simonek shows how the music displays a trans-aesthetic approach that combines and rewrites elements of Western popular culture, Central European culture, and Eastern European culture to develop a new object for a provocative effect. However, this provocative remixing also reflects back on the local culture, for the band also references a montage of Slovene symbols and literature, particularly the work of nineteenth-century poet France Prešeren. They thus display the unique semantic plurality of the Central European region.

In chapter 10, Matthew D. Miller proposes the field of Danubian Studies as an approach that deploys an understanding of the history of Central European transculturality, contested identities, and geographical and political transformations. In particular, the river serves as a "unifying artery of economic, cultural, and international exchanges" as Europe expands eastward (219); the river is a geophysical and transborder connector as well as an open metaphor for fluidity and crossings. Miller displays this by examining the Danube in contemporary transnational cinema, particularly in ex-Yugoslav and Vienna-based filmmaker Goran Rebić's 2003 *Donau, Dunaj, Duna, Dunav, Dunărea*. In his reading of the film, Miller sees a "bottled message" for a politically open Europe, but also an argument for Danubian Studies as a framework for scholarly discussion that looks towards a future-oriented and utopian understanding of Europe in the twenty-first century.

Chapter 11 picks up on these utopian and open understandings of Europe. In it, Carrie Smith-Prei examines the redefinition of confluence and the cosmopolitan for engaging with the personal and political impact of global processes. She looks to Bulgarian-born German author Ilija Trojanow, whose own biography and writings are based in travel (in flight and exile, but also in study and engagement) – encompassing Bulgaria, Germany, France, India, South Africa, and Austria – and who is (self-)positioned as a public intellectual. Using Ulrich Beck's concept of risk and through readings of Trojanow's diverse body of writings, Smith-Prei examines the role of the cosmopolitan public intellectual in calling attention to the negative political, ethical, and social impact of globalization, including its local and transborder resonances. *Crossing Central Europe* thus ends by suggesting that the aesthetic crossings in which the chapters in the volume engaged as well as the continuities and transformations between and among nations historically belonging to Central Europe since the nineteenth century help us grasp the aesthetic repercussions of globalization in the twenty-first century.

By combining case studies from different disciplines and dealing with examples from the turns of the centuries around 1900 and 2000, we shift the focus from nationalist or comparatist narratives towards a more differentiated cultural history of Central Europe. We highlight the diversity of transnational relations, which were already strong in nineteenth century but were interrupted for several decades by the world wars and by the separation of the Iron Curtain. The case studies in the second part of the volume underscore the continuities and ruptures of this widespread cultural network.

NOTES

1 The census of 1910 counted 24 per cent Germans, 20 per cent Hungarians, 17 per cent Czechs and Slovaks, 11 per cent Serbs and Croats, 10 per cent Poles, 8 per cent Ruthenians (Ukrainians), 6 per cent Romanians, 2.5 per cent Slovenians, and 1.5 per cent Italians living in this state (Gisser 19).

2 Unless otherwise indicated, all translations are our own.

3 As of the beginning of 2014, more than a million citizens of foreign countries lived in Austria (total population: 8.5 million). Most of them came from the former Yugoslavia (244,000) and from Germany (165,000) (Austria: Data, Figures, Facts).

4 Between 1818 and 1910, the population of the Austro-Hungarian Monarchy doubled from 26.2 to 51.4 million. Compared to Great Britain and France, the process of urbanization started later. Still, the rural population decreased while cities experienced enormous growth. For example, between 1873 and 1910, the population of Budapest increased from 280,000 to 1.1 million (Wandruszka and Rumpler).

5 The Austrian Foreign Ministry maintains sixty-two Austrian libraries as centres of culture, most of them in Central, Eastern, and Southeastern European cities (http://www.oesterreich-bibliotheken.at).

6 "Durch die neue Mauer zwischen Europa und Nichteuropa wird uns der Blick verstellt auf den unglaublichen kulturellen Reichtum der Regionen im Osten, auf die vielfältigen Literaturen und literarischen Szenen, von denen wir viel zu wenig wissen. Es liegt vor allem an uns, hier Initiativen zu setzen, Versäumtes aufzuholen und Lücken zu füllen." Visit Martin Pollack, 5 March 2014, http://blog.boschstiftung-portal.de/leipziger-buchmesse 2012/18.03.2012/meridian-czernowitz.

WORKS CITED

"Austria: Data, Figures, Facts." Vienna: Statistics Austria, 2015. http://www.statistik.at/web_en/publications_services/austria_data_figures_facts/index.html

Braudel, Fernand. "Histoire et sciences sociales: La longue durée." In *Réseau* 5.27 (1987): 7–37.

Bucur, Maria, and Nancy M. Wingfield, eds. *Staging the Past: The Politics of Commemoration in Habsburg Central Europe, 1848 to the Present.* West Lafayette: Purdue University Press, 2001.

Casanova, Pascale. *La république mondiale des lettres.* Paris: Seuil, 1999.

Czáky, Moritz. "Kultur als Kommunikationsraum. Das Beispiel Zentraleuropas." In *Gedächtnis und Erinnerung in Zentraleuropa,* ed. András F. Balogh and Helga Mitterbauer, 17–44. Vienna: Prsesens, 2011.

David, J[akob] J[ulius]. "Vom Slavischen in der deutschen Literatur." *Die Zeit* 399, 24 May 1902: 120–2.

Feichtinger, Johannes, and Gary B. Cohen. *Understanding Multiculturalism: The Habsburg Central European Experience.* New York: Berghahn, 2014.

Gisser, Richard. "Bevölkerungsentwicklung in der Monarchie nach 1880." *Das Zeitalter Kaiser Franz Josephs* 2.1: 19–25. Vienna: Amt der Niederösterreichischen Landesregierung, 1987.

Grabovszki, Ernst, and James Hardin, eds. *Literature in Vienna at the Turn of the Centuries around 1900 and 2000.* Rochester: Camden House, 2003.

Magris, Claudio. *Il mito absburgico nella letteratura austriaca moderna.* Torino: Einaudi, 1963.

Moser, Lottelies, and Helene Zand. "Die ZEIT, ein 'Wiener Posten der guten Europäer'?" In *Pluralität: Eine interdisziplinäre Annäherung. Festschrift für Moritz Csáky,* ed. Gotthart Wunberg and Dieter A. Binder, 247–57. Vienna, Cologne, and Weimar: Böhlau, 1996.

Polgar, Alfred. "Der Österreicher (Ein Nachruf)." In *Kleine Schriften,* vol. 1: *Musterung,* ed. Marcel Reich-Ranicki and Ulrich Weinzierl, 205–9. Reinbek and Hamburg: Rowohlt, 1982.

Schlipphacke, Heidi, ed. "The Temporalities of Habsburg Nostalgia." *Journal of Austrian Studies* 47.2 (2014): 1–16.

Schwartz, Agatha, ed. *Gender and Modernity in Central Europe: The Austro-Hungarian Monarchy and Its Legacy.* Ottawa: University of Ottawa Press, 2010. Print.

Wandruszka, Adam, and Helmut Rumpler, eds. *Die Habsburger Monarchie 1848–1918,* vol. 3: *Die Völker des Reiches.* Vienna: Verlag der Akademie der Wissenschaften, 1980.

Zweig, Stefan. *The World of Yesterday: An Autobiography.* New York: The Viking Press, 1945. Print.

PART ONE

1900

1 Beyond Aesthetic Borders: Theory – Media – Case Study

HELGA MITTERBAUER

This chapter surveys *fin-de-siècle* Vienna's transnational and transcultural relations in the arts with cultural centres in Western and Northern Europe, as well as with the rising movements in Central Europe. After providing the social, historic, and technical context, I elucidate the theoretical foundation of this chapter by outlining a concept of cultural transfer based on the idea of networks as a tool for analysing the complexities of transnational relations around 1900. In contrast to models of reception, the theory of cultural transfer focuses strongly on the transmitters of information and the forms of media they use. Around 1900, technical innovation and social transformation turned journals and magazines into pivotal means for transmitting new ideas. After giving a short summary of the theoretical concept, I will describe the transfers within the network of (Central) European literary and cultural journals and how those journals popularized movements and artists all around Europe and beyond. I will complement this empirical analysis with a case study: that of the Budapest-born writer and journalist Rudolf Lothar, in particular, his successful play *König Harlekin* (King Harlequin, 1900). This one-act play features Pierrot, an important character signifying problems of identity around 1900.

Introduction: *Fin-de-siècle* Vienna at Large

The processes of modernization in the nineteenth century resulted in a form of world citizenship that involved exchanging information personally in cafés, by travelling, through technical means such as print media, mail, and telegraphy, and eventually by telephone. Literary and cultural journals contributed greatly to the accelerated circulation of the new modernist trends in art, music, and literature. In his essay "Die demolirte Literatur" (The Demolished Literature), Karl Kraus, the Viennese writer and editor of the journal *Die Fackel* (The Torch, 1899–1936), emphasized these journals' importance for the spreading of information; he even complained of a "nearly overwhelming abundance of newspapers and journals" (19).[1] Scholars agree that the aesthetic quality of Viennese modernism resulted from its transcultural and cross-disciplinary borrowings and their creative transformation. As early as 1980, in his pioneering book *Fin-de-Siècle Vienna*, Carl Schorske noted: "The aesthetic movement was, of course, no Austrian creation, and its Austrian protagonists, both in poetry and in painting, drew inspiration from their western European predecessors, French, English, and Belgian. The Austrians readily captured the languorous sensibility of a Baudelaire or a Paul Bourget" (393).

Jacques Le Rider (1993) argues that German, French, Italian, Scandinavian, and American ideas were driving forces in Viennese modernism. In this regard Bachleitner discusses the writer Hermann Bahr, who travelled to Berlin, Saint Petersburg, and Paris and then returned to Vienna with the newest trends, at the same time popularizing new Austrian talents abroad. Dagmar Lorenz (2007) and Jens Rieckmann (1985) emphasize the influence of international writers such as Ibsen and Maeterlinck, Barrès and Bourget, Baudelaire, Barbey d'Aurevilly, and Huysmans, and Wilde and Swinburne, as well as Ola Hansson and Jens Peter Jacobsen on the Young Vienna group. Lorenz and Rieckmann discuss transcultural relations only briefly, whereas more recent studies focus on this topic: Peter Sprengel and Gregor Streim (1998) concentrate on the interactions between Berlin and Vienna, and Sylvie Arlaud analyses English references in Viennese modernism, particularly in the works of Hugo von Hofmannsthal, Hermann Bahr, and Karl Kraus (*Les references Anglais*, 2000). Robert Vilain (2000) has unearthed relations between Hofmannsthal's poetry and French Symbolism, and Karl Zieger (2012) describes Arthur Schnitzler's reception in France. Clearly, these scholars acknowledge the transfers from (and to) Western Europe, but only a very few recognize that this process was not oriented solely westwards. William M. Johnston enhances the perspective by exploring the interplay with Czech and Hungarian arts and culture. Stefan Simonek discusses the Slavic modernist movements and the reception of Viennese modernism in Slavic journals (*Distanzierte Nähe*, 2002, and *Die Wiener Moderne*, 2006); Damir Barbarić and Michael Benedikt (1998) analyse the connections between the modernist movements in Vienna and Zagreb.

These studies hint at the heightened interconnectivity of the literary system around 1900. They also show that this very important period in the history of Viennese and Austrian literature arose through fundamental exchanges. Only through competition with the avant-garde movements in other European cities could modernist writers develop their specific ways of writing and eventually gain a position in the literary canon.

When we view *fin-de-siècle* modernism as a complex interplay of constructions of identity, of dissociations and hybridizations, the interconnectivity with other (Central) European cities is not surprising. Remember here that Viennese modernism was embedded in a very specific social and juridical situation. Compared to the German Empire, censorship in the Austro-Hungarian Empire was still strict, and an anachronistic copyright law hindered the growth of a publishing market. Because Austria-Hungary had not joined the Berne Convention, which regulated international copyright, publications were not protected against translations and reprints abroad, and this increased the risk for publishers. In addition to the more difficult conditions for publishers, the long-established Viennese theatres catered to the high nobility and seldom mounted modernist works. For all of these reasons, modernist authors tended to turn to the German literary market, most notably to Berlin. On the political level, the relationship between Vienna and Berlin was quite ambivalent. In 1866, the Austrian army had suffered a humiliating defeat at the hands of Prussia in the battle of Sadowa-Königgrätz (Bohemia); five years later, in 1871, the German Empire was founded. As a result of these developments, the Habsburg emperors lost their leading role in Europe's German lands. Having lost its military influence, Vienna began to recast itself as a city of art, literature, and music (Nußbaumer). From this perspective, the Young Vienna group's tilt towards the (French) Aestheticist and Decadent movements implies a drift away from Berlin naturalism. Clearly, an aesthetic but also a political dimension was at play when Hermann Bahr set out to overcome naturalism ("Überwindung des Naturalismus," 1891).

Technological and social developments during the nineteenth century resulted in a paradoxical situation in the Austro-Hungarian Empire. The nobility still held more power than the increasingly wealthy middle class. The latter oriented themselves culturally to the tastes and habits of the former. The palaces on Vienna's Ringstraße could serve as examples, and also the idea of an "Adel des Geistes" (nobility of spirit) that arose among the Central European bourgeoisie. According to Carl Schorske, actors, artists, and critics became the heroes of the upper middle class: "If the Viennese burghers had begun by supporting the temple of art as a surrogate form of assimilation into the aristocracy, they ended by finding in it an escape, a refuge from the unpleasant world of increasingly threatening political reality" (38). The concept of *Bildung* became very popular, especially among the upper middle class. Around 1890 in Vienna there appeared "a high bourgeoisie unique in Europe for its aesthetic cultivation, personal refinement, and psychological sensitivity" (Schorske 388). Hugo von Hofmannsthal serves as an example: as a student at the *Gymnasium,* he read all the key works of European modernism in French, English, and Italian. A thorough familiarity in Latin and Old Greek was also part of a classical education. This intellectual grounding helped develop a cosmopolitan orientation, which was perceived positively on the one hand, and negatively on the other as pluralism and drift. This tension caused the suffering of modernist societies, which was so often a prominent theme in *fin-de-siècle* literature, art, and philosophy.

Technological progress – as presented at every world exposition after 1851 – accelerated change in living conditions. Railways, electricity, telegraphy, new printing techniques, a more advanced postal system, and other developments transformed the social framework and the economic conditions in which literature and other arts were produced. Given the loosened censorship and the greater variety of options for making a living from publishing books and newspaper and journal articles, as well as for giving public lectures, writers shed their dependence on noble patrons and on the authorities. The transformations of the nineteenth century resulted in a new self-confidence ("nobility of spirit," identified above) as well as in accelerated exchanges of information. By the turn of the century, the café had become a pivotal space for discourse and for exchanging news. At the café, writers, artists, and their audiences, dilettantes and snobs, dandies and *flâneurs,* found, read, and discussed numerous national and international newspapers and weekly and monthly journals. As never before in history, journals had become a venue of accelerated modernism where various movements alternated, overlapped, and competed against one another. They evolved into transnational and cross-disciplinary institutions with complex relations among publishers, editors, authors, critics, and translators. Sylvie Arlaud notes that the first generation of the Young Vienna writers educated themselves by reading foreign literature in newspapers and journals ("Peter Altenbergs *Kunst*" 99). They also used these mass media to promote their own literature and opinions.

In the discursive space of these journals, movements in art, literature, and music were negotiated. These movements had no fixed characteristics; rather, they were characterized by their fluidity as well as their permeability to other movements and trends. In the next section, I investigate *fin-de-siècle* Viennese literature with regard to its transcultural relations with Western, Central, and Southeastern European movements. The structure of this study is based on an enriched concept of cultural transfer that allows us to analyse the complexities of intercultural relations, including the contradictions inherent in the system.

Methodological Approach: Cultural Transfer

Cultural transfer studies analyse processes of intercultural transfers and transmissions of cultural artefacts, texts, discourses, and practices. The bilateral model of intercultural transfers was first formulated by Michel Espagne and Michael Werner; since then, the prominent view has been that it is transmitters (i.e., translators, publishers, scholars, universities, journalists, writers, refugees, and migrants) who relocate cultural elements from one context to another. These cultural elements are not produced for the purpose of cultural transfer; moreover, they are transferred to another cultural context only through the intervention of transmitters. Usually during the transfer, the element or its meanings are transformed, modified, adapted, or adjusted according to the target's requirements. Processes of selection, adaptation, and creative reception occur. Cultural elements cannot be considered neutral carriers of arbitrary meanings; they do, however, allow for different interpretations contingent on the context. Indeed, it is precisely this peculiarity of cultural elements – they are open to different interpretations in different contexts – that qualifies them for cultural transfer.

The bilateral or triangular model of cultural transfers needs to be augmented, by means of ideas taken from postcolonial studies and network analysis, in order to account for the greater complexity of relations around 1900. Especially important are the concepts of hybridity, *métissage*, and creolization, whereby culture is no longer comprehended as stable, consistent, and delimitable but rather as a dynamic process of overlapping and amalgamation. According to Edward Said, cultures are "neither monolithic nor reductively compartmentalized, separate, distinct" (xxii). Based on Derrida's notion of *differance*, Homi K. Bhabha emphasizes the contradictory, polyphonic, and processual quality of cultural formations as well as the global circulation of humans, artefacts, codes, and information. By regarding cultures as "signifying or symbolic activity" (210), Bhabha emphasizes that cultures are always in motion and in interaction with one another. He deconstructs the idea that the nation-state is a homogenous unity and emphasizes the impossibility of demarcating a heterogeneous entity.

The idea of *métissage* developed in francophone cultural studies serves as a metaphor for the postmodern condition of life with its multi-ethnic and multicultural metropolises and its networks of information, communication, and interaction (Turgeon 53–69). Jean-Loup Amselle focuses on a type of mixing where the elements involved in the continuous process are themselves not viewed as pristine elements clearly distinguishable from one another (Amselle 248). This leads to an understanding of cultural elements as units with frayed seams, which are already an outcome of previous transfer processes.

Akin to *métissage*, Eduard Glissant marks, in his concept of *créolization*, the conjunction of several cultures or at least several elements taken from different cultures. He emphasizes that the result of this process is not predictable (37). Tapping into the thought of Gilles Deleuze and Félix Guattari, he revives the metaphor of the rhizome by emphasizing that identity consists not of a single root, but rather of a multitude of relations. This metaphor illustrates the complexity of transcultural relations.

An enhanced notion of culture as developed in postcolonial theories has had a radical impact on the systems of references used in cultural transfer studies: it has moved the perspective from the centre to the frayed peripheries. The consistency of a cultural structure is no longer pivotal; the focus has instead settled on relentless overlappings and blendings. These studies emphasize internal differentiation and a polyphony of cultural structures whose borders are seen as overlapping zones where never-ending transformations lead to new results in unpredictable ways. Cultures are viewed as dynamic multiplex codifications of individual and collective identity and as constantly being transformed depending on the situation and the frame of reference.

Modelling complex entangled phenomena such as cultural transfer using the epistemological figure of the network is as suitable an approach as applying the notion of culture derived from postcolonial studies. Both theories reject the idea of linear constellations and of culture as a unit with a sovereign centre. Networks are decentric structures consisting of elements with relations to other elements, of clusters, and of relations between them. They are highly flexible, adaptable, circular, and contingent, and they can extend in space and time. They are established, maintained, and transformed by individuals or groups whose positions and functions affect the network; at the same time, they themselves are affected by transformations of multiplex relations.

Cultural transfer studies based on a dynamic notion of culture adjust the concept of network analysis as developed by Harrison C. White and Mark Granovetter. Following a postcolonial notion of culture, neither actors nor events nor objects can be understood as uniform, consistent, or delimited. Connecting the metaphor of the network with a dynamic notion of culture helps us describe sequences in which all of the elements change everywhere in the same space and at the same time. In this structure of relations, we are also confronted with partial interrelations, which can be completely different from simultaneous relations. Such relations can be reciprocal, symmetric, or transitive; they can stay relatively stable for a long time, or they can transform very quickly. Networks are spatial metaphors within which social and material elements impact one another; as soon as the relation between elements or clusters transforms, the entire network is transformed.

When we apply this idea of network to processes of cultural transfer, four dimensions become important. First, network analysis is an actor theory. Actors and transmitters in cultural transfer processes, be they individuals or groups, initiate, pursue, and influence the relations in a network. In our case it is important to see them as hybrid in the sense of postcolonial studies. Second, as mentioned above, the network is a spatial concept and therefore builds a geographical or symbolic space of relations, transposing cultural elements among clusters and transforming them. Third, transfer processes take place in a trajectory of time; however, these processes do not always elapse in a linear, chronological line of time; they can also do so in a non-chronological or perhaps in a dys-chronological way. Fourth, thinking of cultural transfers as dynamic networks reflects social, cognitive, and idealistic constellations as well as structures of power affecting the process. It follows that processes of cultural transfer occur on the levels of spatial distance, internal difference, time, and power.

Modelling cultural transfers as dynamic networks allows us to analyse various forms of transfers. These can take place among nation-states and continents, but also among different social or cognitive groups located geographically very near one another. This approach helps integrate detours and intermediate stations encountered by the cultural element; it also emphasizes that the transfer process is multipolar and potentially endless.

The model of the network focuses on the social and cultural agency of transmitters as well as the interactions between the framework, the social structure, and the individual action. Simultaneously, the social milieu influences the actions of the transmitters, whose acts are the foundation from which net structures emerge. By analysing the historical, social, economic, technical, and medial framework, network theory helps deduce the intentions of the transmitters – for example, whether a transmission takes place because of economic need or for moral or aesthetic reasons. Networks are complex structures of interaction resulting from both intentional and random actions of individuals or institutions.

Within a network, a transmitter can have relations of different qualities and different extensions. A transmitter can have many loose ties or only a small number of strong ties. To use an economic metaphor, the availability of information strongly affects its value. Mark Granovetter views large and heterogeneous networks as more efficient than redundant relations, since the latter can lead on indirect paths again and again to the same clusters, even if they do not deliver more information. In networks, not all clusters are connected; if there is only one path between two points, Granovetter speaks of "bridges" that can provide the better interconnected actor with an advantage of knowledge compared to other individuals or groups.

The sources available for analysis bear a clear historical component, because the means of transport that document the processes of cultural transfer are related to the systems of technology and communication of their time. It follows that the sources for documenting a transfer change with the historic framework. Thus, studies of the time around 1800 – so far the most studied period in the field of cultural transfers – are based largely on archival materials or manuscript collections (Espagne and Greiling 12). For this period, Michel Espagne suggested that we combine "individual" sources (autobiographic reports, private correspondence) with "objective" ones such as administrative actions, business letters, and documents (Espagne 315).

For the period around 1900, literary and cultural journals are a rich source for cultural transfer studies. They were available to everyone in all European coffeehouses. Critics had by then acquired an important function in the battle of interpretive dominance. The waves of modernization during the nineteenth century generated keen interest in information from abroad. It had become usual for intellectuals to take long trips to foreign countries; this served as an initiation process in the sense that the traveller accumulated the knowledge and contacts necessary to gain the authority to launch a new artistic style or to acquire the tools to succeed as a transmitter. Journals provided their readers with the most up-to-date news; they documented in detail when and how and what cultural elements were being transferred within Europe and beyond. An analysis of journals shows the importance of transmitters, who often doubled as writers and as critics, and who were well connected with one another. The system of guest writers for journals in different cities or countries proves this abundantly. As these transmitters were strongly connected by correspondence and personal encounters, it is absolutely essential to include sources such as letters and diaries in the analysis. Cultural journals provide key insights into the complexity of the cultural system around 1900.

Mediascapes: The Network of Literary and Cultural Journals around 1900

Thinking of cultural transfer as a network is based on an understanding of identity that implicates differences of gender, ethnicity, and religion, as well as differentiated access to money and (social) power. Around 1900, the idea that individuals encompassed various identities at one and the same time was widely accepted by philosophers and artists; it was also an empirical fact. Migration and rapid technological advances blurred cultural attributions thoroughly; this becomes clear when we consider the editors of cultural journals and newspapers who migrated from the Crown territories to the empire's capital, Vienna. The three editors of the weekly *Die Zeit* were born in Budapest (Isidor Singer), Galati (Heinrich Kanner), and Linz (Hermann Bahr). The founding editor of *Die Wage*, Rudolf Lothar, also came from Budapest, while his successor hailed from Postelberg in Bohemia. The most important journal of Croatian modernism, *Mladost*, was edited and published in the capital of the Habsburg Empire.

It was not just Viennese artists and writers who gathered together in Vienna's cafés; so did those from all parts of the Empire. They included the Polish-Galician writer Thaddäus/Tadeusz Rittner and the Slovenian Ivan Cankar, both of whom published in their own language as well as in German (Simonek). The editors of and collaborators in these journals maintained contact with authors and critics in the French, British, American, Scandinavian, Belgian, Russian, Italian, Czech, Polish, Hungarian, and other centres of modernist movements.

In the early period of these accelerated cultural transfers at the *fin-de-siècle* – the late 1880s – Paris was the centre of innovative trends. Writers such as Hermann Bahr travelled to Paris and founded and edited journals after their return. At this early time, there existed an asymmetrical transfer: Paris became the paragon for the Viennese aesthetic movement. It was several years before Viennese contributions became recognized in Paris. The writers of Young Vienna transferred elements from the French context, adapted them to their needs, and soon developed an internationally recognized style of their own. In this process of cultural transfer, journals and newspapers were pivotal: in the context of accelerated technological advances, they became the main platforms for exchanging the newest information; writers used the journals to glean information and to spread their own ideas. It is striking how many writers published their texts in journals and newspapers, and also engaged in criticism around 1900.

The first journal of Viennese modernism, *Moderne Dichtung* (Modern Poetry), edited by Eduard Michael Kafka, was founded in 1890. It continued in 1891 under the title *Moderne Rundschau* (Modern Review), edited by Kafka together with lawyer Jacques Joachim and journalist Julius Kulka. It contained mostly literary texts written by naturalist authors, and it was here that Hermann Bahr published his programmatic essay "Die Moderne," in which he encouraged his contemporaries to seize the moment and overcome history. The weekly *Die Zeit. Wiener Wochenschrift für Politik, Volkswirtschaft, Wissenschaft und Kunst* (The Times: Viennese Weekly for Politics, National Economy, Science, and Arts, 1894–1904) and its subsequent daily publication *Die Zeit* (1902–19) were important vehicles for establishing Young Vienna. Bahr, who maintained contact with representatives of the French Symbolist and Decadent movements, edited the literature and theatre sections of *Die Zeit* until the fall of 1899. After proposing the "Überwindung des Naturalismus" (overcoming of naturalism), he used *Die Zeit* as a mouthpiece for the Viennese aesthetic movement. The journal became a key platform for these writers and at the same time an important means of cultural transfer.

Most of the literature published in this journal was written by German-speaking authors (64 per cent), with 13 per cent contributed by French and 8 per cent each by Scandinavian and Slavic writers. Italian, Hungarian, and English literatures were also given space. *Die Zeit* played a prominent role in the cultural transfer between Slavic literatures and Central Europe, given that such literature was provided much less space in other German periodicals of that time (e.g., *Kunstwart* and *Freie Bühne*, 4 per cent each, and *Blätter für die Kunst*, 2 per cent) (Moser and Zand).

The issues of *Die Zeit* had a consistent structure: articles on politics, economics, and the sciences were followed by literary and critical writings, including a literary text, often a serial novel, and various shorter pieces under the rubric "Kunst und Leben" (arts and life). This latter section informed readers about current premieres, new releases, and the content of journals from all over the world. As such it was very important in terms of cultural transfer. Under the heading "Premièren der Woche" (Premieres of the Week), the journal reported performances at theatres not only in Vienna but also in Paris, London, Brussels, the German cities, Prague, Brno, Milan, Venice, Trieste, Naples, Rome, Nice, Budapest, and the Upper Austrian capital, Linz. The book review section and the column "Revue der Revuen" – a title copied from French journals – were equally cosmopolitan. The Revue column had a wide geographical spread: besides periodicals from German-speaking countries, *Die Zeit* received recent copies of journals from all over the world. Among these were journals published in Paris, Belgium, the Netherlands, Italy, Spain, Portugal, and North and South America.[2] The reader was also regularly informed about what was being published in Central, Eastern, and Northern European journals as well as in Asia.[3]

The literary and critical contributions did not have such a broad reach. There was an emphasis on articles about politics and literature in France. Between 1897 and 1899, nineteen articles analysed the Dreyfus affair. One of these was written by the Norwegian writer Bjørnstjerne Bjørnson (*Die Zeit*, 30 July 1898, 63–4). Another topic discussed repeatedly was the 1900 Exposition Universelle in Paris. A common rubric at this time was the "Briefe aus ..." (Letters from ...). Most of these letters were sent from Paris, and most were written by the critic and Symbolist writer Camille Mauclair. Others were penned by Rudolf Lothar, who lived in Paris in 1895 and who later became the editor of the Viennese weekly *Die Wage*.

Die Zeit also published literary texts – most of them by French authors – which were always printed at the end of each issue. These serial novels were regularly introduced by biographies and descriptions of each writer. The largest number of these texts were penned by the writer of mystery stories, Jules-Amédée Barbey d'Aurevilly (1808–1889).[4] In addition, several articles were published about him; one of those was written by the Swedish writer Ola Hansson. Critical essays were written on authors such as Prudhomme, Mallarmé, Rimbaud, and Verlaine. Also published were translations of plays by Georges Courteline, a literary portrait of Maurice Donnay, a long report of the performance of Edmond Rostand's *Cyrano de Bergerac* at Vienna's Hofburgtheatre, about Victorien Sardou as well as on Pierre and Jean Véber. The poet, novelist, and influential critic Rémy de Gourmont (a founder of the *Mercure de France*, a leading Symbolist journal published in Paris), and Henri Albert (Haug), who wrote in the *Mercure the France* about German literature, also published articles in *Die Zeit*. From time to time, essays giving a wider overview were published – for example, the analysis "Vom Einfluss der fremden Literaturen auf das junge Frankreich" (On the influence of foreign literatures on Young France, *Die Zeit*, 10 August 1895, 90–1).

Italian literature was dominated by the poet, journalist, and playwright Gabriele d'Annunzio, who published frequently in *Die Zeit*. He was also the subject of several critical essays, one of them by Hugo von Hofmannsthal. Oscar Schmidt surveyed "Die modernen Italiener" (The modern Italians), and several modernist Italian writers, such as the poet and novelist Ada Negri and the short story writer, poet, and playwright Antonio Fogazzaro, also published in the Viennese journal. Vittorio Pica, the most important transmitter of Italian modernist movements, published a portrait of the diplomat and novelist Carlo Dossi.

The English writer and essayist Vernon Lee (Violet Paget), who knew German literature very well, published a serial novel, which was introduced by Hermann Bahr himself. In 1903, Oscar Wilde's "Birthday of the Infanta" was published in German translation. Prior to that, *Die Zeit* reported on the Wilde trial (1895), and Henri de Régnier published his "Erinnerungen an Oscar Wilde" (Memories of Oscar Wilde), at the time when Wilde was serving his sentence in Reading Gaol. Rudyard Kipling, Robert Stevenson, Walter Pater, and H.G. Wells were other British writers who contributed texts to *Die Zeit* or were the subject of essays. Mark Twain, Ralph Waldo Emerson, and Lafcadio Hearn represented the literature of the United States.

Much space was given to Scandinavian literature: six articles were published on Henrik Ibsen, one on Bjørnstjerne Bjørnson. Knut Hamsun, Hjalmar Christensen, and Jonas Lie wrote literary texts for *Die Zeit*. The Viennese translator and Scandinavian expert Marie Herzfeld contributed a study about Ola Hansson, who himself published an excerpt from an autobiographical novel and an essay on Per Hallström.

Hallström also published a text in *Die Zeit*. Oscar Levertin appeared several times, with two serial stories and various other pieces. Literary texts by August Strindberg, Selma Lagerlöf, Georg Brandes, Biggo Stuckenberg, and Amalie Skram were also printed.

Of great importance for Young Vienna was the Belgian playwright, poet, and essayist Maurice Maeterlinck, who published seven texts in *Die Zeit*. Hermann Bahr wrote an elaborate review of Maeterlinck's collection of mystical essays *Le trésor des humbles* (The Treasure of the Humble; *Die Zeit*, 7 March 1896, 157–8). The Belgian writer, poet, journalist, and member of the La Jeune Belgique group, Camille Lemonnier, and the poet Fernand Séverin played a minor role in *Die Zeit*.

Russian writers, such as Leo Tolstoy (two literary texts by him and six essays on him), Maxim Gorky (one literary text by him and three essays on him), Fyodor Dostoevsky (two texts by him), and Anton Chekhov (two literary texts by him), had a presence in *Die Zeit*. Given that this journal mostly engaged with European literature, an overview of Japanese poetry, published in 1899, is striking.

Of great interest is the strong emphasis on the literature from Central Europe. Ludwik Krzywicki provided an article on "Jüngste Strömungen in der polnischen Literatur" (The most recent trends in Polish literature; *Die Zeit*, 26 January 1895, 54–5), and the Czech writer and critic František Václav Krejči became a transmitter of the Czech Decadent movement (Kostrbová et al.). Between 1896 and 1904, the editor of the journal *Rozhledy* published eleven essays about new trends in Prague's literary and cultural life in *Die Zeit*. But among Slavic writers, the one who contributed the most was the Ukrainian Ivan Franko. He studied in Vienna in 1892 and 1893 and published ten literary texts up to 1903. Finally, the Montenegrin Luka Jovović and the Bulgarian Ivan Vazov also contributed to *Die Zeit*.

This list could be extended by examining the *Wiener Rundschau* (Viennese Review), which was published from 1896 until 1901. It was even more internationally and cosmopolitically oriented than *Die Zeit*. All writers of importance around 1900 – from Russia to the United States, from Scandinavia to Italy, and from the different parts of Central Europe – published in this journal. A major emphasis was on French literature, and it is one of the *Wiener Rundschau*'s great achievements that it focused on writers in the early stages of their careers, such as Ernest de La Jeunesse (1897–8) and André Gide (1901). The journal played a large role in the internationalization of Oscar Wilde. Before the broad reception of the Irish-British writer started in the German-speaking countries, the *Wiener Rundschau* had already published the complete translation of *Salomé* (by Hedwig Lachmann) and excerpts from the *Ballad of Reading Gaol*; finally, the critic Rudolf von Kassner wrote an obituary for Wilde, who had passed away in November 1900.

Besides literary texts and criticism from all parts of Europe and North America, the *Wiener Rundschau* published a multitude of letters from various cities. We find important figures of the modernist movements among the writers of these letters, including Rémy de Gourmont, a founder of and collaborator with the *Mercure de France*. Henri Albert, responsible for the "Lettres allemandes" in that same French journal, sent letters as well, but most of the "Letters from Paris" were penned by Camille Mauclair, who established the important Parisian Symbolist Théâtre de l'Œuvre, in 1893, together with Lugné-Poe (Aurélien Marie Lugné).

These letters from various cities are especially revealing of the widespread network of literary critics and translators who co-generated, promoted, and accelerated the diverse European movements in literature, art, and music. This fairly small number of critics and writers from the various centres of modernist movements were tightly linked with one another by mail. As founders or editors of journals, they were able to influence wide audiences. They were members of literary circles, and often authors of literary texts as well; they met frequently with other writers, often on a daily basis, to discuss local and international new releases and theatre productions. The meeting places included private homes (such as Stéphane Mallarmé's famous "Mardis") and cafés such as the Griensteidl, where Young Vienna gathered every day. Well-known to everyone interested in literature and the arts, these meeting points allowed travellers to join the groups. In particular, an invitation to one of Mallarmé's Tuesday salons was perceived as an inclusion in a very distinguished circle.

The close connectedness of the literary groups within Europe can be described as a network rather than in terms of mutual relations. The Viennese journal *Die Wage. Eine Wiener Wochenschrift* (The Balance: A Viennese Weekly), founded in 1898, was another piece of this network. The Danish writer Georg Brandes published an obituary here on Stéphane Mallarmé (12 November 1898, 760–1); Swedish writer and critic Oscar Ivar Levertin published an article about Paul Bourget, a review of Zola's novel *Travail*, and a literary portrait of French writer and Orientalist Joseph Ernest Renan (*Die Wage* 3.42 [1900], 247–8; 4.33 [1901], 521–2; 6.44 [1903], 1193–6; 6.45 [1903], 1213–16; 6.46 [1903], 1239–41; 6.47

[1903], 1260–3). Austrian translator Marie Herzfeld was an important transmitter of Scandinavian literature (Gallagher 2000, 2007). She not only published articles about and translations of Scandinavian writers in all of the important Austrian journals, but was also quoted abroad – for example, in the *Mercure de France*, where Henri Albert informed his readers about her article on Ola Hansson and republished important parts of it (*Mercure de France* 15.69 [September 1895], 364–74). Another article by Henri Albert explains that Czech philosopher and politician Thomas Masaryk was received in Paris only after a study published in *Die Zeit* in February and March 1898. In the very same "Lettres allemandes," he emphasizes that the many translations published in the *Wiener Rundschau* gave an excellent overview of the contemporary European literary movements (*Mercure de France* 26.101 [May 1898], 315–20).

All of these examples point to the close interconnectedness of literary and cultural journals at the turn of the century: editors informed their readers about articles published in other journals, premieres in theatres, and book releases in other cities and countries. Very often, they invited guest writers or translated articles from foreign journals.

Case Study of a Transmitter: Rudolf Lothar

Among these guest authors and editors, we find the writer, playwright, and journalist Rudolf Lothar Spitzer, who published under the pen name Rudolf (or Rudolph) Lothar. His career is very typical for a writer-journalist around 1900, a time when technological and social transformations resulted in high mobility for the middle class. Born into a Jewish family in Budapest in 1865, he studied philosophy and Romance literature at the universities of Vienna, Jena, Rostock, and Heidelberg. After graduating, he lived in Paris and became acquainted with the French naturalist writers Edmond and Jules de Goncourt. Lothar also made longer journeys to Spain, Palestine, and the United States. He wrote for the feuilleton pages of the *Neue Wiener Presse* (New Viennese Press). After 1907, he worked as a journalist in Berlin, where he also founded a theatre.

At the turn of the century, he kept in close contact with the members of the Young Vienna group; in particular, he was a friend of Arthur Schnitzler. In literary circles, Lothar became well-known for his study *Kritische Studien zur Psychologie der Literatur* (Critical Study on the Psychology of Literature, 1895) and for his book *Das Wiener Burgtheater*

(The Vienna Burgtheatre, 1899). He wrote novels and novellas, as well as plays and librettos. For example, he wrote the libretto for *Tiefland* by Scottish-born German composer Eugen d'Albert, which premiered in Prague in 1903. His best-known work for the theatre was the mask play *König Harlekin* (King Harlequin, 1900). After being banned by Habsburg censorship initially, it was quickly translated into fourteen languages and performed on stages all over Europe.

Lothar founded the weekly *Die Wage* in 1898 and was its editor until 1902. According to an invitation for subscription, his goal was to inform its readers about contemporary politics, literature, arts, and sciences from a very up-to-date and radical point of view (*Die Wage* 2.13 [1899], 219). In March 1898 the Paris-based journal *L'Ermitage* declared in a biographical note following the publication of a translation of Lothar's play *La Fin du Borgia* that *Die Wage* already held a prominent place in Austria's intellectual life (*L'Ermitage* 9 [1898], 183–205). In fact, though, whatever its ambitions to become one of the top German-language weeklies, its quality was not consistently maintained at a high level.

Die Wage reflected Lothar's cosmopolitan interests. In it, he published a great number of articles about or by foreign authors; in common with *Die Zeit* and *Wiener Rundschau*, many of those articles focused on the political situation in France, in particular the Dreyfus affair and the trial of Émile Zola. It is striking for how long and in what exhaustive detail this scandal of anti-Semitism was discussed in the capital of the Austro-Hungarian Monarchy. In these texts, he also illuminated the social context for the birth of the Zionist movement. Besides focusing strongly on literature and the arts, *Die Wage* published political articles from Paris ("Pariser Briefe"). And it covered everyday events, such as the gossip about the divorce of Victor Hugo's granddaughter Jeanne from Alphonse Daudet's son Léon. These items point to the editor's deep insight into Parisian society as well as the reading public's interest in it.

Reflecting Lothar's own literary bent, *Die Wage* informed its readers not only about the newest trends in avant-garde literature but also about light-hearted comedies from Paris vaudeville playwrights such as Victorien Sardou, Ludovic Halévy, Augustin Eugène Scribe, Pierre Veber, and Maurice Hannequin.

Die Wage published articles about English, Scandinavian, and Central European literature – for example, about Czech literature (by František Václav Krejčí) and the newest trends in Polish lyric (by Ludwik Szczepánski) and Italian literature (by Vittorio Pica). However, much more emphasis was placed on everything coming from Paris. Although he was born in Budapest and spent most of his life in Vienna, Lothar was strongly oriented towards Paris, and he drew his evaluation criteria from the aesthetic norms of the Symbolist and Decadent movements. Even when he published articles on new trends in Czech or Polish literature, such as the ones by Krejčí and Szczepánski, these informed readers about youth movements that drew from French Symbolism or Decadence.

Pierrot, a stock character in Symbolist and Decadent literature, has his roots in the Commedia dell'arte. Antoine Watteau's painting of the lonely fellow-sufferer from 1718 inspired Decadents as well as Symbolists. For the Decadents, his naive idealism, distaste for women, and disillusioned attitude, resonating with Schopenhauer's philosophy, represented their own position. Symbolists were moved by Pierrot's soulful sensitivity and by his close relationship with the distant moon, as well as by his complete inability to connect with the crude reality around him. All of these things made him a model for the modernist artist, who was devoted to a life of loneliness outside society, in an artistic and aesthetic environment.

Lothar's *König Harlekin* was part of the international Pierrot trend around 1900. In German-speaking countries, most of the works featuring Pierrot were written by Viennese. One of the best-known works around this theme is Arnold Schönberg's composition after Albert Giraud's *Pierrot Lunaire*, from 1912. This reflected a more general tendency: the naturalist movement was stronger in Berlin and Munich, whereas Vienna was more oriented towards Symbolism and Decadence.

As early as 1893, Richard Beer-Hofmann had written the drama *Pierrot Hypnotiseur*, in which he connected the character with the rising interest in psychoanalysis. In this text, Pierrot is an elderly physician who uses the new technology of hypnosis to seduce Colombine. But hypnosis does not make the young spouse really love her husband, and she functions like an automaton. As soon as Pierrot releases her from hypnosis, she returns to her earlier love Arlequino and spends all her husband's money with him. *Pierrot Hypnotiseur* combines Decadent themes with naturalist elements, such as alcoholism, poverty, contemporary medical practice, and psychology. He contrasts those features with pantomime, then a new style in Austrian avant-garde theatre, based on French models.

Lothar transformed the pantomime into a masquerade play. In *König Harlekin*, Harlequin is an actor playing the king of a fictitious empire so well that nobody realizes the fraud. This explains why the play was banned by the Habsburg censors before it was performed on numerous European stages. In the opening scene, Prince Bohemund returns to his father's palace in the hour of his death. The father has not been a good king to his subjects, and neither Bohemund nor his brother shows promise to rule any better. The prince returns home with a group of actors, including Harlequin and Columbine. Harlequin is assigned the masque of the prince whenever Bohemund gets into trouble, and Columbine is supposed to soothe the prince's ennui with her attractiveness. Harlequin, who is in love with Columbine, kills the prince in an act of jealousy when Bohemund approaches her. Precisely at this moment, the father dies. Harlequin, wearing the mask of Bohemund, becomes king. He soon realizes that being king is only an abstract idea. He changes back into the role of Harlequin, and in a play within the play, he performs his experiences at the court. During the performance, Harlequin disappears with his boat.

This mask play reveals several characteristics of Symbolism. In particular, the emphasis on the mask refers to the problems of identity and the fragmentation of the subject. For example, Harlequin answers this question:

> Who are you? Who is Harlequin? Are you the miserable servant, the weak-kneed and venal slave of this master? [...] Who are you? You play all roles, you wear the masks as if they were your own face. What is your true face? In what role are you yourself?:
>
> Who am I? If I would know that! If a man would know that! Who does not play a role? Who has the right to say: I am I?! [...] Sometimes I imagine myself as a king, I feel so great, so powerful, so majestic. Sometimes I think, I imagine myself as a miserable beggar, separate from all generous and noble-minded people. (Lothar 24–5)

In Symbolist and Decadent literature around 1900, questioning identity was often connected with mourning for a lost unity. Furthermore, playing with masks ranks among the pivotal topoi of these authors. For example, in Oscar Wilde's novella *The Picture of Dorian Gray* (1890–91), the main character keeps the same impeccable face in spite of all the infamous actions he commits. Only his portrait in the hidden attic distorts into an ugly grimace, mirroring his immoral way of life. His face works as a mask hiding the identity of Dorian Gray, just as it points out the constructedness of any idea of a holistic identity. The mask draws our focus to the problem of identity, following ideas formulated by philosophers such as Friedrich Nietzsche and Ernst Mach, the latter of whom asserted that "the ego cannot be saved" ("Das Ich ist unrettbar"). In his play, Lothar reflects on the mask directly when Harlequin says in Act Two: "we play, we wear masks" (61). In Act Three, he states precisely: "One has to be able to wear the mask! One has to be a master of his mask as I am" (123). The mask turns into a symbol of real nobility (in the sense of "nobility of spirit," identified above) as eventually the comedian Harlequin proves to be an upstanding person while all the noble characters in the play demonstrate weakness and dishonesty: "It is easier to steal the mask of a king than those of a Harlequin. It is easier to play a king in a way the populace believes it is the real king than to try bamboozling the people with a fake Harlequin. You can trick the populace but not the audience" (123–4).

This passage reflects a common topic in Symbolist literature: the reality of literature and the arts. In times when certainties become blurred, the idea of reality is contested and its constructedness becomes visible. As a result, fiction becomes one form of reality – for artists and writers around 1900, an even more important one than reality as it is usually understood. Along these lines, Rudolf Steiner, a critic of the performance of the play by the ensemble of the Vienna German People's Theatre (Wiener Deutsches Volkstheater) at the German Theatre (Deutsches Theater) in Berlin in 1900, declared that the play should not be evaluated for its accuracy. He interpreted the play as a humorous fiction illuminating the conditions of life and doing so without pessimism. On the occasion of a performance in Paris in November 1902, the *Mercure de France* praised Harlequin's intrigue at the end of the play when he takes off the mask of the king. Now himself, Harlequin unveils the swindle, but nobody believes him, so he escapes on the boat. The critic Henri Albert even compared Lothar's play with writings by Nietzsche and Ibsen. This was not the only time that Albert was fulsome in his praise of a work by Rudolf Lothar; in 1908, he commended the writer as one of the few Viennese to have succeeded as a feuilleton writer in Paris (*Mercure de France*, 1 November 1908, 172–7). Lothar was so positively received in Paris largely due to his efforts to transmit French art and literature in the German-speaking world.

Lothar's *König Harlekin* influenced later Pierrot texts – for example, the pantomimes *Die Verwandlungen des Pierrot* (Pierrot's Metamorphosis, 1908) and *Der Schleier der Pierrette* (Pierrette's Veil, 1910) by Arthur Schnitzler. Especially in *Die Verwandlungen des Pierrot*, we find again an actor as the main character. The dandyish Pierrot intrudes into the bourgeois idyll of well-educated and well-dressed Eduard and his fiancée Katharina, who is dreaming of a passionate love relationship as described in the novel she is reading. Pierrot slips into several masks to seduce the young girl, and thus Schnitzler multiplies the motive known from his friend's play. But unlike in Lothar's text, it is not Pierrot himself who unveils his identity as actor, but his fellow players. At the end, Katharina returns to Eduard and Pierrot marries the impresario's daughter. Jealousy, loneliness, and uncertain identity are characteristics of all of these texts about Pierrot.

Conclusion

By analysing journals published around 1900, and their editors as transmitters in the processes of cultural transfer, this study has demonstrated that Pascale Casanova's claim that Paris was the capital of a world republic of literature is only partly persuasive. Certainly, around 1900, Paris was the pivotal location for many movements in literature and painting. It inspired poets and artists from all over Europe, and being recognized in Paris was a precondition for prominence in the arts. But this constellation must not be seen as a simple centre–periphery relation; rather, it reflected a multi-directional network with several centres of increasing or decreasing importance.

Switching the focus from Paris to Vienna – especially to the Young Vienna group and its surroundings – reveals that not only Parisian but also Belgian, English, Italian, Russian, Scandinavian, German, and Central European movements inspired the Viennese writers. By participating in the transfer of innovations from movements within the Austro-Hungarian Monarchy or from Scandinavian literatures to Paris, Vienna itself turned into a significant hub. In this way, Viennese critics and journals acquired authority and influence in other centres of literature. The journals published in Vienna became a point of reference for critics within the Dual Monarchy, but also in Paris and London. The reception of Ola Hansson and the Czech modernist movements by French critics via Viennese journals, and other examples, verify this claim.

The case study about Rudolf Lothar and his play *König Harlekin* featuring Pierrot, a key character in the Symbolist and Decadent movements around 1900, illustrates this thesis on an individual level. Lothar clearly focused on Paris, but he also kept an eye on other Western and Central European cities. In particular, the positive reception of his work in Paris reveals the mechanics behind the network: based on the mutual promotion of literary texts of a certain movement, an original transformation of an established subject was well received – in the different centres as well as by his fellow-writers in his own city.

NOTES

1 All translations into English by H.M. unless otherwise noted.

2 *Die Zeit* informed its readers about the content of periodicals from German-speaking countries (*Gegenwart*, *Grenzbote*, or *Preußiche Jahrbücher*), from Paris (*Revue des Revues*, *Revue des deux Mondes*, *Mercure de France*, *L'Ermitage*, *La Revue blanche*, *L'Idée libre*, *D'Art*), and from New York (*The Forum* and *The Nation*). Also, about the *North American Review*, the *Fortnightly Review*, and *Annals of the American Academy*. Also, about Belgium's *Société Nouvelle* and *Le Coq Rouge*. Also, about *De Vlaamsche School* and *Elesvier's Geillustreerd Maandschrift* (Amsterdam), the Italian journals *Revista de Sociologia* and *Vita Italiana*, and Spain's *Espagna moderna*. Also, about *Arte* and *Revista de Portugal*. *La Biblioteca* (Buenos Aires) was described as the premier South American review – one that could compete with the foremost European and North American journals (*Die Zeit*, 5 December 1896, 162–3).

3 It also informed its readers about what was published in the Czech journals *Naše doba* and *Rozhledy*, in *Kraj* (published in the Polish language in Saint Petersburg) and in *Sevierny Viestnik*, in the Russian *Istoričeskij vestnik*, the Danish *Tilskueren*, and the Norwegian *Samtiden*, as well as in *Asiatic Quarterly Review* and the Japanese review *Waseda Bungaka*.

4 "Das Glück im Verbrechen" (Le bonheur dans le crime / Happiness in Crime) and "Der rothe Vorhang" (Le rideau cramoisy / The Crimson Curtain), from the collection of short stories *Les Diaboliques* (The She-Devils, first published in 1874) were printed there as serial stories. Several articles were contributed by François Coppée, the poet of the Parnassian school. Anatole France, Sybille Gyp, Ernest Hello, Paul Hervieu, Jules Lemaître, Pierre Loti, Stéphane Mallarmé, Guy de Maupassant, Marcel Prévost, and Villiers de l'Isle-Adam as well as Émile Zola published serial novels.

WORKS CITED

Amselle, Jean-Loup. *Logiques metises. Anthropologie de l'identité en Afrique et ailleurs*. Paris: Payot, 1990. Print

Arlaud, Sylvie. *Les references anglais de la modernité viennoise.* St Denis: Editions Suger, 2000. Print.

– "Peter Altenbergs Kunst – das Ende der anglophilen Moderne in Wien?" In *Übergänge und Verflechtungen: Kulturelle Transfers in Europa.* Ed. Gregor Kokorz and Helga Mitterbauer. Berne: P. Lang, 2004. 99–127. Print.

Bachleitner, Norbert. "Eine soziologische Theorie des literarischen Transfers. Erläutert am Beispiel Hermann Bahrs." In *Ent-grenzte Räume. Kulturelle Transfers um 1900 und in der Gegenwart.* Ed. Helga Mitterbauer and Katharina Scherke. Vienna: Passagen-Verlag, 2005. 147–56. Print.

Bahr, Hermann. *Die Überwindung des Naturalismus.* Dresden and Leipzig: Pierson, 1891. Print.

Barbarić, Damir, and Michael Benedikt, eds. *Ambivalenzen des Fin de siècle. Wien–Zagreb.* Vienna, Cologne, and Weimar: Böhlau, 1998. Print.

Bhabha, Homi. *The Location of Culture.* London and New York: Routledge, 1994. Print.

Casanova, Pascale. *La république mondiale des lettres.* Paris: Seuil, 1999. Print.

Csáky, Moritz. *Das Gedächtnis der Städte. Kulturelle Verflechtungen – Wien und die urbanen Milieus in Zentraleuropa.* Cologne: Böhlau, 2010. Print.

Deleuze, Gilles, and Félix Guattari. *Kafka: pour une littérature mineure.* Paris: Édition de Minuit, 1975. Print.

Espagne, Michel. "Die Rolle der Mittler im Kulturtransfer." In *Kulturtransfer im Epochenumbruch. Frankreich – Deutschland 1770 bis 1815.* Ed. Hans-Jürgen Lüsebrink and Rolf Reichardt. Leipzig: Universitätsverlag, 1997. 309–29. Print.

Espagne, Michel, and Werner Greiling, eds. *Frankreichfreunde. Mittler des französisch-deutschen Kulturtransfers (1750–1850).* Leipzig: Universitätsverlag, 1996. Print.

Espagne, Michel, and Michael Werner, eds. *Transferts. Les Relations interculturelles dans l'espace franco-allemand (XVIIIe et XIXe siècle).* Paris: Editions Recherche sur les Civilisations, 1988. Print.

Gallagher, Karen. "Marie Herzfeld: German Nationalist or Modern Cosmopolitan?" In *Cosmopolitans and the Modern World: Studies on a Theme in German and Austrian Literary Culture.* Ed. Suzanne Kirkbright. Munich: Iudicium-Verlag, 2000. Print.

– *Marie Herzfeld (1855–1940) and European Modernism.* Ann Arbor: U of Michigan P, 2007. Print.

Glissant, Édouard. *Traité du Tout-Monde. Poétique IV.* Paris: Gallimard, 1997. Print.

Granovetter, Mark S. "The Strength of Weak Ties." *American Journal of Sociology* 78 (1973): 1360–80. Print.

Kostrbová, Lucie, Kurt Ifkovits, and Vratislav Doubek. *Die Wiener Wochenschrift Die Zeit (1894–1904) als Mittler zwischen der Tschechischen und Wiener Moderne*. Prague and Vienna: Masarykův ústav a Archiv AV ČR, Österreichisches Theatermuseum, 2011. Print.

Kraus, Karl. "Die demolirte Literatur." *Wiener Rundschau* 1 (15 November 1896): 19–27. Print.

Johnston, William M. *The Austrian Mind: An Intellectual and Social History 1848–1938*. Berkeley: U of California P, 1972. Print.

Le Rider, Jacques. *Modernity and Crises of Identity: Culture and Society in Fin-de-Siecle Vienna*. New York: Continuum, 1993. Print.

Lorenz, Dagmar. *Wiener Moderne*. 2nd ed. Stuttgart and Weimar: Metzler, 2007. Print.

Lothar, Rudolf. *König Harlekin. Ein Maskenspiel in vier Aufzügen*. 2nd ed. Munich and Leipzig: G. Müller, 1904. Print.

Mach, Ernst. *Die Analyse der Empfindungen*. 7th ed. Jena: G. Fischer, 1918. Print.

Mitterbauer, Helga. "König Harlekin oder die Degeneration. Zur Position zweier Budapester Autoren im europäischen Fin de Siècle." *Studia Caroliensia* (Budapest) 1 (2004), Special issue "Ungarn in Europa." 72–84. Print.

– "Der bleiche Mond über dem Wiener Prater. Zur Pierrot-Rezeption in der deutschsprachigen Literatur um 1900." In *Pierrot lunaire: Albert Giraud – Otto Erich Hartleben – Arnold Schönberg. Une collection d'études musico-littéraires: A collection of musicological and literary studies: Eine Sammlung musik- und literaturwissenschaftlicher Beiträge*. Ed. Marc Delaere and Jan Herman. Louvain, Paris, and Dudley: Peeters, 2004. 159–72. Print.

– "Dynamische Vernetzungen: Theoretische Prolegomena zu kulturellen Transferprozessen." In *Weltbühne Wien: World Stage Vienna*, vol. 1: *Approaches to Cultural Transfer*. Ed. Ewald Mengel, Ludwig Schnauder, and Rudolf Weiss. Trier: WVT, 2010. 51–75. Print.

– "Postkoloniale Konzepte in der Erforschung kultureller Transferkonzepte." In *Überbringen – Überformen – Überblenden. Theorietransfer im 20. Jahrhundert*. Ed. Diethild Hüchtker and Alfried Kliems. Cologne, Weimar, and Vienna: Böhlau, 2011. 75–89. Print.

Nußbaumer, Martina. *Musikstadt Wien. Die Konstruktion eines Images*. Freiburg and Breisgau: Rombach, 2007. Print.

Rieckmann, Jens. *Aufbruch in die Moderne. Die Anfänge des Jungen Wien: Österreichische Literatur und Kritik im Fin de Siècle*. Königstein: Athenäum, 1985. Print.

Said, Edward W. *Culture and Imperialism*. London: Vintage, 1994. Print.

Schnitzler, Arthur. "Die Verwandlungen des Pierrot. Pantomime in einem Vorspiel und sechs Bildern." In *Der einsame Weg. Zeitstücke 1891–1908*.

Afterword by Hermann Korte. Frankfurt am Main: S. Fischer, 2001. 491–512. Print.

– "Der Schleier der Pierrette. Pantomine in drei Bildern." In *Die dramatischen Werke*, vol. 2. Frankfurt am Main: S. Fischer, 1962. Print.

Schorske, Carl. *Fin-de-Siècle Vienna: Politics and Culture.* New York: Vintage, 1981. Print.

Simonek, Stefan. *Distanzierte Nähe. Die slawische Moderne der Donaumonarchie und die Wiener Moderne.* Berne et al.: P. Lang, 2002. Print.

–, ed. *Die Wiener Moderne in slawischen Periodika der Jahrhundertwende.* Berne et al.: P. Lang, 2006. Print.

Sprengel, Peter, and Gregor Streim. *Berliner und Wiener Moderne. Vermittlungen und Abgrenzungen in Literatur, Theater, Publizistik.* Vienna, Cologne, and Weimar: Böhlau, 1998. Print.

Steiner, Rudolf. "'König Harlekin.' Ein Maskenspiel in vier Aufzügen von Rudolf Lothar." *Magazin für Literatur* 69.22 (1900): 382–84. Print.

Turgeon, Laurier. "Les mots pour dire les métissages. Jeux et enjeux d'un lexique." *Revue germanique internationale* 21 (2004): 53–69. Print.

Vilain, Robert. *The Poetry of Hugo von Hofmannsthal and French Symbolism.* Oxford: Clarendon, 2000. Print.

White, Harrison C. *Identity and Control: A Structural Theory of Social Action.* Princeton: Princeton UP, 1992. Print.

Zieger, Karl. *Arthur Schnitzler et la France 1894–1938: enquête sur une reception.* Villeneuve d'Ascq: PU du Septentrion, 2012. Print.

2 The Aesthetics of Change: Women Writers of the Austro-Hungarian Monarchy

AGATHA SCHWARTZ AND HELGA THORSON

The *fin de siècle* was a time of great aesthetic upheaval in literature and the arts in many countries, including the Austro-Hungarian Monarchy. This dramatic shift in aesthetics – one that represented a break from the past and its traditions, as well as a new awareness of the self and its relationship to the world around it, an awareness that manifested itself in formal innovation and experimentation – has commonly been referred to as literary modernism. But modernism was never a unified movement, be it in literature or the arts; rather, "there were many different movements, all of which were later placed under the umbrella term *modernism*" (Parry 2). Although Amie Elizabeth Parry's statement was in reference to the United States, the same could be said about modernist writing in general. Parry continues by stating that the canonical definition of modernism has rested mainly on a set of shared aesthetic characteristics, above all else on "a difficult, experimental, and fragmented form, combined with a highly subjective response to perceived breakdowns in realism's developmental narrative, its underlying sense of progress, its unified subject, and its faith in objective knowledge" (2). In this chapter we argue that literary modernism should be viewed more in terms of a "geography of mobility and interculturality" (Friedman 428) rather than as a unified movement or even a set of literary movements based solely on formal experimental attributes. The privileging of literary form above all else negates the importance of those authors who chose through their texts to question the past and its norms differently; this includes those authors who, while perhaps not experimenting with form in significant ways, nevertheless addressed emergent themes of modernity in their work.

This chapter challenges traditional literary historiography as well as theoretical scholarship on literary modernism in the Austro-Hungarian Monarchy by posing the following questions: What happens when you look beyond the cultural "centres" and regional divisions of this large, multi-ethnic, and multilingual empire and analyse its modernism(s) in a transcultural way? And what happens when the focus is on women writers and their narratives, which have largely been left out of the modernist canon? According to Griselda Pollock, modernism was co-constructed by both women and men; yet the canon of modernism has erased women. Pollock views transformations of gender as central, not supplementary to both modernism and modernity (n.pag.). Our study places gender and geography at the forefront by addressing the role women writers played in shaping literary modernism throughout the ethnically and linguistically diverse regions of the monarchy. By presenting works of fiction by five women writers from different ethnic and/or linguistic backgrounds – Grete Meisel-Hess (writing in German in Vienna and later Berlin), Terka Lux (writing in Hungarian in Budapest), Olha Kobylianska (writing in Ukrainian in the Bukovina), Nafija Sarajlić (writing in Bosnian in Sarajevo),[1] and Zofka Kveder (writing in Slovenian, Croatian, and German in various cities of the monarchy) – we offer a new perspective on the ways in which modernism was written across this multi-ethnic empire. We argue that modernist feminist ideas were multi-directional, travelling not only from the urban centres of the monarchy outward, but also from various points within the Habsburg monarchy to the main urban centres, from one remote region to another, and also across borders with other nations and empires.

In our analysis we rely on the concept "geomodernisms," coined by Laura Doyle and Laura Winkiel in their edited volume with the same title, as well as the work of Susan Stanford Friedman. These scholars emphasize the importance of location (in both time and space) and suggest that, to a large extent, it is the dynamic interplay and multiple interconnections between modernisms that have shaped modernist literature:

> To emplace modernism in this way – to think, rather, in terms of interconnected modernisms – requires a rethinking of periodization, genealogies, affiliations, and forms. To some degree, this rethinking estranges the category of modernism itself. The term *modernism* breaks open, into something we call geomodernisms, which signals a locational approach to modernisms' engagement with cultural and political

> discourses of global modernity. The revelation of such an approach is double. It unveils both unsuspected "modernist" experiments in "marginal" texts and unsuspected correlations between those texts and others that appear either more conventional or more postmodern. (Doyle and Winkiel 3; emphasis in the original)

Drawing on the work of Fredric Jameson, Friedman reminds us of the importance of historicizing modernism. Yet she contends that this historicization must go hand in hand with spatialization (Friedman 426), or with the *emplacement* of modernism as suggested by Doyle and Winkiel. The historical and spatial contexts of the Austro-Hungarian Empire are crucial for understanding the inner workings of modernisms within the vast territory ruled by the House of Habsburg and whether an author or literary protagonist portrays "a sense of speaking from outside or inside or both at once, of orienting toward and away from the metropole, of existing somewhere between belonging and dispersion" (Doyle and Winkiel 4). These locational positionalities and geographical contact zones are also shaped by conceptions of gender, race, class, ethnicity, sexuality, and religion, among other factors, so that what it means to be inside or outside hinges on both an intersectional context and a situational one.

Before we focus on selected literary works of these five writers, we would like to address several key points that highlight the fluidity of boundaries within the empire so as to better position the writers themselves. To begin with, Austria-Hungary represented a Dual Monarchy established in 1867 that – despite the two declared centres of political power, Vienna and Budapest, being under Austrian-German and Hungarian domination respectively – consisted of a complex configuration of linguistic, ethnic, and emerging national groups. As we have written elsewhere,

> most regions of Austro-Hungary were multiethnic and multilingual: in some one nationality constituted a majority, for example, the Czechs in Bohemia or the Romanians in Transylvania. In others, like the Vojvodina, this was not the case. To complicate matters further, some ethnic groups had sizeable minorities in more than one region. Some examples are: the Romanians in Transylvania and the Bukovina; the Slovenians in Trieste and in Carinthia; the Ukrainians in Galicia and the Bukovina; the Serbs in Vojvodina, Croatia and in Bosnia-Herzegovina; etc. (Schwartz and Thorson 3)

Second, what was known as Austria-Hungary was not a stable entity. Its boundaries shifted and its identity changed. For example, at the Congress of Berlin in 1878, convened after the Russian–Turkish War (1877–78), Austria-Hungary was given the mandate to occupy and govern Bosnia-Herzegovina. The occupation was followed by annexation in 1908. One of the authors whose work we are analysing, Nafija Sarajlić, provides literary sketches addressing issues faced by Bosnian Muslim women at the time, a group that earlier would not have belonged to the empire.

Third, although the monarchy's various regions differed greatly from one another, at the same time many differences existed even within the same geographical areas (whether due to education, socio-economic issues, religion, ethnicity, or languages spoken). Scholars such as Jacques LeRider, Steven Beller, Abigail Gillman, and Hillary Hope Herzog have shown that the (male) Viennese Jewish experience of the modernist crisis was especially intense and that this manifested itself in various attempts by male Viennese Jewish authors to negotiate both modernism and Jewishness in their literary works. This short chapter cannot possibly do justice to the complexity of voices within each city or region. Our focus is on addressing the lack of attention given to women writers in much of the scholarship, especially that scholarship which tends to universalize the male experience even when limited to the experience within a specific group, such as the above-mentioned Jewish experience in Vienna. Thus, we must look beyond the achievements of "Freud, Schnitzler, Mahler, and other cultural giants" when trying to understand the Jewish community in Vienna (Rozenblit 2), and no matter what community we are investigating, it is important to analyse the points of intersection of categories such as gender, class, and, in this context, Jewishness. Historians such as Marsha L. Rozenblit and Marion A. Kaplan have shown that depictions of cultural tendencies such as assimilation become distorted when one fails to analyse Jewish society in an intersectional way; when we focus on the interconnections of gender, ethnicity, class, religion, and other characteristics, the picture becomes not only more complete but also very different (Kaplan viii). In our opinion, it is not just a matter of "adding" women to the analysis, but rather of changing the focus of analysis so that these points of intersection are explored simultaneously across time and space. This is especially important in the various regions of the multi-ethnic and multicultural Habsburg Monarchy.

Finally, many modernist writers, including women writers, did not have a fixed place of residence, and this brought about a dynamic system of networks and influences. For example, two of the authors we include in this chapter, Grete Meisel-Hess and Zofka Kveder, moved several times during their lifetimes. Meisel-Hess was born to Jewish parents in Prague in 1879, moved with her family to Vienna where she began her writing career, and then moved on her own to Berlin in 1908. Zofka Kveder was born in Ljubljana (Laibach) in 1878, where she published her first texts, lived for a short time in Trieste, and then moved to Prague, where she worked as a writer and translator. In 1906 she moved to Zagreb (known in the German-speaking world at that time as Agram), where she published a weekly supplement to the newspaper *Agramer Tagblatt* called *Die Frauenzeitung* (The Women's Paper) and later edited her own proto-feminist journal *Ženski svijet* (Women's World, later retitled *Jugoslavenska žena* [The Yugoslav Woman]). Her own writings appeared in Slovenian, Croatian, and German; she also translated works from many languages, including Czech. These examples demonstrate how women writers actively participated in and shaped the expressions of modernism and modernity throughout the empire and beyond. By embracing the concept of geomodernism, we hope to track the multiple directions and dynamic interplay of modernist ideas across the monarchy as manifested in women's writing and fostered through women's contacts and networks.

Little comparative research has been conducted on literary modernism across the Austro-Hungarian Empire beyond the so-called major authors (which excludes most women writers). Most studies focus on the arts and literature of one or two – at best, three – linguistic groups;[2] when women writers are at all central to the analysis, it is usually through the lens of post-monarchy nation-states.[3] According to Ilona Sármány-Parsons, "the publications of Czech, Polish, or Hungarian scholars tend to move within the framework of their own national discourse and neglect the comparative dimension with other cultural centres of the monarchy" (220). This narrow focus reflects in many cases a desire to form a distinct national literary tradition disconnected from the Austro-Hungarian past. The other reason may be simply the linguistic challenge: a comprehensive analysis of the literature of the vast territory of Austria-Hungary is nearly impossible without the assistance of a team of scholars and translators, not only because of the sheer quantity of texts, but also on account of the number of languages in which this literature was written: German, Hungarian, Czech, Slovak,

Polish, Ukrainian, Slovenian, Serbian, Croatian, Romanian, Italian, Yiddish, and Ladino.

Across the linguistically and culturally varied Austro-Hungarian Monarchy, modernisms emerged in inter-relational and multi-directional ways. In specific contexts and situations, the terms *inside* and *outside* could take on many meanings. For example, some women's organizations within the Dual Monarchy turned to cities in Germany, Scandinavia, or the United States for support and collaboration rather than Vienna or Budapest, and often these alliances were formed in reaction to the women's movements in the capital cities within the monarchy.[4] This does not, of course, negate the fact that influences existed beyond what was officially acknowledged; this can be concluded from the content of the various women's magazines – for example, women followed and read the works of their peers in other parts of the monarchy. Similarly, because of the Habsburg Empire's vast size and geographical location, notions of "East" and "West" could be conceived as either embedded in the empire itself (a vast territory that covered both "East" and "West") or as existing outside of its perimeter (in which case Austria-Hungary, and particularly Austria, would be "Western" and juxtaposed to the "Orient" both outside and often within its own borders). But it could also be viewed as "Central" in relation to the two extremes "East" and "West". In the words of Friedman, the "geography of mobility and interculturality is not a utopian fantasy of peaceful integration, but rather recognizes that the contact zones between cultures often involve violence and conquest as well as reciprocal exchange, inequality and exploitation as well as mutual benefits, and abjection and humiliation as well as pride and dignity" (428). As in many other parts of the world, the interactions among specific geographical spaces, group identities, and conceptions of modernity in the Habsburg Empire were complex and ever-changing.

As previously stated, modernist fiction has predominantly been described as representing a crisis of identity, one that is characterized by a break from the past leading to a sense of alienation and fragmentation. But as Brigitte Spreitzer reminds us, it is important to specify *which* crisis and *whose* identity are being discussed (57). Agatha Schwartz writes that one critical difference in the texts by women writers "is the particular cause for the crisis of the female self, which is rooted in male sexual violence or other forms of inhibition imposed on the free expression of female sexuality and creativity" (198). In what follows, we analyse this and other expressions of a crisis of the female self in selected literary works to reflect on how women writers from different linguistic and geographic backgrounds within the monarchy positioned themselves as creative subjects and agents of change.

The five authors discussed in this chapter were born in the latter half of the nineteenth century, between 1863 (Kobylianska) and 1893 (Sarajlić). They were educated middle-class women who expressed feminist concerns in their writing and were professionally active as writers, editors, or teachers for at least a part of their lives: Kobylianska was a founding member of the Society of Ruthenian Women (*Obshchestvo Ruskykh Zhenshchyn*) in Chernivtsi in the Bukovina; Terka Lux (born 1873) was an established feminist writer in Budapest;[5] Zofka Kveder (born 1878) was a professional writer, translator, journalist, and editor from Slovenia who lived in many different parts of Austria-Hungary, including Trieste, Zagreb, and Prague; Grete Meisel-Hess (born 1879) was an active member of the League for the Protection of Mothers (*Bund für Mutterschutz*) in Berlin after growing up in Bohemia as a child and beginning her writing career in Vienna; Sarajlić was a primary school teacher in Bosnia.

We have chosen these five authors for two important reasons. First of all, they were situated in different geographical locations in Austria-Hungary and thus represent two dominant linguistic groups from the two political centres (Vienna and Budapest) as well as several other languages spoken in other parts of the Dual Monarchy that did not have the same political power as Vienna and Budapest but that, nevertheless, had their own cultural centres and flourishing literary life. These situational locations tended to shape their awareness of issues affecting women in diverse ways. Notions of feminism were quite different in the two large urban centres and administrative capitals of Vienna and Budapest, as opposed to other regions that were struggling for national independence. Second, these authors highlight three important points we would like to make regarding the ways in which women writers from across the monarchy helped shape a modernist feminist aesthetic: (1) by emphasizing that the crisis of identity was often a sexual one, (2) by focusing on negotiations of gendered identity within real and imagined geographical locations, and (3) by creating genre innovations that reflected women's struggles in society. This chapter by no means provides a comprehensive analysis of women's writing throughout Austria-Hungary; rather, it offers traces of the diverse roles that women writers with a feminist consciousness played in shaping literary modernisms throughout the various regions of the monarchy.

In what follows, we briefly turn to a short selection of fictional texts by the writers introduced above. We begin with an analysis of two novels by Grete Meisel-Hess set (or partly set) in Vienna and point out that, for Meisel-Hess, the modernist crisis was primarily a sexual one. In our analysis, we address traditional definitions of literary modernism to show that a singular focus on formal characteristics tends to negate important gendered notions of modernism and modernity. Through a literary example of autobiographical self-referencing, however, we illustrate that literary modernism can take many forms, from first-person experimental fragmented writing to third-person realist narratives. Despite different formal qualities, both of Meisel-Hess's texts under analysis emphasize a female protagonist caught in a modernist crisis of identity. We then turn our attention to the other political capital of the Dual Monarchy, Budapest, by focusing on the Hungarian writer known through her pen name Terka Lux. We analyse one of her novels together with a short literary piece from the Bukovina, an ethnically diverse region of the monarchy, written in Ukrainian by Olha Kobylianska. Formerly part of Moldavia, the Bukovina was an administrative division on the eastern border of the Habsburg Empire and later the Dual Monarchy consisting primarily of Ruthenians (Ukrainians), Romanians, and Germans, with smaller populations of many other ethnic groups. In this section, we focus on the interplay of "imagined communities," to borrow Benedict Anderson's term, both within and outside the empire. Finally, we turn our attention to texts by Nafija Sarajlić and Zofka Kveder to illustrate their use of genre as a means of emphasizing women's experiences. By taking this geomodernist approach, we highlight the gender dimension of the transcultural and transregional aesthetics of modernism in the Austro-Hungarian Empire.

Modernism, Modernity, and the Sexual Crisis

Grete Meisel-Hess's 1902 best-selling novel *Fanny Roth, eine Jung-Frauengeschichte* (Fanny Roth: A Story for Young Women) is in many ways representative of the concerns raised by other fellow women writers who wrote in various languages of the empire in that it questions the limits placed on women's agency, be it sexual or creative. The novel tells the story of Fanny's failed marriage, a marriage she eventually leaves in order to escape her controlling husband and dedicate herself to music again. The novel's original German title reveals a double meaning: *Jungfrau* can mean both young woman and virgin. In fact, the scene in Meisel-Hess's text where the female protagonist loses her virginity – when her husband rapes her on her wedding night – is in the very middle of this book, appearing at the end of the first of its two parts (see Schwartz 107–8; Thorson, "Confronting Anti-Semitism" 85–6). It is also the point where the author addresses the silence surrounding sexual violence and marital rape in literature, which positions her novel as an important attempt to fill that gap:

> She lost all awareness for pleasure and aversion; she only knew that everything in her was wild, despairing defense. And why – why?! Hadn't she waited fervently for this redemption? And now – instead of the exhilarating, blissful oblivion of which she had dreamt – horror.
>
> Had they all lied, the poets, who spoke of the blissfulness of this night? Hadn't anybody, anybody been honest? (56)[6]

As illustrated by these lines, when thinking back to the questions posed earlier – Which crisis? Whose identity? – for Meisel-Hess the crisis at hand is first and foremost a sexual one. In fact, in 1909 she coined the very term in the title of her book published in 1909: *Die sexuelle Krise* (*The Sexual Crisis: A Critique of Our Sex Life*, 1917). In it, Meisel-Hess developed her own theory of sexology. In a time dominated by Freud's male-centred theories of sexuality, she challenged several of Freud's theories, such as that of female hysteria; indeed, she developed a theory of *male* hysteria, which she saw as an expression of what she termed male sexual degeneracy. And in *Fanny Roth*, instead of portraying Fanny as a sexually frustrated, "hysterical" wife, she portrays Fanny's husband as a hysterical, degenerate man in that he is unable to leave behind his sexual escapades and relate to his wife beyond an initially brutal and later purely physical dimension. Meisel-Hess further challenged Freud's widely accepted paradigm by stating that women rather than men were the more complete sex. For Meisel-Hess, the identity crisis of the time was but a reflection of a sexual (or in today's terms, gender) crisis – a crisis that she claimed caused the fragmentation and alienation of both men and women, but one from which her female characters (such as Fanny) are able to emerge with the potential of becoming whole again. According to Meisel-Hess, the New Woman could lead the way out of the sexual crisis, both as an active subject and as a creative artist. Thus, Fanny's womb becomes the metaphor for this cultural and figurative rebirth, as formulated in the closing lines of the novel: "A thousand possibilities lay dormant in her: the unborn child in her womb that would come into this world once she found the right partner – or when she would be strong enough to create her own destiny. And a thousand joys of the soul and a thousand happy forces were sleeping in her violin" (Meisel-Hess 133). And thus, although in this novel Meisel-Hess does not experiment on the formal level – she chooses a linear third-person narrative – *Fanny Roth* inscribes itself into modernist discourses by breaking a taboo topic in literature – marital rape – and by challenging some of Freud's theories on sexuality through a literary depiction of female sexuality, desire, and creative potential. Meisel-Hess thus occupies an important although neglected place in one of the key modernist discourses, the discourse around the crisis of human sexuality and gender.

Unlike *Fanny Roth*, Meisel-Hess's 1907 novel *Die Stimme* (The Voice) contains many of the aesthetic features associated with canonical literary modernism: an experimental and fragmented form, a conscious self-reflexivity that highlights the fictionality of the work, and allusions to the metatextuality of the work that draw attention to the process of the novel's creation. Helga Thorson argues that in *Die Stimme*, through the use of these formal devices as well as intertextual self-referencing, "Meisel-Hess was attempting to position herself as the first [Austrian] modernist female writer of her time" ("Regarding the Voices" 4). By blurring the boundaries between fiction and life-writing and by having her protagonist Maja Hertz directly refer to the earlier novel *Fanny Roth*, Meisel-Hess draws attention to various manifestations of the sexual crisis (e.g., sexual violence in *Fanny Roth* and the difficulties of female self-development in sexual relationships both in *Fanny Roth* and in *Die Stimme*). In addition, she highlights her own contribution to Jewish literary modernism in Vienna.

Both of Meisel-Hess's early novels point to the "Jewishness" of their respective protagonists, thereby commenting on the distinct Jewish influence that characterized much of Viennese literary modernism. Although neither of these novels reveals the protagonist's Jewish background as directly as Meisel-Hess's later Berlin novel *Die Intellektuellen* (The Intellectuals; 1911), these two novels hint at this connection through the use of typical Jewish names in the former and through a complex form of intertextual self-referencing in the latter (Thorson, "Regarding the Voices" 11–13), in which Jewish identity is simultaneously absent – the protagonist is depicted as Christian – and present through a textual performance of Jewish childhood memory.[7] In this way, Meisel-Hess's novels express and perform complex notions of modernism, feminism, and Jewishness.

By having the protagonist of *Die Stimme* state that, although *Fanny Roth* addressed important dimensions of the modern sexual crisis, the novel was not particularly well written (*Die Stimme* 254), Meisel-Hess seems to imply that her first novel lacked the playful yet sophisticated aesthetic features that characterized her later work. The difference is not so much that one novel was more modernist than the other, but rather that they expressed modernism differently. Whereas *Fanny Roth* challenged and expanded some key concepts in modernist discourses around sexuality, *Die Stimme* built on the author's earlier ideas and indulged in more experimentation on the formal level.

Imagined Communities: The Geography of Interculturality

Olha Kobylianska, a writer from the Bukovina, a region on the far east of the Dual Monarchy between Galicia and Transylvania, is considered today one of the most prominent Ukrainian modernist writers. Her short prose work "A Conversation" (1902) was published the same year as Meisel-Hess's *Fanny Roth.* We are discussing this text here together with a novel by the Hungarian writer Terka Lux (alias Dancsházi Oláh Ida) in order to explore the geography of interculturality and imagined communities within and outside imperial boundaries. Terka Lux lived in Budapest and explored that city's gendered urban spaces in many of her works (most notably in her 1908 novel *Budapest*). Unlike Margit Kaffka, the *grande dame* of Hungarian modernism, whom many critics consider the best Hungarian woman writer of all time and who is included in all major Hungarian literary histories, Lux was "forgotten" after the Second World War (like so many Hungarian women writers) and has only recently experienced a certain comeback.[8]

Like Meisel-Hess's *Fanny Roth*, Lux's novel *Leányok* (Girls), published in 1906, features the New Woman of the early twentieth century. In this novel Lux establishes "the image and prototype of the intelligent, hard-working, creative woman" (Fábri 166), as seen in her protagonist Juli, who comes to Budapest as an orphan in order to secure an advanced education, which had just become possible for women in the monarchy.[9] This eventually leads her to medical studies and a career in medicine. Yet this "success" is not described in overly positive terms. Emancipation, although important in that it allows Juli to lead an independent life, does not bring about complete self-realization. Instead, the road into the future for the New Woman – unlike the one Meisel-Hess envisages – seems to be one of self-sacrifice and solitude.

In Budapest, Juli's life intersects with that of two other young women who come to the capital to pursue their dreams: Baba (meaning doll in Hungarian), who dreams of becoming an actress, and Janka, whose life goal is marriage (see Schwartz 113–16). Baba, the beautiful, sensual, and naive girl, gets seduced by the city's false promises and meets a tragic end, while Janka, the haughty offspring of an impoverished gentry family, sacrifices her personal happiness to her racial prejudices. By providing a glimpse of three intersecting paths, Lux's *Leányok* highlights female gender roles in a state of transition as well as three expressions of what Meisel-Hess termed the sexual crisis: Juli opts for abstinence (for lack of an adequate partner for the New Woman); Baba's pregnancy from a relationship with an irresponsible man ends fatally following an illegal abortion; and Janka chooses marriage without love.

In its depiction of the fast-growing and modernizing Hungarian capital, the novel features several Jewish characters as reflections of the city's multi-ethnic landscape and its pervasive anti-Semitism, which at the time was very much present in Budapest, just as much as in Vienna and in other urban centres of the monarchy. In fact, the very first words of the novel are spoken by Mrs Flesch, the girls' Jewish landlady, in her broken Hungarian. It is Janka, the third young woman of the trio, who tends to treat non-Magyars as outsiders, and she is especially prejudiced against Jews. During her courtship with a young doctor, Janka learns of his Jewish background and calls off the relationship. She is very much in love, but "the voice of her class drowns out the voice of her heart" (Schwartz 115) and she ends up in an unhappy marriage of convenience. In this way, Lux highlights the existence of imagined communities of belonging: in this novel, some residents are viewed as internal outsiders within the urban space in which they reside. Thus, like Meisel-Hess's *Fanny Roth*, Lux's *Leányok* assumes its place within literary modernism through the topics it thematizes and the intersection of discourses around gender, class, and ethnicity/religion[10] rather than through its form. It also addresses other important topics of modernism, such as notions of inside and outside and tensions between the urban political centres of the Dual Monarchy and the rural areas that many of the characters have left behind and to which some will return.

The topic of insiders and outsiders is also very much a part of Kobylianska's text "A Conversation." In this prose piece, a gentleman (He) and a lady (She) are conversing about the *Rusynka* (Ukrainian woman) while the man smokes and the woman knits a sock. He suggests that the Ukrainian woman is lacking a certain Europeanness:

> I shall say that our middle class woman – it's no use trying to deny the fact – is not yet fully "cultured" in the true meaning of the word; she is not self-reliant in her heart – she is still a puppet, and one that is not fashioned all that artistically. As for becoming educated, she is just taking her first steps. But what offends me most greatly about her is her lack – as I said earlier – of that energetic consciousness of her own "I" that marks a Russian, German, Swedish, or French woman. (220)[11]

Throughout their conversation, both the man and the woman conceive of the Ukrainian community in relation to other national communities and races (referred to as Europeans, Orientals, Kafirs). They thus express an important aspect of our discussion of geomodernism. The ever-shifting physical borders had placed some Ukrainians within the Habsburg Empire – mainly in eastern Galicia, the Bukovina, and Transcarpathia – while a large part of the Ukrainian-speaking population lived in the Russian Empire. In the words of Mary Neuburger: "On the margins of maps, one inevitably finds conceivable centers for 'others'" (18). Although Neuburger was specifically referring to the situation in Bulgaria, the same can be said about other communities. This raises questions such as the following: Who and what are conceived of as being geographically and topographically "on the margins"? Who defines what is similar and what is different? What are they similar to or different from? Who is viewed as on the inside and who is viewed as on the outside? Kobylianska's fictional discussion between a man and a woman illustrates the intensity of these real and imagined contact zones that existed on the edges of the Habsburg Monarchy. The gaze is simultaneously Northern- and Western-looking (what they want to become), Eastward- and Southward-looking (what they do not want to be), and inward-looking (proud of their Ukrainian background but also aware of a supposed lack of self-development).

Influenced by Western Europe's "condescending eastward gaze, cast upon the Orient as well as on Eastern Europe," notions such as "East and West, progress and backwardness, along with the concept of 'nation' were like stones dropped in a pond whose ripples lapped against the outer edges of Europe" (Neuburger 1). Drawing on Edward Said's discussions of Orientalism as well as on notions of in-betweenness and ambiguity, Maria Todorova in her analysis of Balkanism outlines how various ethnic and linguistic communities within the monarchy were often viewed not as other by the Western eye (such as is the case in Orientalism), but rather as an "incomplete self" (18). The discussion between Kobylianska's fictional characters revolves around notions of native and foreign, familiar and strange, progressive and backward, as well as the ambiguity and in-betweenness these pairs of terms suggest. The characters negotiate this "self" from within, while being simultaneously affected by discourses defining the "self" from without. The exchange is friendly; the two conversation partners are not in an antagonistic or adversarial relationship and seem to reach many of the same conclusions. One of these conclusions is that a woman is "the flower of a nation" (227), the symbol of the health of the nation as a whole. This is reinforced by another textual metaphor, that of mother of the nation. This role emphasizes a woman's responsibility in biological reproduction as well as her function as a transmitter of intelligence and culture. As the female partner in the conversation notes, "the level of her intelligence testifies to the intelligence and culture of her *entire nation*" (227). In this way, the conversation partners point to the sense of community belonging within a national or ethnic group and what was widely considered at the time to be a woman's main cultural role as the symbolic mother of that group.[12]

During their conversation, the man and woman set up an imagined Ukrainian community that exists both within and outside the borders of the Austro-Hungarian Monarchy. This community of "Rusynka" and "Rusyny" simultaneously exists inside and outside a larger European community as well as in juxtaposition to an Oriental one. In certain contexts they can be considered European, for example, when He claims "I, praise God, am a European!" (220). In other contexts they are characterized in racial or ethnic terms as Slavs, such as when She states that if a Ukrainian woman "does not marry before she turns twenty-five, people will begin to call her 'an old maid,' even though, not being of the Turkish race, she does not grow old all that quickly, but matures slowly like a strong, well-tempered Slav" (221–2). At one point the woman maintains that Ukrainians are still "Orientals" (222) in terms of how women are treated in society; later the man suggests that the woman's view of Ukrainian men places them on the level of "Kafirs" (226), the implication being that Ukrainian society needs to become more European as a means to strengthen its own "national culture and history" (231). Without once mentioning the Austro-Hungarian Empire, Kobylianska's prose piece discusses the importance of preserving the Ukrainian language and culture by educating Ukrainian women in art, literature, and science. In this way the geography of interculturality demonstrates a sense of gendered and racialized national belonging among geographically dispersed "Ukrainians" both within and beyond the borders of the monarchy as well as an internal negotiation and struggle between a "European" mindset and an "Oriental" one as part of an imagined Ukrainian national identity.

Both Lux's *Leányok* and Kobylianska's "A Conversation" suggest that the contact between cultures, be it real or imagined, is a vital part of the situational geography of inclusion and exclusion. Whereas Lux's novel highlights the Jewish internal outsiders of Budapest and criticizes the growing anti-Semitism, Kobylianska's narrative points to the complex negotiations of identity within an ethnically diverse empire that exists at the crossroads between "North" and "South" as well as "East" and "West." It is the negotiation of these dynamic, unpredictable, and sometimes volatile contact zones that is brought to the fore in these two examples of modernist prose.

Engendering Genre

Nafija Sarajlić and Zofka Kveder fit into our discussion of Austro-Hungarian women writers and modernism in two ways in particular: first, they both illustrate attempts to create new genre forms, and second, they both show how these genre experiments accentuated gender-related realities or inequalities. Nafija Sarajlić, a teacher by training who worked at a school in Sarajevo, was known for her short pieces titled *Teme* (Themes). These short prose pieces were published in the magazines *Zeman* and *Biser* (Hawkesworth 255). They were slated to be published in a collection, but the First World War put a halt to the printing process. Like the other women writers discussed in this chapter, Sarajlić was neglected in literary historiographies for many decades, only to be recently proclaimed Bosnia's "first woman prose writer in the Muslim community" (Isaković qtd. in Hawkesworth 256). Her "comeback" is also reflected in the fact that an elementary school in Sarajevo was named after her in 1993.

Her short piece titled "Teme" (Themes) is a first-person narrative that thematizes a female writer's struggle to define herself as a writer. Similar to Kobylianska's "A Conversation," much of the narrative consists of a dialogue between a man and a woman, this time the narrator and her spouse, a writer himself. Seeking his opinion, she asks him to read "a few themes that [she's] tried out" (262). The text concludes with his response:

> "I have read them," he said, "and I also crossed out some things."
> "Is it worth anything?"
> "Beginners should not ask this question. When a person feels a drive to work toward the greater good, he should do so, all possible recognition notwithstanding."
> And I understood that he approved.
> Therefore, here I have strung together a few themes that could be expanded if there were only more leisure time, but that is unattainable for me. (Sarajlić 263)

In her short fiction, Sarajlić developed a new prose form called "Teme," illustrated in the above excerpted passage. In the words of Emina Memija, "each of her themes could be developed into a story rich in observation and messages" (258). But, we argue, through this short prose piece, "Teme," Sarajlić is attempting to show that the genre she has created is not one that *should* necessarily be expanded.

Sarajlić's creation of this genre is significant for two reasons: first, its brevity as such is new and modern (even to the very critical writer husband), and second, it is gendered. This new genre enables the first-person narrator to fit writing into her busy schedule as a mother and wife. Her short manuscripts share space on her desk with her embroidery and the household bills to which she must attend. On the textual level, the creation of a new genre is significant because it is different from those other genres (poetry, debates, dramas, novels) that her husband considers uninteresting and ineffective in leading society forward. By combining a hypothetical statement ("if there were only more leisure time") with the textual reality ("but that is unattainable for me"), Sarajlić emphasizes a gendered aspect within her formal innovation. The female writer's lack of time justifies the protagonist's choice of the short prose form. By placing the story within a genre that her protagonist reflects upon from the perspective of a woman writer, Sarajlić emphasizes the effectiveness of this modernist literary genre and offers an implicit criticism of women's double-burden. By framing her story in the same genre as that of her character, Sarajlić allows her readers to experience her genre innovation in a reflective way that emphasizes gender on the level of both form and content.

Much like Sarajlić, Zofka Kveder was a literary innovator who experimented with both the genre she created and the topics she wrote about, topics that very much express a gendered sense of crisis. Like Meisel-Hess, Zofka Kveder discussed topics that were previously taboo in Slovenian literature and that only began to be addressed in literature across the monarchy as a whole, such as violence against women and the moral double-standard. Her collection of short sketches *Misterij žene* (Woman's Mystery) was published in her own edition in 1900. Like Sarajlić's "Teme," her snapshots provide glimpses into the issues affecting women in her society; yet Kveder's sketches, which appear one after another in a collection, come together to provide a collage of experiences confronting women from different family backgrounds and socio-economic circumstances.

Kveder portrays the general misery of women, from her depiction of the bleak life cycle of a working-class girl named Toni (who has the double-burden of factory work and household chores), to the life of the young female shop assistant longing for love, to the suicide of a young, well-to-do eighteen-year-old newlywed (who jumps into the river after an evening with guests). According to Kveder herself, this literary approach consisted of "seeing, knowing, and understanding" ("Sehen, wissen und verstehen!," qtd in Linhart 452). At another point she writes: "I don't know why the writer should avoid all shadows, especially the most black ones. To conceal the secret wounds of our societal life, which are still well-known to the world, our patched, rouged morals, is the same as when one tries to mask a manure pile with a valuable blanket" (qtd in Linhart 452–3). Using language traditionally associated with women such as "patched" or "darned" (*gepflickt*) or "made up with rouge or other make-up" (*geschminkt*), Kveder emphasizes that her texts are attempts to unmask the darkness (the blackest shadows) and the smell (the manure pile) of women's misery, instead of covering these up in a conventional female way (i.e., through darning or cosmetics). Through her short sketches she provides a naturalistic aesthetic for doing so (see Mihurko Poniž 37). But unlike most naturalistic texts, which focus exclusively on the life of peasants or the working classes, Kveder's unveil the suffering of women from all walks of life. Three of the sketches were translated by Carl Linhart in 1901 for the Austrian feminist journal *Dokumente der Frauen*, the journal of the *Allgemeiner Österreichischer Frauenverein* (General Austrian Women's Association). Given that Kveder was also involved in the Slovenian women's movement, this translation is an example of how feminist ideas and women's writing in various languages of the monarchy crossed linguistic borders, and not only outward from the political centres of Vienna and Budapest, but also the other way around, thus creating a gendered Austro-Hungarian geomodernist space.

Conclusion

Although each of the texts discussed above uses a different narrative form, one theme seems to run through these works – namely, the attempt to position crisis and identity as gendered. Setting aside differences in ethnic, geographic, and linguistic backgrounds, all five authors portray women as caught between two worlds, either by showing the destruction and violence to which they are exposed (Meisel-Hess, Kveder) or by portraying the New Woman in her attempts to overcome culturally imposed limitations (Meisel-Hess, Lux, Kobylianska, Sarajlić). The term "aesthetics of change" seems justified when we attempt to find a common denominator for these women writers' literary experiments and their ways of inscribing themselves into transcultural modernist debates as they simultaneously helped shape these debates. Such an aesthetics seeks change not only by "gendering" genre through the exploration of new literary forms (as seen particularly in Sarajlić and Kveder) but also by offering constructive gender criticism, and by repositioning women from objects to subjects of literary inquiry, as important but largely neglected players in modernism across the various regions and linguistic, ethnic, and national cultures of Austria-Hungary. Thus by viewing modernism as both a critical inquiry into and a self-fashioned and gendered break from the past rather than an exclusive and unique set of formal characteristics, we expand our understanding of Austro-Hungarian literary modernism. Placing literary modernism in a transcultural and transregional context within the Austro-Hungarian Monarchy through this interplay of locational positionalities and intersectionality helps us understand not only the aesthetics of change at the *fin de siècle* but also our own way of theorizing it today. We can thus establish a more differentiated literary and cultural history of this vast geographic area, one that takes into account the marginalized voices of women in addition to and next to the established canonical writers and that discovers common modernist threads in their works across existing political, linguistic, and intellectual boundaries beyond the dominant narratives of national imagined communities.

NOTES

1 We are adopting here the term "Bosnian" for the language that is today used by the people of Bosnia–Herzegovina although, linguistically speaking, the correct term would be Serbo-Croatian or Croato-Serbian. However, this term has been rejected to a large degree due to more recent political developments and ethnic divisions across the territory, which, except for Serbia and Montenegro, belonged at the time to the Austro-Hungarian Monarchy and, following its break-up, together with Serbia and Montenegro formed the Kingdom of Serbs, Croats, and Slovenes, later renamed Yugoslavia.

2 See for instance Claudio Magris, *Der habsburgische Mythos in der österreichischen Literatur* (Salzburg: Otto Müller, 1966); Carl Schorske's classic *Fin-de-Siècle Vienna: Politics and Culture* (New York: Vintage Books, 1981); Péter Hanák, *The Garden and the Workshop: Essays on the Cultural History of Vienna and Budapest* (Princeton: Princeton UP, 1998); Robert B. Pynsent, ed., *Decadence and Innovation: Austro-Hungarian Life and Art at the Turn of the Century* (London: Weidenfeld and Nicolson, 1989); and Steven Beller, ed., *Rethinking Vienna 1900* (New York: Berghahn, 2001). In the latter, Ilona Sármány-Parsons in her chapter "The Image of Women in Painting: Clichés and Reality in Austria–Hungary, 1895–1905" (220–63) points out a Vienna-centrism in the history of Austro-Hungarian culture, on the one hand, and a too narrowly, nationally defined approach on the other: "most references to Austro-Hungarian culture of the *fin de siècle* have tended to project the Viennese pattern onto the whole region. It is only local scholars who have attempted to correct this perspective when writing on Czech, Polish, or Hungarian culture, but they often have narrowed the focus by discussing one nation only" (220). Sármány-Parsons's approach can be considered the closest to ours, but it is applied to painting, not literature, and unlike our study, Sármány-Parsons discusses major artists, not "forgotten" female ones. The volume *Frauenbilder, feministische Praxis und nationales Bewusstsein in Österreich-Ungarn 1867–1918*, edited by Waltraud Heindl, Edit Király, and Alexandra Millner (Tübingen: Francke, 2006), is an important step in the direction of a more inclusive analysis of the various national women's movements in the Dual Monarchy. Discovering relatively unknown (Jewish) female modernist writers has been an important contribution to the scholarship on modernism and women writers. See, for example, Agatha Schwartz's contribution on Juliane Déry, "Living and Writing as a Cultural Hybrid: The Case of Juliane Déry," in *Jewish Intellectual Women in Central Europe 1860–2000: Twelve Biographical Essays*, ed. Judith Szapor, Andrea Pető, Maura Hametz, and Marina Calloni

(Lewiston: Edwin Mellen, 2012): 59–92. In the volume edited by Agatha Schwartz, *Gender and Modernity in Central Europe: The Austro-Hungarian Monarchy and Its Legacy* (Ottawa: U of Ottawa P, 2010), a multi-regional approach is reflected in the contributions, which cover various disciplines, from literature and painting to sociology, history, and psychoanalysis.

3 See for instance Harriet Anderson, *Utopian Feminism: Women's Movements in Fin-de-Siècle Vienna* (New Haven: Yale UP, 1992); Anna Fábri, *"A szép tiltott táj felé": A magyar irónők története két századforduló között"* (1795–1905) (To the Beautiful, Forbidden Land: A History of Hungarian Women Writers between 1795 and 1905; Budapest: Kortárs, 1996); Dunja Detoni Dujmić, *Ljepša polovica književnosti* (Literature's Better Half; Zagreb: Matica Hrvatska, 1998); the series *Women's Voices in Ukrainian Literature*, ed. Sonia Morris, trans. Roma Franko (Saskatoon: Language Lantern, 1998–2000); Brigitte Spreitzer, *Texturen: Die österreichische Moderne der Frauen* (Vienna: Passagen, 1999); and Kathleen Hayes, *A World Apart and Other Stories: Czech Women Writers at the Fin de Siècle* (Prague: Karolinum Press, 2001).

4 For a comprehensive overview of the women's movements and a selection of women writers across the Austro-Hungarian Empire as well as the contacts that emerged between them, see our book *Shaking the Empire, Shaking Patriarchy: The Growth of a Feminist Consciousness across the Austro-Hungarian Monarchy* (Riverside: Ariadne Press, 2014).

5 We consider Lux to be a feminist writer based on her novel we are discussing here. Her feminism, however, as demonstrated by Judit Kádár, went through various phases and at times was not void of traditionalism. See *Engedelmes lázadók: Magyar nőírók és nőideál-konstrukciók a 20. század első felében* (Obedient Rebels: Hungarian Women Writers and Constructions of the Ideal Femininity in the First Half of the Twentieth Century; Pécs: Jelenkor, 2014, 52).

6 Unless otherwise indicated, all translations are our own.

7 For a detailed discussion of the textual staging of Jewish memory, see Gillman 176.

8 See József Földvári's two chapters "'Egy hazug asszony nem hazug asszony.' Lux Terka nem Lux Terka" [A woman who lies is not a liar: Terka Lux is not Terka Lux] and "Nóra – segédszínésznőkkel: Lux Terka és Ritoók Emma közös színpadán" [Nora performed by assistant actors: On Terka Lux and Emma Ritoók's joint stage], in *Nő, tükör, írás. Értelmezések a 20. század első felének női irodalmáról*, ed. Virág Varga and Zoltán Zsávolya (Budapest: Ráció Kiadó, 2009), 82–88 and 107–11, respectively, as well as Judit Kádár's chapter "Two Austro-Hungarian Women Writers, Anna Tutsek and Terka Lux, Creating New Urban Identities in Early Twentieth

Century Budapest", in *Hungarian Cultural Studies* 8 (2015): http://ahea.pitt.edu/ojs/index.php/ahea/article/view/214/319.

9 The Faculties of Philosophy (Arts) and Medicine and Pharmacy were opened for women in the Hungarian half of the Monarchy in 1895, admitting the first female students in the fall of 1896, whereas in the Austrian half the Faculties of Philosophy opened in 1897 and Medicine a few years later, in 1900.

10 Although Jews were officially classified as a religious group in Austria–Hungary, according to Marsha L. Rozenblit they can be regarded as an ethnic group in that they shared the same history, culture, and religion. See *Reconstructing a National Identity: The Jews of Habsburg Austria During World War I* (Oxford: Oxford UP, 2001) 9.

11 The translation of Kobylianska's "A Conversation" is by Roma Franko.

12 This image of the woman as mother and educator of the nation is frequently found throughout the nineteenth century in movements of national awakening within the Monarchy, an image also embraced by many women. See Schwartz and Thorson, *Shaking the Empire, Shaking Patriarchy*, in particular pages 23, 32, 41, 63–5, 68, 80, and 86.

WORKS CITED

Anderson, Benedict. *Imagined Communities: Reflections on the Origin and Spread of Nationalism.* London: Verso, 1983. Print.

Beller, Steven. *Vienna and the Jews 1867–1938: A Cultural History*. Cambridge: Cambridge University Press, 1989. Print.

Doyle, Laura, and Laura Winkiel. "Introduction: The Global Horizons of Modernism." In *Geomodernisms: Race, Modernism, Modernity*. Ed. Laura Doyle and Laura Winkiel. Bloomington: Indiana UP, 2005. 1–14. Print.

Fábri, Anna. "Hungarian Women Writers, 1900–1945." Trans. Alexander Hervey. In *A History of Central European Women's Writing*. Ed. Celia Hawkesworth. Houndmills: Palgrave, 2001. 87–109. Print.

Friedman, Susan Stanford. "Periodizing Modernism: Postcolonial Modernities and the Space/Time Borders of Modernist Studies." *Modernism/Modernity* 13.3 (2006): 425–43. Print.

Gillman, Abigail. *Viennese Jewish Modernism: Freud, Hofmannsthal, Beer-Hofmann, and Schnitzler*. University Park: Pennsylvania State UP, 2009. Print.

Hawkesworth, Celia. *Voices in the Shadows: Women and Verbal Art in Serbia and Bosnia*. Budapest: Central European UP, 2000. Print.

Herzog, Hillary Hope. *"Vienna Is Different": Jewish Writers in Austria from the Fin de siècle to the Present*. New York: Berghahn, 2011. Print.

Kaplan, Marion A. *The Making of the Jewish Middle Class: Women, Family, and Identity in Imperial Germany.* Oxford: Oxford UP, 1991. Print.

Kobylianska, Olha. "A Conversation." In *For a Crust of Bread: Selected Prose Fiction by Nataliya Kobrynska, Olena Pchilka, Lyubov Yanovska, Olha Kobylianska, Yevheniya Yaroshynska, Hrytsko Hryhorenko, Lesya Ukrainka.* Ed. Sonia Morris. Trans. Roma Franko. Saskatoon: Language Lanterns, 1998. 219–31. Print.

Kveder, Zofka. "Drei Skizzen aus Zofka Kveders *Mysterium der Frau.* In das Deutsche übertragen von Linhart Karl." *Dokumente der Frauen* 4.19 (1901): 617–19. Print.

–. *Misterij žene* (Woman's Mystery). Private edition, 1900. Print.

LeRider, Jacques. *Das Ende der Illusion: Die Wiener Moderne und die Krisen der Identität.* Trans. Robert Fleck. Vienna: ÖNV, 1990. Print.

Linhart, Carl. "Slovenische Frauenbewegung." *Dokumente der Frauen* 6.16 (1901): 449–58. Print.

Lux, Terka. *Leányok.* Budapest: Légrády, 1906. Print.

Meisel-Hess, Grete. *Fanny Roth, eine Jung-Frauengeschichte.* Leipzig: Hermann Seemann Nachfolger, 1902. Print.

–. *Die sexuelle Krise: Eine sozialpsychologische Untersuchung.* Jena: Diederichs, 1909. Print.

–. *The Sexual Crisis: A Critique of Our Sex Life.* New York: The Critic and Guide Company, 1917. Print.

–. *Die Stimme: Roman in Blättern.* Berlin: Wedekind & Co., 1907. Print.

–. *Die Intellektuellen.* Berlin: Oesterheld, 1911. Print.

Memija, Emina. "Medaljoni života Nafija Sarajlić" [Medallions of Life Nafija Sarajlić]. In *Šemsudin Sarajlić, Iz bosanske romantike and Nafija Sarajlić, Teme.* Ed. Emina Memija and Fahrudin Rizvanbegović. Sarajevo: Preporod, 1997. 247–58. Print.

Mihurko Poniž, Katja. "Nation and Gender in the Writings of Slovene Women Writers, 1848–1918." *Aspasia* 2 (2008): 28–43. Print.

Neuburger, Mary. *The Orient Within: Muslim Minorities and the Negotiation of Nationhood in Modern Bulgaria.* Ithica: Cornell UP, 2004. Print.

Parry, Amie Elizabeth. *Interventions into Modernist Cultures: Poetry from Beyond the Empty Screen.* Durham: Duke UP, 2007. Print.

Pollock, Griselda. "The Return of the Repressed: Feminism and Failure in Re-gendering International Modernisms in the Visual Arts." Alternative Modernisms Conference. Cardiff University. 18 May 2013. Keynote Lecture.

Rozenblit, Marsha L. *The Jews of Vienna 1867–1914: Assimilation and Identity.* Albany: SUNY P, 1983. SUNY Series in Modern Jewish History. Print.

Said, Edward W. *Orientalism.* 1978. New York: Vintage Books, 1994. Print.

Sarajlić, Nafija. "Teme." In *Šemsudin Sarajlić, Iz bosanske romantike and Nafija Sarajlić, Teme*. Ed. Emina Memija and Fahrudin Rizvanbegović. Sarajevo: Preporod, 1997. 261–63. Print.

Sármány-Parsons, Ilona. "The Image of Women in Painting: Clichés and Reality in Austria-Hungary, 1895–1905." In *Rethinking Vienna 1900*. Ed. Steven Beller. New York: Berghahn, 2001. 220–63. Print.

Schwartz, Agatha. *Shifting Voices: Feminist Thought and Women's Writing in Fin-de-Siècle Austria and Hungary*. Montreal and Kingston: McGill–Queen's UP, 2008. Print.

Schwartz, Agatha, and Helga Thorson. *Shaking the Empire, Shaking Patriarchy: The Growth of a Feminist Consciousness across the Austro-Hungarian Monarchy*. Riverside: Ariadne Press, 2014. Studies in Austrian Literature, Culture and Thought. Print.

Spreitzer, Brigitte. *Texturen: Die österreichische Moderne der Frauen*. Vienna: Passagen, 1999. Studien zur Moderne 8. Print.

Thorson, Helga. "Confronting Anti-Semitism and Antifeminism in Turn of the Century Vienna: Grete Meisel-Hess and the Modernist Discourses on Hysteria." In *Jüdische Identitäten: Einblicke in die Bewußtseinslandschaft des österreichischen Judentums*. Ed. Klaus Hödl. Innsbruck: Studien Verlag, 2000. 71–94. Schriften des David-Herzog-Centrums für jüdische Studien 1. Print.

–. "Regarding the Voices of Viennese Literary Modernism: Grete Meisel-Hess's *Die Stimme. Roman in Blättern* (1907)." *Modern Austrian Literature* 44.3–4 (2011): 1–18. Print.

Todorova, Maria. *Imagining the Balkans*. Oxford: Oxford UP, 1997. Print.

3 Border, Transborder, and Unification: Music and Its Divergent Roles in the Nineteenth-Century Habsburg Territories

GREGOR KOKORZ

Introduction: Some Theoretical Reflections on Music, Border, and Space

How can we think of Central Europe? How can we understand the Central European space, and what are its characteristics? Often we tend to conceive geographical as well as cultural spaces as fixed and stable entities with specific structures and borders. Rather than outlining such a space, I maintain that it is more appropriate to think of Central Europe in dynamic terms, focusing on changes and transformations and asking questions as to where, when, and how such transformations took place, what role music played in those processes, and how those processes can contribute to the shaping of Central Europe as a common aesthetic space.

Earlier studies on space such as those by Durkheim or Lefebvre (68–168) outlined the importance of constructivist notions, arguing that space is socially produced. They thereby introduced a topic that has become central in recent debates on space and that has created what Bachmann-Medick has called "the spatial turn." This turn in cultural studies has spurred the recent attention to the spatial dimension of culture. This spatial discourse, however, has not automatically generated increased attention to the role and function of borders. Space is often conceptualized without its margins. In the larger context of the ongoing processes of increased transnationalization and the debates over the consequences of globalization, borders have slipped out of focus (Lefebvre; Schroer). The situation is similar for studies on cultural transfer. As a result of the deconstruction of national narratives through a focus on transnational aspects and connections, the once absolute national frames and borders have been, if not completely erased, then strongly reduced with regard to their importance for conceptualizing cultural processes. Yet space does not exist without borders. Space can indeed be defined, conceptualized, and analysed through a focus on its margins, by examining what is included in a certain space and thus constitutes a common cultural ground, as well as what is excluded, that is, ignored or rejected. Just as individual identity is built on the construction of its Other and therefore on mechanisms of exclusion, the constitution of space is driven by similar mechanisms, the implication being that the discussion of space and its construction can be informed by the analysis of these dynamics.

In the past decade, this dynamic understanding of borders has been adopted within the interdisciplinary field of border studies, which has been taken up mainly by geographers and political scientists, who started out investigating borders as given realities (Kolossov) but later shifted their focus to the dynamics of border construction, with an increased interest in the processes of "bordering" and the discursive construction of borders through the influence of postmodern theories. In this context, borders are understood as "strategic representations of the marking and claiming of difference in space" (Berg and Van Houtum 2). In this chapter the terms "border," "transborder," and "unification" serve as analytical tools for examining the role of music in the cultural restructuring of the Central European space, based on such a dynamic understanding of borders; at the same time, this approach underscores the ambivalent and reciprocal quality of borders. That is, borders constitute both moments of separation and zones of contact and exchange. Particularly in this latter aspect, border studies overlap with studies of cultural transfer (which focus on transnational cultural dynamics of exchange, emphasizing the deconstruction of dominant national narratives) but without broaching the issue of borders and their function (Mitterbauer and Scherke). My goal here is to bring the border back into the field of cultural transfer, both in the sense of the bracketing of borders and in the sense of border construction. I am interested in border experiences as particularly spatial, as experiences in which exclusions as well as transitions and unifications take place. The inclusion of "unification" as a third element of this research (the first two being the more common "border" and "transborder") is spurred by my focus in this article on the specific time and space of nineteenth-century Central Europe. It is based on the assumption that nineteenth-century processes of nationalization that shook the entire continent can be understood as a profound restructuring of space in the social, cultural, and, finally, political and military senses. This reorganization was strongly built on mechanisms of homogenization, on the model of the nineteenth-century nation-state as a unified but also homogenized entity. For this reason, nineteenth-century nationalism can be regarded as part of a process of modernization (as, indeed, it was argued at the time) in the sense that it unified previously separate smaller territories into larger and more modern states, which then needed to develop discursive mechanisms and practices of unification.

In the past few years the issues of border and space have received some attention in historical research (Roll, Pohle and Myrczek; Reininghaus and Walter) and have been explored in the context of Central Europe (Fischer). So far, the most important study that gives evidence for the importance of the cultural construction of space and borders in the Central European context is Peter Judson's study on the language frontiers of the Habsburg Empire (Judson; Judson and Rozenblit). Judson describes and analyses the efforts of German nationalist activists after 1880 to nationalize the heterogeneous and multilingual communities in the rural areas of the Habsburg Empire by establishing associations for defending German culture at the "linguistic frontier." His detailed study highlights the importance of culture for the construction of national identities and for the construction and imagination of space. According to Judson, language and the uses to which it is put contribute to the formation and transformation of frontiers and space.

Just like language, so too can music contribute to the social construction of space. Indeed, music can be a highly efficient instrument because of some of its specific qualities. Music's fluidity, its semantic openness, and its collective power can be particularly useful for the restructuring of spaces that are themselves in flux and subject to different and divergent interpretations. Unlike visual constructions of space, be they architectonic or monumental, musical constructions are created by performative acts and thus exist in the moment of singing or playing. Consequently, what makes music a problematic area of research (given that we depend on sometimes scarce information for the historic reconstruction and analysis of such fleeting moments) also makes music an extremely potent medium for the construction of space. Because of its immediacy, its spontaneity, and its potential collective mode, music is able to unite large groups of people in common and highly emotional actions; it can even affect those who are distant from such actions as acoustic waves penetrate windows and walls. Aural space transgresses the boundaries of visual space and follows its own criteria of construction.

In the rest of this chapter, I explore music's role in the restructuring of Central European space. I focus on what border experiences can tell us about where and how borders have been perceived and what they can contribute to the understanding of space. I start with a brief section on Felix Mendelssohn Bartholdy, who, on his trip to Italy, pierced what can be described as the outer crust of Central Europe. His observation of bordering and transbordering serves as an introduction to the topic and as an exemplification of the above outlined reflections. I will then extend my argument in two more detailed case studies, one on Buda and Pest, and the other on Trieste, observing these two Central European urban spaces while they undergo transformations in which music plays a significant role.

Mendelssohn's Border Experience

In the autumn of 1830, Felix Mendelssohn Bartholdy, like so many Germans before him, set off for Italy. In an early letter to his family about his travels, we find the following passage:

> At last morning broke, and as we drove into Resciutta [*sic*!] the driver said that on the other side of the bridge there, no one understood a word of German. I therefore took leave of my mother tongue for a long time to come, and we drove over the bridge. The style of the houses immediately beyond was entirely different. The flat roofs with their convex tiles, the deep windows, the high white walls, and lofty square towers, all betokened another land. The pale olive faces of the men, the innumerable beggars who besieged the carriage, the various small chapels, brightly and carefully painted on every side with flowers, the nuns, monks, and so forth, were all symptomatic of Italy. (Mendelssohn-Bartholdy 32)

Mendelssohn's experience of entering the town of Resicutta can qualify as a border experience. However, it is not geographical or political borders that are involved here but cultural ones; architecture, physiognomy, and language shape the difference experienced by Mendelssohn and create for him a sense of otherness. At the same time, culture creates a common space and bridges potential differences. This becomes quite evident when, only a few lines later, Mendelssohn writes of his encounter with Venetian art. His description of Titian's paintings in

Venice, just as with Goethe's of his contact with Roman monuments in his famous *Italienische Reise* (*Italian Journey*), does not reflect an experience of difference or otherness; rather, it represents an admiring encounter with a cultural heritage that he perceives as part of his own cultural tradition and space.

Travel experiences such as these show that culture is a powerful force for shaping space and creating borders in terms of inclusion as well as exclusion, and that culture, more than politics and geography, contributes to the construction of space. This aligns well with the understanding of space as discussed in cultural studies (Bachmann-Medick), in which space is not treated as a natural fact but rather is conceptualized as a cultural construction. Embracing this conception and focusing on music and Central Europe, my objective then is less about music than it is about how music as a cultural force has helped construct and shape a Central European cultural space, or perhaps several cultural spaces.

Mendelssohn's experience of clearly divided cultural spheres was not necessarily the typical border experience for a traveller in the Habsburg territories at that time. Other travellers, such as Johann Georg Kohl, a distinguished nineteenth-century German travel writer who released five volumes on his journeys in the Habsburg territories in the early 1840s, described his border experience on his journey to Hungary in terms of opacity, reflecting the vagueness of transitions within areas of cultural ambiguity characterized by the simultaneous presence of different ethnic groups and cultures.

At the same time, these border experiences are not limited to border areas. Kohl carefully noted the cultural plurality of the entire region. Indeed, according to Csáky ("Ambivalenz des kulturellen Erbes"; *Das Gedächtnis der Städte*), such plurality can be described as the real unifying element of the entire region: "For centuries the Central European region has been defined by a multiplicity of peoples, languages, and cultures. This was its characteristic marker, and one could say, that the agreement, the unity of the region, is grounded in its multiplicity, i.e. its heterogeneity"[1] ("Ambivalenz des kulturellen Erbes" 35). In particular, the rising urban centres of the nineteenth century became the culmination points of such heterogeneity. This pluralistic urban space and the question of how music contributed to national restructuring, especially towards the middle of the century, are at the centre of the following two case studies. The first focuses on a concert tour by Franz Liszt to Buda and Pest in the winter of 1839; the second, on the year 1848 in Trieste. Both cities were heterogeneous urban spaces where nationalism became a topic of social debate and political conflict. Buda and Pest had German- and Hungarian-speaking communities, while the population of Trieste, the main port of the Habsburg Empire, was a mixture of Italians, Germans, and Slavs, as well as several other communities, such as the Greeks and the English, owing to its role as a international trading port. I demonstrate in what follows how a focus on the processes of bordering and transbordering can inform both an analysis of music (for it allows a richer and thicker description of musical situations) and an analysis of the construction of space (for music contributes to processes of spatial restructuring). Thus music is both the subject of this research and a tool for analysing such historical processes.

Liszt's Hungarian Identity: Music and National Identity Construction

Franz (Ferenc) Liszt travelled to Buda and Pest, the not yet united sibling cities, for a four-week concert tour in late December 1839, arriving in Buda on Christmas Eve. He would return to Vienna at the end of January after a triumphant series of nine concerts. At the time of Liszt's Hungarian sojourn, political tensions were running high. These were the years preceding the 1848 revolutions, and beyond any doubt, Liszt's public appearances were strongly perceived and exploited in that nationalistic context. Liszt took advantage of this by helping to orchestrate his visit as a nationalist project. He helped set this tone by publishing in a local newspaper a private letter he had written to Count Leó Festetics in which he expressed love for his home country (see Schober 14–16). This nationalist discourse was reinforced by discussions of Liszt's own noble pedigree, which culminated in the sharply criticized award of a Sabre of Honour – the sword being a symbol of the Hungarian nobility – during one of his concerts. Also, by Liszt's appearance on stage in national Hungarian costume, by his letters of thanks, and by his frequent speeches during the tour. Clearly, nationalism was being orchestrated during this journey. In turn, Liszt's biographers have drawn heavily from this sojourn, thus adding a further layer of national representation.[2]

But a different perspective is revealed when we focus on this question: Which aspects of this visit have received attention and been included in the narration of Lizst's tour, and which have remained untold? The biographers who discuss Liszt's music on this journey to Hungary pay particular attention to his transcription of the "Rákóczi March,"[3] a piece that was regularly welcomed with thunderous applause. But the audience was reacting in the first place not to Liszt's virtuosic interpretation or to the quality of the composition, but rather to what it signified: it was named after the eighteenth-century Transylvanian Grand Duke Ferenc Rákóczi II, who battled against the Habsburg rulers, a fact that gave the march a revolutionary scent and made it, in effect, an anthem for a free and independent Hungary (Slottman).

In this sort of interpretation, looking at a single piece of "truly national music" takes the place of a closer and more complete analysis, one that provides a different outcome. Surprisingly, only a very small portion of the repertoire Liszt presented at these concerts could be described as "Hungarian" and thus as contributing directly to a distinct Hungarian national discourse. Besides the "Rákóczi March," given twice during these concerts, only two other pieces – "Hungarian Melody and March" and a "Hungarian Rhapsody" – were in this category. Liszt's repertoire in these concerts was dominated by Italian opera, for example, by his "Fantasie sur des motifs favouris de l'opéra *La Sonnambula*" and his "Réminiscences de *Lucia di Lammermoor*." Overall, there was more Beethoven and Schubert than Hungarian music in the programs.[4] This was true even for his performance at the Hungarian National Theatre, where the harshly criticized presentation of the Sword of Honour took place, during an evening when Liszt was celebrated and crowned as a national Hungarian hero. That same evening, the audience could listen to Liszt's transcriptions of Donizetti's *Lucia de Lammermoor* (a piece he had already given twice in concert); his own "Grand Galop Chromatique"; and two of Schubert's songs, "Der Wanderer" and "Gruppe aus dem Tatarus." This is how Walker, based on contemporary reports, describes the events of the evening: "Since the tumult which followed his performance showed no signs of diminishing," Liszt presented the "Rákóczi March" as an encore, which produced a "furor 'almost enough to have awakened the dead'" (Walker 324).[5]

These facts are easily ascertained. But my concern here is less with Liszt's biography than with how national and supranational aspects were intertwined in Liszt's performances and how a closer reading of them can help us understand the Central European space and the dynamics of its reshaping in the nineteenth century. Liszt's Hungarian concerts point to an interesting and highly significant opposition between a supranational aesthetics on the one hand, and an ongoing process of nationalization on the other. The former was represented by his repertoire, which in fact contributed to a Central European or even a larger European aesthetic space; the latter took place largely on a performative level, outside the music: Liszt's Hungarian costume, the awarding of the sabre (whose inscription reads "the great artist Ferenc Liszt, for his artistic merit and for his patriotism, from his admiring compatriots"), and Liszt's response.[6] Whereas these performative practices pointed towards the local and created a distinct national Hungarian space, Liszt's music did not – indeed, it referred to a larger European space. Given that Beethoven and Schubert were a large part of his repertoire, one might be tempted to address that space as Austrian or Central European. However, the musical world mirrored in Liszt's compositions went very far beyond these borders. His "Reminiscences" – piano fantasies based mainly on Italian opera themes – which were in fact the core repertoire of Liszt's recitals, reflected the most recent developments in European music of the time. Bellini's *La sonnambula* was first staged in 1831, Donizetti's *Lucia di Lammermoor* and Bellini's *I puritani* both in 1835, and Meyerbeer's *Les Huguenots* one year after that, in 1836. It was in those same years that Liszt began composing his fantasies, thereby transposing the operatic world into his piano recitals. In this way he presented modern European music in his concerts; indeed, as the most famous and most admired virtuoso of the coming decade, giving hundreds of concerts all over the continent, he helped create and shape a common European musical space. Liszt became a major representative of this modern (musical) world, whose centre lay not in Central Europe but in Paris, which Walter Benjamin so rightly defined as the European capital of the nineteenth century. The music, as well as its virtuoso, shone from what was viewed at the time as one of Europe's most modern places. It was in Paris that Meyerbeer's *Les Huguenots*, Bellini's *I puritani*, and Rossini's *Guillaume Tell* had their premieres; it was in Paris that Liszt himself first encountered this music; it was there that we can locate other parts of his repertoire such as his *Hexaméron Variations*.[7] And it was in Paris that Liszt spent his formative years and that he launched his international career. The Hungarian audience's thunderous welcome for Liszt did not stem solely from his patriotism and his outstanding artistic virtuosity; it also reflected his role as a representative of this modern musical world. In this picture the national and international, while represented by strikingly different patterns, expressed not an insuperable conflict but rather a necessary complementarity. Liszt represented both the national and the international, but he could become a national icon only because he was the admired representative of the modern European world.

This conjuncture of the national and the international became a constitutive element of a Hungarian national identity. Evidence for this can be gathered from Franz von Schober's description of Liszt's Hungarian journey. Schober accompanied the pianist on his journey to Buda and Pest as his private secretary and published his travel report *Briefe über F. Liszt's Aufenthalt in Ungarn* (Letters on F. Liszt's Stay in Hungary) in 1843 as a literary defence of the international criticism of Liszt's visit to Hungary, which risked damaging the artist's reputation. Schober's description is that of a close eyewitness and sharp observer, who provides his readers with a subtle analysis of the Hungarian situation:

> Liszt embodies much that wins him the Hungarian hearts. He was born Hungarian and educated by Hungary through continuous participation; he was proudly calling himself a Hungarian and proved it by his deeds and empathy for the fate of the country. And even though he did not speak the Hungarian language, he appeared before them in their national costume, and no disturbing signs of a foreign nationality affronted them in his beautiful art; they could declare as Hungarian his ravishing achievements, without offence to the Magyarism. How he must have pleased them as they were striving for education and acknowledgement, to declare as theirs such a European celebrity, the foremost in his field. (Schober 24–5)[8]

Two aspects of Schober's analysis are particularly striking. First, among the many elements that contributed to Liszt's capacity to serve as a figure of national identity, music itself was less important than other, non-musical aspects. Second, Schober points to Liszt's international reputation as a core part of this national identification. Liszt's celebrity functioned as compensation for Hungary's perceived backwardness and marginality in European culture. In this way, Liszt connected the Hungarian periphery with the centre and allowed Hungary to participate in modern European culture; he also made it possible for Hungarians to perceive themselves as at the centre. The international thus became a constitutive part of the national.

This idea was already being publicly expressed during Liszt's sojourn in Pest in a cantata of welcome written by the musical director of the German theatre, Janos Grill, which was performed twice during Liszt's stay. The lyrics, which von Schober provides, summon nationalist sentiments and centre on three possible homelands for Liszt: nation, art, and world. Art and world, which symbolize Liszt's great fame, have provided much for him. But not surprisingly, Liszt develops his strongest ties with the nation, lost in early childhood, never forgotten, and now regained in triumph:

Whatever fate declared,
Art, Fame, Pleasure, Happiness;
You still remembered faithfully
The land that gave you birth. (Schober 28)[9]

To underscore Liszt's heartfelt patriotism, Schober inserts a juxtaposition between nation and world, creating a tension between the previously described glory of the world and Liszt's poor, because artistically underdeveloped, homeland: "You come to us, where life is hard / The arts still in their cradle."[10] Liszt's return leads to the climax of the final verse: "Franz Liszt, your fatherland is proud of you!"[11]

Patriotism runs through the cantata like a leitmotif. The terms fatherland (*Vaterland*) and homeland (*Heimat*) are heard in no less than seven of the nine stanzas of von Schober's text: from the loss of the fatherland in the first stanza ("Go on, you have no fatherland"), and of the artistic homeland in the second stanza ("This is the home of great minds"), to the central opposition of world and homeland in the fourth and fifth stanzas ("Liszt, your homeland is the world" – "The land that gave you birth"), until the final climax of the proud fatherland in the last line of the ninth stanza ("Franz Liszt, your fatherland is proud of you").

The cold hand of fate took hold of you
While you were still a tender boy, pulling you
To distant realms, and said:
"Go on, you have no fatherland."

Then Art's transfigured wings
Led you into her magic realm
"This is the home of great minds,
It is yours too, just like theirs."

And with adulation life beckoned you
Into its glittering terrain;
It adorned you with its gifts
And bade you: "Now stay and rule here."

Then, transported by fame, you were
Placed on its pinnacles:
"Do you hear," he spoke, "the people rejoicing?
Liszt, your homeland is the world!"

Whatever fate declared,
Art, Fame, Pleasure, Happiness;
You still remembered faithfully
The land that gave you birth.

You come to us, where life is hard,
The arts still in their cradle,
Yet our heart is rich and pure,
It calls to you: "Be welcome here."

Be welcome with the laurel wreath
Which you deserve so valiantly,
You the great artist, nobleman, the faithful
Franz Liszt, your fatherland is proud of you! (Schober 27–8)[12]

Liszt, as a figure, mediates not only between the national and the international but also between different ethnicities and conflicting concepts of national identity. Setting aside for now the question of what made Liszt a figure of national identity, it is worth focusing on what constituted Liszt's own Hungarian identity. It was not language. When Liszt spoke of himself as Hungarian, he used neither Hungarian nor German, but French, which had become his first language. Liszt, who lived in France after the age of twelve, spoke and wrote mainly in French. He was of German ethnicity, but uneasy with the German language,[13] and he did not speak or understand Hungarian. Even so, he described himself as Hungarian. Liszt's Hungarian identity was based on birth rather than language, a concept of national identity that is also reflected in the Grill/Schober cantata: "You still remembered faithfully / The land that gave you birth." Homeland, here, is the country that gave one birth, not the country whose language one speaks. In the ethnically pluralistic context of Central Europe, with its intermingled ethnicities and languages – a situation that was particularly true for the Kingdom of Hungary (Csáky, *Das Gedächtnis der Städte* 273 ff.), this was an important concept, although in the late 1830s it was no longer universally accepted. Liszt's visit came during a period of transition in which a language-based national concept was gaining dominance over conceptions of national identity based on birth, and in which, in 1844, Hungarian finally took the place of Latin as the kingdom's official administrative language (*Das Gedächtnis der Städte* 273 ff.; Csáky, "Hungarus-Konzeption"). Indications of the presence of these diverse conceptualizations of national identity accompanied Liszt's entire Hungarian sojourn. The lyrics to the Grill/Schober cantata reflect a pluralistic situation – that is, the presence of an important German-speaking community as well as the continuity of a tradition in which language, clearly, was not understood as a signifier of national identity. The repeatedly symbolic use of Hungarian and Liszt's own apology for being unable to address his audience in Hungarian together express the idea of a language-based conception of national identity. The Hungarian language was strongly perceived as an indicator of Hungarian identity, but not yet as an indispensable factor, as Liszt's case perfectly demonstrates.

In situations where language creates a potential conflict, music provides a powerful locus of national identification, one that is not afflicted by the tension that the use of a specific language can cause. Music functions as an inclusive space of identification. Whatever ethnic group one belongs to, whatever languages one speaks, whatever concept of national identity one believes in, music bridges these differences. The musical space that lies beyond the conflict of languages becomes then a space of common national identification. This was especially true for Liszt's piano recitals, during which even language-based pieces, such as opera arias, were transformed into pure sound; in this way, as Schober shows in his analysis, every last sign of foreignness was set aside. Liszt may not have been able to communicate with all Hungarians (as indicated by his constant need for translators), but through his music he spoke to all Hungarians. Thus, in his hands, music became an inclusive factor with the potential to bridge not only linguistic but also social and political differences.

Music, then, has the capacity to bridge social gaps and thereby create a communal national space; but in Hungary, it was not music and its specific qualities alone that made this transformation possible. My analysis would be incomplete without an examination of the intentions of the various actors in the musical field. In the case of Liszt's concerts, the virtuoso and composer himself was a protagonist who carefully arranged and exploited the situation for his own purposes. As Dana Gooley has shown, Liszt employed a well-calculated strategy of self-representation and throughout his concert career established a bond between himself and his audiences. To that end, he drew on national currents in various places, and not just during his Hungarian concert tour:

> He tapped into their sense of loyalty to a community, paid tribute to that community, elevated their spirit of pride, and thereby made the concert into an extraordinary, memorable event. He was willing to transform his image – his dress, gestures, repertory, touring strategies, and even performing style – to reinforce the impression that he belonged, like a brother, to his audiences. They responded by joining him symbolically to their communities, whether with honorary citizenships [...] or with precious gifts and prestigious honors. (Gooley 117)

Similar processes can be found in other Liszt-related contexts, most strikingly in his role in Weimar as a prominent contributor to the formation of a German national identity (Bahr). Liszt functioned as a figure of identification for different national groups. In this era, the Hungarian as well as other national identity constructions made extensive use of music. Music's specific function, however, can vary with the context, and it is precisely this that makes music a powerful tool for studying space. As the example of Liszt's concert tour of 1839 makes clear, music mediates between spaces and bridges social and cultural groups; it permeates borders and thus displays unifying qualities, which are essential for national identity construction. Liszt was present in the German National Theatre as well as in the Hungarian, in the salons of the nobility as well as among the crowds in the streets. His concerts and indeed his very presence temporarily erased class barriers and led to social fusion, as Franz Schober observes: "At the banquets, that he [Liszt] organized in response to their dinners, all class barriers seemed to disappear, aristocrats and artists, merchants and scholars were sitting all together, and Liszt's bright spirit knew how to merge these people into one cheerful, uninhibited busy company, who otherwise shared little or no contact" (Schober 33–4).[14] In Liszt's case, then, music, understood as an overall performative activity that includes music, musicians, and audience, contributed to the construction of a unified national space.

Trieste's Multitude

The situation of Trieste was different. Trieste's cultural and ethnic diversity was comparable to that of Buda and Pest, but the conception of space there differed significantly from that of Hungary. In Buda and Pest there circulated different ideas on how to construct a Hungarian national identity (i.e., based on birth or on language). That said, among German- and Hungarian-speaking groups the consensus was that a Hungarian identity and space did in fact exist. In Trieste there was no such consensus; instead, the urban space was a locus of conflict among concurrent and opposing national identity constructions, and as a result, Trieste was located in divergent national spaces. The question of the restructuring of space was relevant in both cases, as were the processes of bordering and transbordering as the main forces for restructuring; but whereas in Hungary centripetal forces tended towards a common space, Trieste was in the centre of centrifugal forces that propelled the city towards a plurality of spaces. Thus, in this comparison, space as an analytical category becomes the main criterion for differentiation, given that these two urban settings differed precisely in their construction of space.

Trieste had been part of the Habsburg territories since 1382 and was granted the privileges of a free port in the eighteenth century under Emperor Karl VI, but it was economic growth during the nineteenth century that transformed Trieste into the empire's principal port, as well as the Habsburg territories' fourth-largest city after Vienna, Budapest, and Prague. In the 1830s and 1840s, the population doubled and Trieste became a multi-ethnic and pluralistic centre, owing to its geographical position at the intersection of Slavic, Italian, and German cultures and to its far-reaching international trade contacts (Ara and Magris; Dubin). In this heterogeneous and pluralistic context, the rise of nationalism in the highly politicized environment of the 1848 revolutions seriously jeopardized Trieste's stability. Indeed, all over Europe, the national question became the focus of political and cultural discourse. The more specific question of Trieste's national character provoked multiple and opposing views regarding how to construct its identity and space. In terms of the complex cultural and ethnic situation, public discourse in Trieste reflected five different models of identity construction. Three of these models were mutually exclusive in that they constructed the Trieste region as Italian or Slav or German territory. These positions, intrinsically opposed in content yet formally identical, were confronted with two other kinds of identity constructions. The first gave support to the official Austrian state doctrine, which characterized Trieste as pluralistic and developed a supranational Austrian identity; the other – which amounted almost to a loophole to avoid the possible serious consequences of local tensions – emphasized Trieste's local identity based on the pride the inhabitants took in the town's history.

In this ambivalent situation and heated climate, music became an important means to mentally map this urban ground, to construct and restructure but also to mediate space (Kokorz). I will start my brief analysis of music's function in this context with a close reading of a newspaper article on one of the crucial moments of the year 1848 in Trieste, when on 17 March the news of Chancellor Metternich's resignation and the emperor's decision to grant a constitution arrived in town. Each of these items was enthusiastically celebrated on the streets and in the theatre:

> Today is a national holiday! This phrase could be read on the door of every house on the morning of the 17th. The stores were closed. Dense crowds of people moved through the streets singing and rejoicing. In front of Tergesteo's café, all who live from a daily wage were offered breakfast. Special care was taken that the working class lacked nothing on this happy day [...] In the evening the city and the theatre were brilliantly illuminated and every room of the theatre was filled with spectators. A thousand-voiced "Eviva" resounded as Governor Robert Altgraf von Salm appeared. Handkerchiefs and sashes in the national colours were waved from every balcony to welcome him. The hymn was sung and then had to be repeated by popular demand. Countless "Hurrahs" resounded for the imperial house, the constitution, the National Guard, the generous Viennese, the Governor, the Director of Police, Germany, Italy and others. The public's wish to hear the Hymn to Pius IX was met. Shouts of "Long live the Emperor!" testified to the public's gratitude (*Wiener Zeitung*, 25 March 1848, 392).[15]

Music was present not as an artistic representation but as a collective utterance of the masses. The crowds on the streets and in the theatres were not silent – they yelled, they cheered, and they sang. Yet there remained an enormous gap between the performative presence and importance of music and its frequent but poor representation in the public discourse – music, even though almost omnipresent, remained almost ever at the margins. Who exactly the actors were and what people sang remained largely untold; thus a closer historical or musicological interpretation is impossible. Yet documents such as this newspaper article allow a closer look and provide the historically informed reader with the possibility of something we could describe, following Clifford Geertz, as a thick description of a situation.

The mention of streets *and* the theatre suggests a clear distinction between two social spaces, that of the working class (the streets) and that of bourgeois society (the theatre). Also, the report of singing and cheering crowds points to the importance of music on pivotal political occasions. That report, however, is quite vague; by contrast, the description of the music performed in the theatre is remarkably precise, listing what was said and sung during this celebratory moment. That list includes the national anthem (even twice) and a hymn to Pope Pius IX. Clearly, the report focuses on the loyalty of the people of Trieste to the Habsburg ruler, a loyalty demonstrated not by speeches (such as that of the governor or other representatives) but by symbols, national colours, and national music. Music expresses national loyalty and identity and buttresses important moments of political identification. However, the situation is far more complex and less consensual than the report would have others believe, and an analysis of its musical aspects can provide the key to a more differentiated reading, one that is capable of revealing more about the political tensions and fault zones in Triestine society, which the report itself has tried to camouflage.

Pius IX was the Pope of Hope, at least early in his pontificate, owing to his liberal reforms, and for this very reason he was looked on with suspicion by an Austrian government, which in 1846 had even tried to prevent his election. By early 1848, he was a symbol of hope to the liberals, being a strong supporter of constitutional government. At the same time, he was a symbol of national identity for the Italian nationalist movement and was celebrated as such in many poems and hymns of the time. It is no coincidence that by the spring of 1848, one of Milan's leading revolutionary journals was named after him.

Pius IX

Pius the Ninth is not a name and is not the one
Who cuts the air while sitting on his faldstool.
Pius the Ninth is the son of our brain,
The idol of our heart, a golden dream.

Pius the Ninth is a flag, a refrain,
Is a name good to sing in a choir.
Those who sing in the streets: "Hurrah for Pius the Ninth!"
Mean to say hurrah for motherland and forgiveness.

(But then) motherland and forgiveness mean
That one must die for Italy:
No one dies for a vain sound,
No one dies for a pope or for a throne. (Dall'Ongaro 40)[16]

While the newspaper account says nothing about *which* anthem was sung that evening in Trieste's theatre, there is some likelihood that it was based on a poem by Francesco Dall'Ongaro, a Triestine priest and journalist, who had become a leading poet of the Italian national movement and was expelled from the Habsburg territories shortly afterwards on suspicion of revolutionary activities. However, it is less important to know exactly which anthem was sung than to analyse the poetic images evoked at the time by this and other poems about Pius IX. In the political climate of 1848, the words *bandiera* (flag), *patria* (homeland), and *perdono* (forgiveness or pardon) were such general images – and for that reason so ambivalent – that they were open to different and even opposing interpretations. In the poem just quoted, nowhere is it specified which flag and which homeland are being referred to (unless one reads the third stanza), and the pardon could refer to Pius's amnesty of political prisoners *or* to Emperor Ferdinand's generosity towards the Viennese revolutionaries. It is precisely the vagueness, ambiguity, and openness of poetry and music that makes it possible for potential political opponents to unite in chorus. Speech is capable of igniting conflict, whereas music can serve as a bridge across widening political chasms. Music works to mediate space, creating unity and common ground in times when both are at risk of breaking apart.

Music, however, has multiple possible roles. It can unify, as we saw with regard to Liszt's sojourn in Hungary; it can mediate, as we have just seen; or in the Triestine context, it can trigger national conflicts. In this latter sense, music can create borders, given that it is often perceived as a moment of exclusion, as division, invasion, or occupation of space; and in some situations it can be manipulated in such a way as to construct boundaries. Such was the case when the presence of Slovenian songs on Triestine ground provoked an intense controversy in the local newspapers, as is evident in this extract from one of several polemical articles in the Italian press:

Now tell me: why did you underline the fact that Slavic songs were elevated, and even by women, and even by women of high condition? Do you not see that by doing so you do not make people understand that

> those songs are not common, and that especially the female sex has never enjoyed them? That they are not an emanation and an expression of a Slavic nationality? Why [do you say that] the Slavic kudos uttered in the Slavic tongue were more moving than the ones [uttered] in the Italian? (*L´osservatore triestino*, nr. 109, 9 August 1848, 831)[17]

In all such cases, music functions to territorialize national space. Another example of this arose when the Austrian army's leaders decided to send into battle musicians instead of soldiers. On 23 March, after the Venetians proclaimed the Republic of San Marco, riots broke out in Trieste, and "*then those who had the upper hand put on a show in favour of the Emperor and the government. A joyful Salm* [the governor] *thanked them from the balcony and Gyulai* [the commander] *sent out, instead of troops, the military band*" (Tamaro 340).[18]

The streets are an important locus of identity construction; the theatre is another. In nineteenth-century bourgeois society (Fulcher), the theatre became an important political space, as is clear from the previous extract as well as from Liszt's award of the Sword of Honour in the Hungarian National Theatre. So it is not surprising that prominent national issues found their way onto the stage and that music was used to propogate the political discourse. Trieste's opera house was a purely Italian music theatre, run by Italian *impresari*, with Italian singers and a repertoire dominated by Italian composers; but the musical productions, which reflected problems of national identity construction, painted a larger picture and did not serve only Italian nationalism. Music mirrored the complexity of Trieste's situation, and analysing this can provide insights into the multilayered and ambivalent Triestine identity.

I would like to demonstrate the importance of the theatre's contribution to the discourse on identity and space by focusing on two local music productions: Giuseppe Sinico's opera *Marinella* of 1854 and Ferdinando Carlo Lickl's opera *La Disfida di Barletta*, premiered in 1848. These two productions reflected two distinct visions of Trieste's identity. The plots of both operas revolved around national identity, but they also differed significantly in the solutions they propounded for the national contextualization of the Triestine territory. Sinico's *Marinella* aimed to strengthen a local Triestine identity, a project that was favoured by the Triestine authorities in the aftermath of the 1848 revolution. Lickl's opera supported instead a national Italian identity; yet Lickl was a Viennese-born composer who wrote music in the early

German Romantic style, and this makes *La Disfida di Barletta* both an interesting case of cultural transfer and an ambivalent project of identity construction.

Sinico's *Marinella* presents a love story, set in the late fifteenth century, at a time when Trieste, to escape growing Venetian dominance, opted for the protection of Austria. The opera thus evokes a crucial moment in Trieste's history, when the town was struggling for deliverance from imminent conquest by Venice (which, in the mid-nineteenth century, meant remembering that Triestans were not Italians and recognizing the importance of the Hapsburg presence). For *Marinella,* Sinico wrote a hymn to Trieste's patron saint, San Giusto, which not by accident gained popularity beyond the opera stage and became in effect Trieste's "national" anthem:

> If we shall have to suffer a long siege,
> If your misery becomes unbearable
> We shall give the example of how to face death; we shall fight, for God wills it,
> For our sons, for our honour
> To defend our country.
> (a citizen brings to the centre of the stage the city flag)
> Blessed Saint Justus! The trophy of glory, May this emblem guide us to victory; Even if few, we shall be strong, United by the same love; and against our sacred Insignia the pride of the oppressor will be tamed.
> *(a musical band enters playing the tune of the chorus: many soldiers and citizens follow, bringing banners, halberds, axes, and other arms to be distributed to the people)* (Sinico 18)[19]

The flag-waving citizens who, in the opera, follow the *banda* in Trieste's streets form a picture with which Triestines were certainly more than familiar from the experience of revolution. The stage mirrors the streets and the streets mirror the stage. Taking into the streets an anthem written for the stage is not a simple displacement from one space to another; rather, it is an act of transformation and construction of space. It contributes to the unification of the socially divided spaces of street and theatre (as so clearly happened, according to the newspaper extract provided earlier). Music, first in its presence on stage and then as a performative act by the multitude, becomes a powerful mode of identification and of social as well as national unification that is neither Italian, nor Slavic, nor German, but distinctly Triestine.

Sinico's *Marinella* was strongly influenced by the Verdian model. But it was German Romanticism as employed by the Viennese-born composer Ferdinand Ägidius Karl Lickl (or "Ferdinando Carlo Lickl," as he used to sign his composition; see Wurzbach) that provided the "sound track" for the Triestine revolution in 1848. Based on Massimo d'Azeglio's popular novel *Ettore Fieramosca o La Disfida di Barletta*, which dealt with a heroic sixteenth-century victory by Italian soldiers over the French, Lickl's opera offered a broad space for developing a patriotic Italian national discourse (Banti); that space included the presentation of the *tricolore* as well as patriotic choirs on stage. Composed in 1841 but staged only in the heated political climate of 1848, it became the season's great triumph and the composer's only success in this genre. Indeed, the only known photograph of the composer presents him not as an influential pianist and composer of piano music, which he was, but as the creator of this opera.[20]

Lickl's case provides evidence of how entwined the processes of bordering and transbordering can be in the pluralistic and heterogeneous Central European urban space. Here, a Viennese-born, German-speaking composer brought the German Romantic style to an Italian theatre and is now remembered for the political contribution his opera made to the Italian nationalist movement of 1848. All of this highlights processes of aesthetic transfer as well as the construction of a national exclusive space. This ambiguity is evident in almost all of the cases discussed above. Lickl's opera as well as Sinico's, and even the singing of Slavic songs, show that music is an important factor in diverse national identity constructions and thus in the territorialization of space.

The borders drawn by music remain extremely permeable and are characterized by continuous exchange, both in content and actors. This encompasses changes in style as well as in musicians, composers, and audience. It is paradoxical that music simultaneously constructs and transcends borders – that it helps differentiate space even while mediating *between* spaces.

Conclusions

Space can bring a new perspective to the aesthetic discourse, for it adds a new dimension to the analysis and sheds light on aspects that otherwise would be out of focus. Discussing Central European aesthetics can mean bringing spatial and aesthetic notions into conversation with each other. Taking seriously this spatialization of aesthetics and focusing on the possible interactions of space and aesthetics opens new perspectives, just as it raises new questions in the debate. In this chapter I have tried to develop a double-perspective. I have focused on music from a spatial perspective by adopting the spatial categories of "border," "transborder," and "unification" in order to analyse music and its social and political functions. At the same time, I have used this spatial inquiry of the artistic field in order to draw conclusions in the social and political field because artistic products contribute to the construction of space. All of this is based on a dynamic understanding that conceptualizes space not as a given *a priori*, but as a socially constructed and thus historically variable category. In the nineteenth century, the Central European space was being transformed and newly conceptualized as national space – or better perhaps, it was being shattered into a series of national spaces. National identity constructions always bear a geographical dimension, that is, they relate to a territory, and they imagine and structure space. The artistic fields, and music in particular, reflect but more importantly contribute to such processes.

All the above examples, from Mendelssohn's conception of border, to the spatial (and thus also social) consequences of Liszt's Hungarian concerts, to the Triestine operas, have a spatial dimension. They represent border experiences, which can be analysed by examining the relevance of inclusionary and exclusionary mechanisms, that is, mechanisms of bordering and de- or trans-bordering, and the transformations they may support or even induce. What is included or excluded, what constitutes a common space, and what is excluded from such a space all depend in the first place on space's discursive creation. This can be seen, for example, in Mendelssohn's border experience, in which moments of inclusion and exclusion took place on both sides of the bridge. Borders, in fact, are multiply constructed and transgressed. In Liszt's case, international modern aesthetics were absorbed into the building of the national Hungarian paradigm. In Trieste, Lickl's German Romantic style contributed to the construction of Italian nationalism. How we define a certain space, what we include or exclude, depends on how we perceive it, and thus it is subject to change and transformation. This is true for Central Europe as for any other cultural space. The examples analysed above provide evidence that the discursive construction of this Central European space had strong cultural and thus also aesthetic aspects. These aesthetic aspects even seem to be prevalent. On a theoretical level, such conclusions open a conversation between the discourse of aesthetics and other issues such as nationalism and identity. The analysis of the aesthetic discourse can – to modify a statement from the geopolitical discourse on border constructions – help "to identify the limits of the so-called *informal regions* existing in representations [...] and public opinion (for instance, "Northern Europe," "Central Europe"... etc.)" (Kolossov 625). The analysis of the aesthetic discourse can thus contribute to the knowledge of how Central Europe has been constituted, perceived, and transformed in its extent and meaning over time.

Appendix: Comparison of Liszt's repertoire of the Hungarian and Viennese concerts from 1840/41[21]

The list below shows the titles of the compositions that Liszt presented in his concerts in Vienna, and in Buda and Pest during the winter of 1840–41. In the first part, in which Liszt's own compositions and arrangements are listed, the numbers in brackets refer to Raabe's catalogue of Liszt works, which was used by Legány. The second part of the list brings together the compositions from other composers in alphabetic order. The titles underlined indicate works, given both in Vienna and in Buda and Pest. In these concerts Liszt performed as a soloist, a conductor, and an accompanist for singers and other soloists. For a more detailed overview of the single concerts program, see Legány (*Franz Liszt*, "Liszt in Hungary"). A comparison of the Viennese and Hungarian repertoire shows a large correspondence and mostly an identical repertoire in both places, which is based on what was and was to become Liszt's core repertoire. The large portion of Beethoven works in Viennese concerts, which is the main difference between the Viennese and Hungarian programs, is mostly due to the fact that the Viennese concerts were used to raise funds for a monument to Beethoven.

Compositions of the Viennese concerts	Compositions of the Hungarian concerts in Pest and Buda
Liszt, Etude pour le piano-forte no. 7, in es (R. 1)	**Liszt**, Tarantelles napolitaines from Venezia e Napoli (R. 10d/4)
Liszt, Grande Etude in D-minor no. 4 (R. 2a, 4)	Liszt, Grand galope chromatique (R. 41)
Liszt, Fragments from Dante (R. 10b, 7 or an early version to R. 420, Inferno)	Liszt, Réminiscences des Puritains de Bellini (R. 129)

(*Continued*)

Compositions of the Viennese concerts	Compositions of the Hungarian concerts in Pest and Buda
Liszt, Grande valse di bravura (R. 32a) Liszt, Grand galope chromatique (R. 41) Liszt, Réminiscences des Puritains de Bellini (R. 129) Liszt, Hexaméron, Grandes variations de bravoure sur le marche des Puritains (R. 131) Liszt, Fantaisie sur des motifs favouris de l'opéra La sonnambula (R. 132) Liszt, Réminiscences de Lucia di Lammermoor (R. 151) Liszt, L'orgia from the fantasie sur des motifs des soirées musicales (R. 234)	Liszt, Hexaméron, Grandes variations de bravoure sur le marche des Puritains (R. 131) Liszt, Fantaisie sur des motifs favouris de l'opéra La sonnambula (R. 132) Liszt, Réminiscences de Lucia di Lammermoor (R. 151) Liszt, Septett [Hummel] (R. 172) Liszt, Grande fantaisie sur des thèmes de l'opéra Les Huguenots (R. 221) Liszt, Grande fantaisie sur des motifs de Niobe (R. 230) Liszt, La Serenata et l'orgia, fantasie sur des motifs des soirées musicales (R. 234) Liszt, Ouverture de l'opera Guillaume Tell (R. 237) Liszt, Rákóczi march (R. 105/13) Hungarian Rhapsody Hungarian Melody and March
Bach, Litanei	**Beethoven**, Choral Fantasy op. 80 Beethoven, Adelaide, (Liszt piano accompaniment) Beethoven, Meeresstille und glückliche Fahrt, Choral Work Beethoven, Symphony no. 7, A, 2nd movement (Liszt conductor)
Beethoven, Sonata no. 17, d Beethoven, Sonata no. 23 (Appassionata), f Beethoven, Piano Concerto no. 3, c Beethoven-Liszt, Symphony no. 6 (Pastoral) Scherzo, Orage et Finale (R. 128, VI, 3 movements) Beethoven, Adelaide (Liszt piano accompaniment) Beethoven, An die Ferne Geliebte (Liszt piano accompaniment) Beethoven, Trio Beethoven, Symphony no. 1, C	**Bériot**, Piano-Violin Duet
Bériot, Violinist Tremolo (for solo violin)	**Bellini**, Aria, (Liszt piano accompaniment)
Cherubini, Vocal Quartet	**Grill**, Two Choral Works
Chopin, Mazurka	**Haydn**, Choral Work
Curci, Il Platano (Liszt piano accompaniment) Curci, Il Congedo (Liszt piano accompaniment)	**Herz**, Piano-Violin Duet
Hackl, Die Huldigung (Liszt piano accompaniment)	**Mozart**, Overture The Magic Flute (Liszt conductor)

Compositions of the Viennese concerts	Compositions of the Hungarian concerts in Pest and Buda
Kreutzer, Vocal Quartet	**Schubert**-Liszt, Erlkönig, (R. 243.4)
Kreutzer, Pastorale, Am Waldstädtersee	Schubert-Liszt, Ständchen (R. 243.9)
Kreutzer, Lied aus Enzio (Liszt piano accompaniment)	Schubert-Liszt, Ave Maria (R. 243.12)
	Schubert, Der Hirt auf dem Felsen (Liszt piano accompaniment)
Lickl, Auf dem Calvarienberg aus den Ischler Bildern	Schubert, Der Wanderer (Liszt piano accompaniment)
Randhartinger, Das Erkennen (Liszt piano accompaniment)	Schubert, Der Wegweiser (Liszt piano accompaniment)
	Schubert, Der stürmische Morgen (Liszt piano accompaniment)
Schubert-Liszt, Erlkönig (R. 243.4)	
Schubert-Liszt, Ständchen (R. 243.9)	Schubert, Gretchen am Spinnrade (Liszt piano accompaniment)
Schubert-Liszt, Ave Maria (R. 243.12)	
Schubert-Liszt, Die Stadt, Das Fischermädchen, Aufenthalt (from Schwanengesang) (R. 245. 1–3)	Schubert, Gruppe aus dem Tartarus(Liszt piano accompaniment)
Schubert-Liszt, Der Atlas (R. 245.11)	Schubert, Memnon (Liszt piano accompaniment)
Schubert-Liszt, Die Taubenpost (245.13)	
Schubert-Liszt, Mélodies hongroises d'après Schubert (R. 250)	**Weber**, Piano Concerto, f
	Weber, Overture Oberon, Liszt (conductor)
Schubert, Die Forelle (Liszt piano accompaniment)	
Schubert, Nachtigall (Liszt piano accompaniment)	

NOTES

1 All translations into English by G.K. unless otherwise noted.

2 See for example Walker's biography of Liszt (253 ff.)

3 Emile Haraszti provides a thorough analysis of the Rákóczi March and also points out its ambivalent history as a piece of national identification on the one hand and as a recruiting instrument for the Habsburg army on the other. The first publication of the march can indeed be found as part of a collection of military marches of the Eszterhazy regiments, in *Auswahl der beliebtesten Maersche fuer das K.K. Infanterie Regiment Fuerst Eszterhazy von dessen Kapelmeister Nicolaus Scholl componiert* (Wien, 1821).

4 Besides the *Rackozki March*, Legány mentions a "Hungarian Melody and March" and a "Hungarian Rhapsody" (Legány, "Liszt in Hungary" 9).

For an overview of the entire repertoire of these concerts as well as a comparison with the Viennese concerts from the same concert tour, see the appendix to this chapter. General information on Liszt's repertoire can be found in Gooley.

5 Walker bases his description on the eyewitness account of Julia Pardoe, given in her book *The City of the Magyar*, Franz von Schober's report, and further Hungarian publications (Walker 324n14).

6 In Walker (325–6).

7 *Hexaméron Variations* goes back to a quarrel between Liszt and his contemporary, Sigismund Thalberg, in the late 1830s, just before Liszt left to forge his international career, whose start is generally related to the six Viennese Beethoven memorial concerts in December 1839.

8 "Bei Liszt vereinigt sich Vieles, um ihm die ungarischen Herzen zu gewinnen. Er war geborner Ungar, durch fortwährende Mitwirkung von Ungarn ausgebildet, er hatte sich selbst mit Stolz als Ungar erklärt und sich für das Schicksal des Landes fühlend und thätig bewiesen, und war er der magyarischen Sprache auch nicht mehr mächtig, so erschien er doch in ihrer Landestracht vor ihnen, so trat ihnen doch in seiner schönen Kunst kein störendes Abzeichen einer fremden Nationalität entgegen, und sie konnten seine begeisternden Leistungen für ungarisch erklären, ohne den Magyarismus zu verletzen. Wie mußte es ihnen, nach Bildung und Auszeichnung ringend, wohlthun, eine solche europäische Celebrität, die erste in ihrem Fache, in Besitz nehmen, als die ihren erklären zu können." I thank Dirk von der Horst for the translations of the excerpts from Schober's letters as well as for the text of the cantata.

9 Doch was das Schicksal auch gesprochen, / Die Kunst, der Ruhm, Genuss und Glück; / Du dachtest doch mit treuer Seele / An's Land, das Dich gebar, zurück.

10 "Und kommst zu uns, wo arm das Leben / Die Kunst noch in der Wiege ist."

11 "Franz Liszt, Dein Land ist stolz auf Dich!"

12 Dich fasste, noch ein zarter Knabe, / Schon des Geschickes kalte Hand, / Und sprach, Dich reißend in die Ferne: / "Geh' hin, Du hast kein Vaterland." // Dann führten die verklärten Schwingen / Der Kunst Dich in ihr Zauberreich:/ "Hier ist die Heimath großer Geister, / Auch Deine ist's, der ihnen gleich." // Und schmeichelnd lockte Doch das Leben / Dann in sein glänzendes Revier, / Es schmückte Dich mit seinen Gaben, / Und bat: "Nun weile, herrsche hier" // Dann wurdest Du, vom Ruhm getragen, / Auf seine Gipfel hingestellt: / "Hörst Du, sprach er, die Völker jubeln? / Liszt, Deine Heimath ist die Welt!" // Doch was das Schicksal

auch gesprochen, / Die Kunst, der Ruhm, Genuß und Glück; / Du dachtest doch mit treuer Seele / An's Land, das Dich gebar, zurück. // Und kommst zu uns, wo arm das Leben, / Die Kunst noch in der Wiege ist; / Doch unser Herz ist reich und bieder, / Es ruft Dir zu: "Sei uns gegrüßt!" // Sei uns gegrüßt im Lorbeerschmucke, / Den Du verdient so ritterlich, / Du großer Künstler, Edler, Treuer, / Franz Liszt, Dein Land ist stolz auf Dich!

13 Alan Walker has discussed this question to some extent, and includes a list of references of Liszt's on this topic (11–12).

14 "Bei den großen Diners, die er in Erwiederung ihrer Gastmahle gab, schien aller Standesunterschied verschwunden, Magnaten und Künstler, Kaufleute und Gelehrte saßen da in bunter Reihe, und der glänzende Geist Liszt's wußte diese Menschen, die sich sonst so selten oder gar nicht berührten, zu wirklich heiteren, unbefangen belebten Gesellschaften zu verschmelzen." Deaville argues similarly regarding Liszt's Viennese concerts (Deaville 2003).

15 "Heute ist ein Nationalfest! Las man am 17ten Morgens auf allen Haustüren. Die Laden blieben geschlossen. Das Volk wogte in dichten Scharen singend und jubelnd durch die Straßen. Vor den Kaffehause des Tergesteum ward allen, die vom Taglohne leben, Frühstück gebothen und man hatte überhaupt Sorge getragen, daß es der arbeitenden Classe an dem glücklichen Tage an Nichts fehle und so sehr auch der Freudenrausch der Menge dadurch gesteigert war, fiel doch nirgends die mindeste Unordnung vor. Die National-Garde, welche sich bildete und sofort in Wirksamkeit trat, schritt allenthalben beschwichtigend ein; was jedoch nur in sehr seltenen Fällen nöthig war, denn das Betragen, selbst der niedersten Schichten der Bevölkerung war wirklich bis in diesen Augenblick musterhaft. Abends war die Stadt und das Theater glänzend beleuchtet und letzteres in allen seinen Räumen mit Zuschauern gefüllt. Als der Gouverneur Robert Altgraf von Salm erschien, erscholl ein tausendstimmiges Eviva und aus allen Logen wehten Tücher, Schärpen in den Nationalfarben ihm zum Gruße entgegen. Die Hymne wart gesungen, mußte auf stürmisches Verlangen wiederholt werden und unzählige Mahl ertönte ein Lebhoch dem Kaiserhause, der Constitution, der National-Garde, den hochherzigen Wienern, dem Gouverneur, dem Polizei-Direktor, Deutschland, Italien u.s.w. – Dem Wunsch des Publikums, den Inno Pio IX. zu vernehmen ward entsprochen und der Dank dafür gab sich in dem Es lebe der Kaiser! kund. Mittlerweile dauerte aber auch die Festfreude in allen Theilen der Stadt bis in die späteste Stunde der Nacht ununterbrochen fort."

16 Pio Nono // Pio Nono non è un nome e non è quello / Che trincia l' aria assiso in faldistoro; / Pio Nono è figlio del nostro cervello / Un idolo del core, un sogno d' oro // Pio Nono è una bandiera, un ritornello, / Un nome buono da cantarsi a coro. / Chi grida per la via: – Viva Pio Nono! – / Vuol dir viva la patria ed il perdono. // La patria ed il perdono voglion dire / Cher per l' Italia si deve morire: / e non si muore per un vano suono; / non si muor per un papa o per un trono!

17 "Ora ditemi: perché rilevaste la circostanza che s'innalzarono canti slavi, e persino dalle donne, e persino da quelle di condizione elevata? Ma non v'accorgete che con ciò fate capire che quei canti non sono d'uso e che, specialmente il sesso femminino gli ebbe finora s schifo? Che dunque non sono emanazione ed espressione di nazionalità slava? Perché mai erano più toccanti gli evviva portati in slavo che quelli fatti in italiano?"

18 "Quindi, quelli che avevano avuto il sopravvento inscenarono una dimostrazione al'Imperatore e al governo, Salm giubilante li ringraziò dal balcone e Gyulai mandò fuori, invece delle truppe, la musica militare." Attilo Tamaro's history – written in the 1920s – is part of the fascist's political intention to reconstruct Trieste's history as that of an Italian national territory (Hametz). Still his two volumes remain an important source as they give access to a rich collection of documents and data on Trieste's history.

19 Se un luogo assedio soffrir dovremo, / Se la miseria giunga all' estremi, / Darem l' esempio come si muore; / Combatteremo, che Dio vuol, / Pei nostri figli, pel nostro onore, / Per la difesa del patrio suol / *(alcuni cittadini trasportano nel mezzo della scena la bandiera della citta)* // Viva San Giusto! Trofeo di Gloria, / Questo vessillo guida a vittoria; / Se pochi siam sarem gagliardi, 7 Uniti tutti da un solo amor; / E contro l' orgoglio dell' oppressor. / *(una banda musicale giunge intonando il motive del coro: molti armigeri e cittadini la sequono recando gonfaloni, alabarde, azze edalter armi le quali vengono distribuite e brandite dal popolo).*

20 "Autore dell'opera La Disfida di Barletta. Rappresentato con grande successo politico al Teatro Comunale, Trieste il 2. Febbraio 1848." – Author of the opera *La Disfida di Barletta*, represented with great political success at the municipal theatre, Trieste, on 2 February 1848.

21 This comparison is based on the detailed studies of Legány, "Liszt in Hungary," for the Hungarian concerts, and of Legány, *Franz Liszt*, for the Viennese concerts; see further Liszt's own catalogue "Catalogue of works which Liszt played in public, 1838–48, compiled by himself," published in Walker (445).

WORKS CITED

Ara, Angelo, and Claudio Magris. *Triest. Eine literarische Hauptstadt in Mitteleuropa*. Munich: Hanser, 1987. Print.

Bachmann-Medick, Doris. "Spatial Turn." In *Cultural Turns: Neuorientierungen in den Kulturwissenschaften*. Hamburg: Rowohlt, 2006. 284–328. Print.

Bahr, Erhard. "The Silver Age of Weimar: Franz Liszt as Goethe's Successor." *Goethe Yearbook* 10 (2001): 191–202. Print.

Banti, Alberto M. *La nazione del Risorgimento. Parentela, santità e onore alle origini dell' Italia unita*. Torino: Einaudi, 2000. Print.

Benjamin, Walter. "Paris, die Hauptstadt des XIX. Jahrhunderts." In *Illuminationen. Ausgewählte Schriften 1*. Frankfurt on Main: Suhrkamp, 1995. Print.

Berg, Eiki, and Henk Van Houtum. *Routing Borders between Territories, Discourses and Practices*. Aldershot: Ashgate, 2003. Print.

Csáky, Moritz. "Ambivalenz des kulturellen Erbes. Zentraleuropa." In *Ambivalenz des kulturellen Erbes. Vielfachcodierungen des historischen Gedächtnisses*. Ed. Moritz Csáky and Klaus Zeyringer. Innsbruck: Studienverlag, 2000. 27–49. Print.

– *Das Gedächtnis der Städte. Kulturelle Verflechtungen – Wien und die urbanen Milieus in Zentraleuropa*. Cologne: Böhlau, 2010. Print.

– "Die Hungarus-Konzeption. Eine 'realpolitische' Alternative zur magyarischen Nationalstaatsidee?" In *Ungarn und Österreich unter Maria Theresia und Joseph II. Neue Aspekte im Verhältnis der beiden Länder*. Ed. Anna M. Drabek, Richard G. Plaschka, and Adam Wandruszka. Vienna: Verlag der Österreichischen Akademie der Wissenschaften, 1982. 71–89. Print.

Dall'Ongaro, Francesco. *Stornelli Italiani*. Milan: G. Daelli, 1862. Print.

D'Azeglio, Massimo. *Ettore Fieramosca o La Disfida die Barletta*. Paris: Baudry Liberia Europea, 1833. Print.

Deaville, James. "The Politics of Liszt's Virtuosity: New Light on the Dialectics of a Cultural Phenomenon." In *Liszt and the Birth of Modern Europe: Music as a Mirror of Religious, Political, Cultural, and Aesthetic Transformations*. Ed. Michael Saffle and Rossana Dalmonte. Hillsdale: Pendragon Press, 2003. 115–42. Print.

Dubin, Lois C. *The Port Jews of Habsburg Trieste: Absolutist Politics and Enlightenment Culture*. Stanford: Stanford UP, 1999. Print.

Durkheim, Emil. *Les formes élémentaires de la vie religieuse*. Paris: Félix Alcan, 1912. Print.

Fischer, Wladimir, ed. *Räume und Grenzen in Österreich Ungarn 1867–1918. kulturwissenschaftliche Annäherungen*. Tübingen: Francke, 2010. Print.

Fulcher, Jane. *The Nation's Image: French Grand Opéra as Politics and Politicized Art*. Cambridge: Cambridge UP, 1987. Print.

Geertz, Clifford. "Thick Description: Toward an Interpretive Theory of Cultures." In *The Interpretation of Culture: Selected Essays*. New York: Basic Books: 1973. 3–30. Print.

Gooley, Dana. *The Virtuoso Liszt*. Cambridge: Cambridge University Press, 2004. Print.

Hametz, Maura. *Making Trieste Italian, 1918–1954*. Woodbridge: Boydell & Brewer, 2005. Print.

Haraszti, Emile. "Berlioz, Liszt and the Rákóczi-march." *Musical Quarterly* 26.2 (April 1940): 200–31. Print.

Judson, Pieter M. *Guardians of the Nation: Activists on the Language Frontiers of Imperial Austria*. Cambridge, MA: Harvard UP, 2006. Print.

Judson, Pieter M., and Marsha L. Rozenblit, eds. *Constructing Nationalities in East Central Europe*. New York: Berghahn Books, 2005. Print.

Kohl, Johann Georg. *Austria: Vienna, Prague, Hungary, Bohemia and the Danube, Galicia, Styria, Moravia, Bukovina and the Military Frontier*. London: Chapman and Hall, 1844. Print.

Kolossov, Vladimir. "Border Studies: Changing Perspectives and Theoretical Approaches." *Geopolitics* 10 (2005): 606–32. Print.

Kokorz, Gregor. "Triest 1848. Musik im Spannungsfeld nationaler Diskurse." In *Musik und Revolution. Die Produktion von Identität und Raum durch Musik in Zentraleuropa 1848/49*. Ed. Barbara Boists. Vienna: Holitzer, 2013. 157–76. Print.

Lefebvre, Henri. *The Production of Space*. Trans. Donald Nicholson-Smith. Malden, Oxford, and Victoria: Blackwell Publishing, 1991. Print.

Legány, Deszö. *Franz Liszt. Unbekannte Presse und Briefe aus Wien 1822–1886*. Vienna: Böhlau, 1984. Print.

– "Liszt in Hungary, 1820–1846." *Liszt and his World: Proceedings of the International Liszt Conference held at Virginia Polytechnic Institute and State University, 20–23 May 1993*. Ed. Michael Saffle. Stuyvesant: Pendragon, 1998. 3–16. Print.

Mendelssohn-Bartholdy, Felix. *Letters of Felix Mendelssohn Bartholdy from Italy and Switzerland*. Trans. Lady Wallace. Biographical note by Julie de Marguerittes. Boston: Oliver Ditson, 1863. Print.

Mitterbauer, Helga, and Katharina Scherke, eds. *Ent-grenzte Räume. Kulturelle Transfers um 1900 und in der Gegenwart*. Vienna: Passagen Verlag, 2005. Print.

L´osservatore triestino, 9 August 1848. Print.

Raabe, Peter. *Franz Liszt. Leben und Schaffen*. 2nd ed., rev. F. Raabe. Stuttgart: H. Schneider, 1968. Print.

Reininghaus, Wilfried, and Bernd Walter. *Räume – Grenzen – Identitäten. Westfalen als Gegenstand landes- und regionalgeschichtlicher Forschung.* Cologne: Böhlau, 2013. Print.

Roll, Christine, Frank Pohle, and Matthias Myrczek, eds. *Grenzen und Grenzüberschreitungen. Bilanz und Perspektiven der Frühneuzeitforschung.* Cologne: Böhlau, 2010. Print.

Schober, Franz von. *Briefe über Liszt's Aufenthalt in Ungarn*. Berlin: Schlesingersche Buch- und Musikalienhandlung, 1843. Print.

Schroer, Markus. *Räume, Orte, Grenzen. Auf dem Weg zu einer Soziologie des Raums*. Frankfurt am Main: Suhrkamp, 2006. Print.

Sinico, Giuseppe. *Marinella. Opera in un prologo e tre parti su libretto di Pietro Welponer*. Bologona: Bongiovanni, 2010. CD.

Slottman, William B. *Ferenc II Rákóczi and the Great Powers*. Boulder: East European Monographs, 1997. Print.

Tamaro, Attilio. *Storia di Trieste*. 2vol. Roma: Alberto Stock, 1924. Print.

Walker, Alan. *Franz Liszt: The Virtuoso Years 1811–1847*. Rev. ed. Ithaca: Cornell UP, 1987. Print. *Wiener Zeitung*, 25 March 1848. Print.

Wurzbach, Constantin. *Biographisches Lexikon des Kaiserthums Österreich*, vol. 15. Vienna: k. u. k. Hof u. Staatsdruckerei, 1866. 88–93. Print.

4 History without End(s): The Aesthetics and Politics of the Reading Play

IMRE SZEMAN

Although we have come to talk freely and easily about the politics of literature, it is in fact extremely difficult to name and narrate a connection between the two, *especially* in the most vulgar way in which one might hope to relate them – that is, with respect to the production of *substantive and direct* political change: change in policy, change in government, or change from right to left. Rather, literature has typically occupied a different realm of the political than this vulgar one – a broader, no less important sphere of impact and effect than those just named, and one that concerns a distinct mode and understanding of the political. These have included literature's representations of and interventions into the language of politics, or its explorations of the underlying fantasies, dramas, and narratives of a society that give impetus and shape to collective life and its organizing allowances and prohibitions. Even in the case of those literary texts not explicitly consumed with the political, literary history has assembled an archive of the social and political unconscious of a society, sketched into texts – whether or not their author imagined them to be – through the very act of producing a narrative of individuals and their societies (the very idea of the "individual" in the novel, for instance, always already signals the hopes and fantasies of liberal capitalism). The contemporary concatenation of literature and politics has also generated a whole range of intriguing analyses, interventions, and imaginings that literary criticism has sought to outline and understand. All of these sites of the political have covered over or obscured that first, difficult to name, vulgar hope for a direct connection of literature and politics, which does not mean that this direct link, it, too, is not worth considering or exploring, even if we have come to doubt the one-to-one correspondence between the two terms and the distinct fields they name.

I want to look here at the way in which literature responded to the turmoil of mid-nineteenth-century Central Europe. In particular, I wish to think about the way in which literature responded to the *failure* of 1848. In its attempt to end the persistence of monarchies decades after the French Revolution, the 1848 revolutions fuelled national imaginaries across Europe (see Kokorz's chapter in this volume) and rearranged the social bodies of the nations that pushed to change their political conditions. Through their work, artists and writers involved in 1848 believed themselves to be playing as important a role in generating the conditions for revolution as their brethren in the streets. The energy that fuelled this new-found connection between literature and politics – as exemplified *par excellence* in the Hungarian case by poet Petőfi Sándor's "Nemzeti Dal" ("National Song"), a call to arms read aloud in Vörösmarty Square in the heart of Budapest, kicking off the revolution in that city – was one of many things that came to an end with the failure of the revolutions. In the case of the *reading-play* – a unique form that appeared at different moments in the nineteenth and early twentieth centuries in response to social and political failure – literature's incapacity to accomplish what Sándor hoped it might led it to meditate on the limits of the whole of human experience rather than on the political restrictions of a given national situation. Did the reading-play as a form constitute a critique of nationalism? Did it suggest an abandonment of the political ambitions of literature, or, paradoxically, of the literary itself? Or indeed, did it affirm the incapacity of literature to *ever* have a political outcome in the way that I have deemed vulgar here (a concatenation of literature and politics that affirms dreams of the historical avant-garde)? These questions cannot be answered without understanding the *form* of the reading-play, a form that brings to light various impasses and blockages in the understanding of borders and border crossing in Central Europe in the nineteenth century, as well as how we understand the politics of literature from the nineteenth century to the present day.

The Reading-Play: A Map for Moments of Crisis

The reading-play, while a play in form – comprised of dialogues, soliloquies, asides to the audience, instructions for character movement and position on the stage, descriptions of scenes to be set and backdrops to be built, and so on – is distinguished by its unproducibility. The reading play, in other words, cannot be what it purports to be: *in its purest form*, it is a play that cannot be performed. What makes the reading-play difficult to stage is its excess – excess of characters, with single scenes containing tens, even hundreds of characters; fantastic, impossible shifts of time and place – from scene to scene, and within scenes – that would no doubt bring about states of apoplexy in Corneille or Boileau; and "special effects" that could not be created on the stage in the absence of contemporary technologies. The reading-play can thus *only* be read, its space can be entered *only* by the individual reader.

The form of the reading-play would thus appear to involve a contradiction, a paradox. Why write a play that cannot be performed? Under what conditions and for what reasons did such a curious literary form arise? Was there a connection between the emergence of the reading-play and national-political shifts and changes, tensions and anxieties, that emerged in the mid-nineteenth century? Any new form arises as a result of a wide range of developments in culture and society; such new forms are especially marked, however, by uncertainties about the shape and character of the social forms they seek to represent and comment on. The appearance of the reading-play indicated, I believe, a double-crisis: one crisis in the political sphere (which varied from nation to nation, given the uncertain political dynamics of an evolving Europe), and a second, consequent crisis in the possibility of adequately representing the depth and nature of this crisis in literary form. It was this second crisis that was to be resolved through different forms of the reading-play. Johann Wolfgang von Goethe's *Faust*, for example (and this is true in particular of *Faust II*), was an attempt to deal with nascent capitalism and the strange entities it brought into existence (money as a signifier without a signified, property relations, and commodities), as well as to address the place of the intellectual or artist in this new world where "all that is solid melts into air" (Marx and Engels 38). Gustav Flaubert's *La Tentation de Saint Antoine* (The Temptation of Saint Anthony) can be seen both as a meditation on the failure of realism to depict this new world even in the midst of his attempt to perfect the form – the composition of *Temptation* took the whole of Flaubert's life, "standing alongside his other books, standing behind them" (Foucault 102) – and as a renunciation of the questions of the relations of art to capital that Goethe had announced a mere forty years earlier, in the form of a retreat to the interiority of the artist's own activity.[1] *Faust* and *Temptation* were followed in the twentieth century by Karl Kraus's *Die letzten Tage der Menschheit: Tragödie in fünf Akten mit Vorspiel und Epilog* (The Last Days of Mankind: Tragedy in Five Acts with Preamble and Epilogue, 1922), an obsessively, forensically detailed 800-page interrogation of the human foibles and failures that generated the tragedy of the Great War, and by James Joyce's *Ulysses* (1922). Joyce's contribution to the reading-play is harder to characterize, both because the section of *Ulysses* that most resembles this form – "Nighttown" – appears as a part of the larger whole, and because, like Kraus, he is writing closer to the present, a period in which the effects of the radical experiment with form represented by the reading-play are in danger of being nullified. In this section of *Ulysses* we can discern a concentration and intensification of precisely those modernist effects that Georg Lukács identified as rendering reality "static": "[The hero] does not develop through contact with the world; he neither forms nor is formed by it. The only 'development' in this literature is the gradual revelation of the human condition. Man is now what he has always been and always will be. The narrator, the examining subject, is in motion; the examined reality is static" (21).

We can recognize in the extreme interiorization of *Ulysses* a continuation of the "negation of history" begun in Flaubert's text. In this case, however, it is a negation that arises out of a text that is curiously more real than realism itself, mapping out the subject's phenomenological experience of modernity somehow "accurately," even if it does so in a way that confines this subject to an eternity of these experiences – an eternity, moreover, whose boundaries *and* riches can be experienced in the course of a single day.

There are a number of avenues through which the formal richness of the reading-play might be examined. One could focus on its visual aspects, on the manner in which it brings out an experience of visuality in the *absence* of the materiality common to a play – sets, props, costumes, stage movement, and so on – that might eventually render this experience whole. Indeed, this visual effect of the reading-play is central to an understanding of the form. This is made clear through the focus of the reading-play, both in terms of plot elements and scene-setting effects (e.g., hallucinations, dreams, and illusions) – as if its visual character must be reiterated or reinscribed on multiple levels. The most significant aspect of the reading-play, however, is the manner in which, like Joyce's *Ulysses*, it constitutes a negation of history. This negation is twofold. First, history is negated through the very turn to a form that lacks even the possibility of materiality. This is to understand the reading-play as an intellectual thought experiment visualized, as a place or space to consider *apart* from the world, as changes in the world that cannot be otherwise understood. The reading-play is ultimately, however, a poor laboratory for thought: as there are no material referents, any insights that might be gained resist application to the world. But then again, it is precisely the production of a gap between literature and the world that is part of the desired effect of the reading-play. The second negation of history appears in the desire for this gap, in the negation of a particular historical reality in order to examine a realm of phantasms and spectres. This second negation marks an intellectual retreat from the world into an alternative history, a retreat that takes place because it is no longer clear exactly what the role of the intellectual or writer with respect to history might be. It is, invariably, always with respect to questions regarding the meaning of intellectual activity in moments of historical crisis that the reading-play arises as a form.

This double negation of history can be seen at work in Imre Madách's unduly neglected play (neglected, that is, in the English-speaking world), *Az Ember Tragédiája* (The Tragedy of Man, 1862).[2] In Madách's play, these negations reach their apotheosis: history is negated not only in the form of the reading-play, but explicitly in its content as well. *The Tragedy of Man* exhibits a desire for a radical negation of history *in toto*, a desire that springs from a specific political and intellectual failure that is imagined as a failure of the human as such. In the context of the enormity of the failure of humanity, the relatively diminished significance of the intellectual's failure might be "forgiven," or at least explained and rendered comprehensible. This use of history for the purposes of redemption exhibits an apotheosis of the second negation described above. The intellectual retreat that is a part of every reading-play here reaches its maximum.

The Tragedy of Man: Negation and Negation

> Grace appears purest in that human form which has either no consciousness or an infinite one, that is, in a puppet or a god.
>
> Heinrich von Kleist, "On the Marionette Theater" ("Über das Marionettentheater")

> LUCIFER: How like your human kind! How typical!
> You're sorry for yourself to have discarded
> your fantasies to face reality.
>
> Imre Madách, *The Tragedy of Man*

The Tragedy of Man by Imre Madách is considered one of the most important Hungarian plays. Its relative obscurity, and that of the author himself, necessitates some preliminary description and discussion.

The Tragedy of Man appeared during a period in Hungarian history "when national aspirations ha[d] been stifled" (Reményi 131). G.W.F. Hegel, at the beginning of the French Revolution, had been able to express almost limitless optimism for the course of history (if the apocryphal story concerning the writing of the *Phenomenology of Spirit* can be believed); Madách, after the 1848 Revolution, could muster only disappointment, depression, and sorrow. The title of Mor Jókai's novel, *Szomorú Napok* (Sorrowful Days), written in the aftermath of the failed 1848 Hungarian revolution, reflected the mood of a large part of Hungarian intelligentsia during this period. After the decisive defeat of the revolutionary forces, the permanent exile of revolutionary leader Lajos Kossuth, and the imprisonment, death, or "political unemployment" of many of the most influential literary figures in the country (Petöfi dying on the battlefield, Jókai in hiding, the poet János Arany losing his government employment), the confidence of the Hungarian literary community was severely shaken, with regard both to their artistic powers and to the political influence they had long enjoyed. Arany's experience of the post-revolutionary period was typical: "I fled like one chased; fled from my own soul. No hope was to be seen anywhere in the heavens, only despair, which withheld me from lifting up my hands to those heavens" (qtd. in Reidl 224).

Ill health prevented Madách from involving himself actively in the revolution. He was nonetheless deeply affected (losing both a brother and a sister in the war) and profoundly disappointed by the outcome of 1848. He first expressed his dissatisfaction with Austrian rule in Hungary in the 1859 play *A Civilizátor* (The Civilizer), which he wrote upon his release from prison, to which he had been sentenced for sheltering a distant relative who was a secretary to Kossuth. This play, modelled on the comedies of Aristophanes, ridiculed Austria's imposition of a dictatorial centralized bureaucracy on Hungary through its depiction of an arrogant administrator (a barely veiled characterization of the then Austrian interior minister[3]). In this earlier play, Madách's disillusionment with the outcome of the revolution found an outlet in an attack on his oppressors; in *The Tragedy of Man* – written in the years that followed and in a state of despair as deep as Arany's – finds Madách identifying the source of his despair and oppression elsewhere – not in Austrian rule, but in the history of humanity itself.

While it shares characteristics with those literary works of the nineteenth century identified as *poems d'humanité* (such as Byron's *Cain*, Ibsen's *Peer Gynt*, and Hugo's *Légende des Siècles*), the formal characteristics of *The Tragedy of Man* are better captured by the category of the reading-play. The main action takes place within a dream – indeed, in one scene, in a dream within a dream. An examination of just a few scenes shows it to be all but unproducible. In Scene XI, eight characters appear in rapid succession; Scene VI requires statues to spontaneously disintegrate (54) and a cross to suddenly appear in the sky, while mountains on the horizon glow with the flames of burning cities and "savage hordes" descend from the heights (56); Scene XIII takes place in outer space, while Scene XIV has as its setting a "barren, mountainous landscape, covered in snow and ice" (149). It is perhaps unsurprising then to learn that even though the play achieved great fame in Europe, of the fifty-three Hungarian plays professionally staged in New York City between 1908 and 1940, *none* were versions of Madách's *Tragedy*,[4] which cannot possibly be performed effectively without substantial revisions that would undercut much of the text's originality and intent.[5]

The play has fifteen scenes that together describe the fall of man and the history that this fallen man will have to endure, as told through the interactions of three main characters: Adam, Eve, and Lucifer. It begins in Heaven, with the heavenly host of angels worshipping God for the enormity of His effort in creating the universe. This is a God who enjoys praise, so when Lucifer denies it to Him, he is cast out of Heaven. Lucifer's refusal to offer this "God" praise is based on his belief that God assumes the authorial throne of the heavens only by virtue of His clever opportunism: He saw how matter was evolving on its own, added some of His own innovations – chiefly, humanity – and then took credit for the whole of creation (I.79–83). If there is any credit to be passed around, Lucifer feels that he should receive a share himself, since he, as the force of Negation, existed as "the gaps, / the obstacles to every form of being, / those which in turn compelled you to create" (I.119–21). That we are not, in this play, dealing with an omnipresent God – a fact confirmed in the final scene, in which He is shown to be powerless to assuage the despair of man – is first hinted at here, both by the fact that His one real creation, man, turns out to be something that man himself will eventually be able to reproduce (I.89–96), and by the fact that although He first considers destroying Lucifer, He must be content merely to cast him down upon the world, thereby loosing the powers of Negation on humanity.

Scenes II and III broach the fundamental question that the play will ceaselessly confront thereafter. In Scene I, Lucifer had mocked the childishness of God's creative efforts:

To your own glory you composed a song
And placed the record on a botched machine [...]
Does this become your age, your integrity,
this comedy, which might amuse a child,
to see his clay creation mime the maker,
no likeness, but a crude caricature
that flits between free will and destiny,
lacking the overall intelligence? (I.98–9, 102–7)

When we first encounter them in the Edenic setting of Scene II, Adam and Eve are not yet caught up in the endless to and fro of the questions of free will and determinism – questions that permeate the play. This is because they lack self-consciousness, as is clear from their naive, uncorrupted relationship to each other and to the pleasures of their paradise. In the creation story, the temptation Lucifer offers Adam and Eve in the form of the usual cursed apple represents the opportunity to become self-aware:

There is, indeed, one thing: the power to know,
lying dormant in your subconscious mind.
Now, that could make you come of age: the choice,
the gift of knowing right and wrong, the freedom,
to be master of your destiny,
unshackled from the leash of providence [...] (II.94–100)

Eve – whom Lucifer dubs "the first of all philosophers" (II.163) – reasons that if God had created a specific course for humanity, he would have made it so that "no enticement could prompt us to leave it" (II.156); if, on the other hand, God has fated humanity to trespass his law, then they should go ahead and get it over with as soon as possible. Eve takes the apple, and Adam, ridiculed by Lucifer for his hesitation, follows. The abandonment of their pre-reflective existence is immediately felt as an error; Eve cries out "We're finished!" (II.182); Adam, with more bravado, answers Lucifer's question "You despair?" (II.183) with the response: "Me? Not at all. It's just the shock of my awakening" (II.184).

As in *Faust, La Tentation de Saint Antoine,* and the "Nighttown" section of *Ulysses,* much of Madách's play takes place under dream, dream-like, or hallucinatory conditions. Given that this drama is concerned with consciousness, it is perhaps appropriate that an investigation of it should take place within a dream; Western philosophy, after all, has always understood consciousness as dream-like, which is why, of course, dreams themselves have always posed a threat to consciousness.[6]

Adam's dream of history, which will take the rest of the play to complete, begins in Scene III, which is described as taking place "Before History Started."[7] Now in possession of self-consciousness, Adam wishes to know what he has in fact been granted: "I've learned to master my instinctive urges, / But where's my gain?" (III.17–18). He wants more than that "gaudy show" (Scene III, l. 161) of experience; he wants knowledge: "Time passes: I must make the most of it" (III.175). The "knowledge" he will receive from Lucifer is of humanity's experience of history as a whole and its ultimate end, Lucifer presents to Adam in the form of a series of dreams. That the outcome of the dream-journey of knowledge will be unfavourable is noted in advance:

> So be it. Through my spell you'll have the chance
> to see your distant future in a trance,
> in fleeting visions, even to the end.
> But should they prove so daunting for your mettle
> that you might run away before the battle
> commences – once you've come to comprehend
> how profitless the goal, how grim the fight,
> I'll set before your eyes this beam of light,
> whereby you'll see all things within your scope
> as mere illusion. There's your ray of hope. (III.205–14)

Or, as Lucifer puts it even more bluntly in an aside to the audience that cannot exist for this play: "You'll pay a bitter fee for this tuition, / and long to have your former ignorance" (III.166–7).

The remaining scenes unfold with Adam, Eve, and Lucifer appearing in various guises in different historical settings. But these are not mere guises: Adam assumes the consciousnesses of the others he becomes in a manner that effectively obliterates his own consciousness; he *becomes* these figures, but in such a way that he is nevertheless able to retain his experiences of different moments in history so that, by the end of the play, he has comprehended the whole of history. Adam appears first as a young despotic pharaoh, who frees the slaves under his domain. In the scene that follows, these freed slaves are encountered as the citizens of democratic Athens. The hopes Adam had for a society of free individuals is disappointed, however, when the citizenry, who freely buy and sell their votes and act in other than ideally democratic ways, demand the death of their noble leader, Miltiades the Younger, the role Adam assumes in this scene. Renouncing his high ambitions for humanity, he longs for an age that does not strive for anything beyond simple, base pleasures. The next scene opens amidst the debauchery of Ancient Rome, where the pursuit of pleasure is held up as the chief virtue ("Of course, we have more sense today, / have fun and pleasure while we may" [VI.119–20]). The surprising boredom and emptiness of this decadent existence leads Adam to dream again of a higher goal that humanity might pursue.

Madách makes a point of experimenting with the whole of history, leading Adam and Eve through those stages of civilization that in the nineteenth century were seen as high points in the history of humanity, during which one might assume that some insight into collective living had been gained that could be of use in establishing the ways and means of an ideal human life. Athens and Rome are only the first of these. Scene VII finds Adam as the Crusader Tancred upon his arrival at Constantinople. The freedom for the individual that he hoped to find in the brotherhood of Christianity is frustrated by the hypocrisy of a religion that would shed blood over the letter 'i' – the sole difference between those who profess "Homoiousian" and "Homoousian." Again, Adam abandons his ambitions for humanity and appears in two scenes as Kepler, stuck with his scientific instruments in an age of "decadent decaying puppets" (VIII.142–3). These two scenes are interrupted by a dream within a dream. Kepler dreams that he is Danton during the French Revolution. This scene, which opens with the cry "Equality, brotherhood, liberty" (IX.1), ends as yet another moment in history that fails to live up to its possibilities: the revolution turns against its heroes, and Danton is put to death.

At this point in the play, a shift occurs from history to politics. The next two scenes portray the societies of Madách's present and (imagined) near future – capitalism and socialism. Neither is what it might appear to be. The unrestrained individualism of capitalism turns the world into a market in which everything is for sale; the promised paradise of the communist state turns out to be a completely rationalized world empty of everything that makes life interesting and enjoyable. In an effort "to escape, to shed my earthly fetters / the impediment to my aspiring soul" (XIII.10–11), Adam tries to escape into space, only to realize that he is necessarily bound to the earth; only there can he have experiences appropriate to a human being. In the penultimate scene, he experiences the last remnants of humanity living on a dying earth covered with ice and snow, clinging pathetically to their meagre existence. After seeing the achievements and aspirations of humanity humbled at every turn, Adam, at the end of his dream, asks:

> Was it a dream or am I dreaming now?
> If life is only a dream which for a moment
> visits some lifeless matter and dissolves
> together with its host the moment after,
> why must awareness spoil the brief encounter
> and taint it with the fear of non-existence? (XV.8–14)

The fall of man in *The Tragedy of Man* rests in the very fact of his conscious awareness. That which distinguishes men from beasts, that which traditionally defines man *qua* man, does so only in conjunction with a fear of finitude that disrupts the possibility of enjoying life.

Since the history presented in this series of dreams has not yet occurred, in the final scene Adam realizes that he has "the choice to take another road" (XV.28). He can end history before it begins by performing the first and last historical act: his own suicide. At the last moment, in an effort to comfort him, Eve reveals that she is pregnant. Human history will thus unfold whether or not Adam has the strength to confront it. Adam turns to God for aid in his despair. God can only answer, finally, "have faith and do your best" (XV.202). This is not the help that Adam had hoped for; it also constitutes an affirmation of the structure of religious belief: enduring faith in a divine being who never appears and never offers up His divine power to the subjects who understand their whole reality as constituted by this divine power.

It is not difficult to see why critics have described *The Tragedy of Man* as "a play that is the cry of a soul tormented by loss of hope" (Reményi 129) and one that exhibits "a self-torturing interest in the questions relating to the future of mankind which face both society and the individual" (Czigány 213). If the fall of man and his subsequent inability to find happiness, social order, or even any measure of "metaphysical comfort" in *any* social or historical circumstance is due to the very fact of his consciousness, there is no hope for humanity. If every act, every attempt at reform, revolution, or change, is futile, both because of the ultimate end of man and because of the hypocrisy and contradictions that Madách sees existing in every ideology – every form of freedom masking a form of slavery, the subjugation of the many to the few – then it would appear that no action can, or should, be undertaken at all. Adam's own moments of inactivity in the play do not serve him well. But it is not this form of inactivity that Madách appears finally to recommend. It is, rather, the inactivity that belongs to a being that *lacks* consciousness entirely – the state of being of a thing, pre-aware and, strictly speaking, outside of history. Madách longs to be primitive again, whether this takes the form of a puppet or a god: only in the absence of consciousness can man find the happiness he consciously seeks. In the shift of theme from *The Civilizer* to *The Tragedy of Man*, in the movement from a specific historico-political situation to the universality of the human, and in the context of the lingering disappointment of the 1848 revolution, it is hard not to see this desire for and justification of inactivity as a deeply ideological one that seeks to write politics out of art – indeed, out of history.

The shift from *The Civilizer* to *The Tragedy of Man* is not only thematic, but formal as well. The *Tragedy* has embraced a form that has no possibility of external referents – that is, a form that for all intents and purposes is entirely self-contained and cut off from the world, perhaps even allegorically – and thus the ideological function of the play is repeated in form as well as in content. The negation of history reflected in the formal mechanics of the reading-play genre is repeated in Madách's use of history in the play; in turn, this narration of the entirety of human history is made possible only by the excesses permitted by its form. The play is devoted to an account of temporal moments in human existence, yet the specifics of history are actually unimportant for the play. The movement through successive historical eras is mechanical and unmotivated; one comes away from a reading of the text with a lingering sense that there was no real need to include any particular historical period. Any roughly equivalent division of history into particular moments would have served Madách's purposes just as well. More important than the selection of particular historical periods or Madách's characterization of them is their cumulative effect: together, the scenes effectively exhaust history even before it has had a chance to begin. The need to run through the whole of history is due to the necessity of leaving nothing out, so that there is no place left to turn, no hidden, undisclosed space where hope might exist, where consciousness might finally feel at ease.

The repetitive character of history – with each moment being much like the others, if not in content, then in form – reinforces the point that although time may pass, nothing truly new ever enters into the field of human possibility to add to those first announced at the beginning of Scene III:

> LUCIFER: Momentous words. Family and possession
> will be the two mainsprings of history,
> the source of all the weal and woe to come.
> These concepts will develop and appear
> as industry and nation in the future:
> they'll foster countless splendid, great achievements,
> and yet devour their charges in the process. (III.8–14)

In his brief comments on *The Tragedy of Man*, Lóránt Czigány suggests that the play illustrates "the development of the concept of freedom, in a somewhat Hegelian sense, yet with a considerable difference, because antithesis is not followed by synthesis, but by heterothesis" (213). The pharoah's oppressive monarchy in Scene IV becomes a far from ideal Athenian democracy in the next scene. In Madách's depiction of Ancient Rome in Scene VI, we are returned to a system once again divided between rulers and the ruled: nothing has taken place to alter these terms in the least. The terms of historical thesis and antithesis then shift from this direct treatment of freedom to a consideration of pleasure/decadence (Scene VI) as opposed to asceticism/duty (Scene VII), although these, too, return in the end to questions of the proper relations between the individual and society. Once again, nothing is resolved. In Scene VIII, Adam as Kepler rearticulates the previous dialectic in his denunciation of the decadence of court society. Throughout the play, Madách puts a number of binaries into play in a manner that begs for resolution: society/individual, free will/determinism, male/female, action/stasis, development/regression, consciousness/animality. That no such resolution is forthcoming should not be surprising. The work of *The Tragedy of Man* is to undermine the differences between these terms, thereby reducing all of human social possibility to Hobbesian situations of "continual fear and danger of violent death; And the life of man, solitary, poor nasty, brutish, and short" (Hobbes 186). This means that the dialectic is doubly arrested: its terms are allowed no synthesis, which makes historical development impossible, and its terms are shown to be the *same* rather than antithetical, such that – in an amazing bait and switch – there is no dialectic to bring to a halt.

As a consequence of this arrested dialectic, there is in history nothing that is truly historical. There are, of course, a multitude of technological developments that give each age a unique dimension, but these offer only new ways for mankind to suffer. What is lacking is a similar development of ideas, a movement beyond the binaries in which thought appears to be trapped. Adam as Kepler proclaims,

> Ideas are eternal.
> They will endure where transient forms of matter
> must crumble with the weight of violent forces. (X.45–7)

This is in fact the *problem* with ideas in Madách's world view: they refuse to change or to make themselves susceptible to history. This is also why the confidence expressed by Kepler in the lines immediately following is so misplaced:

> I can foresee my loftiest thoughts refined,
> evolving in a slow but stately progress,
> and stage by stage fulfilled throughout the world. (X.48–50)

But then it is clear that for Madách – in a further extension of the operations of negation that take place throughout the play – that even if ideas were historical, they would still be useless when it comes to devising a solution to the human dilemma:

> Frustrating though it is, you'll never find
> exactness – that's beyond the human mind.
> For take this sword and call it large or small
> it won't affect the sword at all,
> but problems which the differentia stages:
> what's large, what's small – could be argued for ages. (VII.88 93)

Thought is placed in an impossible situation with respect to history. It is, for Madách, neither historical enough nor transcendental enough. Human thought is trapped between the possibilities available to beasts and angels, inadequate to both and without any ground outside of these possibilities.

But the manner in which *The Tragedy of Man* announces a retreat from the world of activity is nowhere as apparent as in Madách's depiction of the present of capitalism (Scene XI) and the near future of socialism (Scene XII). These are the two longest scenes in the play, but they are also the scenes that are the *most* historically unrealized. Madách permits himself a great deal of space in which to articulate these periods, but curiously seems to have nothing of substance to say. Both scenes operate through exemplification. The materiality of capitalist London is shown through a profusion of characters, each selling something, or themselves, exhibiting in their totality the ugliness of a world premised on "the anthem of free enterprise" (XI.25); the life of the communist phalanstery[8] is shown through the examples provided by one guide, a scientist who shows Adam and Lucifer artefacts that have been rendered "historical" (moribund) by science – horses and dogs, roses and poetry, craftsmanship, and anything else that lacks utility and function.

What is missing in these chapters is any sustained examination of the character of these societies, which earlier scenes engage in almost to a fault. For Madách, capitalism and socialism are both inadequate; however, the reasons he provides to make Adam feel this to be the case are themselves inadequate. Adam's distaste for capitalism seems to rest on his abhorrence of an ugliness and poverty never exhibited in the scene itself (albeit that scene ends with a series of characters describing the harshness of their lives). The phalanstery is objectionable to Adam because individual creativity is not encouraged – a point also quickly added at the end of the scene through the anachronistic appearances of Luther, Cassius, Plato, and Michelangelo as workmen censured for the individual approaches they take to their tasks. Adam's usual philosophical claims regarding free will and determinism, and the burden of consciousness, are here mostly absent. Madách's failure to offer details about these two political options leaves each scene dissatisfying and incomplete. It is as if Madách felt the need to make specific ideological claims in these two scenes, and then, out of a fear of implicating himself in the history of the present, failed to fill them with content, so that the overall negation of history in the play would be preserved.

That this is a withdrawal marked by anxiety is clear from the disruption of form that takes place in these two scenes. At the beginning of both scenes, for the first time since the dream of history began, Adam appears as himself. There is a suspension of the blurring of consciousness that Adam undergoes in other historical periods, in which he assumes the consciousness of another person. In these two scenes, Adam and Lucifer first survey the scene as outsiders; then, in disguises that do not alter their subjectivity, they enter into the scene to see history unfold before them, less as participants than as observers or anthropologists of the present. This deviation of form indicates that these histories are still open, that they exist as possibilities not yet closed off to genuine historical development, and so not classifiable according to the system governing the rest of the play. Perhaps this is why Lucifer does not insert Adam into the consciousness of another human being – a being here still extant, full of potentiality and active possibility. Madách desires to keep both the present and action at a distance and to suspend a possible conjunction of these terms. The nature of Adam's dream has been changed at this point in the play, without warning or precedence, in order to separate presence and action from each other.

Madách's reading-play develops a defence of intellectual quietism in the face of the difficulties faced by the Hungarian intelligentsia in the period after the 1848 revolution. That defence has implications for how we understand the specific form of the reading-play. *The Tragedy of Man* seeks to establish the philosophical (i.e., universal) impossibility of action, which it confirms through an investigation of the history of political actions as such. Why history? History constitutes the site of potential change and development, which is, I believe, why the play actively works to suppress and negate it at multiple levels. In the second scene in Kepler's laboratory (Scene X), Adam as Kepler tells his apprentice, Lucifer, a secret. He asks Lucifer to repeat what he had humbly (turning to Kepler for guidance) admitted earlier: "That in effect I know nothing matters" (X.97). Kepler treats this not as an appropriate sign of Socratic humility, but as a comment on the possibility of knowledge itself. Kepler responds:

> Neither do I – and no one does, believe me
> Philosophy is only a flight of fancy
> elaborating on our ignorance:
> a harmless discipline, compared with others,
> it plays about with words, aloof, secluded,
> surrounded by a world of fantasy (X.98–103)

What Madách says here of philosophy – that it is simply a "flight of fancy," the invented discourse of an era that is ultimately without real content, referent, or import – can be taken as a description of *The Tragedy of Man* as well, and perhaps of reading-plays in general.

Madách's reading-play is a document of an interregnum: a period of blocked nationalist and socialist longings that only the trauma of the First World War would release (through the independence of Hungary and the formation of Béla Kun's short-lived communist government), however briefly and incompletely. My reading has suggested that this play constituted a justification for the stasis of this interregnum. But the unusual form of *The Tragedy of Man* and that of other reading-plays must be viewed as a symptom of another historical development as well. The broader social and political change that constituted a condition of possibility for the reading-play was the unprecedented shift of the economy (and the multiple relationships that made up social life) from something perceptible – the activities of the dockyard and city market, the spoils accumulated through European wars and colonial conquests – towards something imperceptible and no longer immediately available to cognition. By the time Goethe travelled to Frankfurt and noted to Friedrich Schiller that "people live in a perpetual whirl of getting and spending, and that which we call mood [*Stimmung*] can neither be produced nor communicated" (qtd. in Schmitz 366), this transformation was already well under way. It is this same imperceptibility that was diagnosed by Marx in his discussion of the commodity, the phantasmal character of which does not permit it to be examined in terms of the physical relation between things assumed in ordinary perception; as Marx wrote, "so soon as it steps forth as a commodity, it is changed into something transcendent" (*Capital* 76). As a new genre for mapping present relations, the reading-play tried to render social relations visible by opening up new narrative experiences through its constitution of an audience for a play able to exceed the limits of the visible and the demands of realist form. It thus reflected, in both form and content, the ways in which capital made reality ungraspable and unsteady, thereby producing a literary space that mirrored – or at least, had the potential to mirror – the fantastic form that social relations had taken within capitalism.

The reading-play has passed into obsolescence; it appears today as the filmscript, a form whose referents, however fantastic, can now be re-created with relative ease. The ubiquity of the filmscript does not suggest that a form has come into being that, finally, might provide the cognitive aesthetic map through which "we may again begin to grasp our positioning as individual and collective subjects and regain a capacity to act and struggle" (Jameson 92). And this is not only because of the purposes Madách devised for the reading-play, as he struggled against the demands of its form in order to render it a map of reality that legitimated political quietism. The moment that the reading-play became actualizable was also the moment we passed over into a form of capitalism that could no longer be named by the dynamics of Marx's commodity. But it *could* be named by Guy Debord's spectacle, which presents challenges to the conjunction of aesthetics and politics that must be properly and differently addressed – if indeed they *can* be addressed. One takeaway from the reading-play is that the abandonment of politics in literature is always suspect. Whenever authors or critics try to make the argument that the political capacity of aesthetics has run dry – as in the recent work of, say, Jacques Rancière[9] – we should be wary, for politics is never absent from literary expression.

NOTES

1 Foucault writes: "In writing *The Temptation*, Flaubert produced the first literary work whose exclusive domain is that of books: following Flaubert, Stéphane Mallarmé and his *Le Livre* become possible, then James Joyce, Raymond Roussel, Franz Kafka, Ezra Pound, Jorge Luis Borges. The library is on fire" ("Afterword" 107).

2 Reference to and quotations from *The Tragedy of Man* will be taken from Iain MacLeod's English translation and adaptation (Edinburgh: Cambridge, 1993). In some respects, MacLeod's translation is not quite as good as Thomas R. Mark's (New York: Columbia University Press, 1989) or J.C.W. Horne's (Budapest: Corvina, 1963). These two, however, tend to emphasize the poetic (i.e., *The Tragedy of Man* as a "dramatic poem") rather than the unusual, dramatic characteristics of the play, which MacLeod's translation brings to the foreground.

3 Baron Alexander von Bach was the Austrian Minister of the Interior from 1849 to 1859. During his period as interior minister, he forced a heavily centralized bureaucratic structure on Hungary.

4 See Gergely. It should also be noted, however, that MacLeod claims that the play – in adapted form – has seen "over one thousand and four hundred performances to date" (vii).

5 The adapted Hungarian version contains 70 per cent of the original. "The parts removed from the original text were not considered to be of inferior quality, but it was recognized that some of the longer philosophical

passages and arguments as well as some of the supernatural occurrences, though very interesting reading material, would have added considerably to the already long stage play, which is about two-and-a-half hours duration in its present form" (Macleod 167n2).

6 Is not the central neurosis of modernity with respect to consciousness, after all, first phrased with respect to dreams?

> I must nevertheless here consider that I am a man, and that, consequently, I am in the habit of sleeping, and representing to myself in dreams those same things, or even sometimes others less probable, which the insane think are presented to them in their waking moments. How often have I dreamt that I was in familiar circumstances, that I was dressed, and occupied this place by the fire, when I was lying undressed in bed? At the present moment, however, I certainly look upon this paper with eyes wide awake; the head which I now move is not asleep; I extend this hand consciously and with express purpose, and I perceive it; the occurrences in sleep are not so distinct as all this. But I cannot forget that, at other times I have been deceived in sleep by similar illusions; and, attentively considering those cases, I perceive so clearly that there exist no certain marks by which the state of waking can ever be distinguished from sleep, that I feel greatly astonished; and in amazement I almost persuade myself that I am now dreaming. (Descartes 113–14)

7 This is the title that MacLeod provocatively gives to this scene. The original Hungarian version of the play contains no scene titles. The setting of Scene III is described very briefly as a region of palm trees outside of paradise ("Pálmafásvidék a paradicsomonkívül"). For an original Hungarian version of the play, see Madách, *Az Ember Tragédiája*.

8 "A building occupied by a phalange or phalanx, a cooperative community of about 1800 persons living in a society reorganized according to the pre-Marxist socialist principles of Charles Fourier (1772–1837) in his *Théorie des quatre mouvements et des destinées généralés*" (MacLeod, 183n1).

9 See, for instance, Rancière's *The Emancipated Spectator.*

WORKS CITED

Byron, Lord George Gordon. *Cain*. Cambridge: Chadwyck-Healey, 1994. Print.

Czigány, Lóránt. *The Oxford History of Hungarian Literature*. Oxford: Clarendon Press, 1984. Print.

Descartes, René. "Meditations on the First Philosophy" (1641). Trans. John Veitch. In *The Rationalists*. New York: Anchor Books, 1974. Print.

Flaubert, Gustav. *The Temptation of Saint Anthony*. Trans. Lafcadio Hearn. New York: The Alice Harriman Company, 1911. Print.
Foucault, Michel. "Afterword to *The Temptation of St. Anthony*." In *Aesthetics, Method, and Epistemology*. Ed. James D. Faubion. New York: The New Press, 1998. Print.
Gergely, Emro Joseph. *Hungarian Drama in New York: American Adaptations: 1908–1940*. Philadelphia: University of Pennsylvania Press, 1947. Print.
Goethe, Johann Wolfgang von. *Faust: Parts I and II*. Trans. Albert G. Latham. London: Dent, 1912. Print.
Hobbes, Thomas. *Leviathan*. New York: Penguin, 1985. Print.
Hugo, Victor. *La légende des siècles*. Trans. G.F. Bridge. Oxford: Clarendon Press, 1907. Print.
Ibsen, Henry. *Peer Gynt: A dramatic poem*. London: G. G. Harrap, 1936. Print.
Jameson, Fredric. "Postmodernism, or, the Cultural Logic of Late Capitalism." *New Left Review* 146 (1984): 52–92. Print.
Jókai, Mór. *Szomorúnapok*. Budapest: Akadémiai Kiadó, 1963. Print.
Joyce, James. *Ulysses*. London: Penguin, 1992. Print.
Kleist, Heinrich von."Über das Marionettentheater." In *Sämtliche Werke*. Vol. 3. Munich and Vienna: Carl Hanser, 1982. 338–45. Print.
Kraus, Karl. *Die letzten Tage der Menschheit. Tragödie in fünf Akten mit Vorspiel und Epilog* (*The Last Days of Mankind: Tragedy in Five Acts with Preamble and Epilogue*, 1922). Vienna: Verlag "Die Fackel", 1926. Print.
Lukács, Georg. "The Ideology of Modernism." In *Realism in Our Time*. Trans. John Mander and Necke Mander. New York: Harper & Row, 1971. Print.
Madách, Imre. "A Civilizátor." *Válogatottdrámái*. Budapest: Unikornis, 1995. Print.
– *Az Ember Tragédiája*. Budapest: Szépirodalmi Könyvkiadó, 1969. Print.
– *The Tragedy of Man*. Trans. Iain MacLeod. Edinburgh: Canongate, 1993. Print.
Marx, Karl. *Capital*. Vol. 1. Trans. Samuel Moore and Edward Aveling. Moscow: Progress Publishers, 1977.Print.
Marx, Karl and Friedrich Engels. *The Communist Manifesto*. Trans. Samuel Moore and Friedrich Engels. London: Pluto Press, 2008. Print.
Rancière, Jacques. *The Emancipated Spectator*. London: Verso, 2010. Print.
Reidl, Frederick. *A History of Hungarian Literature*. London: William Heinemann, 1906. Print.
Reményi, Joseph. *Hungarian Writers and Literature*. New Brunswick, NJ: Rutgers University Press, 1964. Print.
Schmitz, L. Dora, ed. *Correspondence between Schiller and Goethe*. London: George Bell and Sons, 1877. Frankfurt on the Main, August 9, 1797. Print.

5 Kitchen Stories: Literary and Architectural Reflections on Modern Kitchens in Central Europe

SARAH MCGAUGHEY

In his unfinished novel *Amerika* or *The Man who Disappeared*, Franz Kafka describes the futility of accomplishing a task, as he so often does in his literary work. Here, though, failure occurs in an unusual place – an American kitchen:

> [S]he [the cook] couldn't prepare the food, a thick soup was cooking in two gigantic pots, and however often the woman tested it with ladles and poured it down from high up, she couldn't get it right, it must be the fault of the inadequate fire, and so she sat down in front of the door, and raked about in the glowing coals with the poker. The smoke which filled the kitchen gave her a cough which at times was so violent that she would reach for a chair and for several minutes do nothing but cough. (*The Man* 187)[1]

This kitchen is antiquated; the oven is still powered by a coal fire, not gas or electricity. Kafka introduces this kitchen scene by stressing the technical difficulties of cooking in an old kitchen, but by the passage's end it is the impact on the individuals in the room that is more striking. The woman's body is under attack; the smoke causes her painful, debilitating cough. This leads to a failure of both woman and kitchen to produce the needed food. As the text continues, an additional failure appears: the main character, Karl, and his fellow manservant, Robinson, are unable to fulfil their employer's wish for breakfast. The kitchen's aging design thus produces a longer chain of events that impacts the bodies and lives of many.

The extended impact of the work of and in a kitchen was a common topic of public discourse at the time of the many versions of Kafka's unfinished novel (1911, 1914, 1927). The length of time necessary and the physical tolls taken to cook a meal in a traditional kitchen, such as the one described in the passage above, were viewed as a loss of energy and money, two particularly important resources for European nations wanting to re-establish their economies, infrastructures, and industries after the First World War. In *Amerika*, Kafka's American setting allows him to portray and criticize the myth of American progress and freedom. His main character, Karl, leaves the past (i.e., Europe and the scandal of a pregnant housemaid) and attempts to make a better future for himself in the land of opportunity. While Kafka presents the United States in all its stereotypical glory, he adds key moments of failure and absurdity. Among the critical representations of the United States is the failed work in the kitchen. This narrative of the American kitchen stands in stark contrast to the one typically constructed in social, cultural, design, and economic histories of the kitchen in the interwar period. These narratives stress the progressive spatial and technological changes in the kitchen and point to the emergence of scientific theories developed in the United States as the ideas that led to the forward-thinking designs developed in Weimar Germany. While such narratives concentrate on the United States and Germany as the locus of modernity in the kitchen, the daily use of kitchens and literary depictions of kitchens, such as the one described by Kafka, are not considered, despite their emphasis on many of the themes of discourse surrounding the work of women and the modern kitchen. In pursuit of understanding the narrative of modernity constructed around kitchen design in the interwar period, this chapter turns to the Central European context of the former Austro-Hungarian Empire to challenge the current limits of the scholarship on the modern kitchen and its national, aesthetic, and theoretical boundaries.

Kafka's American kitchen is an early example of literary references to kitchen discourse. The interwar years were a time of increasing change in kitchens and their representations throughout Europe and the United States. In the former Austro-Hungarian countries after the First World War, significant architectural innovations and discourses reveal a more complex and nuanced history of kitchens. These kitchens present evidence that requires us to revise the current concept of modernity presented in studies of the kitchen. What the broader Central European context of kitchens contributes to our understanding of the modern kitchen is not just the reiteration of characteristics with which the modern kitchen is usually described: its use of forms of mass production, its ties to certain national histories, its use of modern materials, and its reconsideration of the size and use of the workspace. These Central European kitchens also reveal how the modern aesthetic imagination is created and deployed.

As the passage from Kafka illustrates, the kitchen was ready for modernization. It was the room of the house that at the time could benefit the most from the wider availability of gas, electricity, and new technologies. The household and the kitchen underwent sweeping transformations in the interwar period in Central Europe. The kitchen's construction and design were under scrutiny, and the need for its renovation and modernization was a major topic of journals, newspapers, and household manuals. As Susan Henderson explains in her contribution to the history of modern kitchens in *Architecture and Feminism*, women's groups, industrialists, and social democrats were calling for a new kitchen and home that would enable women to be more efficient housewives (221). The need to change the conditions of housework and the equipment and location of the kitchen within the home came into public and political focus as the work of women within the home and in the workplace shifted. Working-class women sought efficient forms of housing to reduce the time spent on household chores, as more worked outside the home. In addition, bourgeois women faced new demands on their time. With the increase in employment options for women, bourgeois households faced a shortage of domestic servants, and thus the development of new kitchens began to address issues that now crossed class lines. This change in the use of the home took place at the same time that architects and urban planners were confronted with the task of creating new forms of inexpensive housing to accommodate an ever-increasing urban working-class population in cities such as Berlin, Vienna, Munich, Stuttgart, and Breslau. In this context of social change, studies of the modern kitchen have focused heavily on avant-garde and ground-breaking kitchens of the 1920s, their technological innovations, their efficiency, their use of modern materials, and their implementation of scientific research.[2]

In *Architecture of Red Vienna*, her study of developments in urban housing, Eva Blau notes that Germany is the space most often studied with regard to innovations in domestic architecture and design (5–6). Such studies focus on the revolutionary examples of German settlement housing, such as Ernst May's *Neues Frankfurt* (New Frankfurt) and Bruno Taut's *Hufeisensiedlung* (Horseshoe Settlement), and have come to form a canon of modern housing in Central Europe. The exemplary modern kitchen in this context was the Frankfurt kitchen, now represented in the major museums of Western European and American design: the Museum of Modern Art (MoMA) in New York, the Victoria & Albert Museum (V&A) in London, and the Museum für angewandte Kunst (MAK) in Vienna. Designed as a part of May's *Neues Frankfurt* by Margarete (Grete) Schütte-Lihotzky, the Frankfurt kitchen was a narrow, one-room workplace tailored for one person and separated from the home's other spaces by a sliding door. It was a space for the woman of the house to complete the task of feeding the family efficiently and comfortably. Ingredients were accessible at arm's length from the cook's stool; distances between cupboards, counter, and sink were short; the compact size and layout allowed for ease of cleaning. This kitchen's exemplary modernist characteristics, it has long been argued, stemmed from its designer's American and German sources.[3] In developing her model kitchen, Schütte-Lihotzky combined the scientific management theory of Frederick Winslow Taylor (Taylorism) and the regulation theory of Henry Ford (Fordism) with the time-motion studies of the Reich Research Society for Economic Efficiency in Building and Housing (Reichsforschungsgesellschaft für Wirtschaftlichkeit im Bau- und Wohnungswesen [or RFG]) to create a physical environment that improved the housewife's efficiency. More recent studies of the Frankfurt kitchen stress that its modernity was due not just to Schütte-Lihotzky's inclusion of American ideas of scientific management and rationalism but also to her use of forms of mass production (Andernacht 198–99). This kitchen, as post–Second World War scholarship depicts, was unflinchingly modern from conception to production.

More recent criticism of the Frankfurt kitchen – its theory, history, and design – describes it as elite or anti-working class as well as antifeminist. In "'Housework Made Easy': The Taylorized Housewife in Weimar Germany's Rationalized Economy," Mary Nolan discusses the American influence on household design and contends that the parties involved in reform – in particular bourgeois women's groups, social democrats, and industrialists – had interests that did not correspond to working-class needs or women's independence (550–1). Nolan looks to social conditions and motives to criticize the modern design of the household and the kitchen; Henderson does so in the more general terms of modernist studies when she writes that "the private patriarchy represented by the family was gradually given over to a public patriarchy dominated by industry and government. [...] [T]he heroic nature of modernism depended on such comprehensivity, on a universal vision that overrode social and gender differences" (237). Here "heroic" is read as "masculine" and the elimination of "difference" is seen not as a move towards equality but rather as an obstacle to it. With regard to domesticity, a feminist approach is laid out in more detail in Hilde Heynen's introduction "Modernity and Domesticity: Tensions and Contradictions" in *Negotiating Domesticity*. Henderson, Heynen, and others have made strides in including the female and feminist perspectives in modernist studies on the kitchen and domesticity; that said, their works continue to perpetuate the divide between the avant-garde and the quotidian – a trend that persists in kitchen studies, despite the variety of interdisciplinary approaches to the topic.

Thus in broad terms, scholarship on the modern kitchen moves between an embrace of modern design, on the one hand, and a rejection of that embrace, on the other. The emergence of global perspectives in modernism and modernist studies suggests, however, that this is a false dichotomy. In "Geographies of Modernism in a Globalizing World," Andreas Huyssen discusses the need to revisit scholarly distinctions between high and low in order to more adequately address contemporary understandings of modernity, modernisms, and globalization. For Huyssen, the realignment of high and low, and the study of their relationship to each other, requires us to view the works of classical literary modernism on a horizontal spectrum with popular cultural forms and everyday life. This revaluing of the aesthetic domain of literature, he argues compellingly, provides further insight into the heterogeneity of global forms of modernism and cultural exchange (197). Huyssen ties his work closely to that of Arjun Appadurai, who in *Modernity at Large* explores the global dimensions of modernity and modernism further and, in so doing, stresses the role of practice and the work of the imagination. In the post-electronic world, imagination is "a collective, social act" and is no longer limited to the "space of art, myth, and ritual" (Appadurai 5). For Appadurai, globalized modernity is characterized by the ability of individuals to deploy their imaginations as they go about their everyday lives (5). Imagination is no longer simply a form of escape; it is a form of action (7). Appadurai's theory of imagination in globalized modernity can be merged with Huyssen's call for modernist studies to argue for a new understanding of textual forms as forms of imagination. Literature is thereby not reduced to a product of an author and thus representative of individual imagination. Instead, in an audience's act of reading, such texts become a part of the collective act of imagination. Reading constitutes not just a form of escape, although in some cases it may function in that way, but also a means by which readers can expose themselves to a variety of visions and representations of their daily lives. This then informs a collective imagination of the everyday. As a part of daily experience, the kitchen already constitutes a space in which one can begin to understand how daily practice and imagination are developed in modernity; that said, an approach that includes texts of all sorts also expands the aesthetic scope of kitchen studies.

To argue that an examination of the everyday kitchen in the literary and architectural context of countries of the former Austro-Hungarian Empire revises our modernist understanding of kitchens is to assume that simply recasting high modernism as part of the everyday imagination is enough to transform the discipline. This, however, neglects migration and globalization in modernity. Huyssen notes two potential pitfalls when expanding modernist studies that apply to this study in particular: first, limiting attention to a single region can lead to an emphasis on the local and thus to the assumption that culture is shaped in communities; and second, although attention to Central European contexts expands the horizon of kitchen studies beyond its current American and German boundaries, it continues to neglect global contexts and remains a monolingual endeavour (199). Indeed, this study does not challenge the traditional monolingualism of modernist studies in Central Europe; however, the authors whose work will be discussed have been chosen from a large geographical area, are well-travelled, and write about contexts beyond the regional. In addition, Viennese and Central European literary and built kitchens address aspects of economics and politics at the heart of global modernist studies of colonialism and empire-building. So to include such literature and architecture in our view of the modern narrative of the kitchen is to challenge the nation-state–based scholarship that currently shapes our understanding.

Certainly, the Frankfurt kitchen was an international concept, although in their studies many scholars neglect to mention, or severely understate, the (inter)national origins of the designer, the collaborative work that went into the design, and the broader context of experiments in kitchen design. The Viennese-born Schütte-Lihotzky was trained in proximity to much architectural experimentation, in particular with respect to the kitchen and its place in the home. In her autobiography *Why I Became an Architect*, begun in the 1980s and published in 2004, she herself admitted: "It is completely misleading to suggest that one person in the 1920s thought up the 'idea' of the live-in kitchen, which was then followed by everyone else. The form of a dwelling is never achieved through a single individual" (Schütte-Lihotzky). In the case of Schütte-Lihotzky, her environment was Viennese architectural circles, and at the time, articles about experimental kitchens in journals, newspapers, and magazines were readily available in that city. Even before the First World War, Vienna had an apartment building with one communal kitchen meant to house single, working women. Journals such as *Neues Frauenleben* (New Women's Life), published for working women by the Allgemeinen Österreichischen Frauenverein (General Austrian Women's Association), reported on experiments outside the capital, such as those in Hungary, where families formed kitchen co-ops (*Küchengenossenschaften*) in a number of towns (Nagyvárad, Kaposvár, Temesvár). Many articles like these were available to Schütte-Lihotzky, which suggests that her design was informed by changes in kitchens taking place across Central Europe.

As a young architect in the 1920s, Schütte-Lihotzky, who had no experience running a household and who did not cook, began to read American scientific research while she was working with Adolf Loos on Viennese *Gemeindebauten* (social housing projects). The interwar *Gemeindebauten* offer examples of floor plans and innovative uses of small spaces shaped by a variety of architects expressing a multitude of theories on the use of a home. Some of their designs had separate rooms for kitchens; others combined living and cooking spaces. Unlike the Frankfurt kitchen, which was a single-person design and part of the single-family unit in *Neues Frankfurt*, some *Gemeindebauten* included communal facilities such as pre-schools, laundries, and public gathering places (Blau 1–6). One group of prominent Viennese architects also involved in the *Gemeindebauten* created floor plans that were not based on abstract theories of efficiency but rather were made to fit the lives of their inhabitants. In his work on this generation of architects, who included Oskar Strnad, Josef Frank, and Oskar Wlach, Christopher Long quotes the Berlin architect Hugo Häring, who described Viennese domestic architecture as one dominated by "Wohnlichkeit," or livability ("Wiener Wohnkultur" 45).[4] The body's movement through daily life was central to Frank's experimental layouts (Long, "Villa Beer" 481). In turn, this wider view of the role of the home and the place of the kitchen within the family and the larger communal unit informed a broader context of architects working to create housing with a variety of floor plans and different forms of kitchens in the *Gemeindebauten*. These kitchens took advantage of modern developments, such as plumbing and electricity, but – in contrast to the Frankfurt kitchen – chose to consider the space of a house in ways that did not always result in a kitchen separated from the rest of the home.

In an arena marked by such building contexts and newspaper coverage of them, Central European readers found plenty of material for reimagining the cultures of their homes and communities, as did authors of that period. Imaginative conceptions of kitchens appeared in many literary genres of the time. As has been discussed above, studies too often neglect forms of high modernism or position themselves as critiques of such forms by focusing on popular and underrepresented cultural forms. In this regard, some recent works about German-language literature after the cultural turn are beginning to reimagine and redefine the relationship between literature and popular media. For example, in *Mediating Modernity*, Stephanie Harris makes a compelling argument for the importance and utility of reading modernist literature in the context of new media (1–20). Harris's work places literature – including canonical modern novels such as John Dos Passos's *Manhattan Transfer* and Alfred Döblin's *Berlin Alexanderplatz* – on a level playing field with other cultural forms and the everyday in the context of media, a shift analogous to this study's focus on literary examples of kitchens in their architectural design context and cultural history.

While audio-visual media forms such as radio and film, as well as newspapers, have become productive sources for cultural studies, the breadth of German-language literature of the interwar period remains relatively unexplored, especially with regard to its contribution to and reflection of discourses on architecture. Works such as Sabine Hake's *Topographies of Class* and Janet Ward's *Weimar Surfaces* explore the role of urban planning and architecture on the literature of the Weimar Republic and note the influence of architecture on the visual culture of the period, but literature of the former Austro-Hungarian Empire, in particular, is not often linked to architectural history and discourse. In the introduction to their edited volume *Interwar Vienna*, Deborah Holmes and Lisa Silverman note this and suggest that it is due to the focus on the pre–Great War period in Vienna (3) and the dominance of Weimar Berlin (5). According to this view, the major roadblock to integrating Austrian architecture and literature into the current understandings of the interwar period is the dominance of Germany; the focus on Vienna, whether before or after the First World War, creates another significant geographical barrier, for it does not include Central Europe. This is especially the case for studies of the kitchen, yet there are plenty of texts that refer to the Central European kitchen of those times, including feuilletons, Expressionist novels, and popular bestsellers, all of which present a view of the literary kitchen that can lead to an understanding of the imaginative ideas circulating at the time.

Written at the height of his Expressionist period and often ignored even in literary studies, Ernst Weiß's *Tiere in Ketten* (Animals in Chains, 1918, revised 1922) tells the story of the prostitute Olga. After years in the grip of her pimp Michalek, Olga is thrown out of her bordello, Haus Nr. 37, and returns home. There, she meets a lawyer, begins a career as a moneylender, and becomes a wealthy, well-respected woman. At first, Olga's success seems permanent. But after a while, she again becomes consumed by her desire for Michalek. Not knowing the reason for the change in her behaviour and mood, the lawyer suggests a trip to a spa. Olga, however, decides to stop in the small town where she had been a prostitute in order to visit Michalek. The visit proves devastating for her mental and physical health. She spirals into sickness, characterized by hallucinatory experiences and animalistic responses to her environment, especially to metals and colours. As Olga's condition worsens, Weiß's prose becomes more frenetic and the images of her world are sliced with strikingly colourful experiences. Food and physical responses dominate Weiß's depiction of her descent; she is slowly becoming the animal into which her figure transforms in Weiß's next novel, *Nahar*.

As a working prostitute, Olga spent no time in kitchens. In Haus Nr. 37, Michalek had controlled access to food, which was distributed by the cook, an old woman: "'Where is my dinner?' 'What dinner? There is nothing here, Miss, please, I know nothing.' 'Did master not say anything?' The cook did not answer. 'Nothing?...' 'The master always has the keys,' the cook said" (Weiß 60).[5] Although she has not yet left the bordello, her access to food is cut off; her desires and needs have been rejected by Michalek since her attack on fellow prostitute Mizzi. Sugar, in particular, is regulated, for the prostitutes would be unable to control their desire for a substance that would ruin their teeth and thereby affect their value as sexual products (40). Thus, Michalek regulates the bodies of his prostitutes not just by selling their services but also by controlling their food. Olga, like the other prostitutes, is allowed to eat as long as she does what Michalek deems profitable. As an independent and wealthy woman in her later years, Olga still does not spend time in kitchens, but her access to food, especially rich food, takes on an obsessive quality as she succumbs to her sexual desires (Weiß 106). In contrast to the rancid, tough food she had to beg from the cook in Haus

Nr. 37, Olga now experiences food sensually: "Dazzled, she looked down into the kitchen. Fine flesh-coloured dough was being rolled onto white porcelain tables, sugar crushed in mortars, a great big fish, still twitching wildly, sawed into pieces" (109–10).[6] The passage describes Olga's view of the kitchen as she stands on the street; the bright white of the kitchen is dotted with the flesh colour of dough. The use of the word *fleisch* (flesh) elicits religious connotations of the weakness of flesh and stresses the animalistic descriptions of her desire and insanity. In her delusion, Olga's vision of unlimited culinary riches is marked by the violence of twitching, crushing, and sawing.

The association of violence and power with the modernist kitchen intensifies in the depiction of Olga's growing insanity. The intensity of colour pairs later in the passage with the kitchen's gleaming metal objects: "Machines for electric power, beating silently back and forth, with nickel-plated pistons, glistened bright in clean tiled rooms, wall to wall with the kitchen of the great hotels" (109).[7] The reader is drawn to the phallic, nickel-plated pistons; the kitchen is a violent space of masculine physical force. This scene reflects the violence of her sexual desire, a desire that culminates in her murder of a fellow prostitute, Mizzi. Here, the modern kitchen's aesthetics and power reflect and underscore the main female character's unbridled violence and sexuality. The electricity and metal create a kitchen that threatens violence instead of contributing to food production.

The violence of the mechanical, industrial service kitchen and its psychological impact on the woman appeared in an Expressionist novel published almost ten years before the Frankfurt kitchen was put on display at the 1927 Frankfurt exhibit "Die neue Wohnung und ihr Innenausbau" (The New Apartment and Its Interior Accessories). In this exhibit, the domestic kitchen was placed next to the Mitropa railway kitchen; the association with a service kitchen was intended not to associate women and the kitchen with power, but rather to illustrate how the Frankfurt kitchen utilized efficient developments in service and industry. In this case, the service kitchen was in motion and associated the housewife's domestic kitchen with travel and speed. With its emphasis on progress and rationality, this presentation of the kitchen eliminated images of violence.

In 1930, three years after the Frankfurt kitchen exhibit, the metal surfaces of the modern kitchen appeared in a feuilleton in a different relationship to transportation, with references to international influences and cultures. In "Der Koch in der Küche" (The Cook in the Kitchen),

Joseph Roth describes the "white, silver, matte metal" of the hotel kitchen (65).[8] Then, in the underworld of a hotel kitchen, Roth surrounds the cook with three additional elements besides metal: ceramic, water, and glass: "This kitchen could look just like the machine room of a modern ghost ship. The cook could be the captain. The cooks sailors. The assistants cabin boys" (66).[9] Captain, sailors, and cabin boys work in Roth's hotel kitchen, which resembles a ghost ship. Both this kitchen and the hotel kitchen in *Tiere in Ketten* are dynamic spaces of gleaming metal and machine-like processes. This comparison underscores the association between the kitchen's elements and the modern forms of transportation presented in Stuttgart and, when paired with Weiß's *Tiere in Ketten*, reveals the ways in which literary sources evoke a variety of imaginative associations with the kitchen.

In Roth's piece, the images of electricity and of the transportation industry together create an aesthetic of motion in the modern kitchen, and as they do so, they draw attention to the kitchen's capacity to include a variety of peoples and cultures. Of the hotel's head chef, Roth writes: "Of the four peoples, who populated this state: the Czechs, the Germans, the Slovaks, and the Jews, the cook unified all of the positive traditional characteristics" (67).[10] Roth is referring here to the chef, but he could just as easily be referring to the different cultures from which his staff come and to the culinary influences circulating in his kitchen. Indeed, his hotel kitchen is international; it includes "Russian snowfields" ("russische[] Schneefelder") and "turbans" ("Turbane[]," 65, 66). We encounter a similar mix of national identities in the Prague restaurant in Kurt Tucholsky's 1929 "Küche in der Hochsaison" (Kitchen in High Season): "It is a very small kitchen; stove, cooks' heads and waiters' cheeks glow. Calls, yells, angry commands – German and Czech, all of it mixes together."[11] Tucholsky, like Roth and Weiß, places motion at the centre of the kitchen, emphasizing its changing and modernizing forms, but he also imagines the kitchen as a non-national place open to multiple cultural influences. In the literary kitchen, nationalities and languages mix to create a dynamic space of creativity and power. Even when it is small – like the restaurant in Tucholsky's short story – it is not a closed-off, isolated working space like the one so often described as the Frankfurt kitchen. Instead, this description aligns well with the readers' experience of journals and magazines describing communal kitchens throughout the former Austro-Hungarian Empire as they imagine the sounds and chatter of the languages spoken there.

The industrial kitchen as presented in these three texts contributes to the themes of internationalism, technology, and efficiency; at the same time, these texts present the aesthetics of the modern kitchen as threatening. They also draw attention to the relationship between the kitchen and health. However, these works do not address any specific changes in the domestic kitchen, although modern kitchens, such as the Frankfurt kitchen, were designed largely for domestic use. But the impact of the home kitchen on the daily working lives of women is addressed, for example, in Jakob Wassermann's bestselling novel *Laudin und die Seinen* (Wedlock, 1925). Unlike Weiß and Kafka, Wassermann was not an experimental author, and unlike Roth and Tucholsky, his target audience was not readers of feuilletons – that is, his goal was not to provide cultural insights or to illustrate social realities. Instead, as Esther Schneider-Handschin has noted, he focused on attracting a large bourgeois readership by following traditional narrative forms (86). Moreover, in her depiction of his literary production, Schneider-Handschin quotes Wassermann himself. Here, he emphasizes that his novels are about the times in which his readers live: "In conclusion it is expected from the novel to be a 'status image of the time,' a history of its soul, the internal and external development, the conditions of its existence, the setting of its concepts, the interdependency of the fates of its characters who are typified in a heightened manner or refined to the symbolic" (87).[12]

The question here is not whether Wassermann's novels achieved his goal of helping the reader understand his or her own condition. The point here is that he depicted and drew attention to his contemporaries' real lives. Thus his work does much to help us understand women's relationships to the kitchen; in particular, early in *Laudin und die Seinen*, the main female character, Pia Laudin, is described in her domestic sphere. In this way, her character development is linked closely to the structure and tasks of the housewife.

In *Laudin und die Seinen*, the kitchen and its place in the household have psychological implications rather than physical and sexual ones, such as those Olga experiences in *Tiere in Ketten*. Sitting in the kitchen performing the weekly task of organizing repairs and service for the house, Pia is under attack:

> All these things – fences, water pipes, washing machines, stoves, coal, milk cans, kitchen tiles, sofa coverings – besieged her. And each thing had its special claim upon her. [...] People were generally of the opinion that

> man needs things. But this opinion seemed utterly foolish and perverse; in reality, the matter stood quite differently. It is the things which shamelessly and impudently stand in need of man, and demand and misuse his strength and his time, as seems fitting to them. (*Laudin* 52)[13]

In Pia's world, objects become her masters, demand her attention, and determine the order of her daily tasks. This passage highlights the structure of a housewife's life and addresses the question of whether her role leaves her the time and energy to host guests and to be a mother. The same passage places the housewife in a larger context of technological progress and consumption. With regard to this latter context, *how* society expects a household to be run determines not just the daily tasks of the woman who manages that household but also her identity. Importantly, this extended existential moment, in which the narrator questions whether Pia is a person or is herself a thing, is associated with a bourgeois household and a marriage in crisis (*Laudin* 53; *Wedlock* 57). It participates in both a public discussion on the role of the woman in the home and the discussion surrounding design decisions, specifically those about the kitchen's layout and appliances.

Wassermann's depiction of Pia reminds us that women's groups and journals of the time called for a restructuring of the housewife's daily tasks in order to improve efficiency and to allow more time for family and other social activities. In this context, Pia is the typical housewife, and the narrative shows that her exhaustion is caused by household objects that prevent her from enjoying the socially important tasks expected of a bourgeois woman. At the same time, the existential questions posed in the passage just quoted challenge the very idea held by many modern architects and designers that a properly designed kitchen or home can transform housewives' work. Manuals and journals of the time presented rules on how to reduce work time – for example, by limiting knick-knacks and ornaments in the home (which needed to be dusted or cleaned), by changing the kitchen's layout, and by purchasing new appliances such as electric irons and gas stoves to simplify tasks. In Pia's case, however, such changes in the objects of her life would have had little effect, for "Pia was the slave of things" (*Wedlock* 53).[14] Her tiredness would not be solved with a Frankfurt kitchen or new decor; the objects that created so much work for her were sofas and water pipes, walls and tiles, and thus elements of both old and new kitchens. Even new technologies, such as the washing machine, would have required more work for Pia. Thus her story undermines the modernist view that it was possible for architecture to change the shape of life and improve living conditions.

The stories of Pia and Olga underscore that literature can contribute to a vertical study of histories of media such as architecture by highlighting for readers that there are alternatives to the dominant discourse in the field. In the case of Olga, the kitchen's emotional and physical dimensions come to light in depictions of violence and power in association with the kitchen's electric power and gleaming metal; in Pia's case, larger questions about social structures appear in the context of a woman's kitchen. Literary sources also reveal vestiges of past discourses, events, and traditions and in so doing temper enthusiasm over modern design and technological developments.[15] Such a view of literature's role allows the reader to revisit both existential questions and daily experiences and to place these in new contexts. In that, it points to an additional way in which literature has imaginative potential in modernism. In the case of kitchen studies, this imaginative engagement with literature reveals fissures in the history of the modern kitchen that run along emotional, aesthetic, physical, and geographical lines. It also calls into question simplistic assumptions about the success or failure of the modern kitchen.

Most of the scholarship on the Frankfurt kitchen has emphasized that it succeeded in changing both the shape of the kitchen and the work performed there (Kuhn, Henderson). As evidence of the success of the design, scholars refer to the number built (over 10,000) and the post–Second World War acceptance of having a kitchen separate from living spaces (Heßler). But on closer examination, the first claim is tempered dramatically when one realizes that all 10,000 Frankfurt kitchens were produced for homes in May's Frankfurt settlements. Its popularity thus remained tied to the local. And while studies of the Frankfurt kitchen imply that it ushered in the idea of the separate kitchen, in fact that idea may well have originated in Sweden (Heßler 179).

Pia's story suggests that women themselves do not reap the benefits of these changes to their kitchens. With his depiction of technology's inability to improve Pia's condition, Wassermann's novel points to the possibility of resistance. Martina Heßler pursues this possibility in her article "The Frankfurt Kitchen," arguing that the Frankfurt kitchen failed to change housewives' work patterns. That is, the change in the physical design and a pedagogical program that taught women how to use the new kitchen failed to convince women and families to use the kitchen as intended. Heßler views these failures as evidence of "resistant users" and places them within the kitchen's history (164). Furthermore, she contends, the patterns created by these resistant users "thwarted" the designers' and architects' attempts to promote a modern lifestyle (178). She presents evidence that users modified their Frankfurt kitchens in a variety of ways, pointing to residents who moved their dining table into the cramped kitchen space or who simply refused to use the kitchen entirely (176). But Heßler concedes that these interventions were unable to contest the eventual changes in household patterns. In other words, they remained *moments* of resistance. Heßler's study suggests that the Frankfurt kitchen belongs within a larger body of modernist studies in which the everyday is a source of resistance – a resistance that suggests that the dominance of high art is thereby either reduced or rejected altogether.

Instead of suggesting, as Heßler does, that these acts create resistance to the modernized Frankfurt kitchen, I contend that when seen in a broader architectural and literary context, they are further evidence of imaginative modes of engaging with the changes taking place in the kitchen. Certainly, radical transformations of physical conditions, like the Frankfurt kitchen, and the accompanying didactic literature and training, were direct attempts to impose new conditions on the lives of housewives, but this was also a part of the larger process of reimagining the conditions in which housewives lived and worked. Austrian kitchens, such as those of the Viennese *Gemeindebauten* and the literary kitchens of the authors presented here, offer a variety of opportunities to explore varied ways in which the individual engages the imagination with regard to everyday contexts. Such kitchens expose how the focus on the Frankfurt kitchen has limited our understanding of the variety of ways in which the kitchen became a space that was negotiated and renegotiated across Central Europe in many aesthetic forms. In such a context, the kitchen in Central European literature offers insights into how new ideas meet old ideas in the development of users' imaginations. When combined with literature as a creative production and as a space of imagination for readers and authors alike, this new view of the kitchen in Central Europe challenges the assumed singularity of the Frankfurt kitchen as *the* representative of modernity. Instead of one moment of modernity defined as the culmination of American scientific and rationalized discourse, this broadened perspective reveals how such discourses met with resistance, alternative experimentations, and imaginative responses in everyday life, literature, and architecture. This is the modernity of the modern kitchen.

NOTES

1 "[D]as Essen wollte nicht fertig werden, in zwei riesigen Töpfen wurde eine dicke Suppe gekocht, und wie oft die Frau sie mit Schöpflöffeln untersuchte und aus der Höhe herabfließen ließ, die Suppe wollte nicht gelingen, es mußte wohl das schlechte Feuer daran schuld sein, und so setzte sie sich vor der Herdtüre fast auf den Boden und arbeitete mit dem Schürhaken in der glühenden Kohle herum. Der Rauch, von dem die Küche erfüllt war, reizte sie zu einem Husten, der sich manchmal so verstärkte, daß sie nach einem Stuhl griff und minutelang nichts anderes tat als hustete" (*Amerika* 243).

2 For an overview of the reception of the Frankfurt kitchen see Kuhn 150 ff.

3 See, for example, the original review of the exhibit showcasing the Frankfurt kitchen and a later work on the United States in its design history (Meyer; Bullock).

4 An article that stands out in its search for alternatives to the Frankfurt kitchen and the canon of design in modern architecture but still focused within the German national context is Jerram.

5 All translations into English by S.M. unless otherwise indicated. "'Wo ist mein Abendessen?' 'Was für ein Abendessen? Hier ist nichts, bitte Fräulein, ich weiß nichts.' 'Hat der Herr nichts gesagt?' Die Köchin antwortete nicht. 'Nichts? ...' 'Der Herr hat ja immer die Schlüssel,' sagte die Köchin."

6 "Geblendet sah sie in die Küche hinab. Feiner fleischfarbener Teig wurde auf weißen Porzellantischen in Walzen gerollt, Zucker in Mörsern zerstoßen, ein riesengroßer Fisch, noch wild zuckend zersägt."

7 "Maschinen für elektrische Kraft, lautlos hin und her schlagend, mit vernickelten Kolben, glitzerten hell in sauber gekachelten Räumen, Wand an Wand mit den Küchen der großen Hotels [...]."

8 "weiße[s], silbrige[s], matte[s] Metall."

9 "So wie diese Küche könnte der Maschinenraum eines modernen Gespensterschiffes aussehen. Der Koch könnte der Kapitän sein. Die Köche Matrosen. Die Gehilfen Schiffsjungen."

10 "Von den vier Völkern, die diesen Staat bewohnen: den Tschechen, den Deutschen, den Slowaken und den Judenvereinigt er alle positiven traditionellen Eigenschaften."

11 "Es ist eine ganz kleine Küche; Herd, Köchinnen-Kopf und Kellner-Backen glühen. Rufe, Schreie, zornige Befehle – deutsch und tschechisch, das geht alles durcheinander."

12 "Schließlich werde vom Roman 'das Zustandsbild der Zeit,' ihre seelische Geschichte, die innere und äußere Entwicklung, die Existenzbedingungen,

die Ideensetzungen, die Schicksalsverflechtungen ihrer ins Typische gesteigerten oder zum Symbolischen geläuterten Charaktere,' erwartet [...] (87)" Schneider-Handschin quotes Wassermann's *Selbstbetrachtungen*, 162.

13 "Alle diese Dinge, Zäune, Wasserrohre, Waschmaschinen, Ofen, Kohlenladungen, Milchkannen, beschädigte Küchenfliesen und neue Sofaüberzüge belagerten sie, und jedes hatte sein besonderes Anliegen an sie. [...] Die Leute waren im allgemeinen der Ansicht, daß der Mensch die Dinge nötig habe. Diese Ansicht war entschieden töricht und verkehrt; in Wirklichkeit verhielt es sich so, daß die Dinge in unverschämter, aufdringlicher und schamloser Weise den Menschen nötig hatten und forderten seine Kraft [...]" (*Wedlock* 56).

14 "Pia war von den Dingen beherrscht" (*Laudin* 56).

15 For more on literature, memory, and its relationship to history see, for instance Fuchs, Cosgrove, and Grote.

WORKS CITED

Allgemeiner Österreichischer Frauenverein. "Aufruf zur Schaffung eines Einküchenhauses."*Neues Frauenleben*, May 1909: 117–19. Print.

– "Die Gründung eines Einküchenhauses für berufstätige Frauen." *Neues Frauenleben*, September 1909: 228–9. Print.

Andernacht, Dietrich. "Fordistische Aspekte im Wohnungsbau des Neuen Frankfurt." In *Zukunft aus Amerika: Fordismus in der Zwischenkriegszeit: Siedlung, Stadt, Raum*. Ed. Regina Bittner. Dessau: Stiftung Bauhaus Dessau, 1995. 192–207. Print.

Appadurai, Arjun. *Modernity at Large: Cultural Dimensions of Globalization*. Minneapolis,: U of Minnesota P, 1996. Print.

Blau, Eve. *The Architecture of Red Vienna, 1919–1934*. Cambridge, MA: MIT P, 1999. Print.

Bullock, Nicholas. "'First the Kitchen – Then the Façade.'" *Journal of Design History* 1.3/4 (1988): 177–92. Print.

Fuchs, Anne, Mary Cosgrove, and Georg Grote. *German Memory Contests: The Quest for Identity in Literature, Film, and Discourse since 1990*. Rochester: Camden House, 2006. Print.

Hake, Sabine. *Topographies of Class: Modern Architecture and Mass Society in Weimar Berlin*. Ann Arbor: U of Michigan P, 2008. Print.

Harris, Stefanie. *Mediating Modernity: German Literature and the "New" Media, 1895–1930. Refiguring Modernism*. University Park: Pennsylvania State UP, 2009. Print.

Henderson, Susan. "A Revolution in the Women's Sphere: Grete Lihotzky and the Frankfurt Kitchen." In *Architecture and Feminism*. Ed. Debra Coleman,

Elizabeth Danze, and Carol Henderson. New York: Princeton Architectural Press, 1996. 221–48. Print.

Heßler, Martina. "The Frankfurt Kitchen: The Model of Modernity and the 'Madness' of Traditional Users, 1926 to 1933." In *Cold War Kitchen: Americanization, Technology, and European Users*. Ed. Ruth Oldenziel and Karin Zachmann. Cambridge, MA: MIT P, 2009. 163–84. Print.

Heynen, Hilde. "Modernity and Domesticity: Tensions and Contradictions." In *Negotiating Domesticity: Spatial Productions of Gender in Modern Architecture*. Ed. Hilde Heynen and Gülsüm Baydar. London and New York: Routledge, 2005. 1–29. Print.

Holmes, Deborah, and Lisa Silverman. "Introduction: Beyond the Coffeehouse. Vienna as a Cultural Center between the World Wars." In *Interwar Vienna: Culture between Tradition and Modernity*. Ed. Deborah Holmes and Lisa Silverman. Rochester: Camden House, 2009. 1–18. Print.

Huyssen, Andreas. "Geographies of Modernism in a Globalizing World." *New German Critique: An Interdisciplinary Journal of German Studies* 100 (Winter 2007): 189–207. Print.

Jerram, Leif. "Kitchen Sink Dramas: Women, Modernity and Space in Weimar Germany." *Cultural Geographies* 13.4 (2006): 538–56. Print.

Kafka, Franz. *The Man Who Disappeared (America)*. Trans. Ritchie Robertson. Oxford and New York: Oxford University Press, 2012. Print.

– *Die Romane: Amerika. Der Prozess. Das Schloss*. Frankfurt am Main: S. Fischer, 1965. Print.

Kuhn, Gerd. "Die 'Frankfurter Küche.'" In *Wohnkultur und kommunale Wohnungspolitik in Frankfurt am Main 1880 bis 1930. Auf dem Wege zu einer pluralen Gesellschaft der Individuen*. Veröffentlichungen des Instituts für Sozialgeschichte e.V., Braunschweig, Bonn: Dietz, 1998. 142–76. Print.

Long, Christopher. "The House as Path and Place: Spatial Planning in Josef Frank's Villa Beer, 1928–1930." *Journal of the Society of Architectural Historians* 59.4 (2000): 478–501. Print.

– "Wiener Wohnkultur: Interior Design in Vienna, 1910–1938." *Studies in the Decorative Arts* (Fall–Winter 1997–98): 29–51. Print.

Meyer, Erna. "Das Küchenproblem auf der Werkbundausstellung." *Die Form. Monatszeitschrift für Gestaltende Arbeit* 1927: 299–307. Web. http://archiv.ub.uni-heidelberg.de/artdok/volltexte/2009/874

Nolan, Mary. "'Housework Made Easy': The Taylorized Housewife in Weimar Germany's Rationalized Economy." *Feminist Studies* 16.3 (Fall 1990): 549-77. Print.

Roth, Joseph. "Der Koch in der Küche." *Panoptikum: Gestalten und Kulissen*. München: Knorr & Hirth, 1930. 65–70. Print.

Schütte-Lihotzky, Margarete. *Warum ich Architektin wurde*. Salzburg: Residenz, 2004. Print.

– "Passages from Why I Became an Architect by Margarete Schütte-Lihotzky." Trans. Juliet Kinchin. *West 86th: A Journal of Decorative Arts, Design, History, and Material Culture* (2011). Web. http://www.west86th.bgc.bard.edu/translated-text/kinchin-schutte-lihotzky.html

Tucholsky, Kurt. "Küche in der Hochsaison." *Vossische Zeitung* 284 (5 December 1929). Web. http://www.textlog.de/tucholsky-kueche-hochsaison.html

Ward, Janet. *Weimar Surfaces: Urban Visual Culture in 1920s Germany*. Berkeley: U of California P, 2001. Print.

Wassermann, Jakob. *Laudin und die Seinen*. Berlin: S. Fischer, 1925. Print.

– *Wedlock*. Trans. Ludwig Lewisohn. New York: Boni & Liveright, 1926. Print.

Weiß, Ernst. *Tiere in Ketten. Neue Fassung*. München: Wolff, 1922. Web. http://www.archive.org/details/tiereinkettenne00weisgoog

PART TWO

2000

6 Spaces of Unhomeliness: Rereading Post-Imperial Urban Heterotopias in East Central Europe

IRENE SYWENKY

> In strange towns there is an unknown joy,
> the cold bliss of a new glance.[1]
>
> Adam Zagajewski, "In Strange Towns" (8)

Historical processes of reconstruction and rewriting of borders, geophysical or symbolic, have immediate bearing on the narratives of collective identity as a site of ongoing negotiation and cultural transfer. The new and evolving post-totalitarian East Central European identity[2] exemplifies one such contested site, which is being continuously redefined in a geopolitically ambivalent and fluid space of shifting borders. The mythologies inherent in the geopolitical spaces of the region, including urban spaces, are significant in that they form cultural topoi, become important ideological constructs, inspire narratives of nostalgia, and contribute to the reimaginings and retellings of history.

In the context of European history, East Central Europe is one of those peripheral regions whose stories, according to Norman Davies, "historians tend to forget" (*Vanished Kingdoms*, dedication). These geopolitically peripheral spaces and border territories, while often overlooked in favour of metropolitan spaces, are indicative of the complex multi-vectorial political and cultural processes that come to shape their communities as a result of transfer between multiple empires. More specifically, cities become important witnesses of history in that they bear material change (shifts in cultural architectonics, physical destruction and rebuilding, selective preservation) but also become symbolic, discursive constructs that create hypertextual ontologies: the kind of imaginary cities that exist in literary discourses, cultural representations, and spaces of memory. Such constructs and representations often engage in ideologically driven archaeologies of the national, the regional, and the local, thus participating in larger narratives of history and collective identity. The region bears witness to many cities' sociopolitical and cultural transformations, which are then nostalgically revisited and reimagined through literary (re)constructions: Sándor Márai's Kassa/Košice, Chesław Miłosz's Wilno/Vilnius, Günter Grass's Danzig and Pawel Huelle's/Stefan Chwin's Gdańsk, and Elias Canetti's Plovdiv, to name a few.

The former Galician city of Lemberg/Lwów/Lvov/Lviv, which belongs to this sort of geopolitically ambivalent space, has recently been the object of several studies in urban history and urban culture, for it is a city whose multiple identities have been shaped by various historical forces as well as by several languages and cultures, some receding, some moving to the foreground over the centuries (Czaplicka, Davies, Grabowicz, Hrytsak and Susak, Narvselius). In the course of its history of imperial transfers, the city has been part of various peripheral spaces as zones of political, economic, and cultural gravitation towards a succession of capital centres: Vienna, Warsaw, Moscow, and, most recently, Kyiv (the capital of independent Ukraine). This chapter focuses on the way Lviv's historical profile has been constructed through post–Second World War and post-1989 literary narratives – poetic and essayistic – in order to foreground its alterity, its fundamentally off-centric quality, and its condition of unhomeliness, which reflects multiple geopolitical displacements and "extra-territorial and cross-cultural initiation[s]" (Bhabha 9). Comparable to Joseph Cary's project of a "ghost story" about the "ghost town" of Trieste, another former periphery of the Habsburg Empire, writing Lviv's polyglot history means uncovering narrative palimpsests, retracing elusive ghost memories, and "remembering a past known almost exclusively through books" (10). Examining the construction of literary Lviv in the writings of some of the key authors who have defined that city's literary landscape – Józef Wittlin, Stanisław Lem, Zbigniew Herbert, Adam Zagajewski, and Iurii Andrukhovych – I contend that the historically ongoing process of negotiating Lviv's geopolitical profile along the East/West and centre/periphery continuum has positioned this city's evolving identity as a fluid signifying space, a cartographic game, and a locus of the nostalgic desire for an elusive, historically displaced "home."

The transhistorical space of Lemberg/Lwów/Lviv has been defined by transculturation, continuous border-crossing, colliding affinities and divisions, and cultural pluricentrism. As Caryl Emerson once contended,

> in Eastern Europe, one town would commonly speak several native languages, belong to two or three empires in the course of a single generation, and assume most of its residents to be hybrids who carried the dividing-lines of nationality within their selves. [...] Exile, displacement, multi-languagedness, heteroglossia, outsideness to oneself and thus a taste for irony, the constant crossing of borders and the absence of a tranquil, organic, homogenized center that belongs to you alone: all these Bakhtinian virtues and prerequisites for genuine dialogue have long been endemic to Central Europe. (203–4)

Emerson's reflection on Eastern and Central Europe in the context of the conditions of border-crossing, decentredness, and Bakhtinian dialogism is a fitting commentary on the city of Lviv.

Today's western Ukrainian city of Leopolis, Lemberg, Lwów, Львов (Lvov), and Львів (Lviv) has a centuries-long history of colonial transfers: from the Kingdom of Poland (14–18th c.), to the Austro-Hungarian Empire (1772–1918), to the Second Polish Republic (1918–39), to the Soviet Union (1939–91). Since the thirteenth century, the city at various times has been home to a wide range of cultural communities: Ruthenians (Ukrainians), Poles, Armenians, Jews, Tatars, Germans, and Hungarians, to name a few. Today's Lviv – Lemberg, in its Germanized version – became in 1772 the capital of the Kingdom of Galicia and Lodomeria, a Crown land of the House of Habsburg. Austro-Hungarian Lemberg was mostly Ruthenian (old Ukrainian), Polish, and Jewish, with German being the language of government. Thus in Austrian Galicia the scholarly and sacred languages of Latin, Old Church Slavonic, Old Armenian, and Hebrew were complemented by secular Polish, Ruthenian, Yiddish, and German, and being fluent in three or four languages was not uncommon (Davies 460–1). Although initially the Austrian authorities pursued a "policy of steady linguistic Germanization," the city was re-Polonized with the introduction of municipal autonomy in 1870, when Polish became the official administrative language. Owing to its development under Austro-Hungarian rule, by the end of the nineteenth century the city was included in major European tourist guides (459, 470).

Largely untouched by the devastation of the Second World War, Lviv has retained the street plan and architecture of a Central European city, including its prominent late-medieval marketplace. This is a testimony to the city's administrative sovereignty and economic privileges under the Magdeburg Law, which encouraged trade and thereby created favourable conditions for the coexistence of many ethnic communities.

The years of development under Habsburg rule further solidified Lviv's Central European feel. Soviet urban planning had little significant impact on the city's historic core; it was left almost untouched by Soviet architectural modernization. The same cannot be said about the city's demographics. The multicultural image of today's Lviv, a result of numerous border shifts and geopolitical changes, masks many centuries of a troubled past, often marked by ethnic conflicts, political strife, mass violence, and displacement. In the aftermath of the Second World War and the redrawing of Poland's borders, Lviv lost between 80 and 90 per cent of its population due to "the decimation of the Jews, the deportation of the Poles, as well as the persecution and exile of indigenous Ukrainians" (Czaplicka 2005, 15, 18; see also Hrytsak and Susak). This did irreparable damage to the pluri-ethnic composition of the city. Over the following decades, the construction of a monologic narrative of a Soviet Ukrainian city almost obliterated the Austrian cultural legacy along with memories of the Jewish and Polish historical presence.

Lviv's historical identity came to be defined by its geopolitical marginality. Although the capital of the Austro-Hungarian province of Galicia, it was at the same time part of the economically and culturally disadvantaged fringes of the empire. It was also peripheral as part of the Polish and Soviet territories, and it remains so within today's independent Ukraine, where it is sometimes referred to as a major city in or the centre of western Ukraine, which itself is a regional designation. An "(un)usual borderline city" (Narvselius 57), Lviv likely owes its rich narrative memory precisely to the ambivalence and complexity of its geopolitical identity and the many historical displacements that have shaped its past and present communities; such displacements and traumas require a process of looking back, of retelling one's experience and creating a discursive network/community of similar experiences, the kind of Lviv that belongs to different cultural/national/political users. With regard to post-authoritarian cities, Ruble refers to the emergence of "parallel historiograph[ies]" (10) – narrative retellings that claim the city's past through different stories/histories; such polyphonic spaces of memory in the context of the city are inherently linked to its material landmarks and structures, thus creating spaces of what is termed "urban memory." The concept of urban memory is susceptible to the pitfalls of anthropomorphism; more commonly, however, it "indicates the city as a physical landscape and collection of objects and practices that enable recollections of the past" (Crinson xii). The organic symbiosis of spatiality and temporality in the urban imaginary often means that different, temporally incompatible things are juxtaposed in one place, "memories of what there was before, imagined alternatives to what there is. The strong marks of present space merge in the imaginary with traces of the past, erasures, losses, and heterotopias" (Huyssen 7). These intersections of the spatial and the temporal, which are at the heart of the Lwów/Lviv narratives examined below, constitute heterotopic structures that, according to Foucault, are "outside of all places" (4), even though they have a concrete, physical location in reality. Akin to "slices in time," they are "heterochronies," "counter-sites" (3–6), of the sort that are endemic to all human groups both as spaces of the collective imaginary and as sites of resistance (even as a way of reading and interpreting official, "real" places). Foucault privileged a society with many heterotopias "not only because these places affirm difference through its multiple interpretations, but also as a means of escape from authoritarianism and repression" (Boedeltje 5). Literary representations of urban space as a performative space of history constitute heterotopias of a divergent multiplicity of histories, memories, and imaginations, which in turn project different nostalgias and desires.

This chapter is structured around the two most recent historical shifts that have changed the cultural and geopolitical profile of the city: Lviv's transfer from Poland to the Soviet Union (following the region's annexation by Soviet forces in 1939); and its social transformation and reorientation towards the cultural and geopolitical paradigm of Central Europe after the collapse of the Eastern Bloc. The first shift was accompanied by a major change in the city's demographics, with an almost complete disappearance of the Jewish population and the mass expulsion of the Polish population westward (a mass displacement similar to the one along the German–Polish border). The second shift has been marked by a retrospective gaze back to the past, towards recovering the city's identity and history, which had been repressed for decades. The narratives from the Polish and Ukrainian sides, which also engage – implicitly or explicitly – with the city's Central European heritage, are stories that "speak" to each other, not only intertextually but also transhistorically, by contributing to a common heterotopic space, the "other" Lwów/Lviv, the city of the reimagined past.

While Lviv's urban culture has drawn some academic attention, the literary history/ies of the city have not been examined. Considering that Lviv has always been at the periphery of all empires – that it has always been slightly off the map, and aware of its own marginality – it has attracted a remarkable amount of literary attention. The most notable literary representations of Polish Lwów[3] after the Second World War, which constitute nostalgic returns to the "lost" city, include Józef Wittlin's *Mój Lwów* (My Lwów) and Stanisław Lem's *Wysoki Zamek* (Highcastle: A Remembrance), but most importantly the poetic and essayistic writings of Zbigniew Herbert and Adam Zagajewski, two prominent, internationally acclaimed Polish poets whose love affair with the city turned into a lifelong presence haunting their entire oeuvre. These names are well known both in the canon of Polish literature and internationally, yet there has been little academic discussion of their contributions to the collective poetic narrative of the city. These retrospective re-creations of Lwów are significant on several levels: as selective (re)constructions of the city, as selective presences/highlights versus absences/silences, and as specific memories and the emotional landscapes those memories create and perpetuate.

Józef Wittlin, a Jewish-Polish translator and writer, spent only part of his life in Lwów, but this connection inspired a strongly poetic and sentimental tribute, *Mój Lwów* (1946), which explores Wittlin's emotional connection to the city and his youth. In the words of the author, "it's not Lwów we long for after years of separation, it's ourselves in Lwów we long after" (7).[4] In this way he explicitly acknowledges that his narrative is a journey of nostalgia into an imagined, non-existent Lwów, the city that resides in his long-faded memories. Although Wittlin's account of the city's history does not fail to mention its darker, more violent memories (e.g., the Polish–Ukrainian war of 1818–19 and the massacre of Lwów's Jews in 1941), he chooses to construct primarily a leisurely, cultured urban space in which the Austro-Hungarian legacy is foregrounded. He leads the reader through some of the city's architectural landmarks and social spaces that owe much to Austrian cultural influence and to Austria's program of urban modernization in Galicia; he also makes a point of dwelling on some of the better-known – and supported in popular culture – connections between Lemberg/Lwów and Austrian metropolitan culture. In particular, he reminds the reader that Lemberg is associated with the professional life of Mozart's son (who worked there as a tutor and a choir conductor) and with the name of Leopold von Sacher-Masoch; although Sacher-Masoch's connection to the city was rather tangential (he was born in Lemberg and spent his childhood there), in many of his writings he explored Galician culture.[5] These links to Austrian and European culture are discussed with the pride of someone who claims rightful "ownership" of the city. For

Wittlin, *his* Lwów is both a fantasy and a reality, a material existence on which his subjectivity has been superimposed but which retains a form of truth: "We […] have to acknowledge every image of the world, reflected in our memory, as a reality. The reality of our soul. And then it will not matter whether Lwów was really the way we remember it here or whether it was different" (8).[6] Although his essay reads like an excursion to a smaller interwar Central European city that can be appreciated by any reader, his intimate narrative tone constructs a specific audience; his story is implicitly addressed to those who know the city and who share in the emotional and cultural landscape of Lwów's urban space. Various references to its topography, which he uses as memory tags, hail the readers who will recognize and appreciate these references. The frequent use of the first person plural is meant to create a sense of collectivity based on belonging to the city through the intimate knowledge of its cultural code, which can be acquired only by living in it. For all its exclusivity, Wittlin's account creates a transhistorical and transcultural Lwów (he writes as a Pole and a Jew) that transcends time and space (he published the piece after moving to New York) and constructs a discursive space of the city that implicitly invites a dialogue with his literary successors.

Stanisław Lem's autobiographical coming-of-age story *Wysoki Zamek* (1966) is set in the Lwów of his childhood and continues the theme of the "lost" city, albeit in a much subtler way. Although Lem is known primarily as an author of science fiction, his nostalgic memoir of the interbellum Polish Lwów gained immediate critical acclaim. In this autobiographical piece, Lem meditates on the elusive and vulnerable memory of childhood, but also on the impact that the early environment has on one's formative years and later life. Furthermore, Lem writes history in an unobtrusive way: the city and the sociopolitical context are veiled by the more vivid details of his parents' apartment, their library, and his years at the *Gymnasium*. Almost intentionally avoiding the broader context of the 1930s, the writer focuses on the microcosm of his memory and his mind. The story of his childhood, however, is also a story of *his* Lwów, a memento of a world that, by the time he wrote, was no more. Except for the High Castle, a historic landmark in the city, Lem does not dwell on specific locations; compared to Wittlin's, his literary topography of Lwów is rather underdone, perhaps intentionally so. In the inner world of his childhood and youth, the unity of his self and the city (i.e., the apartment, the street, the school, the neighbourhood) is organic; no explicit tours and explanations are necessary; his surroundings are an extension of himself, expanding and growing with his growing world. *Wysoki Zamek* is an introspective narrative; from the perspective of the 1960s, by which time he was living in Polish Kraków, having left Lwów at the end of the war, Lem's reflections on his early inclination towards solitude are also retrospective reflections on the loss and loneliness inherent in the exilic condition. By reaching back to memories of his younger years he also reaches out to a city that no longer exists. Thus the title of the memoir refers to the ruins of the oldest structure of the city; it is both the geographical point of its origin and its foundational myth, its symbolic point of reference. Lem's titular reference foregrounds the role of this landmark in the symbolic space of the city and in the symbolic space of his memory, while also pointing to the role of the city itself as the foundational narrative of his life.

Zbigniew Herbert, an exilic poet with homes in many places, embodies Central European ethnic complexity as well as mobility between the metropolitan regions and the peripheries of the former Austro-Hungarian empire. He was a Pole of some Austrian heritage (whose ancestors moved to Lemberg from Vienna and Graz) as well as a lineage of Polonized Armenians (Herbert, *Collected Poems* 585). He was a quintessentially nomadic figure, both culturally and politically, but at the heart of his unsettledness and lack of belonging had always been his exile from Lwów, the city of his childhood and youth. Having been forced to relocate to the post-Yalta, geopolitically reconfigured Poland, and having escaped the Soviet Union, Herbert nonetheless ended up in a country under a socialist totalitarian regime. With a brief period of political thaw in 1956 and the publication of his critically acclaimed debut collection, the borders of Europe were open for him not only to travel, but also to settle for various periods of time in Germany, Austria, Italy, and France.

According to the younger poet and fellow-migrant Adam Zagajewski, Herbert belonged to "those who had been disinherited from Lvov,[7] cut to the heart by the loss of that extraordinary city" (*Defence of Ardor* 107). The theme of that loss pervades Herbert's poetry, appearing in the first collections and resurfacing well into the 1990s, the last years of his life. It is then, for example in the poem "Time," that he acknowledges living "in several times like an insect in amber" (*Collected Poems* 558), simultaneously existing in past and present, never quite leaving the space of remembrance.

Herbert's nostalgic poetic relationship with Lwów indicates the depth of his connection to the city and the feeling of irreparable loss left after his departure for western Poland. In his 1957 collection, the poem "Never of You" ("Nigdy o tobie") sets the tone for his ongoing intimate meditation on the elusive reality of his childhood and the city's haunting presence in his memory: "I never have the courage to speak of you" (*Collected Poems* 82).[8] The second-person addressee of Herbert's poem (the actual city) creates an illusion of immediacy and reality while also underscoring Herbert's common themes – the unreliability of language, the infinite deferral of meaning, and flawed, dreamlike memories. He is always aware that his reconstruction of the city is merely a fleeting image, subjective, elusive, and already slipping through his fingers, and that he can "use only a cruelly common litany of words" (82).[9] Reflecting on Herbert's language of Lwów, Zagajewski comments that Herbert "never called [it] by name in his poems, he spoke of the 'city' as if the name itself was too painful, as if all other cities – and he knew so many – required names, and only this one city could get by just fine without one" (*Defence of Ardor*, 108).

The topos of the city – an anonymous city – becomes a presence of a haunting memory, an attempt to recover the past and seek meaning in a palimpsest of layers of unreality. Unlike Wittlin's assertively possessive *Mój Lwów*, with its abundance of specific topographic references and vividly material urban reality, Herbert's poem "My City" ("Moje miasto") is about absence, abandonment, and the impossibility of regaining the fragile connection with the place of his birth: as his "fallible memory draws up / the map of a city" (*Collected Poems* 104)[10] in a dream-like state, he sees only fragments and unclear images that inevitably come to an end. In his blurry vision of the inaccessible past, the poet acknowledges only one moment of certainty – his own beginning, which is inextricably connected to the city whose loss he mourns: "in the end a stone is left / upon which I was born" (*Collected Poems* 105).[11] The poignant concluding verse of the poem, stark in its unpretentious simplicity, speaks of non-belonging and exclusion: "every night / I stand barefoot / before the locked gate / of my city" (105).[12] The trope of the (locked) gate as a threshold, a borderline between past and present, imagination and reality, a liminal space of transition and change, also echoes in the texts discussed below.

The poem "Report from a Besieged City" ("Raport z oblężonego miasta," 1983) is both a commentary on the effects of wartime and a reflection on transience and loss. The reference to the city ruins, which can be read both literally and metaphorically, constructs an epistemic space of archaeology, a process of removing layers from the meaning. Ruins/

fragments/gaps, as flawed and unreliable as they are, become a new text and the only possible way of connecting and understanding: "we were left only the place and an attachment to the place / we govern ruins of temples, ghosts of gardens and houses" (*Collected Poems* 416).[13] Continuity rests in memory and in articulating the emotional legacy that comes with memory; in speaking of the survivor who, in his exilic life, will always have the city inside him, the poet certainly speaks of himself.

In the poem "In the City" (1998), written during his last years, Herbert bids farewell to "the borderland city [he]'ll never see again" (*Collected Poems* 551). "Seeing" here probably refers to the space of memory and imagination rather than to an actual visit (after his forced relocation from Lwów/Lvov in 1945, he visited the city only once, in the 1990s). The poet reiterates the importance of memory but also the constructed nature of *his* Lwów, a city "which doesn't exist on any map / of the world" and where "there's bread giving lifelong / nourishment black as an exile's fate" (551). It is also in the last collection – in a rare case where Herbert chooses to identify the city (i.e., he actually refers to Lwów) – that there is presence of history. In "High Castle," the poet discusses Herbert's visit to Lwów (at the time already officially Lviv) and references the city's central landmark but also engages intertextually with Lem's text, thus implicitly establishing an affinity between these two exilic figures. While "High Castle" identifies the city's origins in Ruthenian history, Herbert also refers to Józef Kapuściński and Teofil Wiśniowski, leaders of the Polish-Galician insurrection, who were executed by the Austro-Hungarian authorities in 1847 in the vicinity of the castle's ruins. While bringing together – wittingly or unwittingly – Ruthenian/Ukrainian and Polish forces in the city's history, the poet remains nonetheless in the shadow of the Austro-Hungarian and Soviet empires. Through its theme of loss, Herbert's poetry constructs a complex historical profile of the city that does not belong to anyone – perhaps least of all to him. This anxiety of not belonging also relates to the idea of Central Europe. Although Herbert does not discuss the concept extensively, in the poem "Mitteleuropa" he treats this anxiety both with a touch of cynicism and with disillusionment, as a "painted toy of a child / an old man's nostalgic dream" (485). Always a political construct and a myth, beginning with its roots in German influence, the idea of Central Europe remained so, albeit with new variations, in the aftermath of the Eastern Bloc.

Adam Zagajewski's narrative of Lwów appears to have many affinities with Herbert's loss and nostalgia, yet it is very different: his construction of the city is not based on his personal memories. The poet, translator, and essayist was born in Polish Lwów in 1945, but his family left when he was only four months old. Zagajewski never had any childhood memories of the city, and his personal encounter with post-Soviet Lviv did not take place until the 1990s. His imagined and imaginary Lwów was shaped by the city's pervasive presence in his parents' and grandparents' lives in the small town of Gliwice in western Poland, where they had resettled. Zagajewski's relationship with the city he never knew – yet knew so intimately – is conditioned by its simultaneous absence and presence, its unreality, and its almost mythological nature as sustained by his family's stories. His longing for the city he had not experienced for most of his life and the sense of unrootedness associated with his parents' forced expatriation came to define much of his writing, especially his non-fiction prose. Having grown up with an awareness of cross-cultural influences and bilingualism in his family (e.g., his grandfather was fluent in German), Zagajewski introduced Lwów in his writings both as a space of personal loss and as a geopolitical and cultural space of in-betweenness, a meeting point of differences; historically both a capital and a periphery, it favourably combined Western European cultural influences with an "openness to Eastern emanations (although the East was certainly less obvious here than in Wilno or even Warsaw)" (*Defence of Ardor* 3).

For Zagajewski, living in cultural and geopolitical interstices fostered in him a strong sense of absence of home. In his essay "Two Cities" ("Dwa miasta"), he reflects on his lifelong state of "unhomeliness" (in Homi Bhabha's terms): "If people are divided into the settlers, the emigrants, and the homeless, then I certainly belong to the third category" (Zagajewski, *Two Cities* 3).[14] His condition of unhomeliness is something that can be understood only in a metaphorical sense, as a feeling that took root in him through the stories his parents and grandparents had told him since childhood. Those stories instilled in him a sense of unbelonging in provincial Gliwice and a pervasive desire for the "other" city. He learned early on that his parents' life had been split in two, and for many years afterwards they told him stories about the beautiful city they had to leave. Always aware of the trauma of his parents' displacement, and always living that same displacement through their many storytellings, he was gradually immersed in the world of the ghost city whose presence was so constant in his family's daily life: "I walked the streets of Gliwice with my grandfather [...] but in fact we were strolling two separate cities. [...] I was absolutely certain that [...]

I was where I really was. My grandfather, however, despite his walking right next to me, was in Lvov. I walked the streets of Gliwice, he the streets of Lvov" (*Two Cities* 16–17).[15]

In the poem "Strange Towns" (quoted in this chapter's epigraph), Zagajewski talks about the allure of unknown, unfamiliar urban spaces; written by a well-travelled author, this poem can be read at its surface level. However, the strangest and most foreign city for him has remained the Lwów of his parents' and grandparents' prewar lives. In an essay with the telling title "Should We Visit Sacred Places?," he describes his journey to the most important "strange town" of his life when he is invited to a conference in Lviv in independent post-Soviet Ukraine, a conference ironically dedicated to the issues of the Polish–Ukrainian border, international collaboration, and European integration. The emotional impact of being in the city for the first time is enhanced by the crucial moment of collision between the constructed, imagined world of his parents' Lwów and the real place:

> I had before me a city that was both absolutely foreign and completely familiar, forgotten, forsaken, surrendered, mourned, bullet-ridden, but still truly existing, vividly and persuasively illuminated, solid, living [...]. You shouldn't visit mythic places, there's no way to see them, catch them, seize them. They're easy to recognize, but what then? What's to be done? After a long moment, I capitulated and reached for my Japanese camera in order to eternalize the city's astonishing, early morning performance. (*Defense of Ardor* 169)

"Seizing" images of the city on camera creates an illusion of capturing its fluidity along some seemingly fixed parameters, stabilizing it, even if within the conventional geometry of the photographic frame. However, Zagajewski's discourse about Lwów/Lviv is full of irreconcilable binary opposites and paradoxes: "I found myself in my city, which wasn't mine, about which I knew next to nothing, in a foreign city, about which I knew a good deal" (170). This impossibility of fixing the city in any specific set of terms – historical, cultural, national – informs the poet's stroll along its streets. Zagajewski walks in the Lwów of his parents' memories guided by a prewar city map given to him by his father, "without taking the new, Ukrainian onomastics too seriously" (171–2). His Lwów is a non-existing city of vanished Polish street names, of even older landmarks such as Kajzerwald and Ossolineum, the legacy of the Austrian imperial era. As he peels away the layers of twentieth-century history, he ponders that somewhere in western Poland, along the German–Polish corridor, German tourists may be strolling through the equally unreal cities of Gdańsk or Wrocław, reliving their own and their parents' dreams of prewar Danzig and Breslau, with the new life in these cities appearing "imperfect, accidental, provisional, and finally superfluous" (172). Zagajewski admits that his nostalgic quest for Lwów, fostered by his family's intergenerational stories and memories, translates into a "search for something that doesn't exist, something that may never have existed" (172), a symbolic structure that has strong emotional roots, a hope for an "original" home that can never be realized.

Herbert's and Zagajewski's writings about Lviv are deeply personal and intimate reflections. They also constitute part of the larger discourse of collective memory in Central Europe – specifically, the memory of the twentieth-century mass displacements. On yet another level, these narratives participate in the complex geopolitical play that followed Poland's loss of its eastern territories after the Second World War. These discursive re-creations of the city's historical past produce alternative ontological constructs, such as Austrian Lemberg or Polish Lwów, that may or may not have any real connection with the present-day city; they serve, however, to foster and perpetuate various national sentiments about the city and its belonging to specific national groups.

The historically founded, ongoing debate over the geopolitical image of Lviv was renewed after the collapse of the Eastern Bloc in post Soviet Ukraine, especially with the gradual opening of the borders and development of domestic and international tourism. With the reorientation of the post-socialist satellite states along the East–West axis, the concept of Central Europe has undergone essential changes. If *Mitteleuropa* was associated with the rise of German and Austrian political and economic interests in Europe (see Naumann 1916), the idea of new, post-1989 Central Europe meant, primarily, emancipation from eastern/Russian hegemonic influences and looking towards the West. Thus, in the context of post-Soviet Lviv, Czaplicka contends that for this Ukrainian city, with its history in the former Habsburg province of Galicia, "the association with Europe is based on historical ties to the region of Central Europe" (Czaplicka 2003, 400). He also argues that because of the architectural and cultural legacy of the Austro-Hungarian Empire, the residents of the city, and perhaps of the region, think of themselves as distinct from the rest of Ukraine. In the context of this westward gaze, the last several decades have witnessed concerted efforts to revive the historic urban ambience of Lviv (the revival of ethnic districts, the restoration of Armenian and Viennese coffee houses, the founding of cultural societies, and so on). While most of these ventures have been privately funded, some initiatives have come from public groups and the municipal government. In keeping with these efforts, in 2000 a petition was signed to erect a monument to Emperor Francis Josef I as a "symbol-testimony of our choice of Europe and our will to co-exist in the circle of free and independent nations of Central Europe" (qtd. in Zayarnyuk 15). Such manifestations of westward orientation in the guise of imperial nostalgia have troubled some commentators (for a critical analysis, see Zayarnyuk[16]). In October 2013, a sculptural tribute to Iurii Franz Kulchytckyj, the Galician who introduced coffee to Vienna (from whence it came to Lviv), was erected in the city centre, thus "visibly" reconnecting Lviv to Austria, but also reminding onlookers that influences between the province and its metropolis flowed in both directions. According to Heidi Schlipphacke's recent study of Habsburg nostalgia, the manifestation of this phenomenon is "particularly striking in light of the historical vicissitudes of the twentieth century: World War I, World War II, Nazism, the Holocaust, the rise of independent nation states throughout Central Europe, and the demise of the Soviet Bloc." Significantly, the longing for empire is equally persistent in the cultural landscape of the capital city of Vienna and the former imperial borderlands (such as Lviv) and can be seen as a search for "the elusive stability" associated with the rule of Emperor Francis Josef I (2).

The above examples of the material and visible signs of reorientation of post-Soviet Lviv that affect its current topography go hand in hand with narrative (re)constructions and rewritings of its history and culture. As Ruble points out, while the physical city is being reclaimed by various groups and communities through selective preservation or neglect respectively, "the metaphysical city is restructured by a selective retelling of history through tours, guidebooks, textbooks, films and Internet sites" (14). In the aftermath of the collapse of the Soviet empire, with the promotion of tourism and the regained freedom to circulate texts within and across borders, literature on the city, its regional history, and its culture has undergone a renaissance. The publication of area travel guides, city guides, historical references, and travelogues catering to various audiences (thereby endorsing different perspectives) has become an industry in its own right. Foreign publishers have expressed significant interest in various aspects of the city's history.

German-language publications focus mainly on the Austrian period in the development of Lviv (see Bisanz; Fäßler, Held, and Sawitzki; Woldan). There has been a flurry of publications in Polish; one example is a multi-volume series on Lwów/Lviv edited by Żaliński and Karolczak. Another significant Polish publication is the 2007 collection *Miasto jak brylant* (Grodziska, *A City like a Diamond*). This impressive six-hundred-page compilation of quotations and excerpts about the city from a variety of literary sources represents primarily the Polish perspective, which constructs Lwów/Lviv as a Polish city and an important part of Polish history. The three-volume history of Lviv by Isaievych is representative of the current Ukrainian narrative of Lviv, which emphasizes Ruthenian/Ukrainian historical influence in the city. An example of the literary revival is *Dvanadciatka*, a recently published anthology of Ukrainian urban prose produced in Polish Lwów of the 1930s. For postcolonial Ukrainian culture, such rewritings of local urban histories are important ways to restore a voice that had long been erased from official historiographies of the city. Both in Poland and in Lviv there are publishing houses specializing in regional history and culture (e.g., the Centr Ievropy in Lviv and Kraków), and these have been very active in reviving interest in the city's history. Some publications emphasize the regional context (e.g., *Halyts'ka brama* [The Galician Gate], in which the idea of Galicia is revived as a distinctly geopolitical concept). The 2004 collection *Lviv Leopolis Lwów Lemberg Genius Loci*, published by the Lviv sociopolitical and literary journal/publisher Ji, is notable in that it brings together a wide array of narratives about the city, mostly non-fictional, drawn from different historical periods, cultures, and languages. Some contributions appear in translation and some in the original language, thus acknowledging and reviving the historically polyglot and polyphonic space of Lviv. According to Ruble, "the emergence of pluralistic images of the past, present, and future may open the way for more pluralistic understandings of power and social relations" (5). These publications are important signs of the ongoing process of rebuilding the city's civic identity.

While the historical, journalistic, and tourist publications construct today's city as a contested site of different national and geopolitical orientations, the post-1989 literary discourse has been an equally important contributor to the discussion of Lviv's cultural and political space. The dialogue started by Polish writers such as Wittlin, Lem, Herbert, and Zagajewski did not have parallel Ukrainian counterparts during the decades of Soviet rule for reasons of much stricter political censorship and suppressions of local (anti-Soviet) nationalism. Privileging Lviv's Central European/Austrian heritage, acknowledging its Polish history, recognizing the role of important ethnic communities such as the Armenians, or emphasizing the presence of Jewish or Ukrainian historic agency in the area would have meant subverting its totalitarian monologic character as constructed by the Soviet regime.

One prominent Ukrainian literary figure who has contributed to the post-totalitarian, pluralistic narrative of Lviv is Iurii Andrukhovych, whose oeuvre has also become associated with the discourse of Central Europe in today's western Ukraine. Andrukhovych's poetic work of the early 1990s engages in the archaeology of imperial history and emphasizes the process of repeated recontextualization and displacement of the national self. Maura Hametz's argument regarding the function of Habsburg memories in the sociocultural landscape of Trieste can be extended to the case of Lviv, another borderland city where a return to the narrative of Austro-Hungarian imperial history "provides a vehicle to reconcile the city's Central European past with its position on the geographic periphery" (131), in this case the periphery of both Ukraine and Europe. Andrukhovych's poetry of this period features much of Lviv's actual historic topography; in this way, he identifies both the setting (for those familiar with the city) and the historical context. His exploration of Lviv's multilayered colonial past is performed on the thematic, allegoric, and linguistic levels. A representative poetic cycle is "Три балади" ("Three Ballads"), in which the poet sketches scenes from the life of Austrian Lemberg based on actual events and referencing real historical figures. In a matter-of-fact description of the collapse of the city tower[17] in "Лемберзька катастрофа 1826 р." ("The Lemberg Catastrophe of 1826") as a "minor apocalypse" of the "tragic city" (Andrukhovych, *Бу-Ба-Бу* [Bu-Ba-Bu] 18), the poet's focus is on the connotation of the "minor" and "small"; these qualifiers can be read in terms of the city's and its people's unimportance both in the general course of history and in the system of imperial hierarchies. In its use of specific details, the poem references the actual archival document in which the event was described; the mock German accent used to offset the document text emphasizes the critical distance imparted by the archivist's neutral/indifferent official language. The second poem of the cycle, "Дидактична вистава в театрі Богуславського" ("A Didactic Show in the Boguslawski Theatre"), refers to Wojciech Boguslawski, who is considered to be the founder of Polish national theatre and who lived and worked in Lemberg for part of his career. Here, again, the poet emphasizes the distance between the imperial elite and the lower classes, but also a history built on human losses and tragedies ("we all walk on dead bodies," 19). In the explicitly parodic commentary of "Нашіптування з віків" ("Whispering across the Ages"), the figure of the Austrian Emperor Francis Josef I – significantly referred to just as Emperor or Joseph – becomes not only symbolic of the imperial power of Austro-Hungary, but also an allusion to another Joseph to come (Stalin). The poet adopts the form of a ceremonial praise/eulogy, one that is heavy with ironic double-meanings – for example, in its reference to a "happy nation" ("щаслива нація," 20) and in its celebration of the emperor's visit to Lemberg. The poem juxtaposes two historical imperial spaces where both rulers (Francis Josef I and Joseph Stalin) are part of the same political structure; thus, addressing the ambivalent Joseph, the poet comments in anticipation, "it's still a while before the twentieth century, when you die" (20).[18] Frequent intrusions of other linguistic spaces (German, Polish, Russian) into the poetic space result in layers of nuanced subtexts of the imperial structures of the past.

Furthermore, the poet's treatment of Lviv's historical context is somewhat contradictory: he acknowledges the city's colonial past and its geopolitical peripherality, but he is also fascinated by its cultural and aesthetic complexity, which is precisely a consequence of its historic legacy. For the Polish authors discussed earlier, pre-Soviet Lwów was part of their personal experience and personal memory (or, as in the case of Zagajewski, his parents' and grandparents' stories of Lwów were an integral part of his childhood and of what can be construed as his "historical" identity). Andrukhovych's nostalgia for Lviv, however, is a nostalgia for a mythic construct, for the pre-Soviet Lviv he never knew. Under the Soviet program of modernization, Lviv had never become an industrial and "proletarian" urban centre as envisioned by the state (Narvselius 63); it always remained primarily a cultural, educational, and administrative centre. Nonetheless, during the totalitarian years the emphasis was on an ideologically monologic and mono-ethnic construction of the city's narrative. The poet's reading of the Lviv that he knows intentionally goes beyond the years of totalitarian control; it is a process of reimagining and rediscovering the city, whose past was neglected, if not suppressed, for decades. His poetry of the 1990s uncovers a palimpsest of voices and discourses and explores Lviv in its connection between the past and the present, lost "somewhere … / between the renaissance and the baroque" (10[19], see his poetic cycles such as "Faustian Celebration," "Medieval Menagerie," "Exotic Birds and Plants," *Бу-Ба-Бу*). Andrukhovych's construction of the different cities of Lviv and the problematic hermeneutics inherent in their historical opacity is strongly reminiscent of the development of the same theme in China Miéville's recent *The City & the City*, where one physical, material city (ambiguously situated somewhere in post-totalitarian Eastern Europe) houses two ontological constructs, two superimposing urban imaginaries that remain both contiguous and irreconcilable.

The theme of the city, so pervasive in Andrukhovych, remains for him primarily the theme of *the City* as a Galician and a Central European cultural space. Andrukhovych was born in western Ukraine, but not in Lviv, although he would spend his student years there. For the poet, as a western Ukrainian, Lviv had always been the centre of cultural gravitation, the space that largely defined the identity of what constituted the historical region of Galicia.[20] Andrukhovych's construction of Lviv is therefore also a search for the roots of his historical identity, for the kind of collective belonging that is defined against, and opposed to, the years of officially imposed totalitarian, Soviet collectivity. But his archaeology of memory and history is far from unproblematic and is dominated by silence, amnesia, and semantic opacity; it is a mutable, discursively constructed space: "it is only through us that cities pass / into un-memory. / We pronounce them / and find them different" (46).[21] A character in one of his untitled poems collected "impressions / of castles, dungeons, monasteries, / ruins, stairs, monks' cells and yards, / and listened to what the stones would say at last ... // But they remained silent ..." (12).[22] Andrukhovych situates the historical space of Lviv as a complex palimpsest of multiple narratives, where the original text is no longer legible and interpretation is becoming ever more problematic and ambivalent. The metaphor of the gate, likely linked intertextually to Herbert's poem – the gate that is both a passageway and an exclusionary divisive line – emphasizes the impossibility of belonging:

> There are cities that are impossible to enter through a gate.
> There are cities that are impossible to enter
> And they bring a huge key, and they look for a place to insert it, but
> there is no gate, the guards all crumbled
> to dust. Seven winds are sweeping
> across its squares and halls. (44)[23]

Andrukhovych's hermeneutic quest for *his* city, a city as a narrative of collective belonging, is a disillusioning experience; the text of the city is constituted by gaps and lacunae rather than a coherent story. The poet's narrative of Lviv is a site of continuous tension between presence and absence, transparency and opacity; it is a fundamentally unhomely and historically nomadic space that resists appropriation through definitive reading.

In his later essays, which often focus on the geopolitical and cultural aspects of the space of East Central Europe and Galicia, Adrukhovych looks back on his earlier experiences of Lviv. Thus, in "Intimate Urban Prose" he revisits, more critically, his first encounter with Lviv and explicitly acknowledges, in this slightly tongue-in-cheek description, that his initial construction of that city had little to do with the real place:

> The imaginary city of Lviv was spread on the picturesque green hills, completely preserving the architectonics and architecture of a city that looked distinctly medieval. From the windows, one could hear harpsichord music [...] and long-haired maidens were waiting for me on the grass by the fountains. In the imaginary Lviv they spoke only Ukrainian, except maybe for some old warlocks or magicians who could throw in a little bit of Latin or Greek. Generally, it was a city of eternal mystery. (*Дезорієнтація на місцевості* [Disorientation on Location] 13)[24]

Although clearly a fantasy, this conceptualization of Lviv nonetheless points to its role both as a Ukrainian national space and as a cultural nexus associated with the West. With its mix of medievalism, national sentiments, and cultural components gravitating towards a Western cultural paradigm, this imaginary, "foreign" cityscape is an escapist dream that is subversive of the poet's everyday Soviet reality. Andrukhovych's actual experience of Lviv as a Soviet city in the 1980s shattered his earlier mythology:

> Ninety percent of the real Lviv was comprised of awful outskirts and new developments. Agglomeration of industrial areas, chaotic piling of factories, monotonous high-rise apartment neighbourhoods of the 70s and later years, concrete, panels, and stench [...]. Its municipality was helpless about the problems with water, sewage, and public transportation. If there was any music coming from its windows, it was Soviet pop; there turned out to be a lot of Russian language spoken in the city. (*Dyjavol kxovajet'sja v syri* 13–14)[25]

Caught between two conflicting, irreconcilable spaces, the poet opted for a different reality of the city: "There was little left for me but to believe in some sort of parallel, secret Lviv. From time to time this city signalled its existence to me" (14).[26] The "parallel," clandestine Lviv of Andrukhovych's preference was a city of political actions against dissidents, underground art exhibitions, rumours of the rock opera "Stepan Bandera" (a forbidden Ukrainian nationalist icon), a screening of a Tarkovsky film, or a midnight climb up the hills of the High Castle (14).

Andrukhovych's typology of the city identifies three planes of existence: as a space of imagination, a mythology; as a real, physical space; and as a space of resistance. All of these have symbolic meanings; in the first instance, it is a site of desire, and, in the others, a site of active subversion and opposition. In some ways, these different visions of Lviv also relate to Andrukhovych's long-standing engagement with the debate over Central Europe and Galicia and show a distinct evolution of his views regarding the reorientation of this post-Soviet space (see also Sywenky, "Romancing the Empire"). If his 1990s writings tend to indulge in a nostalgic search for a "better" empire, western Ukraine's lost home, the next decade witnesses Andrukhovych's rethinking of his platform, as he himself acknowledges:

> I have recently arrived at the conclusion that for me [East Central Europe] is not, by any means, the ruins of the Habsburg-Danube idyll (which could have been easily derived from my earlier writing), and, thus, not the territory of old Austro-Hungary, not the coffee places with the aroma of cinnamon, not the Viennese postcards, not the old Galician anecdotes, not Sacher, not Masoch, not Kafka, not Musil, not Schulz, not Roth, not all the others. (*Dyjavol kxovajet'sja v syri* 87)[27]

Thus the explicit and often superficial aestheticization of the Central European space gives way to a more sober conceptualization of what this spatial and geopolitical construct means to Andrukhovych in historical terms. In the essay "Атлас. Медитації" ("The Atlas: Meditations"), the writer reflects on his reading of the 1996 *Diercke Weltatlas* (Diercke World Atlas) and his own revision of the cartographic narrative. While *Diercke Weltatlas*'s "Mitteleuropa" is limited to the historically traditional concept centred on the German-speaking cultures and the former sphere of Austrian influence, Andrukhovych's revisionist Central Europe includes what he understands as East Central Europe – that is, most of the post-totalitarian region. In his words, this East Central Europe is a space of extreme historical tensions, deportations, displacements, and genocides; an interstitial territory between East and West; a "transitional, inter-imperial seismic zone" (*Dyjavol kxovajet'sja v syri* 119–20). While acknowledging many of the problematic aspects of today's reality in the region, he nonetheless embraces it as his current and only home and as a cultural space that is closer to him than the sanitized nostalgic utopia of the bygone empire.

In the recent *Лексикон інтимних міст* (*Lexicon of Intimate Cities* 2012), an autobiographical exercise in urban studies that includes more than one hundred essay-entries on cities all over the world that he lived in and visited during his life, Andrukhovych understandably devotes significant space to Lviv, the city that defies any clear chronology of his life, a place that is not "before" or "after," but "always." Here, Andrukhovych constructs a kind of Borgesian space that includes every imaginable possibility of this city and thus offers an infinite unrealized potential. Among its many different faces is "Lviv-simulacrum" that is always the "other," and "Lviv-phantasm," a fictional labyrinth that falls into all the other cities, their "fragments, broken pieces and reflections" (250–2). Andrukhovych inevitably revisits the topos of High Castle, the "epicentre" of his youth (96), thus explicitly connecting to Lem's narrative. Zagajewski's and Andrukhovych's intertextual "bonds" with Lem establish a common space of memories that transcend individual linguistic and cultural experience, bringing together the three very different cities of Lwów/ Lviv and creating a transhistorical continuum and continuity, which is constituted by the simultaneous belonging and non-belonging of the three writers in the city. Commenting on the actual castle, which was destroyed several times in its history, Andrukhovych reflects that the very name of High Castle carries in it a phantom presence; it "disorients and assumes that we believe in ghosts and that we agree with any topographic-poetic conventions" (96). It is a pure hyperreal, a symbol that is no longer supported by the real geophysical landmark, a continuous reinvention, an originary act that subverts its own reality. Just like its central landmark, the city is an ongoing experiment in imagination, a construct and a spatio-temporal heterotopia that continues to evolve.

In the late 1980s, when Lviv was formally still a Soviet city but was already starting to recover from the decades of totalitarian stagnation, the German historian Karl Schlögel commented on its elusive identity; he described it as a space of "washed out borders" and expressed a hope that it would be able to regain its multi-voiced nature with which to tell not just a history of Lviv, but a history of a Central European city (258). It seems that this process is under way, from the changes in local topography to literary and cultural dialogues. This is important not just for the reconstruction and rewriting of the historical narrative, but for the current social transformation. In Ruble's words, "the task of rebuilding a civic identity in L'viv following Ukrainian independence has prompted present-day residents to look back once again to their city's multi-ethnic past in an effort to construct a future civic identity that might transcend the Soviet experience" (13). The search for a point of confluence in these emerging polyphonic discourses and for a shared space of historical and cultural experience is a process familiar to many other East Central European cities, uncertain of their identity, unsettled and unhomely. Reflecting on the journey as an interstitial condition, Zagajewski revisits Plato's concept of *metaxu*, being "in between" the commonplace and the transcendent, the physical and the symbolic, between different stories, meanings, ironies, "incurably 'en route'" (*Defence of Ardor* 9). Lviv, among other East Central European cities, is a city "en route," a space of continuous in-betweenness and hesitation, resisting finality through definitive cultural categories and still writing its heteroglot story. The ongoing literary (re)constructions of Lviv participate in the gradual making of today's city as a place and space of belonging; more importantly, however, they also contribute to the broader discussion of the civic future of the city and its community within national and cross-border contexts while renegotiating the legacy of twentieth-century history.

NOTES

1 "W obcych miastach jest radość nieznana
zimne szczęście nowego spojrzenia ..."
All translations into English in this chapter are by Irene Sywenky unless otherwise indicated.

2 Designations such as East Central Europe are always problematic, geopolitically and culturally, if not geographically. However, following the many examples of its use in much of the recent academic literature (see, for example, Czaplicka), I suggest that in the context of the present study, it serves the purpose of foregrounding the dual historical legacy of the region in question: its situatedness between the Austrian-centred *Zentraleuropa* (and western Ukraine's current westward gaze and orientation towards Central Europe) and the legacy of the Cold War and socialist totalitarian regimes.

3 Commenting on the "nomenclature" problem with most Central European cities, Davies and Moorhouse contend that "when a city has a different name for every nationality that lays claim to it, to prefer one version over another is to make a political statement" (11). To acknowledge Lemberg/Lwów/Lviv's situatedness between different cultural legacies, I will

be using different versions of the name depending on the historical context and the perspective discussed. This approach will serve both to acknowledge the city's complex historico-political background and to foreground the different heterotopic spaces of the city that are sustained by its different communities, past and present.

4 "Nie do Lwowa tęsknimy po latach rozląki, lecz do siebie samych we Lwowie."

5 For a detailed discussion of the way Sacher-Masoch's historical figure and legacy are appropriated in today's discourse of the city, see Chernetsky.

6 "Powinniśmy […] każdy obraz świata, odbity w pamięci, też uznać za rzeczywistość. Za rzeczywistość naszej duszy. A wtedy będzie już obojętne, czy Lwów był naprawdę taki, jakim go tu wspominamy, czy inny."

7 Many post-1991 English translations from Polish and other languages use dated (and politically incorrect) Soviet/Russian nomenclature, such as Lvov. In this case, it would have certainly been much more appropriate to use either the official Ukrainian place name of Lviv, or the Polish Lwów (as a way of emphasizing the poet's perspective).

8 "Nigdy o tobie nie ośmielam się mówić" (*Poezje* 106).

9 "powtarzam tylko okrutnie pospolitą litanię słów" (*Poezje* 106).

10 "ułomna pamięć tworzy / plan miasta" (*Poezje* 131).

11 "w końcu zostanie kamień / na którym mnie urodzono" (*Poezje* 132).

12 "co noc / staję boso / przed zatrzaśniętą bramą / mego miasta" (*Poezje* 132).

13 "pozostało nam tylko miejsce przywiązanie do miejsca / jeszcza dzierżymy ruiny świątyń widma ogrodów i domów" (*Poezje* 521).

14 "Jeśli ludzie dzielą się na osiadłych, emigrantów i bezdomnych, to ja należę zapewnie do tej trzeciej kategorii" (*Dwa miasta* 7).

15 "Chodziłem więc tymi ulicami Gliwic z moim dziadkiem […] ale w istocie spacerowaliśmy po dwu różnych miastach. […] byłem absolutnie pewny, że […] znajduję się naprawdę tam, gdzie się znajduję. Mój dziadek jednak, mimo że szedł tuż przy mnie, przenosił się w tym samym momencie do Lwowa. Ja szedłem ulicami Gliwic, on Lwowa" (*Dwa miasta* 15).

16 Unlike the critics of this proposal, some think that, in the context of Lviv's history, such a monument "would not appear out of place" (Czaplicka and Ruble 401).

17 The collapse of the Lemberg Town Hall on 14 July 1826 was a significant and well-documented event, especially in the light of its later rebuilding in a distinctly neoclassical style by Austrian architects; this, at the time, was considered one of the important contributions to the city's change under the Austrian rule (for more discussion, see Prokopovych 152–57).

18 "і де ще той двадцятий вік, в якому ти помреш?"

19 "десь отам, / між ренесансом і бароко...."

20 Galicians tend to see themselves as different from other regions of Ukraine. For discussion, see Narvselius (311–26) and Zayarnyuk.

21 "Тільки крізь нас переходять міста / у непам'ять. / Ми вимовляємо їх / і знаходимо іншими."

22 "збирав колекцію із вражень / від замків, підземель, монастирів, / уламків, сходів, келій та дворів / і слухав, що каміння врешті скаже... // Але воно мовчало...."

23 "Є міста, до яких неможливо зайти через браму // Є міста, до яких неможливо / зайти. // І приносять великий ключ, і шукають, / куди б устромити, але / брам немає, сторожа зітерлась / на порох. Сім вітрів розкошують / на площах і в залах."

24 "Уявне місто Львів лежало на мальовничих зелених пагорбах, цілковито зберігаючи архітектоніку й архітектуру міста ще, либонь, середньовічного. З відчинених вікон там нонстоп лунала клавесинна музика …, а дівчата з довгим волоссям і вінками на головах чекали на мене в траві поблизу фонтанів. В уявному Львові розмовляли виключно по-українськи, хіба що старі відьмаки й чарівниці дозволяли собі якусь латину чи греку. […] Узагалі це було місто нескінченної таємниці."

25 "Реальний Львів відсотків на дев'яносто з чимось складався з жахливих передмість і новобудов. Нагромадження промислових територій, хаос фабрично-станційних закамарків, одноманітна житлова забудова сімдесятих і пізніших років, залізобетон, панелі, сморід […]. Фатальна безпорадність міської влади з водою, каналізацією, транспортом. З відчинених вікон якщо й долинала якась музика, то тільки радянська естрада, російської мови в місті виявилося страшенно багато."

26 "мені не залишалося нічого іншого, крім віри в якийсь паралельний, таємний Львів. Час від часу це місто посилало мені сигнали про своє існування."

27 "Нещодавно я дійщов висновку, що для мене це аж ніяк не уламки Габсбурзько-Дунайської ідилії (про що можна було недалекоглядно виснувати з моїх давніщніх писань), отже, не територія старої Австро-Угорщини, не цинамонові кав'ярні, не віденські поштівки, не старі галицькі анекдоти, не Захер, не Мазох, не Кафка, не Музиль, не Шульц, не Рот, не всі інщі."

WORKS CITED

Andrukhovych, Iurii. *Бу-Ба-Бу* (*Bu-Ba-Bu*). Lviv: Kameniar, 1995. Print.

– *Dezorientatsiia na mistsevosti* (*Disorientation on Location*). 1999. Ivano-Frankivs'k: Lileia, 2006. Print.

– *Leksykon intymnykx mist* (*The Lexicon of Intimate Cities*). Kam'janets-Podil's'kyj: Meridian Czernowitz, 2012. Print.

– *Dyjavol kxovajet'sja v syri*. Kyiv: Krytyka, 2006. Print.

Bhabha, Homi. *The Location of Culture*. London and New York: Routledge, 1994. Print.

Bisanz, Hans, ed. *Lemberg/L'viv 1772–1918. Wiederbegegnung mit einer Landeshauptstadt der Donaumonarchie*. Exhibition Catalogue. Vienna: Museum of History of Vienna, 1993. Print.

Boedeltje, Freerk. "The Other Space of Europe: Seeing European Geopolitics through the Disturbing Eye of Foucault's *Heterotopias*." *Geopolitics* 17 (2012): 1–24. Print.

Cary, Joseph. *A Ghost in Trieste*. Chicago: U of Chicago P, 1993. Print.

Chernetsky, Vitaly. "Nationalizing Sacher-Masoch: A Curious Case of Cultural Reception in Russia and Ukraine." *Comparative Literary Studies* 45.4 (2008): 471–90. Print.

Crinson, Mark, ed. *Urban Memory: History and Amnesia in the Modern City*. New York: Routledge, 2005. Print.

Czaplicka, John. "Lviv, Lemberg, Leopolis, Lwów, Lvov: A City in the Crosscurrents of European Culture." In *Lviv: A City in the Crosscurrents of Culture*. Ed. John Czaplicka. Cambridge, MA: Harvard UP, 2005. 13–45. Print.

Czaplicka, John. "Urban History after a Return to Local Self-Determination – Local History and Civic Identity." In *Composing Urban History and the Constitution of Civic Identities*. Ed. John J. Czaplicka and Blair A. Ruble. Washington, DC: Woodrow Wilson Center Press, 2003. 372–410. Print.

Davies, Norman. *Vanished Kingdoms: The Rise and Fall of States and Nations*. New York: Viking, 2011. Print.

Davies, Norman, and Roger Moorhouse. *Microcosm: Portrait of a Central European City*. JohnLondon: Jonathan Cape, 2002. Print.

Dvanadciatka: The Youngest Lviv Literary Boheme of the 1930s of the 20th century. An Anthology of Urban Prose. Lviv: Piramida, 2006. Print.

Emerson, Caryl. "Answering for Central and Eastern Europe." In *Comparative Literature in an Age of Globalization*. Ed. Haun Saussy. Baltimore: John Hopkins UP, 2006. 203–11. Print.

Fäßler, Peter, Thomas Held, and Dirk Sawitzky, eds. *Lemberg – Lwów – L'viv. Eine Stadt im Schnittpunkt europäischer Kulturen*. Cologne, Weimar, Vienna: Böhlau, 1993. Print.

Foucault, Michel. "Of Other Spaces." Trans. Jay Miskowiec. 1998. Web. http://www.foucault.info/documents/heteroTopia/foucault.heteroTopia.en.html

Grabowicz, George G. "Mythologizing Lviv/Lwów: Echoes of Presence and Absence." In *Lviv: A City in the Crosscurrents of Culture*. Ed. John Czaplicka. Cambridge, MA: Harvard UP, 2005. 313–42. Print.

Grodziska, Karolina, ed. *Miasto jak brylant … Księga cytutów o Lwowie* [*A City like a Diamond. A Book of Quotations about Lwów*]. Kraków: Universitas, 2007. Print.

Hametz, Maura. "Presnitz in the Piazza: Habsburg Nostalgia in Trieste." *Journal of Austrian Studies* 47.2 (2014): 131–54. Web. Project Muse. DOI:10.1353/oas.2014.0029 http://web.b.ebscohost.com.login.ezproxy.library.ualberta.ca/ehost/pdfviewer/pdfviewer?vid=4&sid=373c6bd4-6349-4cc2-84aa-63ec8df2e0d2%40sessionmgr2

Herbert, Zbigniew. *The Collected Poems. 1956–1998*. Trans. and ed. Alissa Valles. New York: HarperCollins, 2007. Print.

– *Poezje*. Warszawa: Państwowy Instytut Wydawniczy, 1998.

Hrytsak, Yaroslav. "Lviv: A Multicultural History through the Centuries." In *Lviv: A City in the Crosscurrents of Culture*. Ed. John Czaplicka. Cambridge, MA: Harvard UP, 2005. 47–73. Print.

Hrytsak, Yaroslav, and Victor Susak. "Constructing a National City: The Case of L'viv." In *Composing Urban History and the Constitution of Civic Identities*. Ed. John J. Czaplicka and Blair A. Ruble. Washington, DC: Woodrow Wilson Center Press, 2003. 140–64. Print.

Huyssen, Andreas. *Present Pasts: Urban Palimpsests and the Politics of Memory*. Stanford: Stanford UP, 2003. Print.

Isaievych, Iaroslav, et al., eds. *Istoriia L'vova v triokh tomakh* (History of Lviv in Three Volumes). Lviv: Centr Ievropy, 2007. Print.

Lem, Stanisław. 1966. *Wysoki zamek*. Kraków: Wydawnictwo literackie, 1975. Print.

– *Highcastle: A Remembrance*. Trans. Michael Kandel. New York: Harcourt Brace, 1995. Print.

Lviv Leopolis Lwów Lemberg Genius Loci. Lviv: Ї, 2004. Print.

Narvselius, Eleonora. *Ukrainian intelligentsia in post-Soviet L'viv: Narratives, Identity, and Power*. Lanham: Lexington Books, 2012. Print.

Naumann, Friedrich. *Central Europe*. Trans. Christabel M. Meredtith. London: P.S. King & Son, 1916. Print.

Prokopovych, Markian. *Habsburg Lemberg: Architecture, Public Space, and Politics in the Galician Capital, 1772–1914*. West Lafayette: Purdue UP, 2009. Print.

Ruble, Blair A. "Living Apart Together: The City, Contested Identity, and Democratic Transitions." In *Composing Urban History and the Constitution of Civic Identities*. Ed. John J. Czaplicka and Blair A. Ruble. Washington, DC: Woodrow Wilson Center Press, 2003. 1–24. Print.

Schlipphacke, Heidi. "The Temporalities of Habsburg Nostalgia." *Journal of Austrian Studies* 47.2 (2014): 1–16. Web. Project Muse. DOI:10.1353/oas.2014.0023 http://web.a.ebscohost.com.login.ezproxy.library.ualberta.ca/ehost/pdfviewer/pdfviewer?vid=6&sid=4a3da2ad-4580-41fa-91a8-6ced87cd1152%40sessionmgr4006&hid=4209

Schlögel, Karl. "The Capital of European Province." In *Lviv Leopolis Lwów Lemberg Genius Loci*. Lviv: Ï, 2004. 252–8. Print.

Sywenky, Irene. "(Re)constructing the Urban Palimpsest of Lemberg/Lwów/Lviv: A Case Study in the Politics of Cultural Translation in East Central Europe." In *Cities in Translation*. Ed. Sherry Simon and Michael Cronin. Special issue of *Translation Studies* 7.2 (2014): 152–69.

– "Romancing the Empire: Central European Nostalgia in Iurii Andrukhovych." *Australian Slavonic and East European Studies* 26.1–2 (2012): 27–55. Print.

Wittlin, Józef. *Mój Lwów*. 1946. Warsaw: Czytelnik, 1991.

Woldan, Alois. "Lemberg – Modell einer multikulturellen Stadt." In *Nezalezhnyj kulturolohichnyj chasopys. Nova Jevropa. Problema jednosti u rozmajitti?* Lviv: Ji, 1998. 57–71. Print.

Zagajewski, Adam. *A Defense of Ardor*. Trans. Clare Cavanagh. New York: Farrar, Strauss and Giroux, 2004. Print.

– *Dwa miasta*. Paris and Kraków: Zeszyty literackie, 1991. Print.

– "In Strange Towns." Trans. Renata Gorczynski and Benjamin Ivry. *Times Literary Supplement*. Web.

– *Two Cities: On Exile, History, and the Imagination*. Trans. Lillian Vallee. New York: Farrar, Strauss and Giroux, 1995. Print.

– *Wierze wybrane*. Kraków: Wydawnictwo a5, 2010. Print.

– *Wobcych miastach. – In fremden Städten*. Kraków: Wydawnictwo Literackie, 2007. Print.

Zayarnyuk, Andriy. "On the Frontiers of Central Europe: Ukrainian Galicia at the Turn of the Millenium." *Spaces of Identity* 1 (2001): 15–34. Print.

Żaliński, Henryk W., and Kazimierz Karolczak, eds. *Lwów: miasto, społeczeństwo, kultura* (Lwow: City, society, culture). 7 vols. Kraków: Wydawnictwo naukowe WSP, 1995–2010. Print.

7 Interdependencies: Migration, (Trans-)Cultural Codes and the Writing of Central Europe in Texts by Doron Rabinovici, Julya Rabinowich, and Vladimir Vertlib

SANDRA VLASTA

Migration implicates cultural transfer and transforms societies from (supposedly) monocultural to transcultural communities. Literary texts on migration describe these processes and discuss the transnational identities emerging from them. In Doron Rabinovici's, Julya Rabinowich's, and Vladimir Verlib's texts, stories of migration are set in Central Europe and negotiate this space. The migratory moves through and in Central Europe, and the cultural transfers brought about therein, are interdependent. Furthermore, in works by these three authors, the aspect of Jewishness is present to varying degrees, intermingling with the motif of migration and thus becoming a part of the cultural transfer described.

Rabinovici, Rabinowich, and Vertlib are currently among the most discussed contemporary Austrian writers.[1] They have been awarded several prizes and are also present as public intellectuals with regular columns in Austrian newspapers. The works of the three authors share a number of qualities and therefore lend themselves to a comparative analysis; many of them deal with the issue of migration and the negotiation of transcultural identities. A number of the works are set both in Austria and abroad and in this way discuss transcultural experiences and cultural transfer between various places. Furthermore, they describe a transcultural collective memory of which they are part, a collective memory that cannot be labelled in national terms (e.g., as "Austrian" collective memory), but that could, if at all, be defined as (Central) European. The imaginary landscape of "Central Europe," in this context, becomes an even larger space, one that includes more than just the regions that formerly belonged to the Austro-Hungarian Monarchy. Indeed, it extends to Saint Petersburg and the Netherlands;

probably even Israel could be seen as belonging to this sphere. Rabinowich, Rabinovici, and Vertlib not only partake in Austrian literature but are also part of a transnational corpus of literature.[2] In this way, their texts transgress borders of "national literature" and become part of a broader entity that can be referred to as (Central) European or even world literature. Moreover, the three authors share a Jewish background that informs many of their works: Rabinovici and Vertlib often discuss modern Jewish life and identity, especially in the German-speaking countries, within and beyond their texts; Rabinowich's prize-winning first novel *Spaltkopf* (Splithead) tells a story of discrimination based in Jewish identity. In academic writing, they are thus often categorized as Jewish authors (see Gilman; Hahn; Lorenz, "A Human"; Lorenz, "Individuum"). Dagmar C.G. Lorenz, for instance, states that at the root of evolving models of Jewish individualism in the works of authors like Rabinovici and Vertlib "lies a self-concept informed by Jewish historical narratives and an intimate knowledge of Jewish culture that does not require but includes as potentialities life in Central Europe, Aliyah, relocation to international Jewish centers, religious and political affiliation, and a secular existence" ("Individuum" 389; on Jewish individualism see also Lorenz, "A Human"). Andrea Reiter reads Vertlib's works (as well as those by others) as "autobiografictions" (424) that are declarations of Jewish identity. The extended notion of "Central Europe" described above can be approximated to the Jewish identity of both the writers and their protagonists in the sense that it is reminiscent of Stefan Zweig's account of his family's distribution over the world cited in the introduction to this volume. However, Rabinowich's, Rabinovici's, and Vertlib's works are also studied as (Austrian) examples of "migration literature."

This chapter highlights the various literary means by which transculturality is depicted in the texts as a concept inherent in notions of culture, identity (formation), and (personal and collective) memory. Attention will be paid to the Jewish elements in the texts as they are inherent in questions of identity and therefore are closely connected to questions of transculturality. Each of the following analyses has a different focus. Discussed are processes of cultural transfer in Julya Rabinowich's *Spaltkopf*, the depiction of Austria's capital Vienna as a transcultural space in Doron Rabinovici's novel *Ohnehin* (Anyway), and Vladimir Vertlib's *Zwischenstationen* (Interstations), as well as the literary negotiation of the ambiguousness of historical events in Verlib's short story "Mein erster Mörder" (My First Murderer). This study also asks whether the space described in the texts can be read as Central Europe and whether the texts simultaneously generate this space.

Julya Rabinowich's *Spaltkopf*: Negotiation of Identities and Transfer of Cultural Codes

Julya Rabinowich was born in 1971 in Leningrad (now Saint Petersburg) and immigrated to Austria with her Russian-Jewish parents in 1977.[3] She studied translation studies, painting, philosophy, and psychotherapy in Vienna. To date she has published several plays, a novella, and four novels. Her first novel *Spaltkopf* tells the autobiographically inspired story of Mischka, a girl who was born in Leningrad and who immigrated to Vienna with her parents and her grandmother at the age of seven. The book was awarded the prestigious Rauriser Literaturpreis in 2009, thus calling public attention to the author.

For the larger part of the narrative, Mischka is the first-person narrator. Her experience of migration raises her awareness of the inconstancy of identities. The text depicts how she "tries out" different identities and how she refuses others. Thus, the text implies a particular concept of identity: it suggests that identity is not a fixed entity, but rather something fluid, dynamic, ever-changing, and that it therefore has to be discussed and negotiated all the time. Identity, as presented in *Spaltkopf*, needs to be understood as including various dimensions, such as relations to different people and to different places, and the traditions and norms connected to these. Mischka's ever-changing identity is closely connected to the motif of travel. Accordingly, Maria-Regina Kecht describes the novel as "a story of a journey full of various traumata into the liberation from fixed identities, a liberation which in the end chooses being on the move as the ideal way of living" (130).[4] The first part of the text, which consists of four non-chronologically structured sections, explicitly deals with travelling. These sections, told out of order, are short impressions of journeys. The first, titled "Lesson 3," shows the young adult Mischka aboard a ship en route from Ireland to Scotland. The next, "Lesson 1," is a flashback to her family's emigration from Russia, during which Mischka thought they would be going to Lithuania for a holiday and the family instead travelled to Vienna. The following, "Lesson 2," is subtitled "Travellers should not be detained" (*Splithead* 5–6) and refers to Mischka's father and his last trip to Russia, where he dies. In "Lesson 4," we see Mischka again on the journey mentioned at the beginning of the text, in "Lesson 3." This time, though, she finds herself in France and declares: "I have arrived," but also: "I'm not home" (7). These first pages of the novel show that travelling is constitutive both for Mischka and for her family. Besides being on an actual journey (from Ireland to Scotland), she characterizes her life as a journey, albeit one without an end: "I never did arrive, not on my first trip, not after my second. The journey is not ending" (3). To her other family members, constant travelling means dispersal all over the world: some stayed in Russia, others live in the United States, or in Israel, South Africa, or Japan. In this way, Mischka's family has experienced what Homi Bhabha has called "DissemiNation," the "moment of the scattering of the people that in other times and other places, in the nations of others, becomes a time of gathering" (Bhabha 139). These "times of gathering" are also described in the novel, for instance when Mischka's mother, sister, and grandmother go to the United States to meet Mischka's uncle and his family (*Splithead* 153–9), or when Mischka's father returns to Saint Petersburg (117). On another occasion, Mischka travels/returns as a young adult to Saint Petersburg (167–85). However, all of these "times of gathering" fail at becoming true moments of togetherness: Mischka's grandmother is not allowed to embrace her estranged son when in the United States; Mischka's father does not return from but instead dies in Saint Petersburg; and Mischka suffers health problems during her stay in Saint Petersburg and finds it difficult to connect to her former life there.

Travelling and migration entail cultural transfer, that is, the transfer and transformation of cultural elements between different (usually spatial-geographical) contexts (Mitterbauer 25). Mischka's constant journey includes forms of cultural transfer: cultural and identity-forming codes that travel with the protagonist and the family. The term cultural codes was coined by Roland Barthes and later taken up by Shmuel Eisenstadt and Bernhard Giesen. In his book *S/Z*, Barthes develops a system of five different codes for the analysis of Honoré de Balzac's narrative *Sarrasine* (Müller-Funk 174–7). One of these codes he calls the "cultural code." He defines this code as "quotations from the treasure of knowledge and wisdom" (Barthes 24), which are woven into Balzac's text as the "voice of scholarship" (26). Barthes's codes are not to be understood as paradigms, but rather as open systems, which become comprehensible only via the literary text. Sociologists Shmuel Noah Eisenstadt and Bernhard Giesen identify collective codes as criteria for distinguishing collective identities. One of these collective codes they determine to be a cultural code. And much like Barthes, they define a cultural code in terms of its particular relation to "the Sacred" (82–3), or something sublime, which could be God, reason, progress, or rationality. Barthes's "voice of scholarship" (26) could also represent "the Sacred." Based on these two definitions, in the following I will use the concept of cultural codes to mean a group's common and mutual agreement on preferred meanings. Cultural codes are socially constructed and hence open to change and new forms. This is particularly true for the cultural codes depicted in Rabinowich's *Spaltkopf*. As they travel with the protagonists, they change and are changed, thereby taking on new forms.

The cultural code of narratives from Russian (folk) tradition is mentioned at the outset of the text:

> WHEN MY MOTHER WAS PREGNANT WITH ME, SHE OFTEN sat at her vanity table, gazing into the mirror for a long time and imagining what her child would look like. Before her lay a book. "Russian Fairy Tales" was stamped on its worn cloth cover in gold lettering. Her hand, small and elegant, rested on an open page below the title "Mistress of the Copper Mountain." There are many stories about her, and all of them open with a majestic flourish of a Cyrillic letter. (11)

In this way, the corpus of Russian fairy tales is mentioned as a point of reference, as a tradition (as something "Sacred"), one that links together the mother and the unborn protagonist. The most prominent aspects of this cultural code as introduced here are the figures taken from Russian mythology, that is, the Mistress of the Copper Mountain and Baba Yaga.

Baba Yaga is mentioned in the text several times. At the beginning, she is defined in a traditional manner: "Baba Yaga, who wades through the swamp in her little hut on chicken legs. Sometimes she helps those who seek her advice because they have no other choice; sometimes she devours them, depending on her mood" (22). Later in the text, though, the concept of Baba Yaga is transformed: she too experiences migration and must be transferred to new conditions. Mischka describes the proprietress of an Austrian bed-and-breakfast as a Baba Yaga: the old and nearly blind woman who is able to predict the weather is called "Austrian Baba Yaga" (125). To give another example, by the end of the novel, Mischka herself has become something of a Baba Yaga. First, her boyfriend starts to call her "Baba Yaga Girl" (131, 140), and later her relatives in Saint Petersburg compare her not only to her grandmother but also to Baba Yaga: "Like Baba Mascha, like Baba Yaga" (198). Thus, through migration, Baba Yaga has been transformed: she has been detached from her original denomination as a mythical figure and has even become part of the identity of an elderly lady in the Austrian countryside and of a young woman in Vienna. Nevertheless, Baba Yaga has retained some of her original connotations despite this migration.

Russian literature is another cultural code, one that is strongly present in the novel. Although it too travels with the protagonists, it is not transformed as greatly as the concept of Baba Yaga. Literature and fairy tales are both important elements of Mischka's childhood. Her grandmother teaches her both, and consequently they play with the various plots and stories: "We play everything she has taught me: Russian fairy tales and classic literature, absurdly blended together and adapted by me into a predictable division of roles. I am the squirrel; she is Hercules. I am Margarita, the Master's lover; she is the big bad wolf" (43).

The cultural code of Russian literature, like that of Baba Yaga, is primarily a female one. The women of the family – the grandmother, the mother, Mischka – occupy themselves with literature. It is a tradition that is handed down by the female members of the family and is dominated by female characters: for instance, Margarita (from Mikhail Bulgakov's *The Master and Margarita*), and Penelope. However, a mixing or hybridization of this cultural code with new elements in migration is only partly possible. While Mischka's grandmother continues to read Russian literature, Mischka is attracted to comic books and tends to ignore Dostoyevsky and the adult family members' distain for Mickey Mouse. In this way, the cultural code of literature becomes an identity-forming element in migration, one that is expressed differently by the different generations. To the adults, it is a link to the homeland they left behind. To Mischka, it is something from which she wishes distance, looking instead for alternatives.

Jewishness is another cultural code in Rabinowich's novel and is present on two levels of the text. At the level of the narrative, Mischka must come to terms with the fact that her (non-religious) family is Jewish:

> "Who are Jews, actually?" I ask, as I stroke the coloured pencils arranged by shade so that they form a moving rainbow under my fingertips. "I think I saw some on TV once. They have a very funny way of singing and dancing and slanted eyes like this, right?"
>
> My mother puts the paintbrush away and sits up straight.
>
> "No, honey," she says firmly. "The Jews, that's us." (59)

To Mischka, this means that her best friend Shenya is not allowed to play with her any longer. On the historical level, Jewishness is discussed in the context of anti-Semitism in Russia. Jews are widely perceived as the scapegoats for all the country's ills, and Mischka's family has escaped the consequences of this by emigrating. After experiencing violent anti-Semitism during her childhood (she watched her father being killed during the war), the grandmother rejected her own Jewishness. She has changed her name from Rahel to Ada and started wearing a golden cross around her neck in order to hide her "flaw" (178). This story of rejected Jewishness serves as a counterpoint to Mischka's paternal family, whose members speak Yiddish in the home. This cultural code loses its significance once the family has left Russia, and later it is hardly ever mentioned. It does not undergo any transformation in migration.

The motif of travel is closely linked to the protagonist's search for an identity. Mischka finds herself on an endless journey and in the end accepts this way of being as her sole viable course: an ever-changing identity becomes the only possible identity for her. Furthermore, the migration depicted in the novel brings about cultural transfer; cultural codes such as traditional narratives, Russian literature, and Jewish elements are transferred from Russia to the family's new homeland. The family depicted in Vladimir Vertlib's *Zwischenstationen* also experiences a migration from Russia to Austria. There, they end up in a house that, owing to its Russian-Jewish inhabitants, becomes a transcultural space in Vienna.

A Russian Castle in Vienna – Vladimir Vertlib's *Zwischenstationen*

Vladimir Vertlib was born in 1966 in Leningrad and left Russia in 1971 with his parents. Vertlib's Jewish family, like Rabinowich's, chose to escape the oppressive anti-Semitic atmosphere in the Soviet Union. Seeking a new homeland, the family travelled to Europe (Austria, Italy, the Netherlands), then Israel, then the United States, and eventually back to Europe, where they settled in Vienna. Vertlib studied economics in Vienna before publishing his first novel, *Abschiebung* (Deportation), in 1995. Vertlib's second novel, *Zwischenstationen*, draws on personal experience in its depiction of the emigration of a Russian-Jewish family. The first-person narrator is the family's young (and only) son, who recounts the family's various "interstations" and his own quest for identity as his circumstances change.

For a long time the image of Vienna has been shaped by its immigrants, who at some point themselves become Viennese, only to view the next generation of immigrants with suspicion. This has been depicted in literary texts, especially those that explicitly address the topic of migration, such as Vertlib's *Zwischenstationen* and Rabinovici's novel *Ohnehin* (discussed below). In Vertlib's book, Vienna is depicted through the eyes of Russian-Jewish immigrants, or to be more precise, through the eyes of the first-person narrator, who at the time is still a child. By choosing the perspective of immigrants, Vertlib is able to narrate a different version of Vienna than the one commonly offered to visitors. Rather than being "Austrian" in a homogeneous, monocultural way, Vertlib's Vienna is a realm of transcultural intersections. As in Rabinowich's *Spaltkopf*, the cultural codes the immigrants bring with them both transform the context and are transformed by it.

Vertlib illustrates this transformation through his depiction of a house in Vienna's 20th district, where the family lives during their first stay in the city. That house strongly characterizes Vertlib's Vienna. When the family arrives in Vienna for the first time, they find shelter in the "Russian castle" (30), which has been pointed out to them by other Jewish emigrants from the Soviet Union. The building's name refers to its function as an "old tenement where almost solely Russian Jews" (30) live. The first-person narrator describes the house in more detail:

> The house belonged to Mister Liebfeld, who was the owner of a prospering fashion store in the city centre. Mister Liebfeld came from Kielce and left Poland for Austria shortly after the war because of the anti-Semitic riots. Now he rented out all the free apartments of his apartment building to Russian Jews. [...]
>
> [I] hardly ever left the building and nearly believed that the funny outside world of this foreign country did not exist, that it was only a myth or a fairy tale. I sometimes thought I was in Israel, then again in Russia until I finally understood that both were true. The building was part of Israel and Russia and it was located in a foreign world called Vienna. No doubt: the world was constructed like a number of boxes, which fitted into each other. (31)

Here, Vertlib opens up a cultural microcosm, the description of which begins with a brief account of the landlord's life: he is a Jewish Pole who fled to Austria and now rents out apartments to Russian Jews. Like his tenants, Mister Liebfeld is someone for whom historical events have led to migration and transcultural intersections. He is also typical of Vertlib's protagonists, in that he is characterized by different identity-shaping attributes, such as "Pole," "Jew," "refugee," and "owner of an apartment building (who rents out to Russian Jews)." In this way, he serves Vertlib's narration of transcultural collective memory, for in his person are to be found cultural and historical intersections of the twentieth century. These intersections, although still characterized by national attributes (Poland, Austria, Russia), remind us that (cultural) identities cannot be restricted to national realms, but instead must be seen through a wider perspective, which could be that of Central Europe.

In this passage, the various cultural entities (Russia, Israel, Vienna) are still neatly separated. Later in the text, however, the situation in the apartment building becomes the source of transcultural mixing, of hybridization, and this allows for the creation of something new. This happens for instance when the twins Chaim and Jankel, "the Kahanovics' children, an ultra-orthodox couple" (42), come to play with the main protagonist:

> To Chaim and Jankel, our house was like a mysterious island. The courtyard was an adventurous jungle, the corridors were streets on which one could experience heroic deeds, engage in battle, or play hide and seek. Chaim and Jankel spoke German, Hebrew, and Yiddish; soon they also knew some words in Russian. Words, which our parents had better not hear. (43)

The narrator also tells how the twins taught him basic German (42). Thus the various languages are mixed in the building; the inhabitants and visitors all learn from one another. In this passage the building itself once more becomes a special realm. It is called an "island," and the courtyard becomes a "jungle," the corridors "streets": the Russian castle becomes a landscape all its own.

In a number of ways, the apartment building resembles a heterotopia, which is Michel Foucault's term for an alternative space that represents a utopia. First, to the first-person narrator the Russian castle is a "localised utopia" (Foucault 10). This is Foucault's term for the counterspaces children discover when playing. According to him, such places are typical heterotopias; as examples, he offers the garden, the attic, or a tent in an attic. Second, the Russian castle becomes for its inhabitants a "real place beyond all places" (Foucault 11), which is another typical feature of heterotopias. Several incompatible places and temporal moments are brought together in this building: Israel and Russia, the past (the Second World War) and the present (Vienna). This simultaneity, and cultural and temporal heterogeneity, eventually positions the building "beyond all other places." The Russian castle has yet another quality that defines heterotopias: they may be connected to temporal ruptures. For Vertlib's protagonist, this rupture has been caused by emigration from the Soviet Union and then the return from Israel. Also, the building itself is marked by the temporal rupture caused by the various incompatible places and temporal moments mentioned above, such as the Second World War and the present. Finally – and again, this is another feature of Foucault's heterotopias – the Russian castle seems to be an open space. However, in its entirety (including the concurrent and contradicting spaces as well as the temporal layers), it reveals itself only to its inhabitants and the narrator.

In the novel there is another site that serves to describe an alternative version of Vienna. It is the building of the insurance company, where the narrator's mother works as a cleaner. As happens so often with immigrants, her degrees in physics and mathematics are initially not recognized in Austria, so as a "foreigner" she is forced to work as a cleaner. Like the Russian castle, the building that houses the insurance company is depicted as a microcosm, this time of Austria. This is revealed in a humorous episode: in her former job with a small producer of traditional loden clothes, the narrator's mother was taught to greet all with the words "Grüß Gott," the typical Austrian greeting, literally a greeting to God. However, the insurance company is politically on the left. The traditional greeting with religious connotations is therefore inappropriate, and "Guten Tag" (good morning) or "Grüssi" (Hello) are more appropriate (*Zwischenstationen* 69–70). The social hierarchy that the narrator's family has already experienced in Vienna is also obvious in the insurance company. This holds true both for the mother's colleagues (two female immigrants from the former Yugoslavia), who are dominated by the (Austrian) head cleaner and for the people working at the insurance company. Their offices have been assigned in order of importance, with the general director's office on the top floor. The floors are connected by a paternoster elevator, in which the narrator (who often has to accompany his mother for lack of child care possibilities) prefers to spend his time. However, he is afraid of the paternoster, about which he has heard various stories. In the elevator, there are ambiguous warnings: passengers are told to leave the cabin on the top floor and the bottom, but the same warning states that staying on presents no risks. Still, the narrator prefers the liminal space of the paternoster, which enables him to go up and down as he pleases. By going past the various floors, he positions himself outside the building's hierarchy. At the same time, he has discovered a space for himself in the big and impersonal building of the insurance company.

In the Russian castle, daily life happens in a similar liminal space, mainly in the corridors. This is where the toilets and the wash basins are, and it is the part of the house where the children are allowed to play. Homi Bhabha, in his commentary on Renée Green's architectural installation *Sites of Geneaology* at the Institute of Contemporary Art in New York, describes the staircase as a "liminal space, in-between the designations of identity" (5). The staircase with its "hither and thither […] prevents identities at either end of it from settling into primordial polarities" (5). In *Zwischenstationen*, the staircase and the paternoster elevator are spaces where the narrator is not exposed to fixed identities imposed on him by others. Possibly, this enables him to create his own hybrid cultural identity. The staircase and the elevator in this way open up "the possibility of a cultural hybridity that entertains difference without an assumed or imposed hierarchy" (Bhabha 5).

In Vertlib's novel, the Russian castle and the insurance company building serve as examples of transcultural spaces in the city. Doron Rabinovici, in his novel *Ohnehin*, also describes a transcultural space in Vienna. However, he falls back on the more prominent location that is the Naschmarkt.

A Transcultural Vienna in Doron Rabinovici's *Ohnehin*

Doron Rabinovici was born in Tel Aviv in 1961. He came to Austria at the age of three with his parents. In 1994 he published his first literary work, a volume of short stories titled *Papirnik*. *Ohnehin* (2004) is his second novel after *Suche nach M.* (Search for M, 1997). His most recent book, *Andernorts* (Elsewhere), was published in 2010. Rabinovici's works often discuss Jewishness and address questions about Israel and modern Jewish identity, especially in Austria. In *Ohnehin* he links these issues with questions about modern-day immigration and the lives of immigrants in Austria, specifically in Vienna.

The main protagonist in *Ohnehin* is a medical doctor named Stefan Sandtner, who privately treats a friend's father, who suffers from Korsakoff syndrome, a form of amnesia. The patient loses his grip on the present and begins to relive the events of the Second World War, during which he was a member of the SS. At the same time, Sandtner gets to know Flora Dema, a young filmmaker from the "former Yugoslavia" who is in Austria supposedly on illegal terms. In this way, the novel mixes Austria's Nazi past with the public as well as private discourse on how to deal with memory and history in today's "multicultural" Vienna. In particular, the Naschmarkt is described as a site in the city where transculturality is negotiated.

The novel is striking for its international repertoire of characters. As Matthias Beilein has noted, "in no other text of contemporary literature [does one encounter] an Austria as cosmopolitan and polyglot as [...] Stefan Sandtner's circle of friends and relatives" ("Auf diesem" 95). The novel's characters include Lew Feininger, a Russian Jew whose parents emigrated first to Tel Aviv and then to Vienna; Patrique Mutabo, the son of a Congolese diplomat; the aforementioned filmmaker Flora Dema and her friend Goran, a Serbian deserter; and Paul Guttmann, who comes from the Bukovina and who survived the Shoah and remained in Vienna after the war. Many of these figures are presented as "Austrians" in the text. Rabinovici thus undermines traditional ideas about "what a genuine Austrian should look like" (*Ohnehin* 157) and instead presents a more realistic image of the city and its inhabitants.

The Naschmarkt, Vienna's biggest market, is a central site in the novel.[5] Indeed, the cover of the book's first edition shows a photograph of the empty market by night. The closed stalls along a neat, clean street depicted on the cover are in stark contrast to the text's descriptions of the lively, always crowded market. The Naschmarkt is described in detail in the very first pages of the novel. A topographical description locates the market for the reader as Sandtner walks from his home in Heumühlgasse towards the Rechte Wienzeile to the market (16). This is followed by a detailed description of the market's general atmosphere and of its architecture: "stalls and pavilions that were painted in moss green and covered with roofs in faint yellow" (16) are mentioned, as well as the fact that these stalls form two streets. The narrator describes in detail how the "fruit, plants, herbs, cheese and bread" (16) are arranged like an arena "made out of wooden boxes, cardboard racks and plastic cupboards" (16). All of this is covered by canvas awnings swelling in the wind (16). After this first description of the market, the narrative outlines in greater detail the range of goods, the hustle and bustle of a Saturday morning, and the various stalls as Sandtner walks past them: "In the window of an oriental merchant he saw hundreds of small bags with spices in them, each of them with a small note with its characteristics and usage. He passed Japanese sushi stalls, Chinese delis, a Moroccan restaurant, as well as an Indian, Persian, and Turkish one, an Espresso bar and an Italian pizzeria" (16–17). The description goes on to name a Viennese pub and a sausage stand as well as several typical market characters.

Referring to Marc Augé, Beilein analyses the Naschmarkt in Rabinovici's novel as a transitory non-place as well as a global village ("Auf diesem" 95). The market's character is expressed by the goods on offer and by the people who work there, but also by its customers (Stefan Sandtner regularly meets his polyglot circle of friends in bars at the market). In this way, the market undermines traditional images of a "typical Austrian" identity. At the same time, the author's references to the market's ethnic and social diversity bring to mind Émile Zola's novel *Le Ventre de Paris* (The Belly of Paris). Indeed, Rabinovici's depiction of the Naschmarkt contains echoes of Zola's depiction of Les Halles in Paris; in both works, descriptions of the goods on offer play a central role (although at no time in Rabinovici's novel are they as detailed as in Zola's text, which is famous, for example, for its description of a cheese stall and the aromas rising from it). These intertextual references to Zola establish a link between the East (as exemplified by the Naschmarkt, but also by Vienna and the further realm that is opened up in the descriptions of the Naschmarkt) and the West (Paris). Thus, Rabinovici's text alludes to a wider European space characterized by links across time (Zola's nineteenth-century Les Halles and the Naschmarkt at the end of the twentieth century). In fact, Rabinovici's text includes a detailed history of the Naschmarkt. Its history – it "already existed before enlightened absolutism" (176) – is described in detail, starting with an explanation for its name and concluding with the remark that the market has become a civic landmark and a popular tourist attraction (176). Its international character is both evident today and reflected in its history: "For centuries, in this area not only German, but also Italian, Yiddish, Greek, Turkish, Czech, Serbian and Polish has been spoken. But it would be too simple to draw an idyllic picture of colourful diversity and merry harmony" (178).

Here, the narrator alludes to Vienna's multilingual past as the capital of the Austro-Hungarian Monarchy and thus to its role as a former centre of Central Europe. However, the narrator rejects the notion that different cultures coexisted peacefully in the market, in the past *or* the present. Beilein states accordingly that it would be "wrong to read the market as the multicultural vision of an unproblematic *different* Austria" ("Auf diesem" 96, italics in original). In fact, in the novel, the market as a site of transcultural mixing is troubled more often than not. An example is the description of Şirin and Theo: this young couple's inter-/transcultural relationship causes problems for them – her family is Turkish, his is Greek-Cypriot. Theo calls the market his real home, but when he is not at his family's stall, he finds himself confronted with opposition that makes it difficult for him to form his own identity. In this way, Rabinovici discusses the gap between Vienna's multicultural panorama on the one hand, and the stereotyping, when not outright hostile, reactions towards others or different ways of living and different identities on the other. He uses the Naschmarkt to illustrate the city's cultural diversity, well aware of the importance of contributing to the ongoing debate about Austrian identity. His text in this way becomes a space for reflecting on current political and social debates.

The Writing of a Central European Collective Memory in Vertlib's "Mein erster Mörder" (2006)

Unlike Rabinovici in *Ohnehin*, Vladimir Vertlib in his story "Mein erster Mörder" (My First Murder) takes his readers into the past. In this text, Vertlib shows how history and memory cannot be told or recounted from a national perspective; they always reveal themselves as more complex, both spatially/geographically and temporally. In this text, as in other writings, he deals with the traumatic events of the Third Reich and, in particular, with the anti-Semitism that lingered after the war. Like Rabinovici, he examines historic events with reference to later points in time. In contrast to his other works, in this short story Vertlib's protagonist is not himself a Jew, but rather a child of the perpetrators. This enables the author to discuss aspects of the past as well as the present from a different point of view than in other works and to address issues that concern the culprits.

The collection *Mein erster Mörder* is Vertlib's fourth book. In a short introduction to the three short stories, the author notes that they are based on actual events but that many of the details he provides are fictitious. "Mein erster Mörder" focuses on a historic event that has never been a prominent topic in Austrian literature or in historical research: the death marches of those Hungarian Jews who in the spring of 1945 were forced to journey on foot from the Austrian–Hungarian border to the Mauthausen concentration camp in northern Austria.[6] In the story, those death marches are linked to the flight of Hungarian refugees eleven years later after the failed Hungarian Uprising of 1956. The narrative is especially interested in the racism the refugees experienced and in linking this to the (still latent) anti-Semitism in Austria at the time. By referring to Hungary and Austria and by underlining those countries' ongoing common history, the story advocates for a Central European collective memory rather than a national one.

The first-person narrator is a young Austrian, Leopold Ableitinger, who grew up in Vienna in the 1940s and 1950s. As was the case in *Zwischenstationen*, the fact that the narrator is an adolescent enables Vertlib to relate the events from close up, with great immediacy, and without evaluation (indeed, he depicts them in a naive manner at times). In this way, the atmosphere of Austria during the postwar period appears authentic and the opinions of the time are related without comment. The ruins of postwar Vienna are part of that atmosphere; so is the racism of the time – both against the Russians as one of the Allied forces in the city and against the Hungarians who arrived in 1956; and so is anti-Semitism. Despite this critical discussion of Austria and its history, Vertlib has chosen a "Leopold" as a protagonist; the shared saint of Austria and Vienna thus links the issues presented to the country's past and present, but also to its future. "Leopold," however, is also reminiscent of the "Leopoldstadt," Vienna's second district and the former "Mazzesinsel," the district where the majority of the Viennese Jews lived until the time of the Nazi regime. The protagonist's name is thus ambiguous: on the one hand, it can be read as a patriotic choice; on the other, it refers to Austria's Jewish population, and Vienna's in particular, and thus subtly (albeit clearly) emphasizes the country's transculturality.

The anti-Semitism still present in Austria eleven years after the war is illustrated by several statements Leopold hears on the streets. When in a scene in a park a bystander states that the Russians did not occupy Austria but instead liberated it from the Nazis, he is insulted and called a Jew (a word intended also as an insult). He adds that he was imprisoned in a concentration camp as a social democratic member of the resistance. The others laugh at him and call the concentration camps an invention of the Allies. Eventually, the man is beaten; a policeman among the bystanders does not help him. In another scene, pedestrians say that the Jews were only greedy and that they will come back and ask for their apartments and their fortunes to be returned. People do not talk about the Jews' displacement and the genocide, but only about their supposedly voluntary emigration. That they were forced from their homes fails to enter this particular equation. Rather than empathy, people express jealousy towards those who sought "a better life" in America; implicit is the sense that they had escaped the suffering faced by those who had not been so fortunate.

Besides all of this, Vertlib depicts anti-Semitism in more individual ways. Leopold's aunt, for instance, hates Jews, believing them to be responsible for the emperor's death (i.e., for the death of Charles I of Austria in 1922). The Holocaust, in her view, was a "rightful punishment" (39) for the Jews. She once tells her nephew Leopold, who is trying to learn about his father's past as a member of the *Volkssturm* (a people's militia founded during the last months of the Second World War): "So what? It was only Jews who were killed" (61).

In addition to this open anti-Semitism, Vertlib describes the unease the second generation feels when talking about Jews. The Nazi regime and its anti-Semitism, the lack of discussion about what had happened, and the forced silence together have caused an uneasiness that has affected people in a peculiar way: talking about the war from the perspective of the complicit is not the problem so much as talking about the *victims* of the war. Indeed, it seems that talking about Jews, and about Jewish life in Vienna, has been prohibited. Saying the word "Jew" seems to be impossible without any negative implications.[7]

The descriptions of anti-Semitic expressions in the text are closely linked to racist attitudes towards Hungarian immigrants in and after 1956. Leopold's father expresses his disgust for Hungarians, whom he calls a "dirty people" (24). By describing the negative reactions towards the Hungarian refugees, Vertlib deconstructs the myth of Austria's unconditional readiness to help its neighbours at the time. He narrates a certain continuum from the end of the Second World War, from anti-Semitic feelings to racist comments. On the more concrete level of the story, Vertlib uses the events of the mid-1950s as a trigger for a flashback to the end of the Second World War and the death marches of Hungarian Jews from the border to Mauthausen, in which Leopold's father was involved as a member of the *Volkssturm*. At one point the SS soldiers desert the prisoners. Fearing the approach of the Allied forces, the members of the *Volkssturm* decide to lock the few prisoners who are still alive in a shed, then set it on fire.[8] In his text, Vertlib shows why it is still difficult for historians to study the death marches. When Leopold tries to learn more about the events from his father, the latter denies any guilt, asserting that he was only patrolling and that although he would sometimes shout at the prisoners, he did not shoot them or help set fire to the shed. At the same time, he urges his son not to talk to anybody about the incident, and in the end he asks his son to forget about it and to act as though it had never happened. Like many others, Leopold's father prefers to keep silent about what occurred. Not only the father's generation but also Leopold's own should try to forget what had been a "bad time" (75) for everyone. Alois, the father, in this way positions himself as a victim. He himself had no other option, he had to participate, he was only carrying out orders, and so he is not responsible for his deeds (which in the end were not his own, but those of a soldier).

Vertlib's "Mein erster Mörder" negotiates the ambiguousness of historical events. It suggests that instead of writing "Austrian" history, we read history in a wider context. In this regard, his example of the death marches of Hungarian Jews in 1945 suggests a Central European context, one that offers an alternative to "national history" – that is, a transnational one. Vertlib's text thereby forms part of collective memory that can be characterized as Central European. Using anti-Semitism as a principal focus, Vertlib traces historical events and thereby shows the continuity of attitudes and mentalities. In this way, Central Europe and Jewishness are bundled together in this text.

Résumé

The analyses of texts by Doron Rabinovici, Julya Rabinowich, and Vladimir Vertlib in this chapter have different foci. Vertlib's *Zwischenstationen* and Rabinovici's *Ohnehin* describe various transcultural spaces in Vienna. Rabinowich's *Spaltkopf* presents a fluid concept of identity and is characterized by a number of transfers of cultural codes. Vertlib's "Mein erster Mörder" negotiates the ambiguousness of historical events and reads them in a Central European context.

All of the works discuss transculturality. Although mostly set in Austria, they are all strongly linked to other places and open up spaces that can be described as European or even Central European rather than national. By opening up such spaces, they generate and express the idea of a transcultural Europe characterized by migration, exchange, and cultural transfer. By referring to Vienna and describing (places in) Vienna as transcultural (a notion also present in Dimitré Dinev's texts), the texts emphasize the connections between the local and the global and show how each is constantly reflected in the other. Jewishness, present in all four texts, is a strong part of such a Central European identity. It is sometimes the trigger for migration, and it is an important element of the protagonists' search for identity. In the texts discussed, a transcultural Vienna as part of Central Europe is characterized by Jewish elements and its Jewish life, both past and present. An analysis that tries to link issues of transculturality, migration, cultural transfer, and Jewishness, and that reads these aspects against the background of the narratives' location, which is Central Europe, reveals their interdependencies.

NOTES

1 On Rabinovici, see Beilein, "Auf diesem"; Beilein, "86"; Beilein, "Unter"; Lorenz, "Verbrecher"; Silverman. On Vertlib, see for instance Hahn; Gilman; Grabovszki; Lorenz, "Individuum"; Lorenz, "Vladimir"; Molnár; Reiter; Taberner; on Rabinowich, see Vlasta.
2 See also Michael Boehringer's contribution in this volume and his discussion of the categorization of works by authors with a migration background.
3 In the Soviet Union, especially after Israel's victory in the Six-Day War of 1967, there was widespread discrimination against the Jews. This fact led to a major emigration wave of Soviet Jews in the late 1960s and the 1970s, who mainly went to Israel or applied for refugee visas to the United States.
4 All translations into English by S.V. unless otherwise indicated.
5 With regard to the Naschmarkt, see also an interview with Robert Menasse, Doron Rabinovici, and Robert Schindel, where they agree that the market is the only urban part of the otherwise un-urban city of Vienna (Beilein, *86*, 321–2).
6 Interestingly, Rabinovici's *Ohnehin* is another literary text in which these death marches are mentioned, albeit only briefly (92).
7 This is reminiscent of a comment in Rabinovici's *Ohnehin*, where the narrator briefly mentions that in Austria one bashfully speaks of Mosaic religion rather than Jewishness (95).
8 Many of the details that are told in the short story about the death march (such as the fact that those who could not walk anymore were shot) can also be found in historical reports on the death marches. In Isenschnibbe in Saxony-Anhalt, an incident similar to the one described in Vertlib's text took place: there, about 1,200 concentration camp prisoners on a death march were burnt alive in a shed. It seems that Vertlib used information from several different incidents and put them together to tell about the death march in which Alois participated.

WORKS CITED

Barthes, Roland. *S/Z*. Frankfurt am Main: Suhrkamp, 1987. Print.

Beilein, Matthias. "Auf diesem Markt ist Österreich. Doron Rabinovicis *Ohnehin*." In *National Identities and European Literatures. Nationale Identitäten und europäische Literaturen*. Ed. J. Manuel Barbeito et al. Bern: Peter Lang, 2008. 93–104. Print.

– *86 und die Folgen. Robert Schindel, Robert Menasse und Doron Rabinovici im literarischen Feld Österreichs*. Berlin: Erich Schmidt, 2008. Print.

– "Unter falschem Namen: Schweigen und Schuld in Doron Rabinovicis *Suche nach M*." *Monatshefte für Deutschsprachige Literatur und Kultur* 97.2 (2005): 250–69. Print.

Bhabha, Homi. *The Location of Culture*. London: Routledge, 2006. Print.

Eisenstadt, Shmuel, and Bernhard Giesen. "The Construction of Collective Identity." *European Journal of Sociology* 36.1 (1995): 72–102. Print.

Foucault, Michel. *Die Heterotopien. Der utopische Körper. Zwei Radiovorträge*. Frankfurt am Main: Suhrkamp, 2013. Print.

Gilman, Sander L. "Becoming a Jew by Becoming a German: The Newest Jewish Writing from the 'East.'" *Shofar: An Interdisciplinary Journal of Jewish Studies* 25.1 (2006): 16–32. Print.

Grabovszki, Ernst. "Österreich als literarischer Erfahrungsraum zugewanderter Autorinnen und Autoren." In *Von der nationalen zur internationalen Literatur. Transkulturelle deutschsprachige Literatur und Kultur im Zeitalter globaler Migration*. Ed. Helmut Schmitz. Amsterdam: Rodopi, 2009. 275–92. Print.

Hahn, Hans-Joachim. "'Europa' als neuer 'jüdischer Raum' – Diana Pintos Thesen und Vladimir Vertlibs Romane." In *Von der nationalen zur internationalen Literatur. Transkulturelle deutschsprachige Literatur und Kultur im Zeitalter globaler Migration*. Ed. Helmut Schmitz. Amsterdam: Rodopi, 2009. 295–310. Print.

Kecht, Maria-Regina. "Multikulturelles Wien. Entweder-und-oder-Existenzen in der neuen österreichischen Literatur." In *Zeitenwende. Österreichische Literatur seit dem Millennium: 2000–2010*. Ed. Michael Boehringer and Susanne Hochreiter. Vienna: Praesens, 2011. 119–38. Print.

Lorenz, Dagmar C.G. "A Human Being or a Good Jew? Individualism in Vladimir Vertlib's Novel *Letzter Wunsch*." In *Beyond Political Correctness: Remapping German Sensibilities in the 21st Century*. Ed. Christine Anton and Frank Pilipp. Amsterdam: Rodopi, 2010. 109–33. Print.

– "Individuum und Individualität in den Werken zeitgenössischer jüdischer AutorInnen in Österreich." In *Zeitenwende. Österreichische Literatur seit dem*

Millennium: 2000–2010. Ed. Michael Boehringer and Susanne Hochreiter. Vienna: Praesens, 2011. 389–409. Print.

– "Verbrecher sind wir uns selbst. Täter und Verbrechenssuche in der Fiktion jüdischer Autoren in Österreich: Robert Schindel und Doron Rabinovici." In *Akten des 10. Internationalen Germanistenkongresses Wien 2000. "Zeitenwende - Die Germanistik auf dem Weg vom 20. ins 21. Jahrhundert."* Eds. Peter Wiesinger and Hans Derkits. Vol. 7. Bern: Peter Lang, 2002. 269–72. Print.

– "Vladimir Vertlib, a Global Intellectual: Exile, Migration, and Individualism in the Narratives of a Russian Jewish Author in Austria." In *Beyond Vienna: Contemporary Literature from the Austrian Provinces*. Ed. Todd C. Hanlin. Riverside: Ariadne Press, 2008. 230–61. Studies in Austrian Literature, Culture, and Thought. Print.

Mitterbauer, Helga. "Mittler und Medien. Reflexion über zentrale Kategorien der Kulturtransferforschung." In *Zwischenräume. Kulturelle Transfers in deutschsprachigen Regionalperiodika des Habsburgerreichs (1850–1918)*. Ed. Matjaz Birk. Vienna: LIT-Verlag, 2009. 25–38. Print.

Molnár, Katrin. "'Die bessere Welt war immer anderswo.' Literarische Heimatkonstruktionen bei Jakob Hessing, Chaim Noll, Wladimir Kaminer und Vladimir Vertlib im Kontext von Alija, jüdischer Diaspora und säkularer Migration." In *Von der nationalen zur internationalen Literatur. Transkulturelle deutschsprachige Literatur und Kultur im Zeitalter globaler Migration*. Ed. Helmut Schmitz. Amsterdam and New York: Rodopi, 2009. 311–36. Print.

Müller-Funk, Wolfgang. *Kulturtheorie. Einführung in die Schlüsseltexte der Kulturwissenschaften*. Tübingen: Francke, 2006. Print.

Rabinovici, Doron. *Andernorts*. Frankfurt am Main: Suhrkamp, 2010. Print.

– *Ohnehin*. Frankfurt am Main: Suhrkamp, 2004. Print.

– *Papirnik. Stories*. Frankfurt am Main: Suhrkamp, 1994. Print.

– *Suche nach M*. Frankfurt am Main: Suhrkamp, 1997. Print.

Rabinowich, Julya. *Spaltkopf*. Vienna: edition exil, 2008. Print.

– *Splithead*. London: Portobello, 2011. Print.

Reiter, Andrea. "Narrating 'the Jew': The Autobiographical in Recent Novels of Jewish Writers in Austria." In *Zeitenwende. Österreichische Literatur seit dem Millennium: 2000–2010*. Ed. Michael Boehringer and Susanne Hochreiter. Vienna: Praesens, 2011. 410–29. Print.

Silverman, Lisa. "'Der richtige Riecher': The Reconfiguration of Jewish and Austrian Identities in the Work of Doron Rabinovici." *German Quarterly* 72.3 (1999): 252–64. Print.

Taberner, Stuart. "Vladimir Vertlib's *Das besondere Gedächtnis der Rosa Masur*: Performing Jewishness in the New Germany." In *Emerging German-Language*

Novelists of the Twenty-First Century. Ed. Lyn Marven and Stuart Taberner. Rochester: Camden House, 2011. 32–45. Print.
Vertlib, Vladimir. *Abschiebung*. Salzburg: Otto Müller, 1995. Print.
– *Mein erster Mörder. Lebensgeschichten*. Vienna: Deuticke, 2006. Print.
– *Zwischenstationen*. Vienna: Deuticke, 1999. Print.
Vlasta, Sandra. "'Abgebissen, nicht abgerissen' – Identitätsverhandlungen auf der Reise in Julya Rabinowichs Roman *Spaltkopf* (2008)." In *Wie viele Sprachen spricht die Literatur? Deutschsprachige Gegenwartsliteratur aus Mittel- und Osteuropa*. Ed. Renata Cornejo, Slawomir Piontek, Izabela Sellmer, and Sandra Vlasta. Vienna: Praesens, 2014. 207–18. Print.
Zola, Émile. *Le Ventre de Paris*. Paris: Gallimard, 2002. Print.

8 Cultures of Memory, Migration, and Masculinity: Dimitré Dinev's *Engelszungen*

MICHAEL BOEHRINGER

Introduction: National Homogeneity and Transnational Literature

It could be argued, and many have done so,[1] that establishing Austria as anything but a country of migrants can be counted among the most successful projects of the Second Republic. The Austrian myth of homogeneity was born out of the need to forge "Ostmark" into an Austrian nation-state and to marshal a specifically Austrian nationalism that was distinct from a pan-German identity. Claiming geographic and *völkisch* continuity on the basis of a document that first mentioned the region commonly known as "Ostarrîchi" in 996, the Second Austrian Republic celebrated its 950th anniversary in 1946(!), and in 1996, one thousand years of continuance from hallowed past to modern Austria (cf. Lamb-Faffelberger 290). Between 1945 and 1994, when Austria joined the European Union, Austrian literature and criticism played, sometimes unwittingly, a central role in this process of nation building, both by developing a specific Austrian literary genre of the *Anti-Heimat* novel (Müller-Funk, "Austrian Literature") and by focusing intensely on an Austrian literature that, as Günter Stocker notes, was preoccupied almost obsessively with Austria's National Socialist past in the aftermath of the Waldheim affair.[2] As Wolfgang Müller-Funk put it so bluntly, "without Austrian literature and culture no Austrian nation" ("Austrian Literature" 47).

With the dissolution of the Eastern Bloc beginning in 1989, Austria faced a sharply increased flow of migrants, most of them from Central and Southeastern Europe. By 2010, this influx – the largest in Austrian postwar history – had brought the number of Austrian "co-citizens with a migration background" (*Mitbürger mit Migrationshintergrund*) to almost 20 per cent of the total population.[3] Austrian society's relationship with the first and second generations of this immigrant population is by no means unproblematic; it acknowledges their right to be accepted but at the same time has established a conceptual division based on place of origin.

The uneasy tension in the phrase mentioned above[4] underscores the realization that after the Cold War, Austria could no longer maintain its treasured isolation. Furthermore, it could no longer uphold the ideological chimera of an ethnically homogenous Austrian nation, which had in fact always included Slovenian, Croatian, Hungarian, Czech, Roman, and Sinti minorities, all of whom had long ago bestowed a transcultural legacy on this imaginary *Insel der Seligen* (Island of the Blessed). By accident rather than by design, Austria found itself once more at the heart of Central Europe.[5] By the turn of the millennium the outdated ideal of an organic, coherent, and bounded Austrian nation, one with roots in a common geographic, historical, linguistic, and emotional centre, was coming under increasing stress. According to Helga Mitterbauer, that stress was a result of the stark contrast between an official *Volk*-ideology and an increasingly pluri-cultural reality (256).

This "new" reality of a pluri-cultural Austrian society – or better, the return to that reality – is being reflected and negotiated more and more strongly in recent literary production. Postwar Austrian literature played a pivotal role in the creation of the Austrian nation; today, literature has again taken the lead, by rising above national identifications and mapping a transcultural imaginary that, as Donald E. Pease notes, does not negate the past, but transcends it, fostering "a rethinking of the national in the light of newly invented spatial and temporal coordinates" (5). Some of the most imaginative approaches to weaving together the recent national past with present-day and historical transnational realities can be found in the works of "immigrant authors," also referred to as authors of "migration literature." Those authors include Magdalena Sadlon (1956–), Radek Knapp (1964–), Vladimir Vertlib (1966–), Dimitré Dinev (1968–), Julya Rabinowich (1970–), Michael Stavarič (1972–), and Anna Kim (1977–).[6] These authors provide a link between the modern Austrian literature that is written predominantly in German and the hybrid space that was Central Europe at the end of the nineteenth century; together (with Homi Bhabha) they constitute a disruptive force that counteracts homogeneous notions of national identities. Their texts explore issues of being-in-the-world in a globalized world and respond to queries that "locations, ethnicities, genders, race and sexuality make in the production of identities" (Jay 6). In the process, these transnational literary texts have reframed the notion of a national Austrian literature. And they do so in a multilingual and transcultural context, thus pointing to a transformation in Austrian literature that recalls, and connects to, the Central European literary tradition of the late Habsburg period (cf. Müller-Funk, "Austrian Literature" 51). In this chapter I examine the writings of perhaps the best-known of these authors, the Bulgarian-Austrian Dimitré Dinev, and in particular his breakout novel *Engelszungen* (Tongues of Angels, 2003),[7] in order to explore some of the continuities and disruptions in the literary transcultural exchange. My goal is to highlight the process of identity formation and the negotiation of subjectivity within a transcultural process that connects the protagonists' decentred postmodern existence to the multicultural past of Central Europe.[8] I will be focusing on three areas of inquiry, moving from more broadly conceived questions of national languages, literatures, and memory cultures towards an increasingly detailed engagement with the text in order to examine the intersections of migration and identity in the context of gender, ethnicity, and sexuality. Specifically, I will reflect on three areas of negotiation of meaning in which Dinev's texts engage.

First, I investigate the multiple vectors of cultural transfer that highlight the interconnectedness of Central Europe beyond the historical ruptures of war and empire. I maintain that Dinev's texts engage in issues of migration, displacement, and identity in order to contest national and originary myths of being. Transnational literary texts, such as *Engelszungen*, aim to open a memorial culture rooted in myths of national and linguistic homogeneity to an emerging transcultural imaginary that engages with a globalized world and features protagonists in pursuit of their own autonomy.[9] Second, I focus on the intersections among language, migration, and identity, arguing that Dinev links experiences of hybridity and performative identity formations with migration, and furthermore, that he shows them to be fundamental conditions of our being-in-the-world, resulting in an existential homelessness that stands in stark contrast to our desire for a "home." Third, I raise the question of gender and identity and reflect on migration as a gendered rather than a universal experience. Specifically, I examine the continuities and disruptions of male gender identity in the migration process. I submit that *Engelszungen* foregrounds the gendered nature of migration, showing how the failure of persistent patriarchal structures and the loss of male gender identity through the process of migration result in the emergence of a different mode of "being male." The result is a "new masculinity" that has been liberated from its traditional reliance on power, violence, and oppression as means to secure its own hegemonic status, and that instead relies on notions of femininity, motherhood, and *Heimat* that transcend both cultural specificity and the historical moment and reintroduce a dyadic, universalist conception of (gender) identity.

Linguistic Boundaries, Cultures of Memory, and Cultural Transfers

Dinev and his above-mentioned colleagues are "migrant writers," as Brigid Haines observes, "in the double sense that they have migrated and that they write of that experience" (136). They give voice to the complex subjectivities that exist at the margins of mainstream society, and they counter the degrading stereotypes of the ideology of a nationalist Austrian superiority; in this way they (re-)present dynamic, heterogeneous concepts of selfhood of the sort that Elisabeth Bronfen's metaphor of the "knotted subject" captures so well, concepts of selfhood that are both symptomatic and a consequence of a postmodern world characterized by mass migration and the global circulation of goods, signs, and services (Bronfen and Marius 8–9).

Considering the prominence achieved by these authors, it is difficult to disagree with Haines when she attests to an "Eastern turn" in twenty-first-century German-language literature. This trend is arguably even more pronounced in Austria, where in 2001 almost 46 per cent of immigrants originated in the successor states of the Habsburg Empire (Bundesregierung für Migration 21), a figure reflected in the prominence of Austrian authors with roots in Southeastern or Eastern European countries (cf. Haines 136). Their texts often reflect on the themes of migration, identity, and language and thus are commonly conflated with the author's personal experience. No matter how long immigrant authors have lived in Austria, the fact of their migration becomes an identity (Kecht 122) as well as the hallmark of their writing: "Where an author comes from, is more important than his language," Dinev comments with some frustration. "In that manner one can decide more easily. The question where one comes from is much easier to answer than the question who one is, or the question where one is going, let alone how well one can write" ("In der Fremde schreiben" 210).[10]

Yet viewing immigrant authors and their works primarily through the prism of personal experience can obscure the full range of topics and poetics that recent scholarship has begun to identify (cf. Vlasta, "Passage ins Paradies?"). For in these works, as Maria-Regina Kecht has argued, the experience of migration is embedded in the pan-European history of the twentieth century – a history that includes the two world wars, the Cold War, the fall of the Wall, the end of Communism, and Austria's entrance into the European Union (cf. Kecht 125). These authors raise questions about language and identity, they create alternative histories of their homelands and adopted lands, they challenge hegemonic concepts of national literatures, and they ultimately call into question all naturalized notions of self and nationhood (cf. Said xxii). In addition, and of central importance in the Austrian context, transnational literary texts by authors from Central and Southeastern Europe provide a link to the pluri-cultural legacy of the Habsburg Empire and thus point to a *longue durée* of history (Braudel) that transcends the postwar focus of pre-1994 Austrian literature on the ruptures and national history of the short twentieth century.

Dimitré Dinev was born in 1968 in the second-largest city in Bulgaria, Plovdiv. He attended the Berthold-Brecht Gymnasium near his hometown, where he studied German and began publishing both in Bulgarian and in Russian. Like a number of his protagonists, Dinev fled to Austria after the collapse of Communism. There, he worked in various odd jobs, studied philosophy and Russian philology, and soon began to write in the German language. In 2000 he won first prize in the contest *Schreiben zwischen den Kulturen*. In 2003 his novel *Engelszungen* appeared and became a bestseller in both Austria and Germany. In 2005 he was commissioned to write a play for the Burgtheater, and shortly after, to adapt one of his short stories, "Die Totenwache" ("The Wake"), as a play for the Volkstheater. In 2008 he reached the pinnacle of his career as an Austrian author (Vlasta, "Angekommen" 247): he was invited to join the Austrian chancellor in his loge for the highlight of the social season, the Vienna Opera Ball; and the Salzburger Festspiele, one of the world's most prestigious theatre festivals, commissioned from him an adaptation of Dostoyevsky's *Crime and Punishment* (Vlasta, "Angekommen" 248). Dinev has made the transition from the margins of the literary marketplace to a position of social and cultural prominence.[11] Today, as Michaela Bürger-Koftis correctly notes, Dinev is part of the Austrian literary elite (146).[12]

What reads as an easy and almost meteoric rise to the top, was – from the author's own perspective – a long and arduous struggle that called into question his very sense of self. In his short essay "In der Fremde schreiben" ("Writing Away from Home," 2006), Dinev writes: "To write away from home, frequently means to write in the absence of family, of relatives, of friends, without a home, without support, without papers, without registration, without a work permit and without a residence permit. It means to write even when you don't have any confirmation of your existence" (210).[13] Here, Dinev is addressing some of the very same points that his fictional characters struggle with – namely, the lack of interpersonal and official markers that produce, in a Foucauldian sense, the very existence of which they speak.

Without a doubt, the turning point in Dinev's journey was the success of *Engelszungen* (cf. Vlasta, "Angekommen" 244). Over almost six hundred pages, that novel interweaves Bulgaria's twentieth-century history with the stories of the families of the two protagonists, Iskren Mladenov and Svetljo Apostolov. Despite its heft and its focus on a Balkan country that was largely unknown to its readers, this intergenerational family novel was well-received by the German-language press and became a bestseller. Expressions such as "Sprachkünstler" ("linguistic artist"), "Einfühlungskünstler" ("artist of empathy"), "Produkt eines gelungenen Kulturtransfers" ("product of a successful cultural transfer"),[14] "leidenschaftlicher Erzähler" ("a passionate storyteller," "Ganove aus Versehen" 6) suggest the hyperbolic tone of most of the reviews. Most reviewers focused on three aspects of the novel (cf., Vlasta, "Passage ins Paradies?" 107–8): how Dinev intertwines his personal experiences and those of his protagonists; his mastery of German as his literary language; and his talent as storyteller – a talent that Martin Hielscher and others trace back to Eastern European oral traditions, which Dinev successfully transferred to German-language literature (Hielscher 205, see also Schweiger "Entgrenzungen," and Vlasta "Passage ins Paradies?" 108).

As Sandra Vlasta notes, these areas of emphasis point back to the author himself as well as to his personal experiences and must be viewed in connection with the literary marketplace: the exotic among us sells, especially if author and the work are linked biographically, as is clearly the case with regard to Dinev's own experiences as a migrant in Austria ("Passage ins Paradies?"). However, the highlighting of Dinev's mastery of the German language and of his use of "foreign" oral traditions of storytelling reminds us of the difficulty that national literatures and their gatekeepers face when coming to terms with transnational literary themes. According to Yasemin Yildiz, "the challenge that this literature poses to conceptions dominated by the monolingual paradigm" is rooted in the fact that "existing categorizations are inadequate for literatures where the language(s) of the author, his or her ethnicity and residence as well as the content and the language(s) of the text no longer fit the monolingual equation of language, ethnicity, and culture" (19–20). In other words, the pervasive presence of multilingual and transcultural contexts in the works of immigrant authors challenges the "very assertion of the unalterable monolingual core of the subject" (Yildiz 16) and, as such, language as the basis of a national literature.

Wolfgang Müller-Funk, too, argues that especially in the Austrian context, "the play of cultural differences" can no longer be based "exclusively on language, on its written and oral use, as was characteristic for understanding culture in the footsteps of Herder" ("Austrian Literature" 51). Rather, a "history of Central European literature" can be traced from the *fin de siècle* to today's multilingual authors writing in Austria, authors who represent "literary actors of a common heterogeneous symbolic space, in which [...] translation is obligatory" ("Austrian Literature" 51). No longer can the German language be posited as the "property of socially sanctioned, ethnically German [or Austrian] subjects" (Yildiz 17); it has become detached from essentialist notions of origin, ethnicity, and nationality, a tool for the creation of post-national narratives.

One example of such a decoupling of language and subjectivity that contributes to a transnational imaginary can be found in Dinev's short story "Spas schläft" ("Spas Is Sleeping"), in which the protagonists Spas and Ilija encounter refugees and migrants from all over the world in an abandoned train in Vienna (108). Regardless of their country of origin or their native language, the occupants of the train share the same concerns: finding work, avoiding police attention, securing a visa, staying ahead of the ever-changing law. The migrants lead a shadow existence that relegates them to the very fringes of society. Success means giving up a child for adoption so that it can stay in Austria, while the father is deported (113). The individual struggles of Dinev's migrants in the face of a society hostile to "otherness" undermine ethnic and linguistic cohesion. In Dinev's texts, the subjecthood of speakers of distinct "mother tongues" is determined not by their language, ethnicity, or culture but by their everyday experiences and their personal struggles for survival. The multilingual and transcultural Vienna of Dinev's migrants effectively shatters any notion of linguistic, ethnic, or national homogeneity, highlighting, as Vlasta notes elsewhere in this volume, the cultural developments that come to transform society.

Clearly, Vienna functions in Dinev's writings as a heterotopic urban space that enables alternative subjectivities within the very centre of the nation. As the capital of modern Austria, Vienna functions, for better or for worse, as the spatial centre of the imagined community that is Austria. As the premier *lieu de mémoire* of the Habsburg Empire, Vienna also functions as a temporal centre that provides historical continuity to an idealized former imperial and cultural greatness, a continuity that was brilliantly captured in Claudio Magris's concept of the "Habsburg myth." Dinev's migrants disrupt these grand narratives. Their very existence demonstrates that the capital – thought to be the very heart of the nation (Bronfen and Marius 17) – contains within it hybrid and heterotopic elements that explode both narratives of the nation and the concept of a homogeneous, autochthonous Austrian subjectivity. Instead, Dinev's tales of migration suggest a new *transnational* cultural imaginary that connects to an Austrian past "as a collective point of diverse, overlapping contexts" (Müller-Funk, "Austrian Literature" 57).

Such a reading is not meant to marginalize the very real experiences embedded in the text, but rather to conceive works by immigrant authors as part of a broadly envisaged transnational literary culture, instead of relegating them to the status of a "minor literature" inhabiting the margins of a national literature.[15] Vladimir Vertlib, too, has called for a new understanding of a "national" literature – for a literature that reflects a society's cultural diversity as the new normal.[16] Literary works that depict and reflect on the large numbers of migrants in Austria are simply acknowledging the reality of society, creating normalcy rather than exceptionality.

Furthermore, if we consider literary works as part of a nation's cultural memory, transnational texts like *Engelszungen* participate in and modify the ongoing project of Austrian cultural memory. Stocker argues convincingly that by integrating extra-national markers of time and place into a national memory, these texts point to the permeability of cultural memory (3). In *Engelszungen*, Dinev creates a vivid image of that permeability when he places the gaudily clad grave of the Serbian migrant Miro, a reformed pimp, extortionist, and murderer, along one of the most prominent avenues in Vienna's principal *lieu de mémoire* (Stocker 6), the Zentralfriedhof:

> He was surrounded by members of the best, most respectable society. A Danube-Swabian poetess […] lay beside him. A few widowed countesses

> also lay beside Miro [...]. In addition, imperial and royal officers were buried there, strewn around Miro like pieces of shrapnel. [...] Even the technical director of the Viennese funeral services was buried not far from Miro, as if he wanted to ascertain into all eternity, that everything about Miro's grave adhered to the proper order. Surrounded by artists, officers, and high officials, surrounded by persons who mirrored Austrian history more reliably than any textbook, there rested Miro. (6–7)[17]

Yet Miro cannot be considered simply an interloper, an uncouth foreigner who has usurped a place that is not his in good Austrian company. As a "Tschusch," a Serbian who can swear fluently in all the languages that are spoken along the Danube (8), Miro, like the river, transcends national boundaries, and in this way reassembles Eastern and Western Europe in the wake of its Cold War divisions, in a process that embeds the other at the cultural centre of Austria's multinational past.[18] That past includes German-speaking minorities as well as native languages and their speakers in the erstwhile far-flung empire, the officers of the supranational army and the supranational corps of state officials and artists, all of whom have found their resting place in the Zentralfriedhof, the capital's central cemetery. By locating this character who transcends linguistic, national, and class boundaries in an exposed position both in the Zentralfriedhof and in the novel, Dinev stakes an unequivocal claim to an Austrian memory culture that is organized around notions of Central European interconnectedness rather than national and linguistic divisions. His characters, migrants living in the shadows of Austrian society, do not belong in the fringes, but are and always have been central to Austria's history as well as its capital. Like the novels by Vertlib and Doron Rabinovici discussed by Vlasta in this volume, *Engelszungen* thus advocates for a *transcultural* Central European collective memory rather than a nationalist Austrian or ideological Western one.

Cultural transfers are not, however, one-directional. While transnational literary texts written by immigrant authors link up to and interact with Austrian memory culture as in the example above, they can also point back to their place of origin and function as "unauthorized biographies of the nation" (Seyhan 96). This is demonstrably the case with Dinev's *Engelszungen*, given that the novel has had an impact on the literary culture of Bulgaria as well, thus highlighting the reciprocal cultural transfer that transnational literature can achieve.[19] The Bulgarian Germanist Penka Angelova comments on this function of Dinev's novel in a Bulgarian literary context (and her excitement is palpable) when she writes:

> For the Bulgarian reader this is the first novel [in] decades to present an unbelievable sweep of the historical panorama of several generations. Neither the Soldier's Uprising, nor Stambolijski's regime are forgotten here, nor the Bulgarian pseudo-revolutions and liberations. For the first time a panoramic novel does not take place against the background of idyllic country life, but is set in a purely urban environment, unfolding in one of the big towns in Bulgaria with a pronounced urban tradition. (Angelova 87)

And while German and Austrian reviews highlighted the novel's links to Eastern European oral traditions, the Bulgarian critic notes the arrival of the urban novel in Bulgarian literature with Dinev's text, demonstrating how this "Bulgarian" novel, written in German, functions very differently in the contexts of the two national literatures: as successful "literature of migration," in terms of both themes and author-biography in the German-speaking literary reception; and as the arrival of the urban novel in Bulgarian literature (87) in a framework that combines urban themes and settings with uniquely Bulgarian sensibilities of "Balkan magical realism" (Angelova 88).

Language, Identity, and the Post-Modern Condition

Dynamic and heterogeneous notions of identity inform depictions of migration and its effects on the protagonists' identities. This brings us to the second aspect of Dinev's writings that I investigate. Regarding this aspect of Dinev's works, it is not surprising that scholars have brought to bear postcolonial concepts of hybrid identities and the iterative performativity of identity as formulated by Homi Bhabha, Edward Said, and Salman Rushdie. Their formulations, after all, serve almost as blueprints for the literary treatment of migrants' shifting identities. Hannes Schweiger, who has argued this point on several occasions, concludes: "[Dinev's] texts outline different notions of identity and show characters who, as a result of their position as immigrants, refugees or nomads, have to question and change time and again their concepts of themselves" ("Entgrenzungen"; cf. Bürger-Koftis, Hipfl).[20] While such notions of hybridity and performative identity formation are certainly fruitful when analysing Dinev's works, they do not tell the whole story. Thus when we examine the portrayal of such "strategies of selfhood" (Bhaba 4) in Dinev's *Engelszungen*, we find that identity concepts derived from postcolonial theory provide an incomplete picture. This becomes especially apparent in the figure of Iskren Mladenov, the son of a prominent Communist Party official and the novel's second principal protagonist. When Iskren is of pre-school age, he is enrolled in a German kindergarten: "'My grandson will attend a German Kindergarten,' his grandmother bragged to the neighbours at every occasion" (210).[21] Even after decades under communism, the German language has retained its status as the language of the elite in Bulgaria and as the bedrock of Central European cultural values. To be taught the language by an Austrian native speaker of German (215) is cultural capital worth acquiring, as Iskren's thoughts reveal: "So German was something that everyone liked, something that could awaken the love of everyone if one could speak it" (210).[22]

Yet Iskren's experience of learning German shows that language learning is not simply a skill to be acquired. It also leads Iskren to discover the arbitrary relationship between sign and signified, the instability of reality as he knows it: "Not even the rabbits were called rabbits, not even the ladybugs called themselves ladybugs anymore. The entire world out there had different names in this room and that scared him" (213).[23] Instead of bestowing love and admiration upon him, the German language unsettles his sense of being-in-the-world by estranging the known and secure: "this German that changed the world so much that it became all of a sudden strenuous and unfamiliar to him" (215).[24] This mutability of reality extends to Iskren's own sense of identity, when his friend Lena suggests that they adopt different names and different identities in the strange new language: "Everything has two different names. Only the two of us don't. That is unfair. We should also have some that are only known to us. You will be called Koko and my name will be Lili" (216).[25]

The childhood experience of the mutability of reality and identity becomes a fundamental realization for Iskren. From this point forward, he inhabits any identity that promises to fulfil his own goals: when he wants to sleep in, he feigns illness; when he becomes tired of his German kindergarten, he fakes a limp so convincingly that his parents drag him from specialist to specialist to find a cure. For Iskren, identity becomes a game, "the best game he had ever played" (234).[26] Throughout the novel, Iskren plays with aspects of his identity, consciously positioning himself for maximum social and personal gain. In the dying days of the communist system, for example, he becomes a con artist, swindling his countrymen out of money and hope and enriching himself in the process. After the fall of the Iron Curtain, he leaves Bulgaria and traverses several countries, adopting different identities along the way: "A few hours later, he looked down onto Germany from the window of an airplane. At some point, one could see nothing but the clouds. [...] He loved them, these clouds, for nowhere in the world [...] was it easier to begin a new life" (484).[27] In the post-communist, globalized world, identity has become an external attribute, tied to the (false) passport he carries, to be performed and dismissed with equal ease. When Iskren arrives in Vienna in 1996, a year after Austria's entry into the European Union, in the guise of "the Italian citizen Vito Berti," he encounters a taxi driver whose Greek identity is as fake as Iskren's Italian one. To the taxi driver, too, nationality is no longer an essential attribute of his subjectivity; it is merely a precondition for surviving within a globalized economy where real borders have dissolved but imagined ones have not: "We just want to live, just as everyone else, too" (498),[28] he says, and adjusts the small Greek flag on the taxi's mirror – a flag that signals he is one of those people with the "right" passport, the "right" identity, that is, a citizen of the European Union.

Yet, while Iskren's performance of ever-changing identities is outwardly successful and results in a life of luxury, his sense of self is deeply split and reflects an existential uneasiness: "I don't feel at home in my own body. I want to be someone else. To have a different home, different parents and a different name. [...] I even want to have a different body" (433).[29] Iskren experiences a sense of radical discontinuity between self and embodiment. The mind/body duality has arrived at its radical conclusion in the postmodern human condition. Like the ladybugs of his kindergarten days, Iskren's self has become a free-floating signifier at odds with the physicality of its referent, the body. When his last venture, a clinic for magnetic healing in Vienna, is firebombed by a disgruntled client, Iskren is left with nothing: "His life had shattered into small pieces, he had no strength left to collect them. He was tired. He felt the stored up fatigue of three existences in himself. He could no longer walk. He went into a public toilet, locked himself into a stall and began to mourn each one, one after another" (506).[30] This fragmentation, Iris Hipfl argues, represents the final stage of his performative existence; he returns to where he came from, eager to reclaim an identity he had inhabited only in his childhood (Hipfl 99).

But Iskren's sense of self is not tied to his nationality, to his social status, or to his immediate family. Rather, it is tied to a sense of home, represented by his grandmother and the love and security she had provided him (404, 326). His affairs with an ever-changing array of women are aimed only at filling the "empty space" (434) that the death of his grandmother had opened up, and it is in the womb-like bowels of a freighter on its way down the Danube – on his voyage to an imaginary home on the river that connects the countries of Central Europe – that Iskren finds peace while thinking of his grandmother and his childhood (590–1). The text's narrative tone loses its ironic distance and becomes solemn at this point; the narrator focalizes exclusively through the character, and represents his thoughts with steadily decreasing narrative pace, until the text quotes directly the lullaby that Iskren's grandmother had sung to him so often (590–1). Only in a childlike state, the pre-verbal return to the mother/land, can a sense of unified selfhood be achieved. The text reflects critically here on the homelessness that is an essential part of the migrant's experience. Iskren's experience is suggestive of a return to the womb and the *Ur*-mother, yet it is also clear that this can be only a temporary solution to his fragmented identity. A return to his childhood and his *Ur*-mother is not possible; all that is left is the voyage itself.

As Iskren's story demonstrates, Dinev does not identify the instability of identity with the experience of migration; rather, he indicates that it is only a symptom of the post-national global condition. Through learning a foreign language, Iskren experiences his very own "linguistic turn," and subsequently he uses his knowledge of the semiotics of reality to fashion a number of identities. The arbitrariness of the attribution of meaning is perhaps best represented by Iskren's name itself: it denotes "the honest one" (Hipfl 99), the implication being that his entire life is marked by deception. Yet for Iskren, these "strategies of selfhood" do not result in a positive space where the "in-between"-ness becomes liveable. Rather, the conscious playing with identity becomes a game of emptiness, one in which the protagonist attempts to fill the void experienced in the hybrid space and ultimately yearns to return to an imagined *real* self, a self that is grounded in the idealized space of the past, in a return to his childhood and the unconditional love of the *Ur*-mother.

Migration and Masculinity

Iskren's metaphorical return to the womb and to the sense of security associated with the female principle points to a zone of cultural interconnectedness in the theme of gender. But rather than construing the experience of migration as transcending, even superseding gender boundaries, as scholars have undertaken thus far, I maintain that the text foregrounds the gendered nature of migration. While the text lays open the social construction of hegemonic masculine identity through the experience of migration, it does not pry open the nexus between sex and gender, commenting only on the invisibility of that male body that cannot lay claim to the social markers of masculinity. This linkage between masculinity and migration can be demonstrated most clearly with the help of the novel's second protagonist, Svetljo Apostolov. Svetljo is born on the same day and in the same hospital as Iskren. They cross paths at different times and through different people without either ever becoming aware, until they meet, broke and despondent, at Miro's grave in the Zentralfriedhof. Their upbringing in communist Bulgaria highlights the continuity of traditional gendered forms of social organization even after radical equality has been proclaimed. Under real-life socialism, patriarchal structures are alive and well and gender relationships are political and predicated on power, ownership, violence, and the trading of women (cf. Rubin). Iskren's father, for instance, selects his wife based on her overall suitability for his career in the Communist Party and his concept of an ideal home life; meanwhile, he bestows his love on an illegal prostitute. Sveltjo's father murders his wife's lover and cuts out his tongue in an attempt to undermine her decision to leave him. Each man has a clear idea of his rights and responsibilities as the head of his family. For both, a wife is a possession that must be controlled, even through extreme violence. At the same time, alternative forms of sexuality that threaten the heteronormative organization of society and patriarchal power, such as homosexuality (353) and bestiality (318), are coded as pathological abnormalities. The heterosexual integrity of male identity is considered sacred, and any violations of this sexual code are violently punished (361).

This patriarchal power is based on a strict binary organization of gender, one that runs through Dinev's Bulgarian society, where all acceptable sexual activity is restricted to interactions between men and women, while homosexuals are denigrated, beaten, and urinated on (cf., Müller-Funk, "Wanderschaft" 7). The two boys are socialized into these traditional structures through their home life; through bouts of group masturbation and extensive discussions of the mystery of intercourse in adolescence; through their first experiences with females at school; and through the public censuring of alternative forms of sexual identity. When Svetljo and his childhood friend Sascho mimic the hairstyles, body adornments, and clothes of Western punks in order to attract women, the militia arrests them, having identified these visual markers of otherness as signs of effeminacy and deviant sexual orientation:

> They were made to get into a car and taken to the police station. They were surrounded, examined, mocked, and jeered at. Then, they were led into a room. They were asked whether they were gay, as they wore earrings. No, they weren't, both declared. To the contrary, they clearly were [came the response]. That could be seen immediately, and they would be well advised not to deny it. (407–8)[31]

In a society that looks upon prostitution and pornography as inventions of the ruling classes and as cynical means of oppression (319), gender codes are still based on a strict binary organization of sex and desire. Men are men: they must know what a man is and behave in accordance with the norm. Their fathers, their schools, the military – all set out to make "true men" out of them. "We'll turn you into real men," promises the commander of Svetljo's army unit, who continues his notions of the gender structure as follows: "One half of you are fags, the others would prefer to be women. But that'll quickly change" (423).[32] The patriarchs attempt to instil manhood in the young men's bodies and minds through cold showers, beatings, and endless marches that turn their feet into pulp, until they have lost the ability to think and to speak. In this way a "clean slate" is created onto which normative notions of maleness can be inscribed. After twenty-seven months of army service, physical privations have erased Svetljo's former self. Thoughts and words that had once come easily to him have become entombed in his physical being: "It was painful to tear [the words] out, some hurt less, some more, but there were some, he believed, that would cause an important inner organ to fail, if he were to utter them" (512).[33] With the loss of his language comes the loss of his former identity. Svetljo's father is pleased that his son has finally turned into a "man" (511) who speaks and, more importantly, stays silent like "a real man" (511, 512). What is left for these "real men" is a profound sense of disorientation in a world in which all their past certainties have been taken from them. The only point of reference that remains is the body and its sexuality; in Svetljo's own words: "Now, I only want one thing ... to fuck" (512).[34] From now on, his existence is marked by a "masculine silence." He ceases to speak with his father, and he remains in communal silence with his best friend Sascho[35] – the two even win the affections of their girlfriends "without having to say a single word" (517),[36] having found them among the deaf community.

When Svetljo flees to Austria on Christmas Eve 1990, his existence and his self-perception undergo a radical change once again. In Bulgaria, having absorbed "masculine silence," he had been able to establish himself within the traditional parameters of hegemonic masculinity in a range of social fields: a job in a factory, money, an apartment, a girlfriend; now, in Austria, he finds himself stripped of all markers of social and economic capital that delineate the field of masculinity (Coles 36).[37] For the next eleven years, Svetljo lives and works in Vienna, both within and outside the constantly shifting legal framework that governs the migrant's existence. As Stocker notes, Svetljo begins to live the sort of shadow existence that dehumanizes migrants and localizes them in a physical no-person's-land (4). Park benches and, later, public toilets are repurposed as shelter by the dispossessed. The search for work becomes the all-encompassing activity of the migrant, whose vocabulary is reduced to a single word: *Arbeit* (work) becomes the most important word in the new language, the word that encompasses their entire existence: "That is what the life of every refugee revolved around. As long as one had no work, there was no need to think about anything else. For without work, one could be deported at any moment" (538).[38] Svetljo increasingly experiences this danger as he moves from odd job to odd job, exploited at some, treated well at others, but always living in fear: "For the fear, to be once again without work, was much greater and stronger than everything else. It controlled their thinking, it determined their being" (522).[39]

The life of the migrant is determined almost entirely by the task of securing and keeping work, ideally legal work. A sense of home, "the protection of the usual and habitual," as Vilém Flusser terms it (12), is forever tied to the official permission to work.[40] In turn, finding work becomes the sole meaning of life: "His only goal had been the same for the last eleven years: to find work. And what would come after that exceeded his imagination. […] In this manner, work had turned into meaning and the search for work had become a way of being" (*Engelszungen* 573–4).[41]

Dinev describes this life at the margins in all its bleakness. This is not Bhabha's dynamic position of the cultural "in-between" that contains a subversive potential for change. Nor do Dinev's characters experience Flusser's celebrated "Freedom of the Migrant" as "human representative[s] of a beckoning future without heimat" (14). Dinev's migrants are in no position to negotiate meaning, Wolfgang Müller-Funk notes, for they are too busy trying to survive an existence that has been drained of all meaning ("Wanderschaft" 72). Dinev captures their loss of identity vividly in the image of the shadow. In their existential despair, the migrants lose the very materiality of their bodies, becoming "uncertain shadows" "with fearful eyes [...] and wavering steps" (*Engelszungen* 11).[42]

It cannot surprise that this fading of a sense of identity also encompasses Svetljo's masculinity. The precarious existence of the migrant does not allow for the luxury of thinking about women ("One hardly thinks of women, if one has only one pair of underwear and no roof over one's head," the narrator of *Engelszungen* comments, 547–8).[43] Instead, he is forced to turn his body into a commodity on the aptly named yet untranslatable "Arbeiterstrich" (546), the last option for out-of-work migrants, who stand on the roadside in order to sell their physical labour to passing potential employers.[44] It is interesting to note the gendered experience of even this last means of earning money: the selling of one's body. For women, bodies are sold for sexual purposes; men's bodies are reduced to a commodity of physical strength. Even when Svetljo's situation improves and he meets Nathalie, a fellow student at the university who shows interest in him, he is keenly aware of the material and spiritual emptiness of his life at the margins of society: "He was afraid to show her the poverty of his lodgings and of his life. He did not even have a dream that he could tell her about. And he began to avoid her [...] and he took cold showers until she did not contact him anymore" (555).[45] Dinev lays open here the social definition and determination of masculinity, which is dependent on the social and economic capital to which a man can lay claim.

To gain access to a legitimate existence in his adopted country, Sveltjo is willing to change all parameters that define the social subject. After working for more than a year in the shoe repair shop of Mosche Unreich, Svetljo agrees with his employer that adoption is the only way in which Sevtljo can achieve permanent residency in Austria. Ten years have passed when his mother receives a brief letter requesting the parents' agreement that Sevtljo be adopted by Mosche. Due to the disappearance of his biological father, the process takes almost a year, and Mosche dies before he can complete the adoption (572). The shop is sold, and Sevtljo is out of work once again. Eleven years after his arrival in Austria, he is back to square one, his resources depleted, his existence as precarious as ever.

But just as Svetljo hits rock-bottom, when he has spent his last money, hope suddenly arrives through a chance meeting with Nathalie. The two spend the New Year's Eve of the New Millennium together and fall in love. Nathalie has had to overcome her personal past in order to be open to the new, while Svetljo, who has lived the shadow existence of a migrant for ten years, without a past or a future and concerned only with the immediate demands of the now, has to reconnect with his own life history. Nathalie's light-heartedness and ease with words enables him to find his own language again. For the first time since leaving the army, Svetljo finds words, is able to speak again, to tell the story of his family, of his grandfathers, his great-grandfather, and his migration. But the pieces of his narrative, his story, do not yet form a whole. His time in Austria is still devoid of meaning; he has not experienced anything that is worth reporting: "I had nothing to report ... I have not experienced anything" (598).[46] It is the woman who returns language to Svetljo, and it is she who is finally able to place the years in Austria within a system of meaning by speaking her love for Svetljo. Having lost everything and having arrived at the limits of his existence, Svetljo is able to fashion a new male identity, one that breaks with the patriarchal model dictating how he grew up. The masculinity that emerges is dynamic rather than static; it is vulnerable, negotiated rather than imposed from a position of power; and it is dependent on the other person for the completion of the self. While Iskren returns to a childlike state in the womb of the *Ur*-mother, Svetljo finds his utopia in the unity of two souls.

Conclusion

The messages we can take from Dimitré Dinev's works, and in particular from his major novel *Engelszungen*, are multiple, layered, and at times ambiguous. Dinev's texts clearly engage in discussions of migration, displacement, impermanence, and shifting identities. They subvert notions of "natural" national identities and classified categories of difference, inserting the existence of the other into the very centre of the national imagined community. Neither the text nor its characters can be considered marginal like their creator; they are part of Austrian culture, not somehow external to it. As such, author and fictional characters alike explode postwar Austrian myths of national homogeneity, provide a link to the transnational and pluri-cultural past that links Austria to its Eastern European neighbours, and draw attention to the interconnectivity of literary systems around 1900 that also arose through fundamental exchanges with different literary traditions. They intervene in the cultures of national memory of both Austria and Bulgaria, creating space for transnational aspects in the respective collective memories. Vienna is revealed as a heterotopic space that exceeds its place in the national cultural imagination, that holds otherness at the very centre, and that bridges the past and present of a multicultural society in the tradition of a Central European interconnectedness. Personal and gender identities are shown to be mutable in the process of migration, but also through fundamental experiences of alterity through language and its loss. In Dinev's texts, but especially in his (so far) magnum opus, *Engelszungen*, selfhood is not a constant, or a given, but rather a constantly evolving relationship with one's sense of being-in-the-world, encoded in language, space, and time, and subject to radical questioning through the traumatic experience of living, and even the destruction of one's gendered identity. Masculinity, long seen as universal and stable, can no longer furnish a sense of security and is shown to be a patriarchal mechanism of power and control. Like the city, the subject of the new millennium must incorporate experiences of loss, disorientation, and suffering in order to fashion a new identity founded in love and acceptance. Yet while Dinev's "knotted subjects" may be subjects of various and ever-changing discursive formations, he provides them with a glimmer of hope, not in the creation of new, hybrid spaces, and the active negotiation of identities, but rather in finding a home in the feminine, in love, in the womb, in the family. In the words of the author himself: "heimat is where one can receive love and where one is allowed and able to love" (qtd. in Renner).[47] And this is where Dinev's texts fall short of their ambition: while rejecting concepts of fixity, compartmentalization, and distinction in favour of permeability and performativity, his texts reserve gender as a separate aspect of identity, one in which subjecthood can return to itself. Even in Dinev's post-patriarchal, transcultural, transnational world of the new millennium, for the shattered and dislocated self, hope for a home lies with the gendered other, in the giving and taking of (heterosexual) love.

NOTES

1 Mitterbauer, for example, argues that Austrian culture, built on the legacy of the pluri-cultural Habsburg monarchy, can be considered one of the most hybrid cultures in Europe (254).

2 Both Elfriede Jelinek's *Burgtheater* (*Burgtheater*1985) and Thomas Bernhard's play *Heldenplatz* (1988) caused major scandals. As well, Gerhard Roth's 7-volume cycle *Archive des Schweigens* (Archive of Silence, completed in 1991) and Elfriede Jelinek's *Die Kinder der Toten* (Children of the Dead, 1995) may serve as prominent and representative examples of the themes and topics that engaged authors and the public alike (cf. Stocker 1).

3 The 2012 report *Migration and Integration: Zahlen, Fakten, Daten* reports the following numbers and breakdown: "Im Durchschnitt des Jahres 2011 lebten rund 1,569 Millionen Menschen mit Migrationshintergrund in Österreich (= 18,9% der Gesamtbevölkerung). Davon gehören rund 1,153 Millionen der 'ersten Generation' an, da sie selbst im Ausland geboren wurden und nach Österreich zugezogen sind. Die verbleibenden knapp 415.000 Personen sind in Österreich geborene Nachkommen von Eltern mit ausländischem Geburtsort (zweite Migrantengeneration)" (9).

4 Note here that the use of the terminology "Mitbürger mit Migrationshintergrund" or "Menschen mit Migrationshintergrund" is not exclusive to Austria, nor are these to be taken only in a negative sense, although the "othering"-effect persists. See, for example, Backhaus.

5 Already in 2007, the 2. *Österreichischer Migrations- und Integrationsbericht 2001–2006 (2nd Report on Austrian Migration and Integration 2001–2006)* stated "Austria has become a country of immigration – neither in a voluntary nor self-determined fashion, but rather via the factual development," ("Österreich ist zum Einwanderungsland geworden ist – nicht freiwillig und nicht selbstbestimmt, sondern durch die faktische Entwicklung.") All translations into English are by M.B. unless otherwise indicated.

6 For a more extensive listing of authors and a discussion of some of the issues associated with the categorization "immigrant authors," see Haines, esp. 143.

7 The novel has been translated into fifteen languages, but English is not among them.

8 I would like to thank the editors of this volume and the anonymous reviewers for the University of Toronto Press for their valuable feedback on earlier versions of this article.

9 The concept of a new transcultural imaginary was proposed by Dagmar C.G. Lorenz in her recent keynote address "Cosmopolitanism in Second Republic Narratives: Revisiting the Vienna 'Orient' Connection."

10 "Die Herkunft des Autors ist wichtiger als seine Sprache. So tut man sich auch leichter bei den Entscheidungen. Die Frage woher man kommt ist

viel leichter zu beantworten als die Frage wer man ist, oder die Frage wohin man geht, geschweige denn, wie gut man schreibt."

11 For a thorough analysis of Dinev's career as a literary author that uses a Bourdieuan framework to determine the accumulation of social and cultural capital, see Vlasta, "Angekommen und anerkannt?" (2012). My comments here are indebted to Vlasta's analysis.

12 Vlasta rightly notes that this cannot be maintained for German-language literature in the broad sense. Despite his success and his function as a literary mediator between cultures, Dinev is still not listed in major literary encyclopedias, such as the *Kritisches Lexikon der Gegenwartsliteratur* or the *Kindlers Literaturlexikon*. See Vlasta, "Angekommen" 249n22.

13 "In der Fremde zu schreiben bedeutet oft, ohne Familie, ohne Verwandte, ohne Freunde, ohne Heim, ohne Halt, ohne Papiere, ohne Meldezettel, ohne Arbeits- und ohne Aufenthaltsbewilligung zu schreiben. Es bedeutet auch dann zu schreiben, wenn man keine Bestätigung seiner Existenz hat."

14 Bürger-Koftis, Schweiger "Entgrenzungen," and Sievers have analysed in detail the reception of *Tongues of Angels*. The attributions listed here are cited in Bürger-Koftis 145, unless indicated otherwise.

15 The general thrust of this argument was first put forward by Stocker. For a recent mapping of transnationalism in literature beyond the biographical, see Tabener.

16 "As all art, literature should portray the cultural and social multiplicity of a country in its entirety. The world of migrants with its peculiarities and perspectives, their cultural and linguistic localization are part of this normalcy." ("Literatur sollte aber, wie jede Kunst, die kulturelle und gesellschaftliche Vielfalt eines Landes in einer Gesamtheit abbilden. Die Welt der Zuwanderer mit ihren Besonderheiten und Perspektiven, ihre kulturelle und sprachliche Verortung sind Teil dieser Normalität." Vertlib, *Spiegel im fremden Wort* 36.)

17 "Von bester, ehrenwertester Gesellschaft war er umgeben. Eine donauschwäbische Dichterin [...] lag neben ihm. Auch einige verwitwete Gräfinnen lagen neben Miro [...]. [E]s lagen auch dort auch k.u.k. Offiziere, zerstreut um Miro wie Granatsplitter. [...] Sogar the technische Direktor der Wiener Bestattung ruhte nicht weit von Miro entfernt, also ob er sich in alle Ewigkeit vergewissern wollte, daß mit Miros Grab alles in Ordnung war. Umgeben von Künstlern, Offizieren und hohen Beamten, von Leuten, die die österreichische Geschichte stumm, doch verläßlicher als jedes Lehrbuch wiederspiegelten, ruhte Miro."

18 For the Danube river's historical and future importance in a transnational imaginary, see Matthew D. Miller's article in this volume.

19 Stocker was the first to apply Seyhan's concept to Dinev's writings (4), although he does not extend this function to the Bulgarian reception. For Dinev's standing in the Bulgarian literary community, see Vlasta, "Angekommen" 250–51.

20 "[Dinevs] Texte entwerfen unterschiedliche Vorstellungen von Identität und zeigen dabei Figuren, die aufgrund ihrer Position als Einwanderer, Flüchtlinge oder Nomaden ihre Selbstentwürfe immer wieder in Frage stellen und verändern müssen."

21 "'Mein Enkel wir einen deutschen Kindergarten besuchen', prahlte bei jeder Gelegenheit seine Oma vor den Nachbarn."

22 "Also war Deutsch etwas, was allen sehr gefiel, etwas, das die Liebe aller erweckte, wenn man es konnte."

23 "Nicht einmal die Hasen hießen mehr Hasen, nicht einmal die Marienkäfer nannten sich mehr Marienkäfer. Die ganze Welt da draußen hieß in diesem Zimmer anders und das ängstigte ihn."

24 "[D]ieses Deutsch, das die Welt so verwandelte, daß sie auf einmal so mühsam und unbekannt wurde [...]."

25 "Alles hat zwei verschiedene Namen. Nur wir nicht. Das ist ungerecht. Wir sollten auch welche haben, die nur wir zwei wissen. Du wirst Koko und ich Lili heißen."

26 "das beste Spiel, das er je gespielt hatte."

27 "Einige Stunden danach blickte er auf Deutschland aus dem Fenster eines Fliegers. Irgendwann waren nur noch Wolken zu sehen. [...] Er liebte sie, diese Wolken, denn nirgendwo auf der Welt, [...] war es leichter, ein neues Leben anzufangen."

28 "Dabei wollen wir auch nur leben, wie alle anderen."

29 "Ich fühle mich dann nicht wohl in meinem eigenen Körper. Ich will dann ein anderer sein. Ein anderes Zuhause, andere Eltern und einen anderen Namen haben. [...] Ich will sogar einen anderen Körper haben [...]."

30 "Sein Leben war in kleine Stücke zersplittert, er hatte keine Kraft sie zu sammeln. Müde war er. Die ganze Müdigkeit dreier Existenzen spürte er plötzlich in sich. Er konnte nicht mehr gehen. Er ging in eine öffentliche Toilette, sperrte sich in eine Kabine und begann, sie eine nach der anderen zu beweinen."

31 "Man ließ sie in ein Auto steigen und brachte sie auf das Revier. Sie wurden umringt, angeschaut, verspottet, ausgelacht. Man führte sie dann in ein Zimmer. Man wollte wissen, ob sie schwul wären, da sie Ohrringe trugen. Nein, das wären sie nicht, erklärten die beiden. Doch, sie wären es. Das sähe man ihnen sofort an, meinte man, und sie sollten lieber nicht widersprechen."

32 "[W]ir werden aus euch richtige Männermachen"; "Die eine Hälfte von euch sind Schwuchteln, die anderen wären lieber Frauen. Aber das wird sich schnell ändern."

33 "Es tat weh, sie herauszureißen, bei manchen weniger, bei manchen mehr, aber es gab auch welche, bei denen er glaubte, ein wichtiges Organ würde aussetzen, wenn er sie aussprechen würde."

34 "Ich will jetzt nur eines ... ficken."

35 "They preferred to remain silent together than to be silent with their fathers, for they knew that they remained silent for the same reason" ("Sie schwiegen lieber gemeinsam als mit ihrenVätern, denn sie wußten, daß sie über das gleiche schwiegen," 512).

36 "ohne ein einziges Wort sagen zu müssen."

37 It is important to note here that Svetljo retains his access to cultural capital, which is closely linked to language. As a high school graduate he is entitled to enrol at the university (538), where he will meet his future girlfriend and through whom in turn he will be able to reclaim his masculine identity.

38 "Darum drehe sich das Leben jedes Flüchtlings. Solange man keine Arbeit habe, brauche man an gar nichts anderes zu denken. Denn ohne sie könne man jederzeit abgeschoben werden."

39 "Denn die Angst, wieder ohne Arbeit zu bleiben, war viel größer und stärker als alles andere. Sie bestimmte ihr Denken, sie bestimmte ihr Wesen."

40 "Life could never appear free from care [...] as long as one did not have a work permit. This piece of paper was his only goal" ("das Leben [konnte] nie sorglos erscheinen [...], so lange man keine Arbeitsbewilligung hatte. Dieses Stück Papier war sein einziges Ziel." 569; cf., also Stuiber, "Schreiben" 46).

41 "[S]ein einziges Ziel war seit elf Jahren immer das gleiche, eine Arbeit zu finden. Und was danach kommen sollte, überstieg seine Vorstellungskraft. [...] So war die Arbeit zu Sinn und aus der Suche nach ihr eine Seinsweise geworden." On the same page: "What was there left that made life worth living? Svetljo asked himself that question more and more often, and although he considered suicide at least three times a week, he began once again to leave the house in search for work. For, as for so many people in this world, the search for work had replaced the search for meaning. And Sevtljo was one of them" ("Was gab es denn noch, wofür es sich zu leben lohnte? Diese Frage stellte sich Sveltjo öfter und öfter und obwohl er mindestens dreimal pro Woche an Selbstmord dachte, begann er wieder das Haus zu verlassen und Arbeit zu suchen. Denn für viele Menschen dieser

Welt ersetzte die Suche nach Arbeit die Suche nach Sinn. Und Svetljo gehörte dazu," 573).

42 "unsichere[] Schatten" "mitängstlichenAugen [und] schwankenden Schritten."

43 "Man denkt fast kaum an Frauen, wenn man nur ein Paar Unterhosen und kein Dach über dem Kopf hat."

44 For an overview of the situation faced by illegal migrants in Austria in the 1990s, see Jandl et al., esp. 47–8.

45 "Er hatte Angst, ihr die Armut seiner Wohnung und seines Lebens zu zeigen. Nicht einmal einen Traum hatte er, von dem er ihr hätte erzählen können. Und er begann sie zu meiden, [...] und duschte solange kalt, bis sie sich nicht mehr bei ihm meldete."

46 "Ich hätte nichts zu berichten gehabt ... Ich habe sonst nichts erlebt."

47 "Heimat ist, wo man Liebe empfangen und selbst lieben darf und kann."

WORKS CITED

2. *Österreichischer Migrations- und Integrationsbericht 2001–2006*. Ed. Heinz Fassmann. Klagenfurt: Drava, 2007. Web. http://cdn2.vol.at/2007/11/Migrationsbericht.pdf

Angelova, Penka. "The Other Road: On the Bulgarian Topos in the Works of Three Writers Awarded the Adalbert Von Chamisso Prize." In *Shoreless Bridges: South-east European Writing in Diaspora*. Ed. Elka Agoston-Nikolova. Amsterdam: Rodopi, 2010. 83–95. Print.

[Anon.]. "Ganove aus Versehen." *Tiroler Tageszeitung* 652 (2005): 6. Print.

Assmann, Aleida, and Ute Frevert. *Geschichtsvergessenheit – Geschichtsversessenheit: Vom Umgang mit deutschen Vergangenheiten nach 1945*. Stuttgart: Deutsche Verlagsanstalt, 1999. Print.

Backhaus, Jürgen G. "Mitbürger mit Migrationshintergrund sind unersetzlich für die Soziale Marktwirtschaft. Ein Blick in Werner Sombarts *Modernen Kapitalismus*." In *Kapitalismus. Kritische Betrachtungen und Reformansätze*. Ed. Hubert Hieke. Marburg: Metropolis, 2009. 167–80. Print.

"Daten – Fakten – Trends: Deutschland im Europäischen Vergleich. Stand 2004." Beauftragte der Bundesregierung für Migration, Flüchtlinge und Integration. Berlin, 2005. Web. http://www.efms.uni-bamberg.de/sembdf_d.htm

Bhaba, Homi. *The Location of Culture*. New York: Routledge, 1994. Print.

Bronfen, Elisabeth, and Benjamin Marius. "Hybride Kulturen. Einleitung Zur Anglo-amerikanischen Multikulturalismusdebatte." *Hybride Kulturen: Beiträge zur anglo-amerikanischen Multikulturalismusdebatte*. Eds. Elisabeth

Bronfen, Benjamin Marius, and Therese Steffen. Tübingen: Stauffenburg, 1997. 1–30. Print.

Bürger-Koftis, Michaela. "Dimitré Dinev: Märchenerzähler und Mythenflüsterer der Migration." In *Eine Sprache—Viele Horizonte. Die Osterweiterung der deutschsprachigen Literatur. Porträts einer neuen europäischen Generation.* Ed. Michaela Bürger-Koftis. Vienna: Präsens, 2008. 135–53. Print.

Dinev, Dimitré. *Engelszungen.* Munich: btb, 2003. Print.

– "In der Fremde schreiben." *Text und Kritik. Sonderband Literatur und Migration* 9 (2006): 209–10. Print.

– "Spas Schläft." In *Ein Licht über dem Kopf.* Vienna: btb, 2005. 93–121. Print.

– "Die Totenwache." In *Ein Licht über dem Kopf.* Vienna: btb, 2005. 171–83. Print.

Flusser, Vilém. *The Freedom of the Migrant.* Trans. Kenneth Kronenberg. Ed. Anke K. Finger. Urbana: U of Illinois P, 2003. Print.

Haines, Brigid. "The Eastern Turn in Contemporary German, Swiss, and Austrian Literature." *Debatte* 16.2 (2008): 135–49. Print.

Hielscher, Martin. "Migrantenliteratur in Verlagen und Dinevs *Engelszungen.*" *Text und Kritik. Sonderband Literatur und Migration* 9 (2006): 196–208. Print.

Hipfl, Iris. "Zur Hybridität von Migrantenliteratur anhand Dimitré Dinevs Roman *Engelszungen.*" In *Österreichische Literatur zwischen den Kulturen.* Eds. Iris Hipfl and Raliza Ivanova. St Ingbert: Röhrig, 2008. 89–106. Schriftenreihe der Elias Canetti Gesellschaft 4. Print.

Jandl, Michael, Christina Hollomey, et al. *Migration and Irregular Work in Austria: A Case Study of the Structure and Dynamics of Irregular Foreign Employment in Europe at the Beginning of the 21st Century.* Imesco Reports. Amsterdam: Amsterdam UP, 2009. Print.

Jay, Paul. *Global Matters: The Transnational Turn in Literary Studies.* Ithaca: Cornell UP, 2010.

Kecht, Maria-Regina. "Multikulturelles Wien. Entweder-und-oder-Existenzen in der neuen österreichischen Literatur." In *Zeitenwende. Österreichische Literatur seit dem Millennium 2000–2010.* Ed. Michael Boehringer and Susanne Hochreiter. Vienna: Praesens, 2011. 119–37. Print.

Lamb-Faffelberger, Margarete. "Beyond 'The Sound of Music': The Quest for Cultural Identity in Modern Austria." *German Quarterly* 76.3 (2003): 289–99. Print.

Lorenz, Dagmar C.G. "Cosmopolitanism in Second Republic Narratives: Revisiting the Vienna 'Orient' Connection." In *Contemporary Austrian Literature, Film and Culture: International Conference.* University of Nottingham, 13–15 April 2015.

Migration and Integration: Zahlen, Daten, Indikatoren 2012. Ed. Statistik Austria and Staatssekretariat für Integration. Vienna: Kommission für Migrations- und Integrationsforschungder Österreichischen Akademie der Wissenschaften, 2012. Web. http://www.oeaw.ac.at/fileadmin/kommissionen/KMI/Dokumente/Migration_und_Integration._Zahlen_Daten_Indikatoren/statistisches_jahrbuch_2012.pdf

Mitterbauer, Helga. "De-placement. Kreativität. Avantgarde: zum innovativen Potential von migratorischer Literatur." In *Polyphonie: Mehrsprachigkeit und literarische Kreativität*. Ed. Michaela Bürger-Koftis, Hannes Schweiger, and Sandra Vlasta. Vienna: Praesens, 2010. 255–72. Print.

Müller-Funk, Wolfgang. "Austrian Literature in a Transcultural Context." In *Zeitenwende. Österreichische Literatur seit dem Millennium, 2000–2010*. Ed. Michael Boehringer and Susanne Hochreiter. Vienna: Praesens, 2011. 43–63. Print.

– "Auf Wanderschaft. Dimitré Dinevs Roman *Engelszungen*." In *Und kein Wort Deutsch: Literaturen der Minderheiten und Migrantinnen in Österreich*. Ed. Nicola Mitterer and Werner Wintersteiner. Innsbruck: Studien-Verlag, 2009. 64–75. Print.

– "Zungenkuß und kultureller Zwischenraum. Überlegungen zu Dimitré Dinevs Roman *Engelszungen*." In *Komplex Österreich. Fragmente zu einer Geschichte der modernen österreichischen Literatur*. Ed. Wolfgang Müller-Funk. Vienna: Sonderzahl, 2009. 393–403. Print.

Pease, Donald E. "Introduction: Re-mapping the Transnational Turn." In *Re-Framing the Transnational Turn in American Studies*. Ed. Winfried Fluck, Donald E. Pease, and John Carlos Rowe. Hanover: Dartmouth College P, 2011. Print.

Rubin, Gayle. "Thinking Sex: Notes for a Radical Theory of the Politics of Sexuality." In *Pleasure and Danger: Exploring Female Sexuality*. Ed. Carole S. Vance. London: Pandora, 1992. 267–93. Print.

Said, Edward. *Culture and Imperialism*. London: Vintage, 1994. Print.

Schweiger, Hannes. "Entgrenzungen. Der Bulgarisch-österreichische Autor Dimitré Dinev im Kontext der MigrantInnenliteratur." *Trans: internet-Zeitschrift für Kulturwissenschaften* 15 (2004). Web. http://www.inst.at/trans/15Nr/03_1/schweiger15.htm

– "Identitäten mit Bindestrich. Biographien von MigrantInnen." In *Spiegel und Maske. Konstruktionen biographischer Wahrheit*. Ed. Bernhard Fetz and Hannes Schweiger. Vienna: Zsolnay, 2006. 175–88. Print.

– "Mächtige Grenzen. Von (literarischen) Verwandlungsmöglichkeiten in Dritten Räumen." "Meine Sprache grenzt mich ab ..." In *Transkulturalität und kulturelle Übersetzung im Kontext von Migration*. Ed. Gisella Vorderobermeier and Michaela Wolf. Vienna: Lit, 2008. 111–26. Print.

– "Zwischenwelten. Postkoloniale Perspektiven auf Literatur von Migrantinnen." In *Eigene und andere Fremde: "postkoloniale" Konflikte im europäischen Kontext*. Ed. Wolfgang Müller-Funk and Birgit Wagner. Vienna: Turia and Kant, 2005. 216–27. Print.

Seyhan, Azade. *Writing Outside the Nation*. Princeton: Princeton UP, 2001. Print.

Sievers, Wiebke. "Von Elias Canetti bis Dimitré Dinev oder Was ist Migrationsliteratur?" *ÖGL. Österreich in Geschichte und Literatur* 53.3 (2009): 303–12. Print.

Stocker, Günther. "Neue Perspektiven. Osteuropäische Migrationsliteratur in Österreich." 2009. *LebensSpuren*. Web. http://www.lebensspuren.net/medien/pdf/Guenther_Stocker.pdf

Stuiber, Peter. "West-östlicher Dinev." *Die Presse*, Schaufenster. 19 September 2003, 10–13.

Tabener, Stuart. "Transnationalism in Contemporary German-Language Fiction by Nonminority Writers." *Seminar: A Journal of Germanic Studies* 47 (2011): 624–45. Print.

Vertlib, Vladimir. *Spiegel im fremden Wort. Die Erfindung des Lebens als Literatur*. Dresdner Chamisso-Poetikvorlesungen 2006, Dresden: Thelem, 2007. Print.

Vlasta, Sandra. "Angekommen und Anerkannt? Die Rezeption des Autors Dimitré Dinevs im deutschsprachigen Raum." *Aussiger Beiträge. Germanistische Schriftenreihe aus Forschung und Lehre* 6 (2012): 237–56. Print.

– "Passage ins Paradies? Werke zugewanderter Autorinnen in der österreichischen Literatur des 21. Jahrhunderts." *Zeitenwende. Österreichische Literatur seit dem Millennium 2000–2010*. Ed. Michael Boehringer and Susanne Hochreiter. Vienna: Praesens, 2011. 102–18. Print.

Yildiz, Yasemin. *Beyond the Mother Tongue: The Postmonolingual Condition*. New York: Fordham UP, 2012. Print.

9 Remixing Central European Culture: The Case of Laibach

STEFAN SIMONEK

Track I: Intro

Crossing Central Europe, both at the beginning of the twentieth century and at its end, implies as a rule intensified mutual exchanges among a broad range of languages and cultures that differ significantly from one another but at the same time are linked together by a rather similar circumstance – each language has a limited number of speakers and in most cases remains relatively unknown outside the country itself. This specific cultural setting of several "small" cultures, languages, and literatures that overlap and interfere with one another can be considered a hallmark Central Europe[1] into the present day. The European empires of which those cultures had been a part all collapsed after the First World War. For all of these cultures, an essential question is: How are they seen from outside? Because there are few outside experts in them, the Hungarian, Slovak, and Ukrainian cultures are transmitted and received in a highly unified and simplified manner, much more so than with French or English culture, and as a consequence, some entire cultures are represented abroad by only a handful of well-known writers or artists. As for Slovenia (a country of only two million people), Slovene popular culture nowadays is known mainly through two very different musical ensembles: the Original Oberkrainer, a highly skilled but also highly commercialized group of folk musicians that until the 1990s was led by Slavko Avsenik; and a band called Laibach (the German name for the Slovene capital, Ljubljana) and its lead singer Milan Fras. Laibach was founded in 1980 in the Slovene industrial town Trbovlje and became a key player in the cultural underground of the former Yugoslavia. Avsenik's compositions represent a rather commercialized form of easy listening music. Laibach's somewhat provocative musical activities more often than not dance along the edge between popular and elitist high culture and combine the aesthetics of contemporary pop music with the tradition of the *fin-de-siècle* European avant-garde.

By embracing Central Europe's highbrow avant-garde heritage and by deliberately irritating and provoking its listeners, Laibach played a role in the collapse the communist regime. Similar had occurred in other Central and Eastern European countries beginning in the 1960s (especially in the former Czechoslovakia, where the underground band The Plastic People of the Universe, fronted by the poet and singer Ivan Martin Jirous, also known as "Magor," played a role similar to Laibach in the former Yugoslavia). In Central and Eastern Europe, this essential critical function has not always been linked solely to pop or rock music; jazz and folk have also had a hand in it (for example, the famous Russian singer-songwriter, Bulat Okudzhava). It would be oversimplistic, though, to focus exclusively on the politically subversive impact of music in Central and Eastern Europe and to ignore its possible value as nationalist propaganda. Croat rock star Thompson and Serb turbo-folk star Ceca Ražnatović, among others, have shown that pop music can also be used in ways that are the opposite of subversive – that is, to *strengthen* its listeners' political aspirations and national consciousness. In this regard, Laibach never played a distinct dissident role in directly challenging political power; rather, it operated in an underground, partisan-like manner by weakening official political power from within.[7]

A video about Laibach titled *Pobeda pod suncem* (Victory under the Sun), for example, clearly demonstrates the kind of avant-garde allusions mentioned earlier, given that the title is distinctly reminiscent of the Russian Kubo-Futurists' anti-opera *Pobeda nad solncem* (Victory over the Sun), staged in Saint Petersburg in 1913 (Monroe 35; Hanser 80–2). As a consequence, any attempt to decode Laibach's artistic strategies that does not reflect the fact that the band strongly perpetuates the avant-garde heritage does not do full justice to the band's specific aesthetic devices. The same can be said with regard to a significant metatextual strategy employed by the band – it constantly fits together new melodies with older texts and, furthermore, comments on this device in an avante-garde manner. A declaration titled *10 Items of the Covenant*, written in 1982 and published by the band in 1983, offers a good illustration of this strategy. This text (available online in English), which perpetuates the tradition of the avant-garde manifesto often encounterred in Slovene literature (such as one by the Constructivist poet Srečko Kosovel), points to how the band deals with an extreme heterogeneous montage (Bürger 98–116) of cultural material. That montage includes Bruitism (the provocative accidental production of noise to challenge elitist Classical music), "Nazikunst" (Laibach deliberately uses the German term here), and disco. According to point 6 of the manifesto, all of these serve as material for Laibach to manipulate. The same text even negates any idea of originality by declaring that "LAIBACH excludes any evolution of the original idea" (*10 Items*).

This approach to cultural values and ideological discourses represented in the 1983 manifesto makes it possible for Laibach to tap into a multitude of texts from very different layers of Russian, Slovene, and German culture as materials for its own highly manipulative artistic game. This chapter, then, sets out to demonstrate how these somewhat abstract and provocative programmatic positions – which deny any form of cultural authority – have been realized in the work of Laibach and how the programmatic approach is linked in turn to the band's artistic practice. That practice, furthermore, is strongly linked to a genuine trans-aesthetic approach, one that combines various heterogeneous elements of Western popular culture (rock and pop), Central European culture (German, Austrian, and Slovene), and finally East European culture (Russian) to form something new. As a result of this kind of jarring intercultural montage, Laibach could be viewed as an outstanding illustration of this volume's central point. Moreover, the band's ironic rewriting of and montage-like combining of discourses, ideologies, and literary elements harks back to innovative avant-garde devices from the early twentieth century; at the time they first appeared, these devices were meant to supersede traditional high-culture values along with the nineteenth-century literary canon. Yet the avant-garde stayed mired in the realm of high culture and merely upended that culture in an iconoclastic way. Laibach's aesthetics are deeply rooted in an era that envisioned an apocalyptic end to cultural traditions that had been seriously weakened as a result of new technologies such as the airplane and the telegraph.

These avant-garde allusions notwithstanding, Laibach is, in the end, a band and therefore belongs not to high but to popular culture. Thus, in tandem with avant-garde notions of montage and collage, Laibach's strategy of fitting together heterogeneous materials from different layers of culture and ideology could also be called a remix. This approach to the specific way pop music is produced – that is, by using older material and mixing it together – also demands that we consider the methodological reflections of Lev Manovich (a leading American scholar of new media theory), who views sampling and remixing not simply as technical procedures for producing new pop songs in the studio, but much more broadly as a reflection of new models of authorship. In his seminal essay "Who Is the Author? Sampling/Remixing/Open Source," Manovich rejects the notions of collage and montage in favour of remix: "In the last few years people started to apply the term 'remix' to other media: visual productions, software, literary texts. [...] Remix culture has arrived." For him, the term remix itself "suggests a systematic re-working of a source" and also stands for "systematically rearranging the whole text"; at the same time, it differs from sampling, which according to Manovich entails merely importing external material into a basic structure that for its part remains more or less stable and unmodified.

Laibach's artistic aspiration to constantly split up and reshape various cultural traditions and works of art thus has its roots in a European avant-garde tradition that encompasses, among other things, Slovene Constructivism and Expressionism, German dada, and Russian Futurism and Suprematism – and only then pop culture. The addition of Bruitism and disco (see Laibach's 1983 manifesto) joins notions of montage and remix and in so doing places the band's specific aesthetic position in the realm of elitist avant-garde high culture, Kazimir Malevich, the German dadaist John Heartfield, and famous German bands like Kraftwerk and Rammstein (Poschardt).

In part 3 of his essay, Manovich quotes Roland Barthes, who defined the cultural text as a tissue of quotations drawn from innumerable founts of culture without any privileged centre of meaning. This specific notion concerning the general openness of the text also includes the traditional role of its author, whose function as the essential creator of his own text Barthes radically denied in his famous 1968 essay "La mort de l'auteur" ("The Death of the Author"). In it, Barthes splits the author's position in two: the *auteur* plays the traditional role as the privileged and authorized creator of text, who is able to live a life also *outside* the text; whereas the modern *scripteur* exists only *within* the text, as more its product than its creator, and does not claim to be imposing any first-hand interpretation of that text. On the contrary, according to Barthes, the *scripteur* acts less as a writer creating something essentially new than as a collector of cultural material that already existed; the *scripteur* has merely to fit those materials together in a new manner (493–4). In its 1983 manifesto, Laibach deliberately excludes any evolution of original ideas and treats different layers of culture (e.g., Bruitism and disco) merely as materials for its own game of manipulation; consequently, it rejects the traditional role of authorship and acts much more as a *scripteur* in Barthes's sense; this *scripteur* does not generate any additional cultural value, but only rearranges already existing materials in a hitherto unknown manner (an idea that in a postmodern way excludes the possibility of progress that was a core notion of the early-twentieth-century high modernists).

Having taken up the overall function of a *scripteur* (in Barthes's sense of the term), the members of Laibach act less as creators of something genuinely new and more as collectors of already existing material. This collection process could be viewed initially as a sort of ecological recycling of decayed and useless cultural elements. Unfortunately, Laibach in no way tries to recycle those elements – or, for that matter, all of the ideological (totalitarian) garbage it has collected – in order to make the world a little bit better; instead, it further composts them and then remixes them in such a way that the poison within them is suddenly released. This device has often led to misunderstandings among the public (especially in Germany) as well as to accusations that the band, in its songs and videos, glorifies totalitarianism and fascism. But Laibach is not simply glorifying political ideas; rather, it is deliberately exposing those ideas.

But if we are explore Central European literatures and cultures in a more detailed manner, we need to reshape the methodological concepts of remixing and the death of the author, for Manovich and Barthes do not really take Central European cultures into account. For Barthes, the author, in the traditional and outdated function as *auteur*, is doomed to vanish into the fabric of the text, but nevertheless remains a writer of a privileged (assumedly French) literature at the very heart of the Western canon and not outside of it; such cannot be said for nearly every literature in Central Europe. One could argue that the death of the author as outlined by Barthes is simply a luxury that Western literature can afford, indeed a kind of privilege. When we take into account the specific structure of Central European cultures under high modernism at the beginning of the twentieth century, we can link remix and the decay of the author to the concept of cultural plurality as proposed in 1996 by the Austrian historian Moritz Csáky. Taking a semiotic approach, Csáky interprets Central Europe – and particularly its major cities such as Prague, Budapest, and Vienna – as places of especially high cultural density, where several cultures, literatures, and languages came together and inspired one another in ways such that the basic codes of these cultures began to overlap and influence one another (a process characterized by mutual benefits and mutual conflicts). According to Csáky, the strongly pluralistic situation in Austria's-Hungary's major cities allowed for inspiring cross-cultural encounters and at the same time for a multitude of differences and oppositions ("Pluralität" 9).[3] However, Csáky in his writings foregrounds modernist Austrian writers like Hermann Bahr, Hugo von Hofmannsthal, and Robert Musil, and for that reason we must reshape his notions about cultural plurality so that they reflect the postmodernist paradigm of the 1980s and 1990s, decades to which Laibach certainly belongs. In remixing Russian, German, English, and Slovene layers of popular and elitist high culture (which again appeals to Manovich's concept), the Slovene band Laibach reflects the situation of cultural plurality at the beginning of the twentieth century but has also reshaped it in a highly specific and confusing manner. The band combines elements of its avant-garde heritage – for example, by deliberately provoking the public with its videos, albums, and live performances – with pop culture commercialism. Laibach's double-album *Krst pod Triglavom* (Baptism below Triglav), released in 1986, one year after *Nova akropola* (The New Acropolis) and prior to *Opus Dei*,[4] serves as a good example here.

Track II: Remixing the Slovene Literary Canon

The album title *Krst pod Triglavom* may seem somewhat enigmatic for those who are unfamiliar with Slovene culture, but Slovenes themselves do not find it at all difficult to decipher its hidden subtexts, nor to grasp Laibach's strategy of deconstructing cultural values from within through a deliberate overidentification with those values. First, the title evokes the Triglav, Slovenia's highest mountain, which is at the core of Slovene identity, a kind of holy mountain for the whole nation, a mountain on whose summit every Slovene should stand at least once in their lifetime – such is the national world view. The Triglav is also important for economic reasons – it is in the middle of a popular national park around Bohinjsko jezero (Lake Bohinj), a famous centre of summer tourism.

Krst pod Triglavom also alludes to a central work by France Prešeren, the Slovene national poet, who wrote during the nineteenth century and who along with the modernist writer Ivan Cankar is regarded as the most influential writer of Slovene literature. In 1836, Prešeren published the epic poem *Krst pri Savici* (Baptism on the Savica) about the Christianization of the Karantanians during the eighth century. Laibach taps into this traumatic episode in early Slovene history by mentioning on its album the years 819 to 822, which Alexei Monroe tells us allude to the victory of the German armies over the pagan Slovenes; as well as the years 1095 to 1270, which Monroe notes preceded Habsburg rule in the Slovene region (220).[5]

Krst pri Savici came to be viewed as a central text in Slovene literature, one that would be reworked and alluded to in an intertextual manner throughout the nineteenth century, during the period of Slovene modernism around 1900, and finally in Slovene literature after the Second World War (Juvan). Consequently, we find in Laibach's title *Krst pod Triglavom* two essential national symbols: Slovenia's highest mountain, and Prešeren's epic poem. But these symbols do not complete each other; rather, they mutually reduce their meaning in a deconstructivist manner. In addition, *Krst pod Triglavom* fits together select official symbols of the Slovene state, given that the three peaks of the Triglav are an element of the national flag of Slovenia and that Prešeren's poem "Zdravljica" (A Toast) delivered the text for the Slovene national anthem. In addition, both the poet and the first verse of the seventh stanza of the "Zdravljica" are depicted on the Slovene €2 coin.

On Laibach's album, Prešeren's epic poem serves as a key central intertextual source, one that maintains its semantic relevance throughout several tracks and also has a specific textual function in the CD booklet. This booklet offers a series of photographs documenting the staging of *Krst pod Triglavom* by the Slovene stage company Scipion Nasice, which alongside Laibach has been part of the larger art collective Neue Slowenische Kunst (New Slovene Art); these photos display how the company staged *Krst pod Triglavom* in February 1986 more or less in the manner of a futurist avant-garde opera (similar to, for example, how *Pobeda nad solncem* was staged in Saint Petersburg by the Russian Futurists in 1913). Furthermore, the booklet includes a short dramatic scene, also titled *Krst pod Triglavom*, that brings together two of the central characters of Prešeren's poem: Črtomir, the leader of the pagans, and his beloved Bogomila, who at the very end of the poem persuades Črtomir to be baptized at the waterfall of the Savica. The third character in this short scene is a cardinal, seemingly replacing the original priest in Prešeren's poem, who helps Bogomila convert Črtomir at the waterfall.

This scene certainly alludes to the dialogical construction at the end of the poem, where several characters speak for themselves. But

Prešeren's characters are also transferred to a different context: the discussion between Bogomila, Črtomir, and the cardinal touches less on religious than on aesthetic problems. The cardinal, for example, characterizes Črtomir as a prisoner of the form and of the spirit of art ("On je ujetnik Oblike. / On je ujet v duch Umetnosti"; Laibach, *Krst*, booklet). In addition, the scene's characters are used as objects of defamiliarization: Prešeren's heroes are placed not in their original romantic setting next to the waterfall of the Savica, but in an urban context typical of European modernism. As the reader is informed by Bogomila at the very beginning of the scene, she met Črtomir strolling through the cafés of the city ("Srečala sem ga, ko je begal po mestnih kavarnah"; Laibach, *Krst*, booklet). Črtomir, therefore, is no longer a medieval pagan hero as in Prešeren's poem, but a city dweller following the tradition of Charles Baudelaire and of *fin-de-siècle* Slovene modernists like Ivan Cankar and Oton Župančič.

Besides appearing in the booklet, Prešeren's poem serves as a reference for several tracks on Laibach's double-album. As for the intertextual relationship to *Krst pri Savici*, the album's tracks can be divided into two groups: an outer and an inner circle, according to the quality of the track's different intertextual allusions to poem and author. The last part of the album's first track, "Jezero/Valjhun/Delak" (The Lake/Valjhun/Delak) and the eleventh and final track, "Rdeči pilot" (The Red Pilot), would therefore be placed in the outer circle of intertextual references to Prešeren and his poem. Both tracks are clearly linked to the Slovene avant-garde of the 1920s. Ferdo Delak, a radical stage artist and theatre director and the editor of the journal *Tank*, was especially interested in Russian Constructivism and Futurism; *Rdeči pilot* was the title of a short-lived journal edited by the Slovene avant-garde poet Anton Podbevšek, who managed to edit only two issues of his journal in 1922. On top of these avant-garde allusions, Laibach's title track, with its montage-like threefold structure, points clearly to avant-garde artistic devices. Embedded between the lake as a main setting in *Krst pri Savici* and Ferdo Delak, we find the Christian leader Valjhun, who is the third central figure of Prešeren's poem, along with Črtomir and Bogomila. The song "Jezero/Valjhun/Delak" again offers a brilliant example of how Laibach mixes together a multitude of heterogeneous musical traditions: in a remix, the band uses the beginning of the "Inferno" from Franz Liszt's *Dante Symphony* and the Slovene partisan song "Počiva jezero v tihoti" (The Lake Rests Peacefully).

A further intertextual relationship between the album *Krst pod Triglavom* and France Prešeren's biography involves the fact that some of the album's tracks have German titles: track 3 is titled "Jägerspiel" (The Hunting Game), and track 5 "Wienerblut," alluding to the famous waltz "Wiener Blut" (Viennese Blood) by Johann Strauss the Younger. This significant and often deliberately defamiliarized use of German, which characterizes the works of Laibach in general, can also be linked to the use of the German name Laibach for the Slovene capital of Ljubljana – a reference to the city's multilingual and multinational past as part of the Austro-Hungarian Monarchy, a past that had been excluded from the official Yugoslavian discourse. This multinational past of the Slovene capital leads us to parallel moments in Prešeren's biography, in that the writer's canonization as the Slovene national poet necessarily had to place in the background the fact that his life and works were closely linked to Vienna, where he worked as a teacher, acquired a law degree in 1828, became acquainted with the European literary canon, and became friends with the Austrian poet Anastasius Grün (Hafner 266; Baum 107–17). Indeed, besides having these biographical ties to the Austrian capital, Prešeren wrote some of his poetry in German; a small collection of those poems were published simply as *Deutsche Gedichte* (German Poems) in Ljubljana in 1902 (and reissued in 1999). Prešeren was hardly the first Central European Slavic writer in the nineteenth and early twentieth centuries to write poems, stories, and essays in German to reach a broader or a different public; in fact, this was a widespread practice, especially among Slovene authors like Anton Tomaž Linhart (whose historiographic works were an important inspiration for Prešeren when he was writing *Krst pri Savici*), Simon Jenko, Fran Levstik, Josip Stritar, and Ivan Cankar (Spieler). What is unique about Prešeren is that when writing in German, he reflected on the social hierarchies between the two languages. At the very beginning of one German sonnet, he did so through a relation of dominance and subalternity:

> The masters and mistresses who give the orders
> As a rule are speaking German in this land,
> But anyone speaking Slovene belongs to the servants.[6]
>
> Deutsch sprechen in der Regel hier zu Lande
> Die Herrinnen und Herrn, die befehlen,
> Slowenisch die, so von dem Dienerstande. (Prešeren, *Zbrano delo* 2.85)[7]

In the stanza quoted above, Prešeren presents the two major languages used in Slovenia during the nineteenth century, German and Slovene, not as an equals, but rather as social targets to reflect the hierarchies within Slovene society during his lifetime. The "superior" German language is clearly linked to the dominant social groups ("die Herrinnen und Herren"); the subaltern Slovene language, by contrast, belongs to the lower social classes ("die von dem Dienerstande"). Thus the social difference between German and Slovene underscores the contrast between master and servant. In commenting on this in German (and not, as it might be supposed, in his mother tongue, Slovene), Prešeren was using the German language in an unusual and provocative way.

As mentioned earlier, some tracks on the Laibach album *Krst pod Triglavom* directly link to France Prešeren's poem *Krst pri Savici* by creating an inner circle of allusions. Embedded in those same tracks are references to the Slovenian avant-garde artists Ferdo Delak and Anton Podbevšek. Other tracks on the album constitute an outer circle of intertextuality through the use of the German language, which Prešeren himself also used. The very inner circle of allusions to Prešeren's *Krst pri Savici* is developed in a seemingly simple manner by three tracks that all refer to the three main characters in Prešeren's poem – Črtomir, Bogomila, and Črtomir's antagonist Valjhun; the latter's fight against the pagan Črtomir is described in detail in the first part of that poem.[8] Beyond this, the order of the tracks on Laibach's album reflects the central triangular constellation of the three main characters (Valjhun, Bogomila, Črtomir) in Prešeren's text, and not only by bearing the names of these medieval heroes in their titles. In the case of Bogomila, for example, the song title is completed with a second German word, *Verführung* (Seduction). This technique of putting together heterogeneous elements to create a whole perpetuates the avant-garde device of the montage, since the second part of the title does not fully correspond with the first; as a result of this combination of different semantic layers, the title gains an ambivalent meaning that is not easy to interpret. Bogomila is neither seduced by Črtomir nor vice versa; her faith in God is so deep that she refuses to marry Črtomir here on earth in order to meet him later in paradise. Thus she speaks to him: "At the other side of the grave / the purity and faith of my love will be revealed to you" ("Odkrila se bo tebi únstran groba / ljubezni moje čistost in zvestoba"; Prešeren, *Zbrano delo* 1.195).[9] Track 6, titled "Črtomir," completes the triad; thus, we find Valjhun on track 1, Bogomila on track 4, and Črtomir on track 6.

In addition to the tracks directly devoted to the poem's main characters, the second part of the album offers at least two tracks that can be linked directly to either Prešeren or *Krst pri Savici*; each has a distinctly

German dimension. Track 7, "Jelengar," is a brief, pretty melody played solo on a zither and refers to the principal character of a Slovene folk song, the plot of which came to Carniola from Germany. Prešeren evidentially knew this song, since he noted some corrections on a copy of it kept in his archive.[10] Track 10 is the longest track on the album. In its title "Krst, Germania" (Baptism, Germania) we find intertextual allusions to Prešeren's *Krst pri Savici* as well as to German language and culture, which had been so important to Prešeren. Whereas the poem up to this track is represented on Laibach's album by the names of its three main characters – Valjhun, Bogomila, and Črtomir – near the end of the album it is evoked directly by the noun *Krst* (Baptism); this noun places Prešeren's *Krst pri Savici* and Laibach's *Krst pod Triglavom* in a single semantic unit, one on the textual surface and one encrypted as the essential subtext. Track 10 thus places side by side Slovene and German as well as man and woman, since in the first part of "Krst" one band member sings in Slovene. Especially on this track, Laibach comes very close to Prešeren's poem: more than half the lyrics of "Krst" are taken directly from the "Uvod," the poem's introduction; the rest of the lyrics are a montage-like remix of various other elements of Prešeren's introduction, so that *Krst pod Triglavom* literally perpetuates *Krst pri Savici* by means of the text's most famous lines. Laibach chose stanza 17 from the "Uvod" for the song text; that is the stanza in which Črtomir speaks to his tired and disheartened men and encourages them not to give up, but to keep fighting against Valjhun. Later on, these three lines of the poem become a kind of political slogan against foreign oppression throughout the nineteenth century. During the Second World War, the polytheism of the pagan Slovenes that Črtomir evoked in his speech served as a visible contrast to the Christian monotheism of the German enemies:

> But should the gods decree for us damnation,
> Less fearful the long night of life's denial
> Than living 'neath the sun in subjugation! (Baptism on the Savica)
>
> Ak pa naklonijo nam smrt bogovi,
> Manj strašna noč je v črne zêmlje krili,
> Ko so pod svetlim soncam sužni dnovi! (Prešeren, *Zbrano delo* 1.177.)[11]

Yet in the song's second part, "Germania," it is a woman, not a man, who sings a hymn to the power of love, and she does so in German.

This twofold structure (man/Slovene language, then woman/German language) clearly reflects the plot of Prešeren's poem, which is based on the opposition between Slavic (original) paganism and imported Christianity, between old and new (Črtomir to Valjhun), male and female (Črtomir to Bogomila), *terza rima* and *ottava rima* (the introduction to the main part of Prešeren's poem). In addition, the combined track once again foregrounds the overall relevance of *Krst pri Savici* for *Krst pod Triglavom*. Generally speaking, the track "Krst, Germania" is at the very core of the album's aesthetics, since in depicting the forced and tragic Germanization of the Slovenes in the Early Middle Ages, it also reflects Laibach's specific notion that the German language is closely linked to totalitarianism, provocation (ideological as well as artistic), and, finally, taboo.

Besides reflecting philosophically on Slovene history and its problematic relationship to German culture, "Krst, Germania" points to Laibach's specific position between time-honoured avant-garde montage and the technical device of pop cultural remix. The fact that the Slovene band apparently deliberately chose this ambiguous position produces a specific moment of confusion that by no means should be mistaken for the gesture of provocation so typical of the avant-garde, since it encompasses both negation and affirmation. Thus "Krst, Germania," more than any other track on *Krst pod Triglavom*, can be interpreted simultaneously as montage and remix. By fitting together two very different tracks under a Slovene (*Krst*) and German title (*Germania*), "Krst, Germania" clearly perpetuates the avant-garde heritage of artists like Anton Podbevšek and John Heartfield, who are included on *Krst pod Triglavom* either directly ("Herzfeld") or implicitly (as the editor of *Rdeči pilot*).

Furthermore, the two parts of "Krst, Germania" differ radically from each other in style: "Krst," with its monotonous and sinister musical phrases and its presentation of text not as song but as incantation spoken by a man, clearly belongs to the industrial style (for which the industrial region around Trbovlje offers a perfect setting); "Germania," by contrast, is based not so much on repetitive electronic beats; rather, it has been arranged for full orchestra and a female singer. In accordance with the poetics of montage, the track itself is divided into smaller sequences and, as a result of this, brings to question the overall validity of the content of its text, which offers a hymn to the overwhelming power of love. To start with, the song is not sung by a man, as on "Krst," but rather by a woman whose native language obviously is not German and who therefore sings in a defamiliarized and unclear manner that makes it difficult to understand (this fact could also be interpreted as a deliberate attack on the track's use of the high-flying "Germania" in its title). Moreover, the song is cut into smaller pieces by means of the singer's sudden, manifesto-like declaration about the exceptional position of love: "Discern just one thing: love. And discern that nothing else is worth any effort" ("Erkenne nur eines: die Liebe. Und erkenne, dass nichts Anderes der Mühe wert ist"). At the very end of "Germania," this declaration appears again, only this time in an unctuous, priest-like manner spoken by a man.

A closer look at this second declaration on the power of love also reveals the overlapping of montage and remix that defines Laibach's unique position between avant-garde and pop culture, since it offers a link to the album *Nova akropola* (The New Acropolis), released in 1985, a year before *Krst pod Triglavom*. In the song "Die Liebe" (Love), the declaration is not located at the very end of the track; on the contrary, it opens the song, which underscores the prominent role of love already apparent through the use of the German word. The title suggests a joyful hymn to the power of love, as is also the case in "Germania"; but in fact, "Die Liebe" is a deeply sinister song arranged in a typical monotonous industrial manner and presents love more as a frightful totalitarian power than as a spiritual grace from heaven.[12] The power of love is supposedly the mightiest force that can bring about anything, as is declared in the lyrics of "Die Liebe" and "Germania" ("Die Liebe ist die größte Kraft, die alles schafft"). This interpretation of love as a force (i.e., one with the power to manipulate its object) again generates an intertextual link to Prešeren's *Krst pri Savici* as the primary subtext for Laibach's *Krst pod Triglavom*; in stanza 39 of the main part of the poem, Črtomir finally submits to Bogomila and accepts conversion. But he does not confess his love, instead merely declaring that he will not resist Bogomila's faith in love: "I do not resist Bogomila's faith, / the faith of love" (Ljubezni vere, [...] / ne branim se je vere Bogomile" Prešeren, *Zbrano delo* 1.191). Črtomir's silent conversion in *Krst pri Savici* (as we read late in stanza 52: "Molče v to prošnjo Črtomír dovoli" Prešeren, *Zbrano delo* 1.196), therefore, can be interpreted as a good example of the overwhelming (but somehow totalitarian) power of love that makes any resistance impossible, as glorified in "Die Liebe."

Track III: Remixing Austrian Pop Music

Remixing older tracks and re-editing them under new titles, as with "Die Liebe" on *Nova akropola* (1985) and with "Germania" on *Krst pod Triglavom* (1986), is by no means an exceptional practice for Laibach. On the contrary, the Slovene band often remixes material from earlier albums to include in later ones; and on *Opus Dei*, released in 1987, one year after *Krst pod Triglavom*, it even provides two parallel versions of a song. The ambiguous title *Opus Dei* alludes to contemporary pop music, which plays an important role on this album and reveals a new side to Laibach's creativity: whereas *Krst pod Triglavom* relied heavily on a text from the Slovene literary canon and on the avant-garde device of the defamiliarized montage, *Opus Dei* is much more focused on pop songs such as Queen's "One Vision" and the smash hit "Live Is Life," composed and performed by the Styrian band Opus. This latter example adds another semantic layer to the title *Opus Dei*. The lyrics of "One Vision" and "Live Is Life" are translated by Laibach into German in misleading ways, and as a result, the two German versions, titled "Geburt einer Nation" (Birth of a Nation) and "Leben heißt Leben" (Life Means Life), sound like totalitarian art; in this way, they differ radically from their apparently harmless original English versions.[13] *Opus Dei* starts with "Leben heißt Leben" as track 1; the original English version of "Live Is Life" then appears on the album as track 5. In contrast, Queen's song "One Vision" is included only in its German version "Geburt einer Nation," as track 2, thus suggesting that Opus has been more important to Laibach than the famous British rock band.

To show how Laibach deliberately mistranslated the English text of "Live Is Life," we need only compare the first two stanzas of their German version with the English original:

Laibach: "Leben heißt Leben"	Opus: "Live Is Life"
Wann immer wir Kraft geben	When we all give the power.
Geben wir das Beste	We all give the best.
All unser Können, unser Streben	Every minute of an hour.
Und denken nicht an Feste	Don't think about a rest.
Und die Kraft bekommen alle	Then you all get the power.
Wir bekommen nur das Beste	You all get the best.
Wenn jedermann auch alles gibt	And everyone gives everything.
Dann wird auch jeder alles kriegen	And every song everybody sings.

Leben heißt Leben!	Live is life Na na na na na
Leben heißt Leben	Live is life Na na na na na […]
Wenn wir alle die Kraft spüren	When we all feel the power.
Leben heißt Leben	Live is life
Wenn wir alle den Schmerz fühlen	Come on stand up and dance.
Leben heißt Leben	Live is life
Heißt die Mengen erleben	When the feeling of the people.
Leben heißt Leben	Live is life
Heißt das Land erleben	Is the feeling of the band.

In its German version of "Live Is Life," Laibach omits the musical or textual elements that made the English version by Opus a lightweight summer hit with largely meaningless lyrics. To transform the song, Laibach performs "Leben heißt Leben" at an unnaturally slow pace, thereby robbing it of commercial viability. Also, in translation and in performance, the band omits all the stanzas of "Live Is Life" that begin with the line "Live is life Na na na na na." As a result, the song loses its initial harmlessness; Laibach instead deliberately emphasizes the song's text, whose hidden ideological dimensions reach far beyond those of a simple-minded summer hit. In this way, Laibach's interpretation of the Opus song becomes to a certain degree a work of art, one that demands a serious approach. As a work of art, however, "Leben heißt Leben" shifts towards a different set of (ideological and aesthetic) rules that were unimportant to the original version of "Live Is Life," which was intended as a commercial pop culture product. Ivan Novak, a member of Laibach, declared in a 2004 interview that Laibach is Rammstein for adults;[14] thus we can read Laibach's "Leben heißt Leben" as a "Live Is Life" version for a sophisticated adult audience capable of reflecting on the song's lyrics.

When translating the lyrics of "Live Is Life" into German, Laibach had no interest in being faithful to the original text; instead, it deliberately foregrounded philosophical and ideological terms that clearly alluded to totalitarian thinking. Thus "power" is translated as "Kraft," and the third line of the first stanza "every minute of an hour" is transformed by means of abstract intellectual terms like "Können" (skill) and "Streben" (striving). The stanza's eighth line, "and every song everybody sings," has been, because of its banality, replaced in its entirety so that lines seven and eight of the translation can be interpreted as a call for self-sacrifice towards insurrection: "Wenn jedermann auch alles gibt / Dann wird auch jeder alles kriegen" (When everybody also gives everything / Then everyone will also get everything). By replacing the original line eight with this promising yet at the same time ominous prophecy, Laibach is demonstrating that line seven of the original ("and everyone gives everything") hides a totalitarian idea beneath its surface, one that reveals itself when combined with the altered line eight. As a result, a rather simple-minded pop song composed and sung by a provincial Styrian band has been stripped of its apparent innocence and appears instead as a crypto-fascist hymn to power (in German, physical power, "Kraft," also means symbolic power, "Macht"). In this way, Laibach refutes the naive assumption that pop culture revolves around mindless amusement. On the contrary, if the line "when everybody also gives everything" can be logically continued with "everybody will also get everything," then at every turn pop culture verges on totalitarianism, thereby always appearing as its own "adult version" whose innocence is only alleged. This also becomes obvious at the end of the second stanza of "Leben heißt Leben," quoted above. In "Live Is Life," an emotional tie between the people (perhaps as fans or listeners) and the band is evoked: "When the feeling of the people / Is the feeling of the band." Laibach transforms this relationship in order to perpetuate its hymn to power, for according to the German translation, life means experiencing the masses ("Heißt die Mengen erleben") and land replaces band ("Heißt das Land erleben"). The vocabulary of political mobilization is completed by the terms "Mengen" and "Land" in addition to "Kraft" and "Streben." This replacement of the interaction between the band and the people by a further set of political concepts on a semantic level also corresponds to Laibach's efforts to turn the lyrics of "Live Is Life" in the German translation into a monologue-like, solipsistic declaration; in "Leben heißt Leben" there is no place left to directly address the public, as is frequently the case in "Live Is Life" (in "You all get the best" or "Come on stand up and dance," among other lines).

All of these modifications demonstrate clearly that Laibach did not set out to translate the English text precisely so as to create an accurate parallel version of "Live Is Life"; rather, the Slovene band deliberately reshaped the text to unmask its hidden totalitarian subtext by means of the German language and the taboos linked to that language. A closer look at the song's English lyrics as interpreted by Laibach in *Opus Dei*, however, underscores the ongoing validity of the manifesto *10 Items of the Covenant* and the statement that Laibach excludes any evolution of the original idea (and, as a logical result, any original text).

Consequently, in the English version of the song as well, Laibach does not make use of the original lyrics written by Opus, but instead undermines the meaning of the text through a series of small modifications; those modifications are mostly based on the lines of the German version "Leben heißt Leben" as quoted above. As a result, the German text brings into question the validity of the original English version and at the same time any general idea of originality or a privileged position of text. According to the German version of lines seven and eight, Laibach's manipulated English text reads: "When everybody also gives everything / And everyone will also get everything."[15] Since Laibach already in its German translation deliberately misread "band" for "Land," the English version "is the feeling of the band" is replaced by "is the feeling of the land." This line of the song is especially emphasized in the highly individualized performance of Milan Fras, so that it acts as the very core of the song. However, while we can therefore interpret Laibach's version of "Live Is Life" as a deliberate device to unmask the totalitarian message of the original lyrics, the performance again undermines such reading. This artistic strategy cannot be mistaken for a naive protest against right-wing politics, for the distinct overexaggeration of the performance by Milan Fras turns Laibach's interpretation of "Live Is Live" into a parody.[16]

Track IV: Last Exit Laibach/Ljubljana

A comparative analysis of the lyrics from "Live Is Life" and "Leben heißt Leben," or of the original version performed by Opus, and the deconstructionist rewriting of the song as arranged by Laibach again demonstrates the specific position of the Slovene band between the avant-garde heritage of the first decades of the twentieth century (Futurism, Expressionism, Constructivism, and Dadaism in Russia, Germany, and interwar Yugoslavia) and consumerist contemporary pop culture with its unsophisticated public and avoidance of shock in reception (a feature, according to Peter Bürger, of avant-garde montage, 108). To draw a sharp line between those two realms of high and pop culture, however, would be overly simplistic, besides suggesting a clear classification that does not reflect Laibach's aesthetics, which leverage the confusion generated by occupying the dual position of being avant-garde and pop at the same time. Thus, the way that Laibach mistranslates the Opus original into German, thereby "reinventing" a song that was originally in English, seems to be a perfect example of a remix that in turn is a specific technical device in pop music. Laibach makes use of this specific device not only in English pop songs but also in other highly symbolic forms of music. On the album *Volk* (2006), for example, Laibach remixes several national anthems, in this way using German, French, Italian, Russian, and Slovene in addition to English. And on its album *Opus Dei*, Laibach makes use of the remix in such an impressive manner that the device is laid bare; in doing so, they channel the way the Russian Formalists defined it for the Russian avant-garde ("obnazhenie priema"). In this same vein, Laibach titled a selection of its best remixes, released in 2012, not *Greatest Hits* (as a genuine rock band would do), but in an emphatically highbrow manner, *An Introduction to ... LAIBACH*, which is more suggestive of an academic textbook for undergraduate students than a commercial product of pop culture.

In his famous essay "Cross the Border – Close the Gap," which became a kind of early manifesto of postmodernism, Leslie Fiedler declared that "the old distinctions are no longer valid, and that critics will have to find another claim to authority more appropriate to our times than the outmoded ability to discriminate between high and low" (285). Fiedler's provocative and at the same time prophetic essay was published in 1969 in *Playboy*, before the new media were established as global distributors of information. In the meantime, owing to the new media, Fiedler's efforts to overcome the difference between high and low by closing the gap have largely succeeded. There are no more gaps on the surface of culture; there is only a vast plain of garbage awaiting Barthes's *scripteur*, who would pick something up in order to recycle it later. Laibach easily moves on this surface by resorting to devices of pop culture, but at the same time it draws the public's attention to the things that have been lost as building material to fill the gap (e.g., France Prešeren's nineteenth-century romantic poem *Krst pri Savici*). The unique semantic plurality of the Central European region as described by Moritz Csáky brought forward writers like Prešeren, who were bilingual and thus able to switch between several cultural codes, often for provocative aims. Laibach did much the same when it chose the German name of the Slovene capital Ljubljana. Laibach launched its approach in the early 1980s in the former Yugoslavia, where it did much to found the underground culture and provoked officialdom through a series of semi-illegal concerts. (During one of those concerts, the band cross-faded a portrait of the state leader Josip Broz Tito with a porn movie.) In 1986, however, Scipion Nasice, the theatre section of the art collective Neue Slowenische Kunst, managed to stage *Krst pod*

Triglavom in the prestigious Cankarjev dom in Ljubljana, a well-known cultural centre. Within a couple of years, Laibach had apparently made its way into the elitist realms of high culture. In the interim, however, the plurality that forms the main cultural background for Laibach has been largely erased by the forces of globalization. On the road that crosses Central Europe, where many different cultures come together, Laibach/Ljubljana, therefore, seems the last possible exit to take.

NOTES

1 Due to its essential dynamic and open character, it is not possible to deliver a clear definition of the term "Central Europe" in this essay; the term possibly should not be fixed by a clear-cut definition at all, so that it can be used less in a geographical than in a methodological way. In any case, the region of Central Europe at least up to the Holocaust is characterized by a specific cultural density as analysed by Moritz Csáky and by a high degree of mutual interaction between the different cultures of this region (which should not be confused with a naive multicultural idea of a mutual enrichment of these cultures without any sort of conflict). The Czech scholars Ivo Pospíšil and Miloš Zelenka in 2002 defined Central European literatures as a whole, which geographically and geopolitically are characterized by their basic variability (184).

2 For the link between politics and contemporary music in Eastern and Central Europe, see Stefan Michael Newerkla, Fedor B. Poljakov, and Oliver Jens Schmitt, which offers highly informative essays on Thompson and Serb turbo-folk. In Andrej Leben and Marija Wakounig's essay on the political song in Slovenia, Laibach is mentioned in passing (271).

3 In a range of other essays on this topic, Csáky later specified and deepened his initial concept of cultural plurality within Central Europe ("Die Wiener Moderne"; "Zentraleuropa").

4 All three entries in *Wikipedia* offer more detailed information on the three Laibach albums, including, for example, a track list for each album, which also shows the major differences between the CD versions and the LP versions (an altered order of the songs, bonus tracks, etc.).

5 Earlier in his monograph, Monroe underscores the traumatic experience of an imposed Germanization in Slovene history as opposed to the deliberate and provocative use of the German language by Laibach: "Laibach's assertive 'Slovenism' was inextricably linked to its performance of 'Germanism' or 'Germania' (German[ic] mania), and this represented a major symbolic reversal of the assimilation of Slovene culture into the German sphere" (18).

6 All translations into English by Stefan Simonek unless otherwise noted.

7 Taking into account this relation and the totalitarian subtext that Laibach's use of the German language generally bears, the title "Wienerblut" suddenly seems bereft of the serenity for which the waltz of Johann Strauß the Younger has become famous.

8 This first part of "Krst pri Savici" is written in *terza rima*. For the second and main part of his poem, Prešeren used the *ottava rima* stanza with the pattern a-b-a-b-a-b-c-c.

9 The love between the two main characters of the poem, Bogomila and Črtomir, and the possible link to the Christian faith due to Črtomir's conversion at the waterfall of the Savica, have been interpreted by Slovene critics in very different ways (Zupan Sosič). The frequent use of the word "love" in Prešeren's poetry is shown in Peter Scherber's helpful dictionary of Prešeren's poetical language (129–32).

10 The text of this Slovene folk ballad is published in Kumer 350. I thank Peter Scherber (Vienna) for a copy of this text.

11 According to Alexei Monroe, *Krst* (Baptism) is the most utopian and sinister song on Laibach's album *Krst pod Triglavom*; since he characterizes the text of *Krst* only as a "solemn spoken incantation" without any reference to "Krst pri Savici," it becomes clear that Monroe does not know that the text is based primarily on Prešeren's poem (221).

12 See also Monroe's precise interpretation of the song: "*Die Liebe* [...] is equally nightmarish, and transforms 'love,' perhaps the key signifier of pop ideology, into a demonic all-conquering totalitarian force. The fanatical delivery of the lyrics [...] evokes love's fanatical, totalitarian aspects. The punitive militaristic percussion, sinister orchestral samples, and hunting horns show love as applied to notions of nation or state as a blind, merciless source of sublime terror" (218–19).

13 According to Alexei Monroe, "Laibach produced paramilitarized versions of Western pop" (226).

14 Aside from the songs of Queen and Opus, Laibach also remixed the Rammstein-song "Ohne dich" (Without You).

15 This video again leads back to France Prešeren's epic poem "Krst pri Savici" as the central intertextual inspiration for Laibach's album *Krst pod Triglavom*: Milan Fras poses and sings at the front of a very impressive waterfall in the background. It is the waterfall of the Savica, where Črtomir at the end of Prešeren's poem agrees to being baptized because of his love for Bogomila (Simonek, *MC Dorota* 44–5).

16 Alexei Monroe also quotes this line of "Live Is Life" in Laibach's specific interpretation in order to show how "Laibach's subtle modifications and militant interpretation transformed it ["Live Is Life" by Opus] into a paean

to *völkisch* belonging" (229). In addition to Monroe, Eva-Maria Hanser defines in her master's thesis the manipulated text of the song as a hymn that in an exaggerated and almost ridiculous manner praises the land (29).

WORKS CITED

Barthes, Roland. "La mort de l'auteur." In *Œuvres complètes II: 1966–1973*. Paris: Éditions du Seuil, 1994. 491–5. Print.

Baum, Wilhelm. "France Prešeren, ein slowenischer Dichter in Österreich (1800–1849)." *Österreich in Geschichte und Literatur* 43 (1999): 107–17. Print.

Bürger, Peter. *Theorie der Avantgarde*. 14th ed. Frankfurt am Main: Suhrkamp, 2007. Print.

Csáky, Moritz. "Pluralität. Bemerkungen zum 'dichten System' der zentraleuropäischen Region." *Neohelicon* 23.1 (1996): 9–30. Print.

– "Die Wiener Moderne. Ein Beitrag zu einer Theorie der Moderne in Zentraleuropa." *nach kakanien. Annäherungen an die Moderne*. Ed. Rudolf Haller. Vienna, Cologne, Weimar: Böhlau, 1996. 59–102. Print.

– "Zentraleuropa. Ein komplexes kulturelles System." *Études Danubiennes* 13.1 (1997): 1–16. Print.

Fiedler, Leslie. "Cross the Border – Close the Gap." In *A New Fiedler Reader*. Amherst: Prometheus Books, 1999. 270–94. Print.

Hafner, Stanislaus. "Prešeren, France." *Österreichisches Biographisches Lexikon 1815–1950*. Vol. 8. Vienna: Verlag der Österreichischen Akademie der Wissenschaften, 1983. Print.

Hanser, Eva-Maria. *Ideotopie. Das Spiel mit Ideologie und Utopie der "Laibach"-Kunst*. MA thesis, Vienna, 2010. Print.

Juvan, Marko. "Przezwyciężanie romantycznego dziedzictwa? 'Krst pri Savici' jako tekst-klucz literatury słoweńskiej w perspektywie modernistycznej i postmodernistycznej." In *Postmodernizm w literaturze i kulturze krajów Europy Środkowo-Wschodniej. Materiały z konferencji naukowej zorganizowanej przez Uniwersytet Śląski (Ustroń, 15–19 listopada 1993)*. Ed. Halina Janaszek-Ivaničková and Douwe Fokkema. Katowice: Śląsk, 1995. 233–44. Print.

Kumer, Zmaga, Milko Matičetov, Boris Mechar, and Valens Vodušek, eds. *Slovenske ljudske pesmi*. Vol. 1. Ljubljana: Slovenska matica, 1970. Print.

Laibach. "Baptism." Web. http://en.wikipedia.org/wiki/Baptism_(Laibach_album)

– Krst pod Triglavom – Baptism. Klangniederschrift einer Taufe. Scipion Nasice [booklet to the CD-version, without page numbers]

– "Leben Heißt Leben." Web. http://lyrics.wikia.com/Laibach:Leben_Hei%C3%9Ft_Leben

– "Leben heißt leben." Web. http://www.youtube.com/watch?v=LZxE0ttCLnM
– "Die Liebe." Web. http://www.youtube.com/watch?v=u0phln0davs
– "Die Liebe Lyrics (Laibach)." Web. http://www.maxilyrics.com/laibach-die-liebe-lyrics-72b9.html
– "Nova Akropola." Web. http://en.wikipedia.org/wiki/Nova_Akropola
– "One Vision." Web. http://en.wikipedia.org/wiki/One_Vision
– "Opus Dei." Web. http://en.wikipedia.org/wiki/Opus_Dei_(album)
– "Opus Dei/Life Is Life." Web. http://www.youtube.com/watch?v=d5pRLZkJdP8
– *Victory Under the Sun* (1988). Video. Part 1. Web. http://www.youtube.com/watch?v=ZDMK4kW-WGY
– "10 Items of the Covenant." Web. http://www.gla.ac.uk/~dc4w/laibach/covenant.htmlQ1

Leben, Andrej, and Marija Wakounig. "N'mav čriez jizaro. Das politische Lied bei den (Kärtner) Slowenen." In *Das politische Lied in Ost- und Südosteuropa*. Ed. Stefan Michael Newerkla, Fedor B. Poljakov, and Oliver Jens Schmitt. Vienna: LIT, 2011. 251–72. Print.

"Live Is Life." Web. http://en.wikipedia.org/wiki/Live_Is_Life

Manovich, Lev. *Who Is the Author? Sampling/Remixing/Open Source*. Web. http://www.manovich.net/DOCS/models_of_authorship.doc

Monroe, Alexei. *Interrogation Machine: Laibach and NSK*. Cambridge, MA: MIT P, 2005. Print.

Newerkla, Stefan Michael, Fedor B. Poljakov, and Oliver Jens Schmitt (eds.). *Das politische Lied in Ost- und Südosteuropa*. Vienna: LIT, 2011. Print.

Novak, Ivan. "Laibach ist Rammstein für Erwachsene." Web. http://www.netzeitung.de/entertainment/music/315256.html

Opus. "Live Is Life Lyrics Opus." Web. http://www.golyr.de/opus/songtext-live-is-life-22158.html

"Počiva jezero v tihoti (partizanska)." Web. http://www.youtube.com/watch?v=ED3kZopOG3o

Poschardt, Ulf. "Pop und Affirmation bei Kraftwerk, Laibach und Rammstein." *Jungle World* 20 (12 Mai 1999). Web. http://jungle-world.com/artikel/1999/19/30872.html

Pospíšil, Ivo, and Miloš Zelenka. "Zur Kategorie des Raums in der Literaturwissenschaft. Marginalien zu einem Phänomen der mitteleuropäischen Literaturen." *Germanoslavica* 4.1 (2002): 179–89. Print.

Prešeren, France. "Baptism on the Savica." Trans. Tom M.S. Priestly and Henry R. Cooper, Jr. Web. http://spinnet.eu/wiki-anthology/index.php/Baptism_on_the_SavicaQ2

– *Deutsche Dichtungen* (German Poems). Ed. Wilhelm Baum. Klagenfurt: Kitab, 1999. Print.

– "Krst pri Savici." In *Zbrano delo*. Vol. 1. Ljubljana: Državna založba Slovenije, 1965. 173–98. Print.

– *Zbrano delo*. Vol. 2. Ljubljana: Državna založba Slovenije, 1966. Print.

Scherber, Peter. *Slovar Prešernovega pesniškega jezika*. Ljubljana: Obzorja, 1977. 129–32. Print.

Simonek, Stefan. "'Rammstein'-Rezeptionen im postsowjetischen Kontext." In *Kultur und/als Übersetzung. Russisch-deutsche Beziehungen im 20. und 21. Jahrhundert*. Ed. Christine Engel and Birgit Menzel. Berlin: Frank and Timme, 2011. 205–8. Print.

–. *MC Dorota/Noize MC. Text-Bild-Ton-Relationen der slawischen Popkultur*. Passau: Karl Stutz, 2013. Print.

Spieler, Maria. *Zweisprachige Dichtung bei den Slovenen*. PhD diss., 1965.

Zupan Sosič, Alojzija. "Ljubezen v *Krstu pri Savici*." In *Romantična pesnitev: Ob 200. obletnici rojstva Franceta Prešerna. Mednarodni simpozij Obdobja – Metode in zvrsti, Ljubljana, 4.-6. december 2000*. Ed. Marko Juvan. Ljubljana: Center za slovenščino kot drugi / tuji jezik pri Oddelku za slovanske jezike in književnosti Filozofske fakultete, 2002. 267–79. Print.

10 Bottled Messages for Europe's Future? The Danube in Contemporary Transnational Cinema

MATTHEW D. MILLER

In civilizations without boats, dreams dry up, espionage takes the place of adventure, and the police take the place of pirates.

Michel Foucault

Danubian Studies for a Transnational Europe

Amidst the long-standing contestation of Central Europe as a geographical, historical, and cultural concept,[1] the field of Danubian Studies offers a suggestive framework for the study of Europe, in terms of both the legacies of its varied pasts and the openness of its possible futures. The mighty river is Europe's second-longest: from its beginnings in Germany's Black Forest to the Romanian and Ukrainian shores where it reaches the Black Sea, the Danube flows through and/or borders ten countries, while its watershed covers areas of four more. In the context of the European Union's eastward expansion along the river's course and in the wake of Cold War scission, the Danube is again serving as a unifying artery of economic, cultural, and international exchanges in the continent's diverse southeastern regions. The multilingual, multicultural, and multi-national space traversed by the Danube has long figured as a contested site of numerous imperial incursions by Romans, Ottomans, Habsburgs, Nazis, and Soviets, among others. These external pressures have contributed to the hardening of internal divisions within Danubia (Okey 118, 131–2), such that the river has figured more often as a divider than as a connector of Danubian populations.[2] Yet as Europeans continue to work through and towards the elaboration of a continental identity, the coupling of geographical proximity with political integration is placing new demands on negotiating transnational relations through which the connectivity suggested by the river's function as a conduit might be strengthened. In this, the river itself may figure as a quintessential site of transcultural engagement in the new Europe as well as an instantiation of the global present.[3]

This chapter delivers an account of the Danube in contemporary transnational cinema with an analysis of the ex-Yugoslav and Vienna-based filmmaker Goran Rebić's 2003 *Donau, Dunaj, Duna, Dunav, Dunărea*. Its argument, briefly, is that beneath the surface of the film's celebration of a new European identity in the form of the transnational, multiethnic family, Rebić delivers a bottled message for a politically open European future.[4] In spelling out an interpretative appreciation of Rebić's narrative river film, I simultaneously seek to demonstrate the value of Danubian Studies as a framework for scholarly inquiry.

Rationales for the field's purchase can be outlined in advance. First, while the river runs right through Central Europe and has figured prominently as a point of reference in the arts for some time, the Danube has not, in some contrast to *Mitteleuropa*, existed as a geographical concept to be decentred; rather, it has always seemed off-centre, so much so that even in Stanisław Mucha's bitter and comic search for Europe's elusive core in the film *Die Mitte* (The Center, 2004), the river is not featured at all. But the Danube's very ex-centricity may constitute its promise: the unofficial status of "Danubia" as a region denoted and bounded by the river sidesteps the national perspectives through which the region's history has been so maligned and its academic study often filtered. Moreover, by constituting such an area study by way of a prominent feature of Europe's natural geography, Danubian Studies can also take part in the current eco-critical reorientation of the humanities. Challenging culture's separation from nature, eco-critical studies have ranged widely – from rocks and soils to the high seas – in the environments they emphasize. As a river – landlocked Central Europeans' only "sea" – the Danube's flow connects the terrestrial to the maritime, allowing for the analysis of suggestive interplays between water and earth and the signifying regimes associated with their respective pulls. From this perspective, it is notable that "Danubia" has resisted being reduced into the terrestrial classifications of actually existing political states such as the Danube Monarchy, one of the many names for the Habsburg Empire, which staked the greatest symbolic claim to the river.[5] Austria-Hungary has doubtlessly left a profound imprint on the region, and its legacies – as chapters in this volume attest – are still most palpable in the lands of Habsburg Europe today. While that multiethnic state constituted a crucial part of Danubia's history, the signifier can also be freed from this politically important chapter and wielded as a future-oriented construct, even as a space of utopian projection.

As a subfield of European Studies, Danubian Studies also provides a focus for clarifying the discourse of Europeanization, a historically variable and troubled semantics, one that has arguably entered a new phase in the twenty-first century with regard to the (theoretical) openness of the EU project: as an unprecedented experiment in transnational continental identity and sovereignty, this political entity's future is by no means foreclosed, but will continue to unfold in the process of its contestation between its perceived economic agenda (which includes the enforcement of austerity budgets as a manifestation of neoliberalism) on the one hand and emergent forms of democratic transnational solidarity on the other.[6] An important piece of this process, as Étienne Balibar has written in lines evoking the aforementioned tension between economics and politics, is Europe's need for a fictive identity:

> The heart of the aporia [of the right to citizenship in Europe] seems to me to lie precisely in the necessity we face, and the impossibility we struggle against, of collectively inventing a *new* image of the people, a new image of the relation between membership in historical communities (*ethnos*) and the continued creation of citizenship (*demos*) through collective action and the acquisition of fundamental rights to existence, work, and expression, as well as civic equality and the equal dignity of languages, classes, and sexes. (9)

And indeed, the transnational cinema of contemporary Europe – not least given funding structures such as the European Council's EURIMAGES – constitutes an important mass medium for such invention. Rebić's polyglot Danube film is certainly a part of this inventive process.

Finally, as a connector, the Danube's flow straddles the most recently prominent division of the continent into West and East during the Cold War.[7] The traverse of the historical watershed of 1989 is marked powerfully in *Donau, Dunaj, Duna, Dunav, Dunărea,* which I interpret as wresting a faintly perceptible legacy of the Second World from the riparian waters. This interpretation is facilitated by attending to the film's participation in an intertextual and transcultural Central European aesthetic network. Rebić underscores his engagement with literary works by fellow Danubians Claudio Magris and Péter Esterházy, acknowledging them in closing credits.[8] My analysis of the film's intertextuality demonstrates how Danubian Studies can exploit conceptual metaphors of solidity and fluidity in a productive rearrangement of transcultural European Studies to contest the liquidity of late modernity's neoliberal flow, and thereby outfit the continent with horizons of greater futurity.[9]

"Europeanization" and the Danube

If Danubian Studies can serve as a framework for approaches to the new Europe, the writings of Austrian author, publisher, and polemicist Karl-Markus Gauß might constitute a springboard for Danubian Studies. Although it may have no intention of doing so, the suggestive, even programmatic character of Gauß's 1995 essay "The Teachings of the Danube" lends itself well to serving as a lens of the field. In his opening to Inge Morath's photography album, Gauß culturally maps the river in a perspicacious survey of the promises and catastrophes associated with the region's ethnic complexity. Focusing on the "hatred of peoples mutually dependent but periodically set against each other" ("Teachings" 15), Gauß not only frames peaceable cohabitation in Danubia as an experiment teetering between blessing and curse (19), but also endows its multi-national character with allegorical significance for the rest of the world: "The Danube is in itself an experiment that affects the whole world, what goes awry here can fail anywhere and everywhere, that which succeeds here gives us hope for other places" (16). Moreover, eschewing the celebration of continental unification on the one hand and the hardening of small-nation nationalisms and insular regionalisms on the other, Gauß argues as a quintessential Central European after the demolition of Central Europe.[10] If the dissident function of the concept of Central Europe has been eclipsed after 1989, as Gauß writes in 1991 on the eve of the continent's new historico-political phase (Gauß, *Die Vernichtung* 33), "Danubia" serves to replace it. Gauß both taunts the "compulsory idea" of a continent of nation-states with the river's supranational realities, to which the category of nationality will not apply (or apply only by force), and imbues the river with inveterate counter-hegemonic tendencies that spurn any "united Danubian kingdom's" attempt to level the "coexistence of the dissimilar, the sparkling richness of contrast," features that make the entire region so interesting to Gauß in its irreducible heterogeneity ("Teachings" 22).[11] By extension, this line of argument also relates to the prospects of European unification, about which Gauß, mindful of Danubia's resistance to external prescriptions, has disseminated a productive scepticism.

Such scepticism is informed not only by Gauß's keen awareness of the transience of all foreign powers that have attempted to subject the river to imperial rule, but also by the equivocal process of European unification. Danubian Studies can clarify a fundamental ambivalence in the discourse of Europeanization relevant to the region, a clarification that is likewise contextually important for understanding the contribution Rebić's film makes to the continent's cultural identity. At issue is the project's relation to the nation-state. Pitched as a peace project, the EU certainly signals the overcoming of open hostilities between states that so afflicted the history of the continent in the twentieth century. At the same time, the settling of that history has also featured the principle consolidation of nation-states. In their observations thereof, scholars such as Andreas Huyssen and Maria Todorova have attended to the *pas de deux* of nationalization and Europeanization. In coming to terms with Germans' predilection for assuming a European identity over the course of the twentieth century's second half, Huyssen has written that the "decision to opt for a European identity in order to avoid the Germanness in question, so typical of postwar intellectuals, was and remains a delusion. [...] Rather than representing an alternative to the nation, Europe was always its very condition of possibility, just as it enabled empire and colonialism" (Huyssen 72–3). In a related strain of argumentation, Todorova has claimed that "what we are witnessing today [2009] in the geographic Balkans – namely, the eradication of the final vestiges of a historical legacy of ethnic multiplicity and coexistence, and its replacement by institutionalized ethnically homogenous bodies – may well be an advanced stage of the final Europeanization of the region, and the end of the historic Balkans and the Ottoman legacy" (Todorova 199).[12] Europeanization connotes for neither observer any sublation of the nation-state, but rather its deeper mooring. Yet Huyssen and Todorova's reflections are closely wed to twentieth-century experiences, the resulting structure of which may not be written in stone. In her 2003 study on "Eurovisions," the historian Ute Frevert has observed a different valence in the semantics of Europeanization. Without denying the reciprocal relationship between Europe and the nation-state that Huyssen and Todorova criticize (163), Frevert notes the divergence of Europeanization and nationalization after 1989. Europeanization will now be associated with – and celebrated as – denationalization (170). Dedicated Europeans such as Frevert regard this path as full of potential. She welcomes "suggestions for strengthening the supranational elements of the union [which] focus [...] on the European parliament, a common constitution, and European citizenship" (167).

Moreover, a more integrated Europe by no means necessarily entails a loss of democratic legitimation or civic engagement. On the contrary, depending on its structuration, it could circumvent the still powerful forces of the nation-state in their collusion with elites (which may themselves be multinational) that make for the democratic deficits in Europe (and elsewhere) perceived and criticized today. For this reason, European writers such as Robert Menasse and Étienne Balibar continue to focus on the EU's potential as a project of democratic transnationalism. The concern, to speak mutedly, is that without democratic structures, a stronger parliament, and reinforced representation to go along with it, the EU may present an interesting case of transnational experiment. But who or what would steer it? Transnationalism in the service of neoliberalist economics may interest the continents' residents very little. Nor is it guaranteed to enhance the quality of their lives.

If the vagaries of political transnationalism constitute a first challenge in grappling with Europeanization, a second problem arises in the impression of a well-nigh maelstrom of inner European non-contemporaneity (*Ungleichzeitigkeit*). This is also where the divide and power struggle between West and East makes itself felt. In observation of the formerly socialist central and eastern European countries' position in the wake of the Cold War, an astonished Gauß, attending to an ironical twist analogous to what Todorova observed in her critical account of the semantics of Europeanization, writes that those Central Europeans who have "just won sovereignty over themselves, are demoted to the role of suppliants [*Bittsteller*]" vis-à-vis the West and called upon to jettison Central Europe [*Mitteleuropa*] as a possible counter-identification to European integration on the West's terms (*Vernichtung* 32). The problem here is not so much *Ungleichzeitigkeit* itself, which could only be measured by some normative conception of time's linear arrow, but rather the asymmetrical relation of power that such temporalizing rhetoric implies. Gauß may not be primarily interested in any Central European myth as such, nor in continuing the dissident discourse of the 1980s at a time in which the terrain is being swiftly reclaimed. But the erasure of Central Europe in his writings and its replacement with "Danubia" speaks to a timely interest in experimenting with relational concepts through which the potential for resistance against a normative Europe of Western provenance might be multiplied and strengthened.

Gauß's scepticism draws our attention to emergent fault-lines between a transnationalism implemented from above and one stemming from the lived and shared histories of peoples below. Here, the

Europeanization of Eastern Europe recapitulates the contestable process of German unification at the continental level: the European Union's slogan of unity in diversity contrasts with the perception that Europeanization prematurely levels possible political formations on the continent. If integration were to transpire along democratically egalitarian lines, citizens of joining countries might be able to contribute valuably to the process, by drawing on their experiences with actually existing socialism, for example. But the new nation-states are not on equal footing with their counterparts in the West: as the terms of integration are set by belonging members, candidate countries are viewed according to a logic of belatedness (*Nachträglichkeit*). And thus the process of assimilation proceeds in the manner of German unification: the EU expands by sustaining the pre-christened form of its status quo to the detriment of alternative possibilities.

Fluid Signification: The Danube in Contemporary Transnational Cinema

The vagaries of the process of Europeanization are reflected in contemporary European cultural production. Balibar's demand for a new image of Europe resounds especially in and for cinema. The medium of film constitutes a form of symbolic action whereby the process of European unification might be imagined and contested; this includes Rebić's riparian journey eastward.[13] Rebić's film contributes to a predication of the idea of Europe for the twenty-first century by way of its embrace of myth. The source thereof is the river itself, which in the film is endowed with its own agency. To be sure, the Danube has long figured as the site of many myths. From autochthonic pagan tales to modern festivals, Danubian populations have creatively represented the significance of the river's liquid geography for their lives. Very often, the flow of the great river's waters has been symbolized in the medium of music, as in the singularly famous waltz of Johann Strauss II, "An der schönen blauen Donau" (On the Beautiful Blue Danube). As film scholars Jennifer Stob and Robert Dassanowsky have noted, however, the artistic medium privileged for the Danube's representation has shifted significantly to cinema. Stob attests to the ability of moving images to capture and exploit the water's flow (142); Dassanowsky has delivered a short history of the river's reception in Austrian and Central/Eastern European cinema history from Carl Zeska's misguided *Johann Strauss an der schönen blauen Donau* (1913) to the present day ("Taking the Waters").[14]

1 *Nordrand (Northern Skirts)*: Jasmin on the river bank.

To Dassanowsky's focused inventory one could add a host of films from Europe's contemporary cinema in which the Danube plays some integral role. I mention three others to contextualize the uniqueness of Rebić's work. These are Barbara Albert's *Nordrand* (*Northern Skirts,* 1999), Emir Kusturica's *Podzemlje* (*Underground,* 1995), and *The Ister* (2004), made by the Australian team of David Barison and Daniel Ross.[15] Albert's *Nordrand,* to which Dassanowsky elsewhere ascribes a pivotal role in placing Austrian cinema on the international scene (*Austrian Cinema* 268), works towards a micropolitics of futurity for the new Europe by exploring the personal relationship between two young women in Vienna. Inscribing the Yugoslav conflict into the fabric of Central European life, it overlaps with Rebić's traverse of formerly Habsburgian space, but *Nordrand* represents the Danube in only one of its more traditional roles: as a site of violence. Figure 1, a still from a scene that casts the proverbially blue river in shades of *noir,* shows the brutalized character Jasmin on the riverbank, about to be rescued by the Bosnian refugee Senad.

On the whole, trains (Figure 2) remain the privileged vehicle of transportation in *Nordrand,* not least in its figuration of Sarajevo (Figure 3) as the film's vanishing point and afflicted "other" haunting not only the character (of Serbian background) Tamara's dreams but also Central

2 *Nordrand*: Tamara's journey to Sarajevo.

3 *Nordrand*: The Serbian-Austrian Tamara's New Year's Eve question to the Bosnian refugee Senad.

4 *Podzemlje (Underground)*: Yugoslavism on the Danube after Yugoslavia.

Europe itself. Emir Kusturica's well-known – and sprawling – *Podzemlje* embraces as its subject the full sweep of the history of the second Yugoslavia. In this film, the Danube serves as nothing short of a utopian conduit – from cellar to insular daylight – facilitating the assertion of a fanciful Yugoslavism after the country's violent disintegration (Figure 4).

Whereas the Danube serves as a representational placeholder in both *Nordrand* and *Podzemlje*, Barison and Ross's *The Ister* addresses the river itself, which constitutes the main focus of their documentary and philosophical essay-film. In this engrossing work, philosophy sails the river to explore its most haunting chapters during the Shoah and to reckon with far-ranging questions concerning technology in the twenty-first century. In *The Ister*, the Danube provokes thought but will not contain it; thought is schooled on the philosophical imaginaries the river has only entrained.

Only Rebić's *Donau, Dunaj, Duna, Dunav, Dunărea*, to return to the discussion of this feature film, promotes the river to the status of a character in its own right. In other words, Rebić's riverine myth begins with the attribution of agency to the river itself, which does not so much represent other forces as overwhelm and contain them. This is fully in line with a last relevant point to be gleaned from

5 Waiting for signs in *Donau, Dunaj, Duna, Dunav, Dunărea.*

"The Teachings of the Danube," in which Gauß anthropomorphizes the Danube, writing that it "knows everything Europe knows" (15) and, moreover, that it possesses more intelligence than, say, the Rhine (20).[16] To Gauß's appeal to the Danube's superior wisdom, Rebić adds a prominent signifying agency. At a pivotal interval in the film's narrative, the voice-over – "passengers wait for the river to give them a sign" (Figure 5) – recalls resonant lines of Friedrich Hölderlin's "Mnemosyne":

> A sign we are, without meaning
> Without pain we are and have nearly
> Lost our language in foreign lands [...] (Hölderlin 272–3)[17]

This is far from the only appeal to the literary medium by which *Donau, Dunaj, Duna, Dunav, Dunărea* gains its force. Rebić's film thrives on its intertextual interaction with a mini-network of Central European literary aesthetics. Danubian master-writer Claudio Magris likens his own literary journey down the river to a long film: "Is that all, then? After three thousand kilometres of film we get up and leave the cinema [...] but the canal runs on, runs on, calmly and confidently into the sea" (401); whereas Rebić's description of his film as a "poetic journey" acknowledges his debt to the textual hospitality of his literary co-travellers.[18] And the reference to "Mnemosyne" signals more than

Rebić's transformation of the river from a cinematic "Bedeutete" (signified) of representation into a "deutende" (signifying) power of Hölderlinian provenance. The agency Rebić ascribes to the river also enjoys eco-political resonances insofar as the symbiotic relationship between the waters and its travellers in his film constitutes a veritable actor-network straddling the divide between nature and culture, as discussed by sociologists Michael Schillmeier and Wiebke Pohler.[19] In Rebić's actor-network of human and non-human natural elements, the Danube is endowed with the agency of writing.[20] This river-writing will usher journeying passengers into the forms of their new lives.

The Danubian Family of the Future

The attribution of the power of fluid signification to the river itself relates to the irreducible heterogeneity of Danubian space to which Rebić attests. The English translation of the film's title, *The Danube,* fails to grasp its multilingual title, since *Donau, Dunaj, Duna, Dunav, Dunărea* is an eastward encapsulation of the German, Slovak, Hungarian, Serbian (but not Cyrillic), and Romanian names for the river in their juxtaposed plurality. But to associate each of these names with a specific Danubian language already muddles identifications of the region's linguistic complexity, since the Slovak *Dunaj* is identical to the Czech name, and the would-be Serbian appears identical to the Croatian name, given Rebić's use of the Latin alphabet in the opening credits. I thus make these reductive attributions by way of how the characters are identified – again, tenuously, according to their state-defined nationalities – in the film. And while these five are not the only languages spoken, German remains the film's lingua franca. Yet German is not the professed identity of the old ship's captain Franz (played by Otto Sander), whose references to "the Germans" in the film are accompanied by a self-distancing intonation throughout. And despite the symbolic nominal overlap between this captain and the long-reigning helmsman of the Danube Monarchy, Francis Josef I,[21] Franz personally identifies as Danubian rather than Austrian. His ship is the film's other main character, a miniature Kakania[22] *sans* aristocrats in the twenty-first century: over the course of its journey down the river, the riverboat houses a motley crew of diverse Danubians. Some of them work the old ship during its regular short pleasure cruises in the vicinity of Vienna: they include the Ukrainian, Giorgi; Nikola from Belgrade, who holds a Danubian and a Yugoslavian passport; and the Hungarian, Tanya.

Joining the ship on its irregular route towards the delta are passengers motivated by existential questions, life crises, aspirations, or traumas. The first is Bruno, who is intent on honouring his late mother's dying wish to be buried, or rather submerged into the waters, at the Iron Gates, a river gorge some 1,000 kilometres downstream from the Austrian capital. He has been sent to Franz by his mother Mara and has been led to believe that the captain may be his biological father – an assumption disappointed and reconfigured later in the film. After encountering some resistance on Franz's part, Bruno is finally able, in Budapest, to get the captain to commit to this delivery mission. The Afro-Austrian woman Mathilda also boards in Vienna, having been sent by a bird (the good-luck-bearing black stork Grusgrus, one of the film's fairy tale dimensions) to escape past trauma. She eventually meets, befriends, and founds a family with Mircea, a Romanian who had been living illegally in Germany and who is trying to return to Germany in the wake of his deportation. Franz fishes him out of the waters near Bratislava during Mircea's perilous attempt to cross a then still guarded border between Western and Eastern Europe (which indicates to viewers that the film was made before 2004, the year of the EU's first eastward expansion). Farther downstream, the ship serves as a transport vessel for a group of Roma, who orphan an infant to the ship. In a symbolic enactment of adoption, the film's main theme, Mathilda and Mircea accept responsibility for the infant.

Rebić's first message – a quite obvious one – is articulated through his account of a transnational, multi-ethnic European family of the future. As the ship passes the Serbian border, in one of the film's most bitterly humorous moments, the border guard points out that it is carrying one passenger without papers (Mircea), one without a visa (Mathilda), one with a passport from "a country that no longer exists" (the guard's description of Nikola's situation), and one Danubian corpse (Mara, of Romanian background) and declares it to be a ship of fools. Bruno counters by expressing his sincere belief that all of the passengers belong to a single family. Indeed, the constitution of a transnational Danubian family, which comes together by circumstance and choice, is the sign the river is giving the passengers. Through a dreamlike logic of deliverance, past traumas have been reconfigured into new, family-oriented identities (Mircea and Mathilda with their adopted infant; Bruno with Franz and Mara – see Figure 6). Here too, Rebić is undoubtedly in dialogue with one of his co-travellers, the master Magris. For in his book *Danube*, Magris offers an important distinction between two

6 Rebić's Danubian family.

conceptions of familial orientation according to their temporal dimensions. In a comparative review of two epic texts, the *Nibelungenlied* and the *Edda,* Magris contrasts the family of origin with the family of foundation and postulates that in "cultural history, as well as in individual lives, there is often a tension and opposition between the family from which one comes, in which one is son or brother [*sic*], and the family which one founds, in which one is spouse or a parent" (120). Whereas Magris associates the *Edda*'s "iron language" with the natural necessity of the family of origin, the family of foundation is synonymous with freedom, "an arduous and unpredictable odyssey full of pitfalls and temptations, sunsets and new dawns. The hazardous plenitude of conscious, deeply felt family life has not often been adequately represented in poetry, maybe because of the fear that awareness brings disenchantment, that taking refuge in childhood is preferable" to images of "conjugal and paternal love" (121). Upon this pivotal difference, Rebić turns time: his film champions the future Danubian family of foundation by espousing the principle of adoption, which clearly has allegorical resonance for the new Europe. What is more, whereas Magris may still be beholden to a European family bounded by whiteness, Rebić expands the ethnic framework for the continental family not only by including Mathilda but also by having her adopt, with Mircea, a child born of Europe's long racialized and cultural other, as represented by the Roma infant they take in.[23]

7 *Donau, Dunaj, Duna, Dunav, Dunărea*: Bruno reading Mara's diary.

The film establishes a whole matrix of adoption. Mathilda and Mircea adopt a "child of the Danube" (as Franz calls the infant after the Roma abandon him at Turnu Magurele) upon settling into their new Romanian home. In the Bulgarian town of Ruse, Bruno's adoption of a cat underscores the novel reformulation of his identity after learning that neither Franz nor Mara was his biological parent. As the first step in this new identification, Franz takes Bruno in as if he were the son that Franz and Mara lost to the Danube during an attempt to smuggle him out of 1980s Romania, which had bound the Olympic swimmer Mara to her country of origin by refusing her son any exit. Franz even symbolically enacts this adoption of Bruno by having him read from her diary, which includes a passage about a practice in the Caucasus, whereby on the conclusion of blood feuds, sons of former enemies are adopted (Figure 7). While the precise identities in play here are never fully clarified in terms of their genealogy, it is abundantly clear that Rebić is seeking to lessen the impact of lineage on one's destiny (i.e., familial affiliations) for the sake of a more conciliatory continental harmony. As a key part of this, the adoptive family – Magris's family of foundation – replaces the family of origin, and the future comes to hold sway over the past.

Bruno's newfound identification speaks to Rebić's efforts to reduce the power of past hostilities (including the ethnic dimensions thereof) in order to steer the future. In this way, Europe's spells of violence might be broken. But the second step in Bruno's process of identification exposes some of the costs and omissions of the approach being championed here. Franz's sudden death towards the end of the film leaves Bruno orphaned yet again. Giorgi, however, steps in to facilitate Bruno's deliverance into Mara's Lipovan family in the delta in an act that Stob has appropriately termed a form of irresolute dediasporatization: irresolute because Bruno is assuming the identity of Mara and Franz's deceased son Michael, whom the Lipovans take Bruno to be. In this way, Bruno's new identity has been formed in and by the past (at least in the eyes of others) and is also troubled (albeit not absolutely so) by the fact that a mute Bruno, whose native language is German and who possesses no apparent linguistic proficiency in Romanian or Russian (his adoptive mother's tongues?), has completely "lost his language in foreign lands," to cite that Hölderlinian case of estrangement once more. These features of Rebić's film have led Stob to view its characters as "avatars of exilic memory" (151). She thus pinpoints a key demand regarding the challenge his characters present – namely, that in their state of interim occupancy,[24] they must find "the courage to speak, to debate, and to test out the new filiations and allegiances that post-national identity requires to thrive historically in addition to corporeally" (158). At the same time, Rebić's own diminishment of the characters' agency, which works in tandem with the principle of river-writing introduced earlier, also affords viewers breathing room to move beyond the film's ostensible use of the family constellation (into which Bruno is at least provisionally swallowed) as an allegory for the new Europe.

Signifying Regimes: Past and Future through Land and Water

The micropolitical constellation of the family is a curious allegory for an entire continent. In the context of the increasingly racialized debates and conflicts regarding EU citizenship and immigration policies, Rebić's emphasis on the multi-ethnic Danubian family is undoubtedly important. Even so, the family metaphor may have a limited ability to speak to the macropolitical issues Europe faces. If we are to appreciate an additional layer of the film beyond the family structure, we need to conceptually reformulate the foregoing points in two steps. To review: the river writes or rewrites the characters' life courses. Not only do national identities prove to be illusory here, as Dassanowsky writes ("Taking the Waters" 50),[25] but so also do entire trajectories of people's lives. In an apparent reinforcement of this principle, the opening credits roll out the cast's real-life names only to have the print washed away by the river's flow (Figure 8). The film's curious extension of its principle of the power of riverine signification into non-diegetic space points to the fluid transformability of identity itself. With this, we have re-entered the currents of Magris's discussion and the seminal outgoing conceptual move of his *Danube*: "Ever since Heraclitus the river has been the image for the questioning of identity, beginning with that old conundrum as to whether one can or cannot put one's foot into the same river twice" (23). *Donau, Dunaj, Duna, Dunav, Dunărea*'s sustained examination of the signifying potential of river-writing capitalizes on identity's fluidity. As underscored by the voice-over, time on the ship serves for all of the characters as a release from their terracentric and routinized lives.[26] (As for the crew, work on the ship has become their routine.) As Michel Foucault contended in the seminal lecture "Of Other Spaces," "the ship is the heterotopia par excellence" (6). In coining this term, Foucault has provided language for the "other spaces" of reality as interstitial counter-sites – that is, as sites that are set apart from and neutralize the effects of the spaces we usually inhabit.[27] In Rebić's film, the characters' heterotopic experiences on the water serve as preconditions for the transformation of their life courses, as discussed above. To be sure, for some of the characters, such as Nikola, who is returning home to Belgrade after the 1999 NATO bombings, the past will indeed catch up. But for Rebić, the determining instance is not the past, but the riverine present, which reconfigures the past into futures that are perhaps as open as the ability of the river-bound passengers to respond to their riparian experiences. Hence, notwithstanding the film's emphasis on the past, memory, "Mnemosyne-effects," the reconciliation of past feuds, and so on, it is the time they spend on the water (which heterotopians, in contrast to Thomas More's canonical insular utopians, can hardly prolong indefinitely) that remains pivotal and facilitates new landings. Given that the river banks serve as the provisional ends of fluidity, we need to analyse those banks. That is why we must look beyond Rebić's transnational family constellation to see whether *Donau, Dunaj, Duna, Dunav, Dunărea* provides additional possible significations for the new Europe.

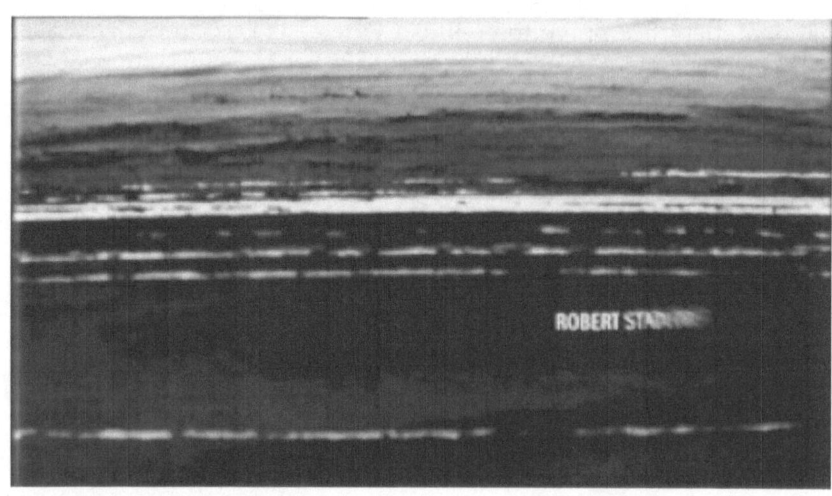

8 The non-diegetic fluidity of identity in *Donau, Dunaj, Duna, Dunav, Dunărea*'s opening credits.

What has transpired here along Rebić's riparian journey is a suggestive reworking of the metaphors of fluidity and solidity, which can be conceptualized one step further. Magris's work likewise makes this possible, since his cultural navigation of the river as a site for the questioning of identity enables him to soak historically accrued and hardened forms of enmity and division long enough for them to become pliable. Magris's book contains a multitude of stories about amazingly stubborn Danubians, but he has a special affinity for those who immerse themselves in non-identity, a term I use for another of Magris's recurring motifs, that of "becoming Nobody," which is part of an Odyssean-cum-modernist search that Magris is undertaking for himself as well (Magris 156–7). The heterotopic neutralization of identity facilitates the realization of non-identity as the substrate of one's (fluid) existence and enables one to reframe "identity" in terms of processes of identification and thereby deal craftily with these. Hence Magris's general predilection for self-determination through (mostly literary) culture and his emphasis on all of those Danubians who either assume multiple "ethno-national" identities over the course of their lives or mesmerizingly mix multiple identities into their own idiosyncratic and even incoherent discourses.[28] In this, Magris is clearly working towards a projected finding, a "chorus of a human race united, despite everything, in the variety of its languages and its cultures" on the Danube (Magris 33). Two competing signifying regimes hold sway over this journey. One can grasp them by exploiting the metaphors of fluidity and solidity. For while Magris deliberately traverses many "borderline cases lacerated by contention" in Danubia (88), and while his literary tour seems to some readers to be "clad in the granite of culture" (Civian-Mihajlova 46), his reputedly "drowned novel" confirms the power of the fluid signifying regime more than it does its counterpart of solidification.[29] Indeed, Central Europe (*Mitteleuropa*) and the Danube can themselves be opposed to each other along these lines. In his chapter "Mitteleuropa: Hinternational or All German?," Magris emphatically rewrites *Mitteleuropa* from a Danubian perspective: "The Danube is German-Magyar-Slavic-Romanic-Jewish Central Europe, polemically opposed to the German Reich" (29).[30] The latter is associated with a terracentric semiotic regime: identifiable bloodlines matched to soil and the Nazi German mission to exert domination over Central Europe; whereas the former speaks to fluid connectivity among Danubian populations in terms of non-identity without hierarchy.[31] Magris's fluviocentric Danubianism is thus not simply some existential appreciation of the transience of human life. More importantly, his reformulation of the static and terracentric concept of identity into dynamic and fluid processes of non-national (self-)identification invites Danubians to wield agency in responding to what the river (i.e., Danubia's cultural history) prewrites in terms of subjects' signifying possibilities. In other words, river dwellers are called upon to complement and fill in frameworks that the river provides in its plurality and vastness, an activity that draws attention to the fluidity of signification in culture's indelible flow. This returns us to the powerfully signifying channels of intertextual practice contained in Rebić's film.

To the extent that Rebić's film never really engages the nuts and bolts of *Vergangenheitsaufarbeitung* (coming to terms with the past), his diminishment of the past's power may seem all too facile. He indeed opts for a restrained silence when passing sites of violence associated with the Yugoslav wars (Figures 9 and 10). Nikola (Figure 11), moreover, returns to Belgrade, where he painfully reunites with his wife, whereupon he rather falls out of the movie's narrative, and his story – unfreed of the past – figures as an anti-*Märchen* juxtaposed to Mathilda's fairytale-like deliverance.[32] Rebić eschews any explicit commentary on Vukovar – the

Danubian city with a majority Croatian population that was besieged and destroyed by the Serbian-controlled Yugoslav army in 1991. His grappling with Europe's transition out of the Cold War and the hot conflicts associated with socialism's passing takes shape through his intertextual engagement with another voice.

9 Vukovar, Croatia, with the water tower in the background.

10 The no longer functional Vukovar water tower as war monument.

11 Nikola at Novi Sad, on his way home to Belgrade.

Bottled Messages

Péter Esterházy is no torch bearer for any distinct substantive political legacy of the Second World. That said, his 1991 novel *Hahn-Hahn grófnő pillantása*, translated from the Hungarian as *The Glance of Countess Hahn-Hahn (down the Danube)*, serves as an intriguing intertext for Rebić's film. Its relevance, however, may not be immediately apparent. For example, the novel's narrator excoriates the dissident discourse on Central Europe (including Magris's less political version of this, which Esterházy toys with elsewhere in his book) as a "sedative tablet" (182). For Esterházy's Danube-travelling narrator, there is indeed truth in that "*other* way of thinking that the world somehow needs [... but] only privately. Within the individual, not within the community" (182). Thus Esterházy's voice – which is not knowledgeable about anything nameable, but rather a self-proclaimed "register, and [...] a colour on the palette of the European chorus" (182) – may prove unlikely to deliver anything of significance to the macropolitical terms missing from Rebić as a result of his focus on the transnational family of the future. Yet it is Esterházy's literary current that Rebić taps for his bottled message. Both Dassanowsky and Stob have noted Mara's collection of jars of Danube water, the contents of which Bruno empties back into the river, and Stob has even directed our attention to the passage's source in Esterházy's novel. In light of the foregoing discussion of signifying regimes as they relate to elements, we can now address the entire passage in terms of its political significance. For Esterházy crafts his own anecdote from another source. In one of *Down the Danube*'s sections inspired by Italo Calvino's *Invisible Cities*, we read the following:

> Cities and Signs. 2.
>
> In the days when the Lenin Ring became the Teréz Ring and some resourceful students made money selling tin cans with the label: "Socialism's Last Breath," there lived in Gozsdu Court [...] a woman who [...] collected the water of the Danube in tiny phials. She had evening Danube, Dawn Danube, Spring Danube, Angry Danube, Drift-Ice Danube (which she kept in the fridge), Green Danube, Fair Grey and Blue Danube, and God only knows how many others. (146–7)

Esterházy's passage performs a number of moves. First, the intertextual dialogue with Calvino raises the issue of the semiotic legibility of urban space. Second, his reference to "Socialism's Last Breath" can be related to the curious market value that *Ostalgie* (nostalgia for socialism in Eastern Europe) garners after socialism's passing, as if such breath could, if not facilitate some resuscitation, then at least be of some personal symbolic significance to those who inhale it. As an opening phrase, "in the days when" projects a very recent social transformation onto a bygone past (146). Interestingly, Esterházy's collector need not travel, as the river's flow allows her to assemble a diverse collection, which is a marker of time. Mara's collection, by contrast, in flasks labelled after each collection site and its distance in kilometres from the delta, is a marker of space, mirroring, as it were, the solid borders of the Cold War's impassable terrain, which are depicted in their new permeability in Rebić's film. Of course, each of these collections remains symbolic, insofar as the air and the waters in question are hardly identifiable in this way (although they may be amenable, in another ecological resonance of the film, to more scientific procedures of data collection). In other words, each collection constitutes a play in signification.[33] Herein lies the significance of Bruno's emptying Mara's flasks: Rebić has the camera linger on certain of these – not only the flask with Iron Gates water, which is of biographical importance to Mara and by extension to her adopted son; but also the Vukovar flask (Figure 12). Given the parallel of this collector's procedure to Esterházy's reference to "Socialism's Last Breath," one cannot help but reflect on what is being assembled here in order to craft cinematic meaning. To be sure, the siege of Vukovar – visible only in the city's damaged sites, on which Rebić lingers without voice-over or further elaboration – is treated not as "Socialism's Last Breath" but rather as a consequence of the asphyxiation of the socialist project in Yugoslavia. From the narrative context of the film, we are given to understand that the water in the Vukovar flask long pre-dates the siege there. A distinction is being made in the waters. In short, and all Yugostalgia aside, the violent disintegration of the socialist federal republic ensued amidst the imperilment of its political project, not before. Up until then, the country had been meant to serve – as part of its founding myth of "brotherhood and unity" – as a vehicle of transnational, multi-ethnic European life. Yugoslavia's fatefully unrealized legacy constitutes an important background to Rebić's resurrection of the ideal of multi-ethnic peace in and for the new Europe.

Mara's bottles contain much water from the Second World. This collection of fluids is a curious mapping project and one that is certainly outside the bounds of any terracentric rationality. Bruno pours the liquids back into the Danube's flow. Given the power of signification attributed to the Danube throughout this film, Bruno's act (Figure 13) signals no absolute farewell, but rather a return of the Second World – and its legacies – to the waters, which continue to figure as sources of possible signification. On this interpretation, *Donau, Dunaj, Duna, Dunav, Dunărea* deftly underscores the need to process and respond to precisely this submerged set of legacies in the waters it traverses and the storylines contained therein. While there is a great deal of pastness in those waters, the film again seems not to be emphasizing the past's determining qualities – how few drops has Mara collected from such a gigantic waterway! – but rather be inviting viewers' (if less so the characters') signifying interaction with what may be contained in the mighty waters of the new Europe's river. The emptied water will demand new flask containers of signifying meaning if Danubia's future flow is to enjoy less cursed trajectories of solidification.

While this appreciation of the Danube as a signifying source of possible human futures on the new continent is not explicitly political, attention to this second intertextual current underlying *Donau, Dunaj, Duna, Dunav, Dunărea*'s celebration of the transnational family at the very least speaks to the larger political and socio-economic issues that overwhelm what family structures by themselves can usually signify. Rebić's family is a provisional landing that may obscure this undercurrent: like the

12 Mara's Vukovar flask.

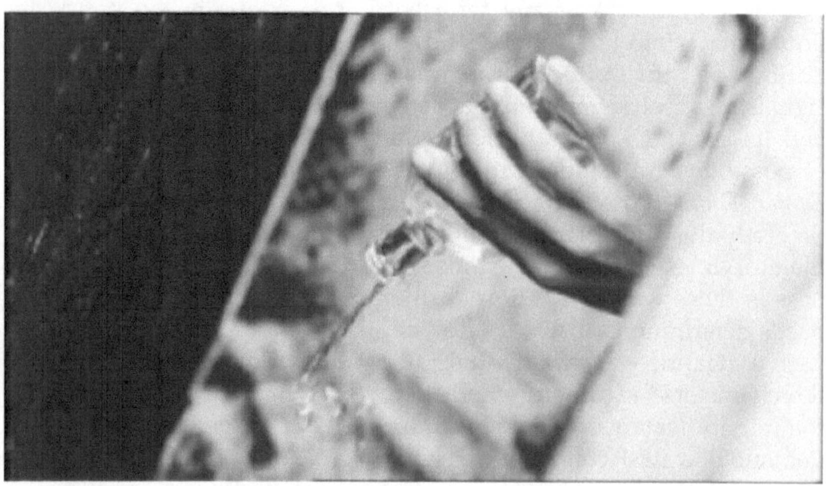

13 Bruno returning storylines to the waters for new signification.

past's ethnic fault-lines it aims to supplant, the family structure – even with its transnational, multi-ethnic Danubian content – is by itself no replacement for democratic politics. Indeed, the foregoing appeal to a fluviocentric regime of signification (operative, in different ways, in Gauß, Hölderlin, Magris, Esterházy, and Rebić's works) places heavy demands on the evaluation of the flask containers and the banks on

14 Whither Danubia? Europe's future at the Iron Gates dam in *Donau, Dunaj, Duna, Dunav, Dunărea.*

which their messages might take more solid shapes. We see the weight of this charge – the critical analysis of solidification – not only in the symbolic status of Vukovar's water tower,[34] and not only in the strands of Magris's own grappling with candidates for Danubia's social glue.[35] Process-oriented interpretation embraces the fluid character of thought, life, and history, but not at the expense of concretion. As Theodor W. Adorno wrote in a different context: "Unleashed dialectics is not without anything solid, no more than is Hegel. But it no longer confers primacy on it" (37).[36] Magris's own appeals to "elusive identity" as "not simply the destiny of children of the Danube, but a general historical condition, the being of each and every individual" (194), may indeed serve to melt past forms of Danubian defensiveness and inner division, but in the meantime they appear dangerously close to what have now become, in our post–Cold War age, fairly transparent and ideologically inflected usages of "fluidity" and "flow" as metaphors for the human condition in increasingly globalized and crisis-ridden market economies.[37] In such contexts, fluidity proves frightening to human beings, who long for banks and sustainable positions – in other words, for more solid and reliable forms of procuring their own livelihoods.[38] But this film's celebration of identity's fluidity and the Danube's power to signify the like does not imply service to neoliberalism; rather, it can be regarded as a means to expand imaginative horizons and thereby make possible futures actual in a transnational Europe in which national, genealogical, and racialized determinations of identity wane. Lending such possible futures additional contours (Figure 14), *Donau, Dunaj, Duna, Dunav, Dunărea* also does well to summon from the waters, however faintly, a larger political sense of Europe's present and future challenges, which can be articulated in terms of two guidelines: first, that reformulations of identity lead to questions of agency; and second, that predications of the new Europe cannot remain merely cultural, but also demand translation (*Übersetzung*: a setting over to other banks) into the economic and political tasks faced by the continent.

NOTES

1 Some of the most instructive overviews include Magocsi; Okey; Schlögel; Stirk; and Todorova.
2 As Klaus Roth has made clear, however, it is not the river itself that forms the barrier (on the contrary, the water often serves as passageway and bridge), but rather the political claims made on and around it.
3 A globalizing age reveals the borders of area studies to be as historical as they are porous, yet such studies continue to provide opportunities for "the analysis of the whole through its parts, and, consequently, of how those components fit together," as Peregrine Horden and Nicholas Purcell have recently written in their methodological justification of Mediterranean Studies (722).
4 For related examinations of or appeals to the social form of the family, see chapters 5, 8, and 11 of this volume.
5 I distinguish "Danubia" from the monarchy in contrast to King, who follows Simon Winder's *Danubia: A Personal History of Habsburg Europe* in attesting this link. After 1918, the signifier in question enters its spectral phase.
6 The problem in the application of "transnationalism" to the European project consists in the term's vagueness: the communicative medium of the labour of the creative arts, for example, is as transnational as that of financial markets. For this reason, it may be useful, if schematic, to wield transnationalism (unmarked) in association with the neoliberalism of which it is an ideological epiphenomenon (a transnationalism from above) and juxtapose to it a marked transnationalism of democratic praxis (a transnationalism from below).

7 Introducing the river's cultural history, Andrew Beattie canvasses the symbolism of the river's potentially unifying traverse of this divide. See Beattie, xix–xx, 114, 119–20.

8 On the pertinence of the term network to Central European aesthetics, see chapters 1 and 11.

9 A keen purveyor of the emerging field of Futurity Studies, Germanist Leslie Adelson encourages us to distinguish the future from futurity. The latter serves as a "a protean abstraction with which we can begin to describe and parse various uses of the future relative to multifaceted frameworks in which the future emerges as an object of thought," as she writes in her introduction to *Germanic Review*'s special issue on "Futurity Now" (215). In his cinematic reconfiguration of the family along adoptive and multi-ethnic rather than genealogical lines, Rebić works on a pivotal condition of the future's emergence, as discussed below.

10 In his opening essay to *Die Vernichtung Mitteleuropas*, a volume dedicated to introducing multilingual Danubian literature to a German-speaking public, Gauß attends to the obsolescence of his titular term amidst the EU's plans for its eastward expansion. For a related deconstruction of the concept of Central Europe, see chapter 6 of Todorova's *Imagining the Balkans*: "Between Classification and Politics: The Balkans and the Myth of Central Europe" (140–60).

11 While Gauß's celebration of Danubian diversity tends to overlook the challenges of extreme economic disparity in the region and the palpable desire to overcome it, his missives against integration into the EU speak to concerns regarding the EU's facilitation of the exploitative reproduction of existing socio-economic inequalities.

12 Still more acerbically in her 1996 conclusion to this work, Todorova had written that "it is, of course, a sublime irony to observe leaders of the cleansed societies of Western Europe fifty years after their ugliest performance raise their hands in horror and bombard (in words and in deed [*sic*], and safely hidden behind American leadership) the former Yugoslavs in preserving 'ethnic diversity' for the sake of securing a *Volksmuseum* of multiculturalism in a corner of Europe, after having given green light to precisely the opposite process" (186). With such lines, Todorova exposes the ideological dimensions of Western Europe's investment in the Balkans, whereby the EU might signify its putatively post-ethnic social model. But Europe's score on this front qualifies it as an unlikely bearer of Nobel peace prizes.

13 On cinema as a form of "symbolic action," see Elsaesser 120.

14 In what follows, I build on both Stob and Dassanowsky's discussions.
15 For a larger inventory, see Stob's study of Rebić's film and her contextualization thereof in twenty-first-century European cinema.
16 Following Hölderlin, Gauß champions the Danube as supporting the myth of life, a path that compels him to ascribe the "death-obsessed" *Song of the Nibelungs* to the Rhine and frame the work and concentration camp at Mauthausen as a despicable aberration from the Danubian melody his essay wishes to sound.
17 "Ein Zeichen sind wir, deutungslos / Schmerzlos sind wir und haben fast / Die Sprache in der Fremde verloren." The editorial history of this poem is complex. Santner's edition provides Sieburth's translation.
18 "The film is a poetic journey […] and the Danube the main character," as he says in an interview with Karin Schiefer.
19 Drawing on Latour's work in their co-authored "The Danube and Ways of Imagining Europe," they write that what we "understand as 'culture', 'society' or 'nature' is an effect of contingent relations of human and non-human relations and cannot be explained away by 'culture,' 'society' or 'nature' as realities on their own. The Danube never becomes socially relevant as an exclusive form of pure and unaffected 'nature,' nor as a 'culture' solely produced by humans. Rather, it is always and at the same time a cultural and a natural object. Neither does the river's nature exist outside of societal reach, nor can we imagine the cultural meaning of the River Danube without its non-human configurations" (27). Their follow-through on this claim adds an ecological layer to the semantics of Europeanization not canvassed above (28).
20 As it happens, this too is a recurring motif in Magris's *Danube*, in which the author wishes to draw inspiration from the water's flow for his own pen: "Writing ought to be like those waters flowing through the grass," he writes near the elusive source of the Breg, one of the Danube's tributaries, "– full of spontaneity, fresh and timid but inexhaustible" (25). The meta-reflective attribution of the signifying power to nature again recalls Hölderlin's poetics.
21 See also Dassanowsky, "Taking the Waters" 51.
22 Following Robert Musil's famous neologism for the Dual Monarchy of 1867–1918 (26–31).
23 It should be underscored that Mathilda's Afro-American identity is introduced via the casting of the character and plays no explicit role in the film's narrative.
24 In this, Stob (152) insightfully modifies Elsaesser's general category of double-occupancy, which he has applied to new European cinema.

25 Dassanowsky accurately notes that ethnic cultures are left intact. But these are not racialized in the film, nor does genealogy necessarily figure as a category of membership. Instead, they merge peacefully as constituent parts of the multi-ethnic family.

26 The film's juxtaposition of this river-time to land-life stages the former as a "parallel temporality" in the sense used by Leslie Adelson in her work on futurity in recent writings by Alexander Kluge ("Future of Futurity" 176).

27 See chapters 6, 7, and 8 of this volume for additional applications of "heterotopia."

28 Memorable examples include Reiter Róbert/Franz Liebhard for the former and of course "Grandma Anka" (the guide of *Danube*'s chapter 7) for the latter. See Magris 291–8.

29 Polezzi cites Magris's description of his book as a "specie di romanzo sommerso" (681).

30 For the sake of extreme contrast, one could compare Carl Schmitt's infamous little 1942 book *Land und Meer* to Magris's project. Schmitt speculatively historicizes the relationship between land- and sea-bound approaches to space. His substantive appeal to these classically conceived elements ominously moves from water through land and air to fire as master determinants of entire ages (see especially pages 104–5 there). By contrast, Danubians such as Magris and Rebić thankfully stick with a semiotic approach to the elements. Rebić especially entertains the reversal of Schmitt's ordering back to a water that baptizes, heals, and cleanses, whereby his film's Christian references, as Dassanowsky has noted, come to overlay the power of the pagan Danube (cf. "Taking the Waters" 51).

31 E.B. Ashton's translation of Adorno's *Negative Dialektik* renders the relevant line as "utopia would be above identity and above contradiction; it would be a togetherness of diversity" (150).

32 Incidentally, in line with my reservations regarding the ability of Rebić's family-focus to speak to larger political issues, it is curious that Mathilda's personal trauma (the loss of her boyfriend in a car accident, in which she would have preferred to die in his stead) admits of fairytale transformation, whereas the political nature of Nikola's trauma (a war-induced ten-year absence from wife and family) brooks no such imaginative rectification. The latter may signal Rebić's view on the EU's inability to come fully to terms with the former Yugoslavia's violent disintegration and the repercussions thereof.

33 This play is not particularly novel either, insofar as we are considering different kinds of containers for elemental substances In terms not terribly distinct from the canonical metaphors of the Christian Testament, as in Matthew 9:17.

34 The tower's symbolism is all the more powerful as a container providing for the liquid sustenance of life in a city plagued by death. Riddled with destructive shots, it no longer serves its primary function, but rather represents the city's suffering.
35 In search of such glue, Magris's masterpiece ranges widely from his considerations of German and Jewish culture as Central Europe's Roman forces (!) to Yugoslavia as an inheritor of the Habsburg myth of a multinational and peaceable coexistence, as he wrote in the 1980s. See Magris 309, 312, 331–2.
36 Ashton's translation renders "Entfesselte Dialektik entbehrt so wenig wie Hegel eines Festen. Doch verleiht sie ihm nicht länger Primat" (48).
37 See the following chapter for a related discussion of these issues.
38 In this, I follow some of Zygmunt Baumann's discussion in chapter 5 of his *Liquid Modernity*, especially pages 168 and 199.

WORKS CITED

Adelson, Leslie. "The Future of Futurity: Alexander Kluge and Yoko Tawada." *Germanic Review* 86.3 (2011): 153–84. Print.

– "Futurity Now." *Germanic Review* 88.3 (2013): 213–18. Print.

Adorno, Theodor W. *Negative Dialektik*. 1970. Frankfurt am Main: Suhrkamp, 1997. Print.

– *Negative Dialectics*. Trans. E.B. Ashton. New York: Continuum, 1983. Print.

Balibar, Étienne. *We, the People of Europe? Reflections on Transnational Citizenship*. Trans. James Swenson. Princeton: Princeton UP, 2004. Print.

Baumann, Zygmunt. *Liquid Modernity*. Cambridge: Polity, 2000. Print.

Beattie, Andrew. *The Danube: A Cultural History*. Oxford: Oxford UP, 2011. Print.

Civian-Mihajlova, Tatjana. "The Danube – Symbol of the Mythical Road and a Mythological Frontier." *Ethnologia Balkanica* 1 (1997): 29–52. Print.

Dassanowsky, Robert. *Austrian Cinema: A History*. Jefferson: McFarland, 2005. Print.

– "Taking the Waters: The Danube's Reception in Austrian and Central/ Eastern European Cinema History." In *Watersheds: Poetics and Politics of the Danube River*. Ed. Marijeta Bozovic and Matthew D. Miller. Boston: Academic Studies Press, 2016. 25–52. Print.

Donau, Dunaj, Duna, Dunav, Dunărea (The Danube). Dir. Goran Rebić. Lotus Film, 2003. DVD.

Elsaesser, Thomas. *European Cinema: Face to Face with Hollywood*. Amsterdam: Amsterdam UP, 2005. Print.

Esterházy, Péter. *The Glance of Countess Hahn-Hahn (Down the Danube)*. Trans. Richard Aczel. Evanston: Northwestern UP, 1998. Print.

Foucault, Michel. "Of Other Spaces (1967), Heterotopias." Lecture. Trans. Jay Miskowiec. Web. http://web.mit.edu/allanmc/www/foucault1.pdf

Frevert, Ute. *Eurovisionen: Ansichten guter Europäer im 19. und 20. Jahrhundert*. Frankfurt am Main: Fischer, 2003. Print.

Gauß, Karl-Markus. "The Teachings of the Danube." Trans. Mary B. Murrow and Tom Appleton. In *Donau*. Ed. Inge Morath. Vienna: Müller Verlag, 1995. 15–23. Print.

– *Die Vernichtung Mitteleuropas: Essays*. Klagenfurt/Celovec: Wieser Verlag, 1991. Print.

Hölderlin, Friedrich. *Hyperion and Selected Poems*. Trans. Richard Sieburth, et al. Ed. Eric L. Santner. New York: Continuum, 1994. Print.

Horden, Peregrine, and Nicholas Purcell. "The Mediterranean and 'the New Thalassology.'" *American Historical Review* 111.3 (2006): 722–740. Web. http://ahr.oxfordjournals.org/content/111/3/722.full#fn-3

Huyssen, Andreas. *Twilight Memories: Marking Time in a Culture of Amnesia*. New York: Routledge, 1995. Print.

The Ister. Dirs. David Barison and Daniel Ross. New York: First Run/Icarus Films, 2004. DVD.

King, Charles. "Excursion and Division." *Times Literary Supplement*, 20 and 27 December 2013, 32. Print.

Magocsi, Paul Robert. *Historical Atlas of Central Europe*. Seattle: U of Washington P, 2002. Print.

Magris, Claudio. *Danube*. Trans. Patrick Creagh. 1989. New York: Farrar, Straus and Giroux, 2008. Print.

Menasse, Robert. *Der Europäische Landbote: Die Wut der Bürger und der Friede Europas, oder, Warum die geschenkte Demokratie einer erkämpften weichen muss*. Vienna: Zsolnay, 2012. Print.

Die Mitte (The Center). Dir. Stanisław Mucha. Strandfilm, 2004. DVD.

Musil, Robert. *Der Mann ohne Eigenschaften*. Hamburg: Rowohlt, 1978. Print.

Nordrand (*Northern Skirts*). Dir. Barbara Albert. 1999. Lotus Film, 2006. DVD.

Okey, Robin. "Central Europe/Eastern Europe: Behind the Definitions." *Past and Present* 137.11 (1992): 102–33. Print.

Podzemlje (*Underground*). Dir. Emir Kusturica. 1995. New Yorker Video, 2003. DVD.

Polezzi, Loredana. "Different Journeys along the River: Claudio Magris's *Danubio* and Its Translation." *Modern Language Review* 93.3 (1998): 678–694. Print.

Rebić, Goran. Interview with Karin Schiefer. *Austrian Film Commission* (2003). Web. http://www.austrianfilms.com/news/news_article?j-cc-node=artikel&j-cc-id=8142

Roth, Klaus. "Rivers as Bridges – Rivers as Boundaries: Some Reflections on Intercultural Exchange on the Danube." *Ethnologia Balkanica* 1 (1997): 20–8. Print.

Schillmeier, Michael, and Wiebke Pohler, "The Danube and Ways of Imagining Europe." *Sociological Review* 58 (2011): 25–40. Print.

Schlögel, Karl. *Die Mitte liegt ostwärts: Europa im Übergang*. Munich: Hanser, 2002. Print.

Schmitt, Carl. *Land und Meer: Eine weltgeschichtliche Betrachtung*. 1942. Stuttgart: Klett-Cotta, 2011. Print.

Stirk, Péter, ed. *Mitteleuropa: History and Prospects*. Edinburgh: Edinburgh UP, 1994. Print.

Stob, Jennifer. "Riverboat Europe: Interim Occupancy and Dediasporization in Goran Rebić's *Donau, Duna, Dunaj, Dunav, Dunărea* (2003)." In *European Cinema after the Wall: Screening East-West Mobility*. Ed. Leen Engelen and Kris van Heuckelom. Lanham: Rowman and Littlefield, 2014. 140–62. Print.

Todorova, Maria. *Imagining the Balkans*. New York: Oxford UP, 2009. Print.

Winder, Simon. *Danubia: A Personal History of Habsburg Europe*. New York: Farrar, Straus, and Giroux, 2013. Print.

11 Ilija Trojanow and the Cosmopolitical Public Intellectual

CARRIE SMITH-PREI

"I was born in Bulgaria. But already at six I was introduced to the foreign. Since the day that I was placed, along with mother and father, in a camp where people spoke many incomprehensible tongues, I am able to trust my memory. At six, I was tossed into the unintelligible. Since then, I try to make sense of it all" (7).[1] Thus begins *Der entfesselte Globus* (The Unbound Globe, 2009) a collection of travel writings dating from as early as 1981 that cover German-language author Ilija Trojanow's[2] experiences in Africa, India, Asia, and Central Europe. Born behind the Iron Curtain in Bulgaria in 1965, Trojanow fled with his family to Germany in 1971, and then on to Nairobi, Kenya, in 1972, where he lived out his childhood. Adulthood sojourns brought him back to Germany as well as to France, India, South Africa, and Austria. Much of the scholarship on his work has approached his writings through his biography, not least because works by authors from immigrant backgrounds are often subject to autobiographical assumptions.[3] Despite his far-flung travels, Trojanow's birth country of Bulgaria receives first, and sometimes sole, mention in these critical and scholarly assessments. Those who approach an author's work through the biographical lens tell us much about the country where the critique originated. Julian Preece writes: "Contemporary cosmopolitan Germany is tempted to see an ideal image of itself reflected in such a writer. Austrians are reminded of a time when the peripheries of the Habsburg Empire produced many of their most celebrated poets and thinkers" ("Ilija" 119). Preece's comments highlight the complexities of discussing authorial national belonging in a global age and for a global author; Trojanow is recoded for a future-oriented Germany or a Habsburgian-focused Austria, belonging simultaneously to both and neither. For the traveller in exile, there can also be no suitable experience of belonging. The essay quoted above continues: "There were times when I longed for return. Until I understood that my origin is not a space that is reserved for me, that I need only fling open and dust off in order to move back in" (8).[4] Such recognition leads to the next departure (*Aufbruch*). Home, in the sense of the German *Heimat*, does not exist and is replaced instead by the body in motion. This movement describes the cosmopolitan subject shaped by the experience of cultural and national confluence.

Thus, notwithstanding the reductive nature of biographical approaches to literary texts, Trojanow's globetrotter background indeed resonates in his writings. In non-fictional texts and novels alike, the author is concerned with the crossing or bleeding together of national boundaries that make up cultural, economic, and personal identities.[5] This confluence has a direct impact on the author's approach to notions such as home, nation, and belonging, but also on the role of the cosmopolitan subject as author. In a 2015 interview, Trojanow claims that cosmopolitan literature brings the international experiences of the author to the fore. "The cosmopolitan approach would be to allow these other influences to coauthor the text" (270). Thus the term cosmopolitanism, he contends, includes also an ideal (266). This chapter considers a small selection of Trojanow's works to offer a portrait of this Central European author as cosmopolitical public intellectual. In the first section, I discuss the travelogue *Der entfesselte Globus*, which illustrates Trojanow's understanding of confluence and its impact on self, language, and writing. Pairing this with the essay *Der überflüssige Mensch* (The Superfluous Person, 2013), the analysis examines the manner in which confluence also drives global crisis discourse and uncovers threats that demand that the cosmopolitical author act. The second section turns to this call to action in the form of creative works: the novel *EisTau* (Ice Thaw, 2011) and the photo-essay *Wo Orpheus begraben liegt* (Where Orpheus Lies Buried, 2013).

This chapter thus closes this volume on Central Europe by taking up two concepts – confluence and cosmopolitanism – that (together with the previous chapters) have suggested we define the region by showing how contemporary globalization has transformed their political, ethical, and utopian implications. It does so by discussing an author who is repeatedly – in critical analyses and in reviews, in popular media and in academic circles – located within Central Europe.[6] It indicates that the aesthetic crossings the chapters in this volume have analysed, including the continuities and transformations between and among

Central European nations since the nineteenth century, may well help us grasp the aesthetic repercussions of globalization in the twenty-first century, including those of the shifting public sphere and the role of the humanist author today.[7]

Confluence and Globalization – *Der entfesselte Globus* and *Der überflüssige Mensch*

In the essay "Das Netz von Indra oder Die Philosophie hinter dem Spiel" (Indra's Net, or The Philosophy behind the Game, 2007), included near the end of *Der entfesselte Globus*, Trojanow utilizes the Buddhist image of Indra's Net to explain the "possibility of a global community" that would arise out of "mixture and amalgamation, flow and confluence" (184–5).[8] He sees such confluence as particularly important for the countries of Central and Eastern Europe, whose identities are dynamic and whose transformations are ongoing (185). He concludes the essay by applying this thought to the whole of Europe:

> If we wish to prepare ourselves for the future, we must understand our borders as confluences that have fecundated us in the past. These borders are playgrounds for mixed cultures, which have had and continue to have critical meaning for the development of the continent. For that which separates us is merely only a momentary difference – a fleetingness in history. Multiplicity has always been the great strength of Europe [...]. In its golden years, culture in Europe has always existed in the plural and it has never stood still. (185)[9]

Here, the experience of travel outlined throughout *Der entfesselte Globus* takes on locational specificity, which Trojanow captures with the term confluence (*Zusammenfluß*). The intersection and cultural exchange is grounded in Europe, led by the cultural histories of Central and Eastern Europe. Furthermore, he compares the confluence of cultures to the process of writing: "When we write, we create networks. Word to word, place to place. We line letters up together, we collect words, sometimes into solid paragraphs and sometimes into flowing stanzas. That which is written down continues on to link itself to the reader" (183).[10] The term Trojanow uses is *vernetzen*, to create a network or to link up, and throughout the essay he continues to utilize the metaphor of the literal and figurative net. The reader ventures out into the world with a net, and through words – written, published, read, thought about, and carried forward – the reader is able to transfer that net into larger nets that lead towards "greater nets that astound and enrich us […] from one level to the next, from one country to the next, and from one language to its neighbouring language" (183).[11] Words are the first step towards creating the network that Trojanow proposes is innate to the region of Central Europe and essential to the European project. In crossing borders, we transform our language and thus ourselves; confluence has a direct impact on the permanence of borders but also on selfhood, communication, and the written word.

Indra's Net offers us a way of thinking about the author as a cosmopolitical public intellectual bound not by national concerns but by larger political, ethical, and empathetic concerns affecting or arising from the confluence of cultures in an era of globalization. The term "cosmopolitan" here I understand in terms of Kwame Anthony Appiah's definition, as referring to our obligation to others in our shared world citizenship and to a recognition of the value of individual human life (xv). When Julian Preece writes that he sees in Trojanow's writing an "empathy for the other" ("Ilija" 131), this is the cosmopolitan moment.[12] In comparison, globalization, following Eric Cazdyn and Imre Szeman, is an "ideological project" (1) and a "vector" for the distribution of goods or technology, but also of "cultural forms and practices" worldwide (9). While "cosmopolitanism" is by no means a synonym for globalization – to equate the two would ignore the long-standing philosophical and ethical reach of the former term's humanistic origins in favour of globalization's economic roots[13] – the cosmopolitical cannot be thought through in this context without taking globalization into consideration. As Stuart Taberner writes in linking transnationalism and cosmopolitanism, today's urgent question has become "how can we live with 'others,' both at home *and* globally?" (44).[14] This question is central to the work of an author like Trojanow, who is not only a traveller by biography and trade but also outspoken with regard to political issues that have cross-national impact. Thus while cultural confluence based on national structures is one aspect of individual development towards the cosmopolitan position, the global resonances threaten the essential utopian quality of the term. The cosmopolitical public intellectual speaks within this moment of threat.

This threat is outlined in *Der überflüssige Mensch*, which is the print version of a lecture Trojanow gave in Austria at the Literaturhaus Graz from 18 to 20 March 2013 for the series "Unruhe bewahren" ("keep agitated," a wordplay on the German *Ruhebewahren*, "keep calm") presented by the Akademie Graz. In this lecture, Trojanow speaks out against the manner in which neoliberal society under late capitalism has deemed certain individuals unnecessary. "Those who produce nothing and – worse yet – consume nothing do not exist according to the current economic balance sheet" (7).[15] Understanding globalization as the end result of colonization, he sees the control of capital as the root of the problem: "The dark side of affluence is the superfluous person" (50).[16] He goes on to bring together the precariat, a social class made up of those living permanently on the edge of economic ruin (including those groups who have always lived outside the sphere of acceptability, e.g., the Roma), with the increasing demands made by globalization on the planet, such as overpopulation.[17]

Ulrich Beck's *World Risk Society* (1999) and *Weltrisikogesellschaft* (World Risk Society, 2007) offer one manner of connecting the threats produced by such waste – whether of people or things – as described by Trojanow with an understanding of the cosmopolitical and, ultimately, with the potential impact of writing conceived as confluence.[18] In his 1999 introduction to the earlier English-language version of the text, Beck explains that all of life's patterns – including employment, progress, and exploitation – are now being determined increasingly by globalization and by global risks that are simultaneously affecting Western and non-Western societies, albeit the latter more heavily (*World* 2, 5). He defines risk in terms of the ways in which societies attempt to control the "various unintended consequences of radicalized modernization" (3). In the 2007 German-language version, he further explains that risk is not the same as a catastrophe; rather, it is the possibility of a future catastrophe that does not yet exist (*Weltrisikogesellschaft* 29). Therefore, society's state of being is one of constant and threatening anticipation, whether of an environmental apocalypse or economic collapse; risk society is a society living in the subjunctive (*German Europe* 8).

The description of the risk society here is in keeping with Trojanow's descriptions of society in *Der überflüssige Mensch*. The superfluous person – the one living on the edge of, or in, destitution – serves as a portent for the consequences of global modernization and capitalism (unbalanced consumption, overpopulation, environmental destruction) and signals pending catastrophe. At the same time, however, world risk societies spur on the type of confluence described by Trojanow in *Der entfesselte Globus*:

> They tear down national borders and mix the native with the foreign. The distant other becomes the inner other – not as a result of migration, but rather as a result of global risks. The everyday becomes cosmopolitical;

> people must add meaning to their lives through exchange with others and no longer through contact with their own kind. (*Weltrisikogesellschaft* 40)[19]

Because of the global nature of risk, borders become invalid and confluence a necessity, confluence that is cultural and political but also banal or everyday. Cosmopolitanism, which once meant elitism and imperialism, helps the individual recognize and interpret his or her own vulnerability and lack of control while at the same time inciting attempts towards "transborder new beginnings" (*grenzüberschreitende Neuanfänge*, 119), for it demands the inclusion of the "other," worldwide (110). This is so, of course, because the risks that can be characterized as global are those that have been delocalized, are incalculable, and cannot be compensated for or dissolved in monetary or other terms (103).[20] They therefore have a transnational character (in that they ignore national borders), are imprecise as to the space and time of their impact, and, finally, have no concrete solution. The reaction to the risk described above must not be refusal or apathy but transformation, which builds the cosmopolitical moment of the world risk society (97).

Trojanow's essay arises out of just such a cosmopolitical moment. In recognizing risk, it simultaneously identifies the transformative capabilities of such risk. In the final chapter, "Ways Out" ("Auswege"), Trojanow emphasizes the cross-border communication inherent in the risk that is embodied by superfluity, as well as the demand to create new alternatives for action at the governmental and individual levels. He warns against blanket calls for critical thought and resistance, for "they spoon-feed to individuals what they should develop on their own impetus" (81).[21] Instead, Trojanow writes: "We need utopian plans, we need dreams, we must breathe daringness. […] The belief in prevailing also belongs to the necessary visions" (82).[22] Similarly, Beck writes of the cosmopolitical chance of the world risk society as that of "reforging global risks into realistic utopias for a threatened world, utopias that allow us to reinvigorate and relegitimate state and politics" (*Weltrisikogesellschaft* 124).[23] These utopias can come about through understanding and listening, both of which also automatically contain the conscious and selective choice to not-listen or not-understand (338). The call is a moral one that demands we engage with the resources at our disposal, accept invitations to act across borders, undermine institutionalized requests for objectivity, and expand our own horizons (338). The utopias of *Der überflüssige Mensch* also come about through understanding the other, which speaks to a deep-seated and ethical position of empathy: "Without empathy the reality of the superfluous person cannot be fought" (85).[24] Through being touched by others, we are shaken out of our navel-gazing and are pushed to engage (86). To use Beck's word, the ethics of recognizing the other creates a *Risikoweltbürgerrecht*, or world civil rights of risk (*Weltrisikogesellschaft* 340). This would suggest that risk demands not only action and empathy but also a different understanding of global human rights that can become the basis for transnational political engagement.

The following questions arise: How must the public self-positioning of the author within the world risk society be understood, particularly when risk is used as the basis for enacting potentially repressive structures of control, and, following on this, how is the role of the engaged author transformed in or by the cosmopolitan moment? The public sphere is structured differently under world risk than within national boundaries. Jürgen Habermas, for example, understands the public sphere as a space of equal participation, one that must follow the principle of rational discourse and that is defined in opposition to the private sphere – this definition works national-specifically (54–5). In contrast, the public sphere in world risk is, according to Beck, a space of emotion and unfreedom, one in which people are put before the media and exposed at will (*Weltrisikogesellschaft* 116). Here, discourse arises out of dissent around the consequences of transnationally reaching decisions (116). This public space defined by arbitrariness and the power of media, by falsehoods and selective thinking, would demand a different intellectual approach than the public described by Habermas, which is confined by boundaries of community or nation. Here, world problems forge international partnerships (*Weltrisikogesellschaft* 268).

But for Trojanow, the public is not constructed out of discourse arising from participation or dissent. Instead, the public is configured in its interaction with text and authorship. In his essay "The Public Role of Writers and Intellectuals," Edward Said traces the coming together of the terms writer and intellectual owing to the increasingly public intellectual work of the writer in the form of writers' congresses that approach global issues, such as civil strife and freedom of speech (PEN International would be one example), and in the "special symbolic role of the writer as an intellectual testifying to a country's or region's experience, thereby giving that experience a public identity forever inscribed in the global discursive agenda" (25). This speaks in part to the manner in which Anke Biendarra, in *German Going Global* (2012), utilizes the term "glocal" (developed by Roland Robertson[25]) to describe the kind of literature that best highlights the relationship between literature and globalization, and particularly in understanding the role the globally engaged author plays in the public sphere, one that is both national and local (9).[26] The three versions of the term *public* outlined by Michael Warner are useful here: *the* public (a social totality), *a* public (a concrete audience), and simply public, which is "the kind of public that comes into being only in relation to texts and their circulation" (50). This last form remains in conversation with the other two forms and presumes an audience that is either specific or concrete, each of these a social imaginary: "Writing to a public helps to make a world, insofar as the object of address is brought into being partly by postulating and characterizing it" (64). The type of public brought into being by Trojanow's writings is one that is simultaneously specific and a totality. Because he writes in German, his assumed public is German-speaking. However, the public called into being by the texts themselves is a more diffuse totality; in their globally relevant topics, they imagine a public that is "virtually without borders" (Said 20).[27] We therefore see a productive tension between an author who, as Preece writes, "embodies a certain vision of Germany and Austria as places of international cultural communication at the beginning of the twenty-first century" (*Ilija* 1) and an author who also "argues with the world" (2). Through that global argument and in contact with his linguistically defined audience, the author enacts the moment of confluence in a first step towards the public's political, ethical, or social enlightenment.

The notion of glocality, which defines the combined force of *the* and *a* public imagined by the texts here, points to the increasing impossibility of disengaging the two terms – global and local – from each other in an age of globalization, but also the coexistence of disunities, discord, harmony, and understanding within the term (Krossa 44). In a 2010 speech at the Lessing Festival in Hamburg titled "Weltbürgertum-heute" ("What Being a Citizen of the World Means Today"), Trojanow spoke to this coexistence specifically as that which the world citizen must embrace. Within the continual cultural encounter or confluence made by increasing worldwide communication and circulation (of people, thoughts, and actions) arises the experience of chaos and increasing inequity. "This is why we need non-systematic, intuitive, paradoxical, fragmentary, conflicting thinking, because only that will do justice to the complexity and diversity of the world in which we live" (35).[28] The cosmopolitan, he went on to argue, is prepared for such a task and must tap into the chaos felt in the encounter with the world in a creative way (41). The author must take up this call as the cosmopolitical public intellectual by harnessing the discord brought about by the mediatization of knowledge through the global spread of texts and the development of disparate publics out of such circulation. This does not mean, however, that the result will necessarily be positive action. Said ends his essay on the public intellectual with the claim that the intellectual's home is the domain of art, which he calls a "precarious exilic realm" into which "one can neither retreat nor search for solutions" (39). It is here, however, that one can "first truly grasp the difficulty of what cannot be grasped, and then go forth to try anyway" (39). Trojanow's writings are thus not necessarily to be understood as "protest actions in prose" (Hamdorf),[29] but rather as attempts to harness this discord between global confluence and the local experience of crisis in creative and aesthetic terms.

The Aesthetics and Cosmopolitics of Despair – *EisTau* and *Wo Orpheus begraben liegt*

The global and local dimensions of that discord are at the heart of two of Trojanow's most recent fictional works, *EisTau* (2011) and *Wo Orpheus begraben liegt* (2013). Both display a different format than that of a traditional novel, the former using the form of a journal paired with polyvocal sections of media discourse, and the latter a selection of short stories thematically linked together by the country of Bulgaria, with pages interspersed among photographs. Moreover, both texts are driven by the sense of crisis and threat dominating the present day. In the earlier novel, crisis – in the guise of global climate change – forms the plot line. In the more recent text, the narrative focus is not on crisis but rather on what might be termed the human impact of economic and political confluence as a country, once on the outer edges of Central Europe and the Soviet Union, finds itself precariously on the periphery of the European Union.

EisTau tells of Zeno Hintermeier, a glaciologist who has left the university after realizing that "his" glacier, the Tiroler glacier in the Alps that he has been studying most of his career, is dying.[30] After his wife Helene leaves him, he takes up a position as lecturer on a cruise ship taking retirees to the Antarctic. In a notebook, which forms the majority of the text of *EisTau*, Zeno documents his emotional distress at the rapidly declining state of the world's glaciers in the face of human-created climate change; his anger over the tourists whose desire to see displays of untouched nature is contributing to environmental degradation; his obsession with ice; and his sexual desire for Paulina, his Filipina co-worker and lover. The plot line of these chapters is straightforward: readers follow Zeno's thoughts, including memories from childhood or his marriage and notes on what occurs around him, as the cruise ship heads into the Antarctic. On board, we meet the international crew, insipid passengers, and camera teams and reporters following the artist Dan Quentin, who wishes to form a massive SOS sign out of the bodies of the passengers on one of the glaciers. At the site of the art stunt, Zeno stays on board, the only person to do so except for one other passenger, a woman who is feverish from a penguin bite. He hijacks the ship, leaving the other passengers and crew stranded on the glacier.

Interspersed with Zeno's first-person chapters from the notebook are short interruptions that are very different in language and tone, which Preece terms the multi-voiced "chorus to the tragedy of the main action" ("Mr Iceberger" 119). Made up of media jargon (from news to pornographic snippets), unrelated conversational (including dialect) language, and headline-like breaking news items written in capital letters. These headlines announce the stranding of the passengers on the glacier, their rescue, and the hijacking of the ship. They also act as warning signals, embedded in the cacophony of everyday language:

> Differences between worms and chimpanzees, between punks and porters depend entirely on culture, warning, attention BREAKING NEWS NATURE NOT ENDANGERED, PEOPLE ALL DEAD? BREAKING NEWS NATURE NOT ENDANGERED, PEOPLE ALL DEAD? keep it up (29)
>
> The fire will finally burn down the world, cut, BREAKING NEWS STRANDED PASSENGERS SAVED FROM ICE BREAKING NEWS STRANDED PASSENGERS SAVED FROM ICE ablaze (110)[31]

In the first example, the headline plays cheekily with the basis of the novel and the reader's own sensibilities: nature in danger is the focus of the novel. The second represents the short attention span of the media (*Klappe*, here translated as "cut"), interrupting a discussion of fire that serves as a metaphor for the end of the world, for which the melting ice is a portent. That the term "breaking news" is used in the original, and not the German *Eilmeldung*, speaks to the international reach of such media organs.

Gerrit Bartels describes the novel as one that does not want to sound the "eco-alarm" (*Öko-Alarm*) but that intends to shake readers awake through descriptions of the transformations of the Antarctic and thesis-like statements related to environmental distress and the risk of pending environmental crisis. These statements speak to a personal despair in the face of futility. "Futility has features full of good intentions, these must be torn apart, each and every one, our methods have failed. We warned, to no avail, it got worse from year to year. Our era industriously cashes in on Cassandra-like prophecies" (88).[32] Thus for Zeno, this crisis is not in the subjunctive – it is *already* in effect a catastrophe. While the reader is offered descriptions of ruined landscapes and dying glaciers to support this contention, the gross negligence of humanity at every turn is at the forefront. Sometimes this negligence is indirect, in the form of his students' apathy (57) or passengers solving puzzles and sipping coffee as glaciers slide by (99); sometimes it is the result of goodwill, as when a passenger attempts to shield an egg from a natural predator only to be bitten and fall on a nest herself, killing a penguin and crushing eggs in the process (143–4); and sometimes it is intentional, as when Argentinian soldiers throw burning cigarette butts into crowds of penguins (114–15). Midway through the novel, when speaking to a reporter, Zeno translates the word *Kälteidiotie* as the stage of hypothermia where the sufferer believes himself to be too warm and begins to take off clothing (102), at which point there is no saving that person. He proposes a similar concept of *Wärmeidiotie*, where the person believes himself to be too warm and strips off clothing, necessitating that the heat be turned up even higher (102). This is of course a statement about waste, delineating the way in which the developed world is consuming energy at unnecessary rates. But it also points to Zeno's own mania: *Kälteidiotie* befell him as a young boy during his first glimpse of an alpine glacier.

Zeno's desire to change his life in the face of his absolute despair can only amount to nothing. That this failure is not merely individual is seen, as Preece notes, in the mediatized choral sections: "The modern media treat all subjects in the same way, in the same voice, and in the same style" ("Mr Iceberger" 125). By the time the ship has been recovered and the passengers sent home, the media (and therefore the public) have moved on. At its core, the novel is telling two stories about global risk, environmental disaster, and media proliferation, bound up in one story about an individual living banally within that risk. As exemplified by Zeno, the individual who tries to make sense of it all fails (117). This returns us to the requirement for fragmentary or paradoxical thinking to deal with the demands of a globalized world suggested by Trojanow above. Such thinking is found in this novel in the representation, but not the analysis, of the imbalance between the developed and developing worlds. In both its crew and its passenger list, and also in terms of the languages spoken, the cruise ship is international. While the novel is written mainly in German, there are markers throughout the text that point to the actual language spoken on the ship as English. Zeno writes in his notebook: "I barely even notice the peppering of English anymore, it sneaks in due to the situation (*communication on board*) [...] my German is becoming Anglicized, *step by step*" (105 [in the original, the italicized words are in English]).[33] To counter the slow creep of English into his German, Zeno recites poetry, which Paulina asks him to translate into English. He claims that a translation would be incomprehensible to her, and "if I instead transfer it into Paulinian, we will both understand it better" (106).[34] He grabs her by the wrist and begins to have sex with her, kissing her with "dogmatic meaning" (*rechthaberische Bedeutung*; 106). "Paulinian," therefore, refers to sexual conquest. That this mirrors colonial conquest is underscored by the reductive racialization of femininity: after sex, he listens to her recounting gossip she picked up from another female crewmate while they were working in the kitchen; Zeno describes their mouths as clattering like sewing machines (106). His desire for her is intertwined with her otherness and stereotypical gendering, both of which suggest a global-north–global-south or developed-world–developing-world divide. This is further solidified when at one point he notes that the memory of Paulina turns him on more than "the sight of scantily clothed long-legged women from the EU barrack countries" (149).[35] Zeno's linking of libidinal desire with highly racist displays of gendered otherness has the effect of muddling the ethical clarity of his climate change warnings.

Wo Opheus begraben liegt, much like *EisTau*, shows the negative consequences of confluence, but this time they are nationally specific, local, and personal. The book is comprised of photographs and texts, which are written as short stories or vignettes documenting Trojanow's numerous trips to Bulgaria with photographer Christian Muhrbeck. With deep empathy, Trojanow and Muhrbeck show in image and word the impact of globalization and waste on the people of Bulgaria, Trojanow's country of origin. The texts are not meant to elucidate the images, although they complement each other thematically. In the above-cited 2015 interview, Trojanow says of the volume's perspective on Bulgaria that " [Christian Muhrbeck's perspective] is dominated by fascination, mine is clearly dominated by pain and disappointment" (268). At the same time, he speaks of the "creative tension between the fascination of the foreign and familiarity with one's own as one of the aesthetic preconditions" for collaboration (269).

The stories and images present aspects of contemporary Bulgaria that reach back to the country's past and position it in the present day. In some of these, the country's transformation since the collapse of the Soviet Union is at the forefront. For example, in the story "Donaufischer" (Danube Fisher) we read: "The men in their wooden boots, who had earlier been welders and turners, were not asked when the carton company and the plant for electric motors and the factory for batteries were closed. They catch fish that barely feed them" (88–9).[36] The story is accompanied by photographs of old men carrying buckets of tiny fish, with the Danube in the background and factories along its bank. Another story speaks to humans perceived as waste and the future impact of this as a result of the European Union. "Dale" describes the experience of Bulgaria's Roma: "'Dale' comes most likely from the Indian word 'Dalit,' the Untouchable. He who lives from garbage becomes garbage" (171).[37] In this story, even the garbage is a potential commodity. "At the entrance of the landfill a sign, placed for pedestrians accidentally passing by, announces that the construction of a sorting processor will be supported by EU funds in the sum of 23 million Euros" (178).[38] The images that are interspersed among the pages of this story show men, women, and children selecting bits of treasure – a shard of mirror, a doll, a cologne bottle – from among piles of garbage that stretch beyond the frame. The implication in both texts is that larger structures of national and political confluence directly – and often negatively – impact those living precariously on their outer edges.

The texts and photographs illustrate the individual and personal dimensions of a country caught somewhere among post-socialism, futile small-scale agrarianism, failed capitalism, and European Union member status. The implications of the words and images extend farther than the local impact. The text that opens the book, for example, focuses on a family debating where they should begin looking for work: in the Canary Islands there is construction work, and in Austria there is work harvesting vegetables; they know an Englishman who buys grandmother's medicinal herbs and a German who buys pine cones (38). While the EU has expanded the possibilities for confluence among nations, this story suggests that such confluence is open only to some. Indeed, the map of the EU and its member nations is drawn according to the chances of finding work. The images that accompany this story, titled "Sippschaft" (Kinship), show large groups of men and women, divided primarily according to gender and wearing traditional dress. The same text offers us two options for understanding territorial borders out of this tension between transformation and continuity, options that together speak to origins and confluences: "I think of my great-great-grandfather's legacy, scribbled on the endpaper of a torn photo-album: 'The borders of my tribe are the borders of my world'" (35).[39] The narrator's father in this same story claims: "He who travels discovers how many relatives he has" (35).[40] In the first scenario, family ties determine national, or at least personal, borders – borders that stretch as far as one's tribe; in the second, the tribe is configured through travel, with each movement across borders gathering new family. Together, these images form an apt, even utopian, metaphor for the persistence of historically founded but nevertheless imagined Central European borders in a contemporary global era.

What we see and read in *Wo Orpheus begraben liegt*, therefore, suggests the staying power of narratives of continuity in a Central European country despite the transformations it has recently faced. These narratives of continuity tell stories of borders and marginality, but also of national identity and cross-cultural history. This is most apparent in a text midway through the book that speaks to a region's self-definition. In "Denkmalvordenker" (Monument Prophet), the narrator describes his city as dominated by a multitude of large monuments commemorating the people of the city and historical events (98, 99). The narrator proposes alternative monuments, for example, a monument to Orpheus: "What could be more appropriate than a monument to Orpheus, there are, after all, seven villages around us here in the south that claim to be his place of birth; yes, our villages are that old. Seven potential monuments, that is, seven attempts to finally get it right for once" (101).[41] The narrator makes other suggestions besides. One is that existing structures be transformed by, for example, placing a Coca-Cola bottle over a monument to the Soviet army (106); perhaps that monument could then be inscribed with the words "Enemy of the Folk" (*Volksfeind*), "Destroyer of National Culture" (*Zerstörer der Nationalkultur*), or "Pornographer" (108). At the end of the story, the narrator is revealed to be a prisoner writing an open letter from his cell. His lawyer, he claims, intends to distribute the letter via the Internet, "to ask for your solidarity. Not for me, but for the freedom to spray our monument-preserved history with contestations" (109).[42] The accompanying photographs show a variety of Soviet monuments, an image of a socialist-era highrise dominated by a large Kermit the Frog in the foreground (104–5), and an interior shot of what seems to be living quarters left in ruins (108). The story thus suggests alternative narratives to those dominating local, regional, or national self-definition while also questioning the truth-value of the mythology at the base of all narratives. At the same time, alternative narratives are founded on those of the past and rely on aesthetic continuity.

During a December 2013 press conference, initiated by Trojanow and his German collaborator Juli Zeh along with other international authors condemning the mass surveillance activities of the US National Security Administration,[43] the Bulgarian-born author commented that, while there had been times in the recent past when authors needed to reflect and analyse at a distance, "there have also been times in which authors needed to act" ("Geht auch anders").[44] Trojanow's call to arms to the global writing community here offers a closing point for this chapter. Ilija Trojanow is an "old-fashioned committed writer who wants to change the world – or at least the ways that we think about it" (Preece, "Mr Iceberger" 112). He wishes to do so through writings that outline the immediate risks facing global society today, whether these are related to mass surveillance, perversion of security, global warming, or the waste produced by capitalism. Taken together, *EisTau* and *Wo Orpheus begraben liegt*, while radically different in subject matter, speak to the modern world's ongoing crisis. Along with *Der entfesselte Globus* and *Der überflüssige Mensch*, they tell the story of their author's deep commitment to narratively uncovering the inequity and chaos caused by global confluence, but in a manner that displays cosmopolitan awareness and empathy for the other while not claiming to provide ways out of the crisis. The task of the cosmopolitical public intellectual is not to imagine solutions for such risks in a reality parallel to our own, but rather to uncover the impossibility of finding solutions; as Appiah claims, "cosmopolitanism is the name not of the solution but of the challenge" (xv). For the cosmopolitical public intellectual, that challenge is deeply rooted in writing that clearly shows its ties to the present. In an interview with Stefan Gmünder following the publication of *EisTau*, Trojanow claims: "Literature must be contemporary in the sense that it reflects the insanity of its own time and aspires to overcome it";[45] in a different interview with Evi Zemanek, he states that the role of an author is to question the "language and ideological constructs of his or her time" ("Endliches" 190).[46] Part of this reflection and questioning entails the representation of chaos in the ostensible harmony of the far-reaching political, ethical, and social consequences of confluence.

NOTES

1 "Geboren bin ich in Bulgarien. Aber schon mit sechs lernte ich die Fremde kennen. Seit jenem Tag, an dem ich mit Mutter und Vater in ein Lager kam, in dem in viele nun verständlichen Zungen gesprochen wurde, kann ich meiner Erinnerung vertrauen. Mit sechs wurde ich ins Unverständliche geworfen. Seither versuche ich mir einen Reim darauf zu machen."All translations into English by C.S-P. unless otherwise noted.

2 Throughout this chapter, I use the German transliteration of Ilija Trojanow's name rather than the English transliteration Iliya Troyanov. I do so in keeping with most other publications on his work, as well as in keeping with the language in which he publishes.

3 Yvonne Delhey uses this as a central point for her article on his self-fashioning in *Die Weltensammler* (*Collector of Worlds*); Julian Preece begins with biography also and goes on to discuss *Die Weltensammler* and intercultural literature (see "Ilija"). See also Dirk Göttsche on Trojanow's relationship to Africa (197). Preece's essay is included in the volume *Emerging German-Language Novelists of the Twenty-First Century*. In the introduction, editor Lyn Marven contends that all of the authors and texts discussed in the collection – whether of immigrant background or not – in their use of intermediality, fall under the category of globalization as "globalized hypertexts" (2). However, in their volume, Marven and Taberner are not concerned with the economic bases of globalization, but instead with the identity-formative contexts of cultural exchange (7). Trojanow's work shows how, under globalization, economic factors cannot be disentangled from culture and identity.

4 "Es gab Zeiten, da sehnte ich mich nach Rückkehr. Bis ich begriff, daß meine Herkunft kein Raum ist, der für mich reserviert ist, den ich nur aufsperren und entstauben müßte, um wieder einziehen zu können."

5 This is apparent particularly in his travel writings, where the traveller's own identity is distinctly intertwined with the experience of the foreign. As Christina Kraenzle writes, Trojanow's travel writings appear "at a time in which models of national culture have lost their credibility and identities are increasingly acknowledged to cut through geographical locations" (128).

6 In keeping with the chapters in this volume, I use the term Central Europe to define an imaginary space within the European continent defined by

fluidity and flux. Bound historically since the late nineteenth century, this region remains culturally intertwined. I would differentiate the contemporary understanding of Central Europe from that of the European Union here due to the legal and economic policies that define the latter.

7 Here I follow Edward Said's lead in conflating writer or author with intellectual in today's society. The writer, in communicating with the global world, places him or herself in the public and contributes to intellectual discourse.

8 "Möglichkeit einer globalen Gemeinschaft"; "Mischung und Vermischung, aus Fluß und Zusammenfluß." In an interview in the volume *Transnationalism in Contemporary German-Language Literature*, he further engages with the term confluence as a more precise alternative to cosmopolitanism and transnationalism.

9 "Wenn wir uns für die Zukunft wappnen wollen, sollten wir unsere Grenzen als Zusammenflüsse begreifen, die uns in der Vergangenheit befruchtet haben, als Spielwiesen von Mischkulturen, die für die Entwicklung des Kontinents von entscheidender Bedeutung waren und sind. Denn das Trennende ist stets nur eine momentane Differenz, eine Flüchtigkeit der Geschichte. Vielfalt war schon immer die große Stärke Europas [...]. In Blütezeiten hat Kultur in Europa stets im Plural existiert und ist nie stehen geblieben." Of course, 2007 marked the further expansion of the European Union to the east with the addition of Romania and Bulgaria.

10 "Wenn wir schreiben, vernetzen wir. Wort mit Wort, Ort mit Ort. Wir reihen Buchstaben aneinander, wir versammeln Wörter, mal zu festen Paragraphen, mal zu vorbeifließenden Strophen. Das Niedergeschriebene vernetzt sich weiter, mit dem Leser, den Leserinnen."

11 "größere, unser staundende und berreichernde Netze [...], von einer Ebene in die andere, von einem Land ins nächste und von einer Sprache in die benachbarte."

12 For a thorough examination of a related term to empathy, that of "tolerance," in the context of globalization, multiculturalism, and pluralities in German culture, see the special issue on tolerance edited by Elisabeth Herrmann and Florentine Strzelczyk. Furthermore, for a discussion of the terms multiculturalism, interculturality, and cosmopolitanism in German discourse, see Yildiz in the same volume.

13 Although Anthony Appiah suggests that globalization no longer refers to economics but "encompass[es] everything, and nothing" (xiii).

14 In this same essay, Taberner offers a discussion of the forms of cosmopolitanism and its resonance for German-language literature today. He looks particularly at moral (we are all part of one human community),

cultural (multiculturalism, diversity, and cultural respect), Romantic (emotional connectedness), and "kynical" (truly global citizens and ironic distance from particularist claims) cosmopolitanism, ascribing the latter to Trojanow's writings.

15 "Wer nichts produziert und – schlimmer noch – nichts konsumiert, existiert gemäß den herrschenden volkswirktschaftlichen Bilanzen nicht."

16 "Die Schattenseite des Überflusses ist der überflüssige Mensch."

17 The precariat is international and describes people from Africa to Eastern Europe to Canada, including seasonal workers, minimum wage employees, and adjunct professors. In many ways, this essay reflects in its broad-based critique of the consumption patterns of late capitalism, the voicelessness of the precariat, as well as the global reach of the dangers of superfluity in many of the discussions of the Occupy Movement. See Mitchell, Harcourt, and Taussig on Occupy. See also Hester Baer's discussion of precarity as distinctly transnational.

18 The German version of the text from 2007 is not a translation of the English-language text printed in 1999, but instead a transposition and massive expansion of the ideas from the earlier text. Most of the following discussion is based on the more recent, German text.

19 "Sie reißen nationale Grenzen nieder und mischen das Einheimische mit dem Fremden. Der entfernte Andere wird zum inneren Anderen – nicht als Folge von Migration, viel mehr als Folge von globalen Risiken. Der Alltag wird kosmopolitisch: Menschen müssen ihrem Leben Sinn verleihen im Austausch mit anderen und nicht länger in der Begegnung mit Ihres gleichen."

20 Of course, despite the international thrust of these border crossings, certain affinities can be kept. Beck explains in *German Europe* how the economic crisis in Europe, while also a worldwide crisis, did affect Europe in specific ways; in particular, he shows how old affinities were dissolved (17, 20).

21 "sie dem Einzelnen das vorkauen, was er aus eigenem Antrieb entwickeln sollte."

22 "Wir benötigen utopische Entwürfe, wir brauchen Träume, wir müssen Verwegenes atmen. [...] Zu den notwenigen Visionen gehört auch die Vorstellung, was es bedeuten würde zu obsiegen."

23 "globale Risiken in realistische Utopien für eine gefährdete Welt umzuschmieden, Utopien, die es erlauben, Staat und Politik neu zu beleben und neu zu legitimieren."

24 "Ohne Empathie ist die Realität des überflüssigen Menschen nicht zu bekämpfen."

25 See Krossa 43–47 for a summary of Robertson's usage.

26 Victor Roudometof speaks of thick and thin cosmopolitanism in relation to glocalization (which he defines as inner globalization), thick being a "rooted" cosmopolitanism and thin favouring movement and detachment from locality (113); it is this latter usage that applies here. This symbolic role has been further impacted by the speed of digital circulation (27) – and increasingly so since 2002, when Said wrote his essay, as a result of the impact of Twitter and other social networks, which in turn have destabilized any clear conception of audience, or of the public for whom the writer writes.

27 This simplifies Warner's distinctions of course, because a public bound together by language is also a totality, one in which smaller and more concrete publics emerge. For ease of argument, I am taking the global public as a totality and the language-specific public as a more concrete public within that totality.

28 In Preece's book on Trojanow, this speech is offered in both German and English. I quote the English translation here by Seiriol Dafydd. In this context, see also Trojanow's speech during the inaugural International Literature Award given out in Berlin in 2009 by the Haus der Kulturen der Welt (House of the Cultures of the World). In this speech, "Das Ende der Einäugigkeit" (The End of Monocular Vision), Trojanow references Kwame Anthony Appiah's notion of "rooted cosmopolitism," which to his mind speaks to the notions of confluence and origins. See also Delhey 335.

29 "Protestaktionen in Prosaform."

30 The text is also a direct allusion to Italo Svevo's novel *Confessions of Zeno*.

31 "Unterschiede zwischen Regenwürmern und Schimpansen, zwischen Punks und Portiers sind rein kulturell bedingt, Achtung aufgepaßt BREAKING NEWS NATUR NICHT IN GEFAHR, MENSCHEN ALLE TOT? BREAKING NEWS NATUR NICHT IN GEFAHR, MENSCHEN ALLE TOT? weiter so"; "[E]s ist das Feuer, das die Welt endgültig niederbrennt, Klappe BREAKING NEWS GESTRANDETE VOM EIS GERETTET BREAKING NEWS GESTRANDETE VOM EIS GERETTET lichterloh"

32 "Voller gute Absichten sind die Seiten der Vergeblichkeit, sie müssen zerrissen werden, jede einzelne, unsere Methoden haben versagt. Wir hatten gewarnt, vergeblich, es war von Jahr zu Jahr schlimmer gekommen. Unsere Epoche löst kassandrische Prophezeihungen strebsam ein […]."

33 "Mir fallen die englischen Einsprengsel kaum mehr auf, sie schleichen sich ein, den Umständen geschuldet (*communication on board*) […] mein Deutsch verenglischt, *step by step*."

34 "wenn ich es hingegen ins Paulinische übertrage, werden wir es beide besser verstehen."
35 "der Anblick von flüchtig bekleideten Langbeinigen aus den Barackenländern der EU."
36 "Die Männer in ihren hölzernen Booten, die früher Schlosser, Schweißer und Dreher waren, haben keine andere Wahl, sie wurden nicht gefragt, als der Kartonbetrieb und das Werk für Elektromotoren und die Fabrik für Batterien geschlossen wurden. Sie fangen Fisch, der sie kaum ernährt [...]"
37 "'Dale' stammt vermutlich vom indischen Wort 'Dalit' ab, den Unberührbaren. Wer vom Müll lebt, wird zum Müll."
38 "Am Eingang der Deponie ein Schild, für zufällig vorbei schlendernde Spaziergänger aufgestellt, der Bau einer Sortieranlage werde mit EU-Geldern in Höhe von 23 Millionen Euro gefördert."
39 "[M]ir fällt Ururgroßvaters Vermächtnis ein, gekritzelt auf das Vorsatzpapier eines zerrissenen Fotoalbums: 'Die Grenzen meiner Sippe sind die Grenzen meiner Welt.'"
40 "Wer sich auf Reisen begibt, entdeckt, wie viele Verwandte er hat."
41 "Was lege näher als ein Denkmal an Orpheus, immer hin gibt es bei uns im Süden sieben Dörfer, die behaupten, sein Geburtsort zu sein, ja, so alt sind unsere Dörfer. Sieben potentielle Denkmäler, also, sieben Versuche, es ausnamsweise einmal richtig hinzukriegen"
42 "um Ihre Solidarität und Unterstützung zu bitten. Nicht für mich, sondern für die Freiheit, unsere denkmalgeschützte Geschichte mit Einwänden zu besprühen [...]"
43 On 10 December 2013, Trojanow, joined by Juli Zeh (Germany), Eva Menasse (Austria), Josef Haslinger (Austria), Janne Teller (Denmark), Priya Basil (UK), and Isabel Fargo Cole (US), launched a widespread organized protest against the mass surveillance activities of the US National Security Administration (NSA). Together calling themselves Writers Against Mass Surveillance, they drafted an appeal for an International Bill of Digital Rights, which was distributed online in multiple languages, signed by 562 authors (including five Nobel Prize winners) from more than eighty countries, and was printed simultaneously in more than thirty newspapers around the globe. The *Frankfurter Allgemeine Zeitung* broke the story, although the newspaper released it on its digital site the evening before owing to leaks; see "Demokratie im digitalen Zeitalter."
44 "es gab aber auch Zeiten in denen auch Schriftsteller handeln müssten."
45 "Literatur muss gegenwärtig sein in dem Sinne, dass sie den Irrsinn der eigenen Epoche spiegelt und zu überwinden trachtet." Quoted also at the outset of Preece, "Mr Iceberger" (111).

46 "Meiner Auffassung nach ist es die Aufgabe des Schriftstellers, die Sprache und die ideologischen Konstrukte seiner Zeit zu hinterfragen."

WORKS CITED

Appiah, Kwame Anthony. *Cosmopolitanism: Ethics in a World of Strangers*. New York: Norton, 2006. Print.

Baer, Hester. "Precarious Sexualities, Neoliberalism, and the Pop-Feminist Novel: Charlotte Roche's *Feuchtgebiete* and Helene Hegemann's *Axolotl Roadkill* as Transnational Texts." In *Transnationalism in Contemporary German-Language Literature*. Ed. Elisabeth Herrmann, Carrie Smith-Prei, and Stuart Taberner. Rochester: Camden House, 2015. 162–86. Print.

Bartels, Gerrit. "Der Mensch muss fallen." *Der Tagesspiegel*, 20 September 2009. Web. http://www.tagesspiegel.de/kultur/der-mensch-muss-fallen/4581838.html

Beck, Ulrich. *German Europe*. Trans. Rodney Livingstone. Cambridge: Polity, 2013. Print.

– *Weltrisikogesellschaft. Auf der Suche nach der verlorenen Sicherheit*. Bundeszentrale für politische Bildung. Bonn: Suhrkamp, 2007. Print.

– *World Risk Society*. Cambridge: Polity, 1999. Print.

Biendarra, Anke S. *Germans Going Global: Contemporary Literature and Cultural Globalization*. Interdisciplinary German Cultural Studies. Vol. 12. Berlin: De Gruyter, 2012. Print.

Cazdyn, Eric, and Imre Szeman. *After Globalization*. Oxford: Wiley-Blackwell, 2011. Print.

Delhey, Yvonne. "Ilija Trojanow und das 'Self-Fashioning.'" In *Auto(r)fiction. Literarische Verfahren der Selbstkonstruktion*. Ed. Martina Wagner-Egelhaaf. Bielefeld: Aisthesis, 2013. 329–53. Print.

"Demokratie im digitalen Zeitalter." *Frankfurter Allgemeine Zeitung*, 10 Dececember 2013. Web. http://www.faz.net/aktuell/feuilleton/buecher/themen/autoren-gegen-ueberwachung/demokratie-im-digitalen-zeitalter-der-aufruf-der-schriftsteller-12702040.html

"Geht Auch Anders: Pressekonferenz #stopwatchingus #gehtauchanders." YouTube.com. 11 December 2013. Web. https://www.youtube.com/watch?v=HmxO_jgOsz8

Göttsche, Dirk. *Remembering Africa: The Rediscovery of Colonialism in Contemporary German Literature*. Rochester: Camden House, 2013. Print.

Habermas, Jürgen. *Strukturwandel der Öffentlichkeit*. Frankfurt am Main: Suhrkamp, 1990. Print.

Hamdorf, Laura. "Kälter wird's nicht." *Spiegel Online*. 19 September 2011. Web. http://www.spiegel.de/kultur/literatur/trojanow-roman-kaelter-wird-s-nicht-a-786508.html

Herrmann, Elisabeth, and Florentine Strzelczyk, eds. *Embracing the Other: Conceptualizations, Representations, and Social Practices of [In]Tolerance in German Culture and Literature*. Special issue of *Seminar* 48.3 (2012). Print.

Kraenzle, Christina. "Rewriting Colonial Travelogues: Cosmopolitan Visions and Colonial Legacies in *Nomade auf vier Kontinenten*/Nomad on Four Continents." In *Ilija Trojanow*. Ed. Julian Preece. Contemporary German Writers and Filmmakers. Vol. 2. Bern: Peter Lang, 2013. 127–52. Print.

Krossa, Anne Sophie. *Theorizing Society in a Global Context*. Basingstoke: Palgrave Macmillan, 2013. Print.

Marven, Lyn. "Introduction: New German-Language Writing since the Turn of the Millennium." In *Emerging German-Language Novelists of the Twenty-First Century*. Ed. Lyn Marven and Stuart Taberner. Rochester: Camden House, 2011. 1–16. Print.

Mitchell, W.J.T., Bernard E. Harcourt, and Michael Taussig. *Occupy: Three Inquiries in Disobedience*. Chicago: U Chicago P, 2013. Print.

Preece, Julian. *Ilija Trojanow*. Ed. Julian Preece. Contemporary German Writers and Filmmakers. Vol. 2. Bern: Peter Lang, 2013. Print.

– "Ilija Trojanow. *Der Weltensammler*: Separate Bodies, or: An Account of Intercultural Failure." In *Emerging German-Language Novelists of the Twenty-First Century*. Ed. Lyn Marven and Stuart Taberner. Rochester: Camden House, 2011. 119–32. Print.

– "Mr Iceberger Runs Amok: The Aporias of Commitment in EisTau/Melting Ice." In *Ilija Trojanow*. Ed. Julian Preece. Contemporary German Writers and Filmmakers. Vol. 2. Bern: Peter Lang, 2013. 111–25. Print.

Roudometof, Victor. "Transnationalism, Cosmopolitanism, and Glocalization." *Current Sociology* 53.1 (2005): 113–35. Print.

Said, Edward. "The Public Role of Writers and Intellectuals." In *The Public Intellectual*. Ed. Helen Small. Oxford: Blackwell, 2002. 19–39. Print.

Taberner, Stuart. "Transnationalism and Cosmopolitanism: Literary World-Building in the Twenty-First Century." In *Transnationalism in Contemporary German-Language Literature*. Ed. Elisabeth Herrmann, Carrie Smith-Prei, and Stuart Taberner. Rochester: Camden House, 2015. 43–64. Print.

Trojanow, Ilija. *EisTau*. München: Hanser, 2009. Print.

– "Das Ende der Einäugigkeit." *Der Tagesspiegel*. 30 September 2009. Web. http://www.tagesspiegel.de/kultur/literatur/ilija-trojanow-das-ende-der-einaeugigkeit/1608468.html

– *Der entfesselte Globus: Reportagen*. München: Hanser, 2008. Print.

– "Interview." In *Transnationalism in Contemporary German-Language Literature*. Ed. Elisabeth Herrmann, Carrie Smith-Prei, and Stuart Taberner. Rochester: Camden House, 2015. 265–70. Print.
– *Der überflüssige Mensch*. Wien: Residenz, 2013. Print.
– "Vor der Katastrophe." *Der Standard* (Album). 27–8 August 2011. Web. http://derstandard.at/1313025257040/Neuer-Roman-EisTau-Ilija-Trojanow-Vor-der-Katastrophe
– "Weltbürgertum heute: Rede zu einer kosmopolitischen Kultur / What Being a Citizen of the World Means Today: On Cosmopolitan Culture." Trans. Seiriol Dafydd. In *Ilija Trojanow*. Ed. Julian Preece. Contemporary German Writers and Filmmakers Vol. 2. Bern: Peter Lang, 2013. 15–43. Print.
Trojanow, Ilija, and Christian Muhrbeck. *Wo Orpheus begraben liegt*. München: Hanser, 2013. Print.
Trojanow, Ilija, and Juli Zeh. *Angriff auf die Freiheit. Sicherheitswahn, Überwachungsstaat und der Abbau bürgerliche Rechte*. München: Hanser, 2009. Print.
Warner, Michael. "Publics and Counterpublics." *Public Culture* 14.1 (2002): 49–90. Print.
Yildiz, Safiye. "Multikulturalismus – Interkulturalität – Kosmopolitismus. Die kulturelle Andersmachung von Migrant/-innen in deutschen Diskurspraktiken." In *Embracing the Other: Conceptualizations, Representations, and Social Practices of [In]Tolerance in German Culture and Literature*. Ed. Elisabeth Herrmann and Florentine Strzelczyk. *Seminar* 48.3 (2012): 379–96. Print.
Zemanek, Evi. "Endliches Eis und engagierte Literatur. Ein Gespräch mit Ilija Trojanow über seinen Roman *Eistau*." *Literatur für Leser* 35.3 (2012): 189–94. Print.

Contributors

Michael Boehringer is Associate Professor of German at the Department of Germanic and Slavic Studies at the University of Waterloo, Canada. He is particularly interested in questions of interculturality, migration, and gender, and is currently working on a monograph on the intersections of migration and masculinity in Austrian literature.

Gregor Kokorz is an Austrian musicologist with an interest in questions of cultural transfer, and music and identity in Central Europe. He has been a member of the interdisciplinary research project *Modernity: Vienna and Central Europe around 1900* at the University of Graz; researcher at the Wirth Institute for Austrian and Central European Studies at the University of Alberta; and a Mellon Visiting Scholar at the University of Chicago. His present research focuses on music in Trieste. Thematically relevant publications include "L'Europe n'existe pas? About the Construction of a European Musical Space" (2014); "Triest 1848 – Musik im Spannungsfeld nationaler Diskurse" (2013); and *Übergänge und Verflechtungen. Kulturelle Transfers im europäischen Raum* (with Helga Mitterbauer, 2004).

Sarah McGaughey is Associate Professor of German at Dickinson College and holds a PhD from Washington University in St Louis. She is the author of *Ornament as Crisis: Architecture, Design, and Modernity in Hermann Broch's The Sleepwalkers* (Northwestern UP, 2016). Along with her work on Hermann Broch, she continues to publish on themes of and challenges to modernism and modernity through the intersection between architecture and literature. Currently, she is interim online editor of *Glossen*, maintains the website and communications of the

Internationaler Arbeitskreis Hermann Broch (IAB), and sits on the editorial board of *Imaginations.*

Matthew D. Miller is Associate Professor of German at Colgate University in Hamilton, NY. He works on twentieth- and twenty-first-century German literary, film, and theatre studies, transnational cultural studies, and critical and aesthetic theory. He has published articles on Peter Weiss and Uwe Johnson, Alexander Kluge, and Christian Petzold, and co-edited *Watersheds: The Poetics and Politics of the Danube* (Academic Studies Press, 2016), which features an multidisciplinary approach to the river as a unifying artery of economic, cultural, and international exchanges in central and southeastern Europe. His book manuscript *Mauer, Migration, Maps: The German Epic in the Cold War* traces the evolution of the literary genre with a focus on works by Weiss, Johnson, and Kluge.

Helga Mitterbauer holds the Chaire de litérature allemande at the Université libre de Bruxelles. Her research interests include German and Austrian Literature in European Context, Cultural Studies, Transcultural Studies, Theory of Cultural Transfers, Network Analyses, and Migration and Globalization. She has published about twenty volumes and numerous articles on German-speaking literature and culture in its transnational context from the nineteenth to the twenty-first century and on the theory of cultural transfers. She is a co-editor of the journal *Germanistische Mitteilungen* (Heidelberg: Winter) and of the book series *Forum: Österreich* (Berlin: Frank & Timme), and a member of the coordinating committee for the Comparative History of Literatures in European Languages Series (Amsterdam: Benjamins).

Agatha Schwartz is Professor of German literature, culture, and language and world literatures and cultures at the University of Ottawa. Her research interests are nineteenth- and twenty-first-century Central European literature and culture, women's and gender studies, cultural hybridity, and narratives of trauma. Her publications include *Shaking the Empire, Shaking Patriarchy: The Growth of a Feminist Consciousness across the Austro-Hungarian Monarchy* (with Helga Thorson, Ariadne Press, 2014); *Gender and Nation in Hungary Since 1919* (special volume of the *Hungarian Studies Review*, co-edited with Judith Szapor, 2014); *Gender and Modernity in Central Europe: The Austro-Hungarian Monarchy and its Legacy* (U of Ottawa P, 2010); and *Shifting Voices: Feminist Thought and*

Women's Writing in Fin-de-Siècle Austria and Hungary (McGill-Queen's UP, 2008).

Stefan Simonek is an Associate Professor at the Department for Slavic Studies at the University of Vienna. His main research interests currently are Russian, Ukrainian, and Czech literature in the early twentieth century (modernism, avant-garde), and contemporary Slavic pop culture. He is the author of monographs on Osip Mandelstam (1992), Ivan Franko (1997, Ukrainian translation 2013), and Slavic pop culture (2013) and (co-)editor of two literary anthologies on Galicia on the depiction of Vienna in Ukrainian literature.

Carrie Smith-Prei is Associate Professor of German Studies and Chair of Modern Languages and Cultural Studies at the University of Alberta. She researches in the areas of digital feminisms, performance art activism, and political affect. She is the author of *Revolting Families: Toxic Intimacy, Private Politics, and Literary Realism in the German Sixties* (2013) and co-author of *Awkward Politics: Technologies of Popfeminist Activism* (2016). She co-edited *Digital Feminisms: Transnational Activism in German Protest Cultures* (2016); *Transnationalism in Contemporary German-Language Literature* (2015); and *Bloom and Bust: Urban Landscapes in the East Since German Reunification* (2014), and served as co-editor of *Women in German Yearbook* (2014–17). She is currently co-editor of *Seminar: A Journal of Germanic Studies* (2017–2022).

Irene Sywenky is Associate Professor of Comparative Literature at the University of Alberta, and editor of *Canadian Review of Comparative Literature / Revue Canadienne de Littérature Comparée*. She has published on postcolonial and post-imperial cultural spaces in Central and Eastern Europe; border identities and border cultures; memory; popular culture; and contemporary Canadian literature. She has co-edited several books and special journal issues, and her articles have appeared in edited volumes and international journals such as *Comar(a)ison: An International Journal of Comparative Literature; Translation Studies; German Politics and Society; Canadian Review of Comparative Literature;* and *Australian Slavonic and East European Studies.*

Imre Szeman is Professor of Drama and Speech Communication and English Language and Literature at the University of Waterloo. He conducts research on and teaches in the areas of energy and environmental studies, critical and cultural theory, and social and political philosophy. Recent books include *Fueling Culture: 101 Words for Energy and Environment* (Fordham UP, 2017; co-editor), *Energy Humanities: An Anthology* (Johns Hopkins UP, 2017; co-editor) and the fourth edition of *Popular Culture: A User's Guide* (Nelson, 2017; co-author).

Helga Thorson is Chair of the Department of Germanic and Slavic Studies at the University of Victoria in British Columbia, Canada. Her research interests include modernist literature, gender studies, German and Austrian literary studies, and Holocaust studies. Together with Agatha Schwartz, she co-authored *Shaking the Empire, Shaking Patriarchy: The Growth of a Feminist Consciousness across the Austro-Hungarian Monarchy* (Ariadne Press, 2014). She has also published on the intersections of sex, gender, and Jewishness in Germany and Austria in the early twentieth century.

Sandra Vlasta is currently lecturing in Comparative Literature at the Johannes Gutenberg-University in Mainz, Germany. She earned her PhD in Comparative Literature at the University of Vienna, Austria in 2008. She taught German at Trinity College in Dublin, Ireland, and at the Università degli Studi Roma Tre, Italy; was a Lecturer in Comparative Literature at the University of Vienna; and was a Research Associate at the Austrian Academy of Sciences. Her main research interests are literature and migration, travel writing, cultural transfer, multilingual literature, and postcolonial literature and theory. Recent publications include *Contemporary Migration Literature in German and English: A Comparative Study* (Brill/Rodopi, 2016).

Index

www.ingramcontent.com/pod-product-compliance
Lightning Source LLC
LaVergne TN
LVHW040152080826
844660LV00014B/928/J

* 9 7 8 1 4 4 2 6 4 9 1 4 9 *